# Montesquieu and His Legacy

# Montesquieu and His Legacy

Edited by
Rebecca E. Kingston

Published by
State University of New York Press, Albany

© 2008 State University of New York

All rights reserved

Printed in the United States of America

No part of this book may be used or reproduced in any manner whatsoever without written permission. No part of this book may be stored in a retrieval system or transmitted in any form or by any means including electronic, electrostatic, magnetic tape, mechanical, photocopying, recording, or otherwise without the prior permission in writing of the publisher.

For information, contact State University of New York Press, Albany, NY
www.sunypress.edu

Production by Eileen Meehan
Marketing by Fran Keneston

Library of Congress Cataloging-in-Publication Data

Montesquieu and his legacy / edited by Rebecca E. Kingston.
　　p. cm.
　Includes bibliographical references and index.
　ISBN 978-0-7914-7621-5 (hardcover : alk. paper)
　ISBN 978-0-7914-7622-2 (pbk. : alk. paper)
　1. Political science—Philosophy.   2. Montesquieu, Charles de Secondat, baron de, 1689–1755.   I. Kingston, Rebecca.

JA71.M654 2009
320.092—dc22
　　　　　　　　　　　　　　　　　　　　　　　　　　　　　　2008000122

10 9 8 7 6 5 4 3 2 1

*To Ronnie*

# Contents

Acknowledgments     xi

Introduction     1
    Rebecca E. Kingston

1. What Montesquieu Taught: "Perfection Does Not Concern Men or Things Universally"     7
    Michael Mosher

## Part I
## Morals and Manners in the Work of Montesquieu

2. Morals and Manners in Montesquieu's Analysis of the British System of Liberty     31
    Cecil Patrick Courtney

3. Honor, Interest, Virtue: The Affective Foundations of the Political in *The Spirit of Laws*     49
    Céline Spector

4. On the Proper Use of the Stick: *The Spirit of Laws* and the Chinese Empire     81
    Catherine Volpilhac-Auger

5. Montesquieu on Power: Beyond Checks and Balances     97
    Brian C. J. Singer

## Part II
### Montesquieu's Legacy in Eighteenth- and Nineteenth-Century Political Thought

6. Montesquieu's Constitutional Legacies — 115
   *Jacob T. Levy*

7. Montesquieu's *Humanité* and Rousseau's *Pitié* — 139
   *Clifford Orwin*

8. Montesquieu and Tocqueville as Philosophical Historians: Liberty, Determinism, and the Prospects for Freedom — 149
   *David W. Carrithers*

9. Montesquieu and the Scottish Enlightenment — 179
   *James Moore*

## Part III
### Montesquieu and Comparative Constitutional Law

10. Montesquieu and the Renaissance of Comparative Public Law — 199
    *Ran Hirschl*

11. Free Speech and *The Spirit of Laws* in Canada and the United States: A Test of Montesquieu's Approach to Comparative Law — 221
    *Stephen L. Newman*

## Part IV
### Montesquieu and Modern Liberalisms

12. Montesquieu's *Persian Letters*: A Timely Classic — 239
    *Fred Dallmayr*

13. Montesquieu and Us — 259
    *Jean Ehrard*

14. Montesquieu and the Future of Liberalism — 271
    *Ronald F. Thiemann*

15. Montesquieu and Liberalism: The Question of Pluralism 279
    *Catherine Larrère*

Bibliography 303

Contributors 323

Index 329

# Acknowledgments

This collection of chapters is the result of a conference I organized at the University of Toronto in the fall of 2005 to commemorate the 250th anniversary of the death of Montesquieu. It seems only fitting that the occasion was used to discuss how Montesquieu has contributed to our established political traditions as well as how his work can aid us in adapting our traditions to new political circumstances and considerations. I wish to thank all those who were instrumental with their good advice and help in making sure that the conference was a great success. These include Sophie Bourgault, David W. Carrithers, Christine Elias, Ran Hirschl, Catherine Larrère, Rita O'Brien, Leanne Thomas, and Rob Vipond, as well as staff at the Munk Centre for International Studies. I also am grateful to the Chancellor Jackman Program for the Arts at the University of Toronto, the Departments of French, Law, and Political Science of the University of Toronto, the French Consulate in Toronto, and the Social Science and Humanities Research Council of Canada who helped to fund it.

I thank all the participants and discussants at the conference, including Mel Richter, Ed Andrew, Simone Chambers, Andrea Radasanu, Simon Kow, Ronnie Beiner, and Thomas Pangle and all the authors represented here, as well as the two anonymous reviewers of this volume, all of whom helped to ensure that the quality of the scholarship presented here is of the highest quality.

In preparing this volume I could not have done without the tremendous skill and patience of my assistant, Katherine Reilly. I also am grateful for the help of my editor, Michael Rinella, of State University of New York Press. In addition, Crystal Cordell translated four chapters for this collection. She deserves recognition for her excellent work.

Chapter 3, by Céline Spector, is reproduced (in translation and with some adaptation) from chapter 1 of her book *Montesquieu. Pouvoirs, richesses et sociétés* (2004) with the permission of her publisher Presses Universitaires de France. Chapter 12, by Fred Dallmayr, "Montesquieu's *Persian Letters*: A Timely

Classic" is reproduced from pages 95–115 of his book *In Search of the Good Life* (2007) with permission from the University Press of Kentucky.

I would like to thank my family, Ronnie, Gabriel, Zimra, Marcus, Mia, Pauline, (uncle) Fred, (aunt) Mouse, (uncle) Paul, and all those who have shown great patience over the last number of years with all things Montesquieuian.

# Introduction

*Rebecca E. Kingston*

This volume brings together many of the best scholars on Montesquieu today, and from a variety of traditions, to reflect on the intellectual legacy left by this formidable thinker of the Enlightenment. Montesquieu's work has been deemed important for the development of liberal democratic traditions in Europe throughout the nineteenth and twentieth centuries. Yet his work has never fully been captured by its ongoing identification with those traditions. This collection of chapters seeks to explore and exploit that tension. In various ways the authors of these chapters bring to light an added complexity to Montesquieu's thinking that allows for a rethinking of his legacy and that generates new possibilities for political lessons in a world that has changed significantly since the mid-1700s.

Most of the traditional focus on Montesquieu's legacy, particularly in Anglo-American circles, stemming from a history of interpretation of his work *The Spirit of Laws* (1748), has been in the realm of formal constitutionalism. However, scholars have recently developed a new interest in Montesquieu's observations of the more informal aspects of community, including the ways in which collective sentiment, manners, and 'moeurs' function in political community. The sensitivity to this dynamic in Montesquieu's work reflects a growing awareness within contemporary liberalism of the inadequacy of the formal mechanisms of law, constitutions, and contracts in being on their own efficient mechanisms for even the minimal demands of peace and order. Recognition of this, with the consequence of greater attention to the role of cultural norms and *moeurs* in politics, raises the possibility of not one but competing paths and manifestations of liberal modernity. One important legacy of Montesquieu's work in this context is to give us some of the tools needed to generate a plural conception of modern liberalism.

In order to highlight many of the significant themes in Montesquieu's work as well as how these themes have been carried into Western traditions of political thinking, the chapters in this volume are divided into four sections. The first section is devoted to the theme of morals and manners, or what we might loosely call "social norms and customs," as portrayed within Montesquieu's main texts. There are discussions of how these features are portrayed by Montesquieu across a number of cultural contexts, as well as how they play into his model of political liberty in the England of his day.

The second section is an exploration of the legacy of Montesquieu's thought in the later Enlightenment and early nineteenth century, with a particular focus on the appropriation and development of the theme of morals and manners. This will help to show a different intellectual legacy than that often supposed by early twentieth-century commentators on Montesquieu's work, commentators who have sometimes reduced his contribution to the history of political thought to the concept of the separation of powers.

The third section focuses on Montesquieu and contemporary studies of comparative constitutional law. Montesquieu's work has largely been studied by political theorists and scholars of comparative literature. This section offers new readings of Montesquieu's work from the perspective of comparative law as a means to assess his impact on contemporary legal scholarship as well as what his work can contribute.

The fourth and final section is devoted to the theme of Montesquieu and modern liberalism. The intent is not to assume that Montesquieu can be read straightforwardly as a liberal thinker. Rather, the idea is that Montesquieu can be seen as an inspiration for later liberalism and that this fact coupled with the recognition that there is a certain parallel to be made between Montesquieu's attempts to think through the fact of diversity and our own attempts within liberalism to do the same today make his thought of particular contemporary interest.

Five important themes cut across virtually all these chapters: the significance of Montesquieu's "anti-Jacobin" ethos; his commitment to pluralism; his interest in uncovering the dynamics through which various communities sustain their unity; the significant, though contested, nature of his methodology; and the need to rethink Montesquieu's legacy in ways that help us to rethink liberal modernity. While the chapters in this collection touch upon each of these themes in quite different ways, the authors generally agree on these fundamentals. Alongside this, there are also a number of issues that are left open by the authors for ongoing deliberation and further study.

All the contributors to this collection recognize the important legacy that Montesquieu has had into the present. Whether it be measured by casual and not so casual remarks by leading European journalists and politicians (as noted by Jean Ehrard) by recognition of the common reflex to attribute to

Montesquieu the modern constitutional notion of a 'separation of powers' (as noted by Michael Mosher, Cecil Patrick Courtney, Brian C. V. Singer, and Jacob T. Levy), or by the acknowledgment of the importance of the work of Montesquieu for foundational thinkers of the modern era, such as Smith, Tocqueville, Hegel, Nietzsche, and Durkheim (as noted by James Moore, David W. Carrithers, Clifford Orwin, Ran Hirschl), there is a general acknowledgment that the work of Montesquieu has been important in helping to determine a number of outlooks that constitute our modern conception of politics. All the authors in this collection share in a general consensus on this point. Furthermore, all the contributors recognize that, despite this important legacy, it is a partial legacy. They acknowledge that in many ways there are further and important resources in Montesquieu's work for rethinking, or at least refining, our liberal modernity and how it has manifested itself in relation to political life. The compatibility of Montesquieu's work with certain key aspects of liberalism makes him particularly well suited for helping us to shed some new light on our current preoccupations, if not to revise our common presuppositions. Still, of course, there will be limits as to how far this can go, and not all the contributors agree on either the extent to which this is possible or the manner in which his thought can be most revelatory.

Another theme acknowledged by the contributors is Montesquieu's resistance to the application of uniform solutions or to the idea that there is one universally best constitutional form. It is recognized in various guises, such as anti-Jacobinism (Fred Dallmayr) or Montesquieu's quarrel with Condorcet (Catherine Larrère), and a number of contributors, including Mosher, note the importance of this point, particularly to deepen the issue of Montesquieu's known commitment to monarchy in France and to judicial independence. Courtney shows how key passages of *The Spirit of Laws* devoted to an exegesis of the English constitution demonstrate this spirit. Levy demonstrates that a focus on Montesquieu in this light is essential, as it not only demonstrates the ongoing importance of regional loyalties and appreciation for diversity and traditional privileges and immunities that characterise our legal systems today but also forces us to rethink the stark divide between ancient and modern constitutionalism that had been a standard idiom of political theory for much of the twentieth century.

Some contributors suggest that the force of Montesquieu's anti-Jacobinism comes more from a consideration of the ontological preconditions for authority than a respect of legal custom per se. For Singer, the fact that Montesquieu separates power from law (the ultimate example being that of despotism where power exists as will without law), shows a sociological approach to the question of political order. In a similar but distinct vein, Céline Spector argues that it is the dynamic of a social network held together by similar passions that is the key to political order for Montesquieu and that laws should be regarded as somewhat instrumental to this task. For both these contributors, law is in essence limited and constrained by what it can effect, given the nature of the social. Thus, there are two ways to view the anti-Jacobinism of Montesquieu: one, as a normative issue vis-à-vis the desirability of a recognition of legal customs and diversity within a single legal framework; and two, as an empirical issue, regarding the constraints of law as an instrument such that it cannot be implemented in the same way in diverse situations.

On a different but related point, there is general acknowledgment among the contributors to the book regarding Montesquieu's commitment to a principle of diversity or pluralism. Like liberal commitments, however, the unity of the commitment hides a multiplicity of concerns. For some, the key is moral pluralism. Larrère shows how Montesquieu's notion of the differing objects of states is an endorsement of moral plurality. While she recognises Montesquieu's invocation of universal norms, such as in his condemnation of slavery, she holds that these universal norms fix limits and thereby stand only as negative injunctions, alongside competing systems of diverse moral characteristics. Dallmayr also acknowledges the importance of Montesquieu in this light but suggests further that Montesquieu's work provides us with some resources to cross over these barriers and engage in cross-cultural understanding, something that indeed Ehrard also seeks to engage in his contribution.

For others, while moral pluralism is certainly important, of more general importance is the question of identity (within which questions of moral pluralism may be embedded). The fact that Montesquieu was a keen defender of preserving the integrity of differing groups within a polity (with certain limits, particularly with regard to religion, as acknowledged by Orwin and others) provides another challenge to modern calls for uniformity and shows how far he remains from contractarian models of liberalism where individual commitments override claims to group preservation. Mosher's contribution is particularly revelatory as to how this plays out in Montesquieu's discussion of monarchies, in contrast to the question of identity in republics.

The issue of group identity is central to Montesquieu also in relation to the more general consideration of how a civil ethos is formed and sustained. While this is looked upon by Spector in terms of the interactive effects of a similar shared passion within one political community, such as an Augustinian might view it, Larrère suggests that Montesquieu comes closer to Aristotle and indeed Machiavelli on this point and that the emergence of a civil ethos is through the interaction and indeed possible conflict of quite different-minded groups. Whatever the dynamic, it is of interest to Singer to acknowledge how this process can work to develop a sense of a symbolic order through which power can be exercised in ways separate from the authority of law. It is precisely through these means that in a monarchy there can be clear, legitimate constraints upon the supposed sovereign authority of the king.

But how can or should we trust the analysis offered by this thinker several centuries ago? It is of interest that the contributors acknowledge that the value of Montesquieu's analysis derives not from the timelessness of his logic—that is from a rationalist framework that survives through the test of time—but rather from his very attention to particular detail. This is shown in a concrete way through Catherine Volpilhac-Auger's discussion of Montesquieu's uses of sources regarding China. Her expert knowledge of the manuscripts allows her to reveal how Montesquieu as a critical thinker did not take his sources at face value but sought to develop an independent perspective by sifting through a number of competing accounts. Similarly Carrithers, Ehrard, and Larrère show Montesquieu as providing careful attention to the characteristics that *distinguish* particulars within a certain category. It is this attention to detail, then, allowing for a complex analysis of a number of social and political phenomena, rather than an *esprit de système*, that has proved to have had lasting value in his work. There may be some, such as Hirschl and Stephen L. Newman, who, from the perspective of contemporary practice of constitutional law, recognize some deficiencies, such as inattention to the politics of law (though Mosher disagrees with this and holds that Montesquieu clearly recognized how the ambitions and preconceptions of the legislator can be pernicious). However, the degree to which the broad contours of analysis offered by Montesquieu can still be followed today to begin to understand legal evolution is significant. And the urge to extend comparative legal scholarship to a greater number of both similar and distinct sample jurisdictions, as suggested by Hirschl, can only be regarded as the spirit of Montesquieu transposed to a scale made possible by modern social science.

In the midst of these general themes, there are a number of issues singled out for further deliberation and study. One issue that remains unresolved in the conversations of this volume is the exact nature and breadth of Montesquieu's pluralism. While some contributors praise his defence of universal justice, an invocation that shapes his injunctions against international aggression and his condemnation of slavery, it is not clear how Montesquieu reconciles this commitment to universalism with his vision of moral pluralism. Larrère and Dallmayr provide important indices as to how one might seek to resolve this apparent paradox.

Another question raised by these contributions is, why has Montesquieu been largely misinterpreted and thereby misappropriated? While Courtney offers some suggestions as to how the history of publishing may have had something to do with it (publishers cutting corners by only publishing extracts of a longer work and assuming that the English would for the most part be interested in the chapters directly describing their own politics), Levy suggests also that there were important political and social reasons for the shift. Ehrard, nonetheless, also reminds us that it is in the nature of Montesquieu's thought itself to be somewhat elusive, something that can never be fully captured and thereby will always lend itself to interpretative swings.

Given the new legacy that is sketched in this collection, what can we draw from Montesquieu for current debates within liberal democracy today? Mosher offers us the paradox of the great thinker who warns us against the lure of philosophy and the search for general answers, while teaching us to embrace, albeit cautiously, a global modernity. Ronald F. Thiemann suggests that Montesquieu allows us to single out the central problem of economic inequalities plaguing contemporary democracies. Larrère further suggests that Montesquieu offers us a valuable perspective in which we can deepen our understanding of pluralism. Montesquieu leads us to recognize the social roots of all individual norms through which individuals define and may choose their conception of the good in contemporary liberal societies. Does this mean, as suggested by Orwin, that we have left nature behind us? Or does "the nature of things"—that sets limits to sovereign and legal authority and allows us to conceive of freedom as the endowed prerogative of communities into the modern era—give us a solid basis on which to define and guide our future progress?

Perhaps we must ultimately return to the more humble acknowledgment of Montesquieu that in the long run human beings are to a large degree unable to control the broader forces that shape their social and political lives. Humans are creatures of community who relate to each other and who appear on the public stage as mainly emotional beings. While this does not suggest that politics will always be unreasonable, it does suggest that the possible number of influential factors and unintended consequences is infinite and that political life can neither be controlled nor predicted. Indeed, this is the message of his image of the ultimately powerless despot. It suggests that it is not a useful enterprise to reflect at a macrolevel on the shape of the most rational society; rather, we need to start from a clearer understanding of the beings that we are and through that achieve a better understanding of possibilities and the limits to the politics we have.

In conclusion, then, this is not a collection of chapters that seeks to retrace or sketch a well-worn and established intellectual trajectory. While articulating the legacy of Montesquieu, these authors are also engaged in an act of what we might call "transformative interpretative reiteration," that is, adapting and reshaping that legacy in the very act of expressing it. It is both the changing circumstances and new challenges of contemporary politics, as well as the richness of Montesquieu's work, that serve as the underlying conditions for this project.

1

# What Montesquieu Taught: "Perfection Does Not Concern Men or Things Universally"

Michael Mosher

Montesquieu's legacy is justly dominated by his thoughts about the separation of powers, whether in his ideal model of the monarchical regime where they are most strikingly presented, or in Madison's, Hamilton's, and Constant's republican adaptations of these monarchical institutions (ably explained in this volume by Levy), or in countless other areas of political, social, and intimate life.[1] But why did he worry so much about the division, distribution, and separation of power? Of course, the political science and constitutional mechanics are understood as well as his fear of state power, but what anxiety lies at the bottom of the argument for the doctrine of a separation of powers? I pursue the meaning of this anxiety and its political and philosophical consequences under four headings, which I take is "What Montesquieu Taught."

First, he stood against what we might call "state-sponsored perfectionist ethics"—a state that engages a citizenry in projects of self-transformation along a known path of development and with a, so to speak, preordained teleological outcome. He offered three counsels for the avoidance of the perfectionist temptation, two of which are cautious in the extreme, one of which is incautious in the extreme and which reintroduces, so to speak through the back door, an alternative version of a self-transformative and perfectionist politics. However, this last counsel possessed no preordained teleological goal and urged restraint only in order to preserve the conditions that allowed these nonstate-sponsored—or only indirectly state-sponsored—transformations to take place, namely, the condition of political liberty in what was later called "civil society." Second, we see that the consequences of these three counsels against state-sponsored perfection play themselves out in a preferred regime, a model of undercommitment to public things, which is monarchy, not a republic. But unlike the official Bourbon regime under which Montesquieu lived, his was a reform model, a monarchy that was secular, more open to internal political resistance, and more able to countenance heterogeneity, that is, pluralism and diversity, which in his understanding the republic could less well tolerate. Third, we see that the republic as a model of overcommitment to public things was, as its many partisans among the readers of Montesquieu had always supposed, a regime that represented political redemption against the drift characteristic of regimes of undercommitment, however unpredictable the self-transformative or perfectionist politics that result. Fourth, we need to highlight Montesquieu's deep-seated animus against large-scale polities and rule from a distance and all the forms of illegitimate rule that often flowed from these endeavors, namely, empire, colonialism, and despotism. These are for Montesquieu related pathologies and an understanding of political things that Hannah Arendt freely adapted into her theory of totalitarianism.[2] However, they can be approached as well from the point of view of Montesquieu's fundamental ambivalence about philosophy, and therefore about the figure of the philosopher who, like the imperial despot, sought a form of rule from a distance. Enlightened philosophical skeptics were heroes of resistance to injustice, superstition, and oppression, and Montesquieu on more than one occasion gave them their due. But he also seemed to detect in their outlook (and in himself, but that is another story) a sort of puritanical abstemiousness, which was the emotional revulsion of the detached skeptical mind, as both Puritanism and skepticism expressed a desire for distance from others. It was an outlook that had something in common with the mental horizon of the imperial administrator or despot.

### First Teaching: The Seductive Lure of Political Perfection, Which Is Cured by the Spontaneous Exercise of Freedom

We begin with three widely scattered passages from *The Spirit of Laws*. We turn first to the "Invocation to the Muses" (added only posthumously and attached to the beginning of Book XX) where Montesquieu pleads with the divinities of seductive prose: "Make it so that one is instructed though I do not teach." He is wary about assuming the pose of teacher. Education is arduous, teaching is easily rejected. Tutelage implies the absence of liberty.

Second, in a chapter from Book XIX whose subject is "How some legislators have confused the principles which govern men," Montesquieu compares the republic of ancient Sparta (or Lacedaemonia) to imperial China, which he officially dislikes because it is too big to be governed other than by despotic means, but which in fact he sometimes quietly applauds. In this instance, the Greek republic comes off worse than the despotic Asian empire precisely because Sparta illustrates only too fulsomely how the republican spirit floods public life with tutorial hectoring. By contrast, China's instruction is minimal and to the point. It encouraged men "to have much respect for each other." This was "civility," a trait superior to mere politeness, since the latter "flatters the vices of others" while "civility keeps us from displaying our own." Sparta encouraged neither politeness nor civility. Its founder, Lycurgus, instead taught Spartan citizens to be teachers. Such a result should have been commendable in the era of *"lumière."* But Montesquieu is clear-eyed about the pedagogical limitations of the importuning characters thus encouraged. "As simple as they were rigid, these people [the republicans of Sparta] were always correcting or being corrected, always instructing or being instructed." As a consequence, "they *exercise virtue* rather than show respect for one another" (XIX, 16; my translation and emphasis).

The practice of "virtue" is the goal of every perfectionist ethics. In Montesquieu's understanding, virtue is also the tutelary ideal of republican citizenship. However admirable the collective results (in the case of Sparta, fierce and loyal warrior-citizens and thus a long-lived regime able to leave its mark upon the world), the perfectionist practice of republican virtue seems to have produced an attendant vice: a tyranny of small souls that is on the face of it far worse than the cosmopolitan "civility" encouraged in a well-ordered expansive empire.

Third, on what was once intended as the last page of the last book of *The Spirit of Laws*—Books XXX and XXXI were an afterthought—the author turns to the issue of personal bias in the legislator. Even for great figures such as Plato, Aristotle, Machiavelli, Thomas More, and Harrington, "the laws" in their texts always reveal, he says, "the passions and the prejudices of the legislator" (XXIX, 19). This is an extraordinary claim to find on the last page of a text that exalts the rule of law. The impersonality of law is evidently in every instance compromised—the examples given suggest it was not a beneficial compromise—by the personality of the lawgiver. The law is law only for and on behalf of its maker. How could the law become law for everyone? Suppose that we credit Montesquieu with the recognition that such a judgment would apply to him as well. He was not exempted from this judgment against the philosopher-legislator. What can we find in his text that would immunize the law, or those to whom the law applies, against the prejudices and imperfections to which all legislators are prone?

The three examples point to difficulties of instruction and therefore difficulties for regimes that required teachers to transform men and women into citizens. Teaching is easily rejected unless accompanied by seduction or coercion. There is a hectoring, importuning quality to this public life that is prejudicial to the basic "civility" arguably owed to each free citizen. Teachers and pupils must always concern themselves with the imperfections and self-interested motives of teachers. The author meets these difficulties by proposing three kinds of self-abnegating instruction for the teacher/legislator.

The first bit of advice confronts the vice inherent in the "counsels" of perfectionist ethics. "Counsels" of perfection are designed to cope with human imperfection but must take into account that human imperfection may have tainted its adherents' understanding of what improvement is required. This problem was most evident, Montesquieu supposed, in those inspired by religious (or as we shall later see, philosophical) idealism. In Book XXIV ("On the Laws in Relations to the Religion Established in Each Country"), the author is blunt. It is perilous to search for perfection. Therefore, one may give advice or "counsel," but the latter should never be made mandatory, that is to say, "law." State authority ought not to enforce religious law. (Even within churches, the religious precepts of perfection ought to be the nonobligatory urging of counsel.) As religion touches on what might perfect us, this can be no concern of the error-prone legislator. The duty of the latter is to make contingent judgments between various understandings of the good and not to impose a standard reading of perfection upon all the souls within the grasp of the sovereign. "When [religion] . . . gives rule, not for the good but for the better, not for what is good but for what is perfect, it is suitable for these to be counsels and not laws, *for perfection does not concern men or things universally*" (XXIV, 7; my emphasis). The contemporary analogue to these cautionary precepts is the political liberalism of John Rawls and others that in the standard deontological manner constrains states to observe rights of the associated members while leaving diverse projects for reaching the public good outside or at least on the margins of state supervision and in the hands of the volunteer associations of civil society.

The second instruction regarding the passions behind the laws is equally cautionary, but goes in another direction. Deliberate change is not always for the better. This Montesquieu announces right at the outset in the preface to *The Spirit of Laws*. "One feels the old abuses and sees their correction, but one also sees the abuses of the correction itself." Edmund Burke, a close reader of Montesquieu, took this advice to heart and with it founded modern philosophical conservatism—which is distinct, of course, from any conservatism with a perfectionist project.[3] The differences, however, between a self-abnegating liberal and a conservative who sees abuses in reform are not as great as they may seem to the partisans involved. Both practice interpretative caution.

By contrast, the third counsel is open to all the innovations talkative human beings can invent. Montesquieu's third counsel is the "talking cure" to borrow the vocabulary of therapy. It comes in two sorts, talking back to power and talking to those one may treat as equals.

Where people can talk back to power there is greater possibility for correcting errors. This argument was to have an illustrious future. It is Tocqueville's central premise for asserting the superiority of democracy, that it can correct its own errors.[4] But talk is not possible where some cringe in fear. Montesquieu's famous separation of powers is a device for neutralizing the distorting effects of power imbalances.

The result preserves conversational (and constitutional) exchange and creates a space for the second kind of talk, the speaking characteristic of "civil society," which is to say the talk among those who may regard one another as equals. We put it this way to avoid claiming that Montesquieu insisted upon a moral or state-enforced requirement of strict equality or equality in every domain. He did not. He understood that the impulse to create and to recreate hierarchy was endemic. But every hierarchy that is not purely despotic—and the hierarchies of monarchy are not, they are what Rawls would call "decent" hierarchies[5]—should contain within them possibilities for challenging or taming hierarchy. Every hierarchy must allow the weaker members not only to talk back to power, free speech in the political sense, but they should also encourage civil society, the possibility of speaking to others as though all were equal. This is again the work of the separation of powers which ameliorates the concentrations of power not only in government but in society.

Let us illustrate this last point by considering the role of the separation of powers in extending women's rights in Europe. Why were women more nearly equal to men in Europe than elsewhere?[6] Such a question might seem bizarre today where the benchmark against which progress in equal rights is measured in precisely the bad old days of the Europe of Montesquieu's time. But Montesquieu asks a comparative question. He was convinced that women were more subordinated both earlier in European history and elsewhere outside modern Europe. He wanted to know why Europe was a relative exception. This conviction lies at the heart of his views on "oriental despotism." Describing France on the model of a harem satirically presented the abuses of Louis XIV against his subjects. French subjects were on this indictment as deprived of liberty as harem women. Montesquieu did not believe Europe was protected from either despotism against subjects or from the enslavement of women. Nevertheless, he had persuaded himself that institutions had arisen early on which gave Europe the potential to be different as the strange and marvelous paragraphs in XXXVIII, 22 explicated below show.

Writing on behalf of heterosexual men, Montesquieu asserts that, "our connection with women is founded" on three kinds of desires. The first and obvious one is sensual desire, but Montesquieu criticizes the impulse that promotes this form of "happiness." The spirit of sensual desire is too close to that of despotic empire. "The prodigious luxury of Rome when it was immense flattered the idea of the pleasures of the senses." The second desire is equally obvious, the sentimental and romantic wish to love and be loved. This, he alleges, was not natural but a social invention, another innovation of the ancient Greeks: "A certain idea of tranquility in the Greek countryside caused the Greeks to describe the feelings of love." But from the perspective of women interested in being acknowledged as having a public existence, neither lust nor love is satisfactory. Physically stronger or more aggressive males are moved to protect both their lusts and their loves from rivals. They do so by defining women as private creatures and by assuring that they are, as far as custom and law will permit, enclosed in a household that, not inaccurately, has been defined as patriarchal. This is why, presumably, Montesquieu found the Islamic *serail* or harem such a perfectly universal expression of men's standard desires about women.

A third male desire, equally a matter of historical invention, comes closer to being in reciprocal accord with a woman's desire for public and not merely private acknowledgment. European late medieval practices, nowhere evident earlier or elsewhere, show that women "are quite *enlightened judges* of a part of the things that constitute personal merit" (my emphasis). Montesquieu draws this lesson from chivalric codes that prescribed, in "a spirit of gallantry," judicial combat. This involves duels between men motivated not by the desire for recognition from each other but from a desire to "please" women who now had public standing as their "judges" (XXVIII, 22).

For women to be public judges of merit among men may not seem like much, but for Montesquieu the spirit of gallantry that brought women into the public limelight was the moment when Europe became potentially different. Burke's famous passages in *Reflections of the Revolution in France* that link medieval chivalry to the spirit of modern Europe, its commerce, its learning, and the standing of women, as illustrated in the cult of the Queen in France, derive from this reading of Montesquieu.[7]

In Montesquieu's description of the *political* separation (or as he says, the "distribution") of powers in England, the independence of judges (i.e., English juries) is the critical factor that decides whether this country or any other is despotic or not, however unwisely united the legislative and executive powers may be. Finding in the history of European *society* a power of judgment distributed to the physically weaker sex as compensation for the effective seizure by men of a monopoly of legislative and executive power suggests how concerned Montesquieu is to see in counterbalances to power the prerequisite for maintaining a free society.

But Montesquieu's "talking cure" for the problem of human limitations has further ramifications. Talking can transform understandings and disagreements since talk transforms the participants who hold these understandings and disagreements. Faithful to the civil society that flourished in the aristocratic salon culture of his day, Montesquieu found conversation transformative only (or at least especially) when men and women together undertook it. Montesquieu invidiously contrasts two kinds of *esprit* or cultures. He pits the gender-integrated communicative and transformative cultures against the noncommunicative and therefore presumptively despotic cultures.

Montesquieu's first two counsels against the search for human perfection were cautious in the extreme. They offered either a self-abstemious liberalism or a philosophically lethargic conservatism. The third counsel, however, shows that Montesquieu is far from being risk averse. By commending a "communication" that flourishes only in liberty and whose outcomes are unknown except that they will constantly change manners and mores, Montesquieu sets humanity on a vast dialectical and transformative adventure. This understanding of history as an unfolding adventure of the human spirit will later be recognized as historicism, the primary conceit of German idealist thought. It is also, as must be obvious, a species of perfectionist politics—straight out of its origins in Plato's *Republic*, where Socrates shows the way of light to dialogue partners mired in the shadows. But there is a crucial difference. For Montesquieu, no one should know in advance where the unfolding of the human spirit was heading, or at least no one should have an effective monopoly in guiding that spirit, so long as the conditions for keeping the conversation open were met. The later historicists (Hegel, Marx) were more anxious about where the human project was heading. Montesquieu seems content to describe the political and social forms that he believes have the best chance of accommodating whatever humans come up with next.

The first of these forms was, as it was for Hegel, monarchy. The second form that both allowed and channeled change Montesquieu called simply "commerce." His defense of it was spun from the same web of understandings that allowed him to exalt the spirit of chivalry and gender-integrated salons into paragons of liberty, reciprocally beneficial exchange, and self-transformative communication. "The history of commerce," he writes, "is the history of communication among peoples" (XXI, 5).

But was Montesquieu like other Enlightenment thinkers more optimistic than he had a right to be about the direction in which commerce was likely to go? Perhaps not. For him, the communication inspired by commerce was not always a pretty business. Immediately following the above cited line, he adds that, "the various destructions of these peoples, the identifiable rise and fall of populations and devastations, form the greatest events of this history" (XXI, 5; my translation). Before Marx called upon the workers to correct the abusive and socially destructive capitalist business cycle, and before Schumpeter ambivalently celebrated capitalism's "creative destruction," Montesquieu evidently grasped the nub of the argument.

If he understood that the history of that form of communication called "capitalism" was simultaneously the history of bloody reversals of fortune, why did he support it? There is in *The Spirit of Laws* ample acknowledgment of commercial exploitation that pits class against class. Aristocratic landowners in Poland were so situated that they were more or less inevitably tempted to exploit the peasantry in order to gain an export advantage. Where law and custom did not rigorously forbid it, well-connected aristocrats and state bureaucrats (including the "prince") were tempted by predatory commercial opportunities (XX, 19–23). In these cases, Montesquieu acknowledges the argument against commerce that was by the mid-nineteenth century to carry so many thoughtful critics into opposition.

Is it then a problem that in Montesquieu we are given no glimpse of the "ends" of life, a sense of achievable perfection? Instead of ends we are left with the idea of a self-abnegating liberty whose sense of adventure and contingency depends upon refusing or being sincerely unable to answer the questions about ends.

In a more prosaic register, this is not unlike the choice that the critics of globalization see before them. They often speak as though they were caught between a liberty that secures citizens in the enjoyment of a diminishing national patrimony—the "end" is the good life for each nation—and a liberty that runs the risk of losing it forever in the global marketplace. The latter may promise access to alternative goods and even to the means by which the original patrimony could be sustained. But the charms of global openness are lost on those for whom anxieties about loss of national tradition or an old social contract loom larger. Globalization is but a new version of what in Book XX Montesquieu suggests "great Atlas taught," namely, that there is nothing but the communicative competencies of commerce and its multihued allies, taste and changing cultural fashions (XIX, 8), that sustain a world composed only of such human reasons for acting. If such communications establish patrimony and contract, they also undo them.

Montesquieu attributes this teaching to Atlas, the mythical creature who holds up the world, and ties it to his thesis about communication and commerce. But it is perhaps better understood as Montesquieu's *own great teaching* in a book that endeavors to hold up to view the world insofar as it can be presented as a whole. The theory that permits us this glimpse of the planet as a sphere of human meanings is itself dependent upon the communications fostered by commerce. The latter have in effect supplemented the inherited particular manners, mores, and laws of each nation with "reasons" that permit humans partially to transcend the horizon established by the nation. A seemingly naturalistic sociology of regimes, founded on tyrannical forces such as climate and terrain, becomes thanks to the "talking cure" an idealist social theory whose agenda is to show how first nature and then the nation (which masquerades as second nature) become self-conscious and endogenously transformative.

This puts Montesquieu on the side of globalization and of the world it is busy fabricating—not according to *les choses* but according to *l'ordre des choses* that spells out along the tracks provided by the separation of powers the distinct influences of manners, mores, and laws, which must never, he warns, be allowed to collapse into one another—the mistake of Chinese and other "oriental despotisms." Within the plural possibilities such separate tracks of influence inevitably permit, humans are free, and not overbearingly determined as Pierre Manent thinks the sociological perspective requires.[8]

There is, nevertheless, much in *The Spirit of Laws* for sovereignty-obsessed foes of globalization to savor. A favorite sentiment will be found in an early line about the significance of republican sovereignty, the anxieties about which seem among the critics of globalization to have reached a new crescendo of despair. However much Montesquieu may have wanted to deflate the pretensions of republicans, he was forced to admire the republican achievement. His and Rousseau's version of the republic, furnished with all the weapons of a mythical sovereignty, are ideas too seductive to dismiss in a world anxious about restoring security to citizens who believe they are under constant threat of being invaded by alien forces—either natural or human. These critics of global commodities and capital flows lament the dismantling of the leviathan state and, in a world of massive immigration flows, deplore the resultant dilution in the meaning of citizenship. Surely some among them will take a certain bloody satisfaction in Montesquieu's first effort in Book II, 2 to discuss the meaning of republican sovereignty: "Libanius says that *in Athens a foreigner who mingled in the people's assembly was punished with death*. This is because such a man usurped sovereignty" (Montesquieu's emphasis).

To reiterate, Montesquieu's first teaching can be easily summarized. He gave his readers two reasons to be cautious about using the state to plan for the improvement of the citizenry. First, perfectionist plans inevitably carry the taint of their designers' personality. They are not therefore for everyone even if they are imposed on all. Second, even if this were not the case, every planned change may go awry, and the costs may end up higher than the benefits. "Corrections" carry their own "abuses." But if this advice is good for creating anxiety about state-planned change, why is Montesquieu less anxious about purely social change? For his third counsel is to participate in the unplanned seemingly spontaneous changes of people in civil society who are talking or seducing themselves into new ways of living. To recur to the theme of the invocation of the muses, there is instruction here, but no dictation, no state power–inspired teaching. Montesquieu evidently trusted the spontaneous self-concerned instincts of free people more than he did the pedagogical encouragement of those organized as the Spartans were, into a political free people. Yet this cannot be our final conclusion about Montesquieu's turn of mind. For if he only celebrated the freedoms possible in a people undercommitted to public projects, which is to say a people who live under what he describes as monarchy, why then does he lavish so much praise, to wit, the above passage on Athenian sovereignty, on a people overly committed to a public project, namely, a republican citizenry?

## Second Teaching: In Praise of Undercommitment—Monarchies That Govern Complex, Differentiated, Open, "Multicultural" Societies

Montesquieu's picture of monarchy draws on Newtonian and Copernican scientific imagery: "You could say it is like the system of the universe where there is a force constantly repelling all bodies from the center and a force of gravitation attracting them to it. Honor makes all the parts of the body politic move ... [E]ach person works for the common good believing he works for his individual interest" (*Laws* III, 7).

Monarchical actors were simultaneously drawn in by the gravitational allure of patriotic service to the state, honor's source, so to speak, and yet strove just hard enough in the centrifugal direction to escape the reputation of dishonorable conformity to those currently in control of state and court, an escape that alone would permit each actor a distinctive identity and therefore the possibility of both making a mark on the world and of contributing to the state. Personal ambitions agitated society but never, Montesquieu thought, the properly constituted monarchical state, which, despite the contrary passions that honor elicited, exhibited, he was confident, the serene celestial permanence of a planet orbiting the sun. This was not a portrait of monarchy as a transitional state tipping toward revolution.

Monarchy's stability was reinforced by its balance of diverse interests and separated powers, which was the on-going task for moderate and prudent legislators: "In order to form a moderate government, one must combine powers, regulate them, temper them, make them act; one must give one power a ballast, so to speak, in order to put it in a position to resist another" (*Laws* V, 14). Not unaware of the shortcomings of the Bourbon regime, the baron proposed an image of a progressive monarchy sufficiently attractive that it became a widely shared partisan view.[9]

On the question of sovereignty, Montesquieu splits the difference with the great predecessor theorists. The author exiles Bossuet's theological justification of the absolutist state. Bodin, however, is another matter. *The Spirit of Laws* affirms Bodinian absolutism: "[I]n a monarchy the prince is the source of all political and civil power" (*Laws*, II, 4). Absolute sovereignty, the ultimate power to decide, rests with the holder of royal authority. Given the fact of his absolute power, however, what happens when the king asserts his Bodinian right to overrule any "intermediary power?" For Montesquieu, "honor" comes to the rescue as a cultural supplement to the law. Honor is the political "principle" that actually undermines the narrowly legitimate exercise of monarchical power. But when it is countenanced rather than suppressed, honor guarantees the wider legitimacy of the regime. In the case of an overruled intermediary power, honorable judges will be expected, when the stakes are high, to continue to resist. Resistance as such is illegal under an absolutist legal code, but under the cultural code of honor, resistance is mandated. Aristocratic honor requires obedience to a king, but it simultaneously makes that obedience provisional by requiring every subject to draw a prior conclusion about the continued worth or honorableness of the higher authority in question. The aristocrat both upholds hierarchy and submits it to democratic censure. Honor discovers that a rebel necessarily dwells in the soul of every obedient citizen. The appeal to honorable dissent is as illegal as it is effective. It necessarily attunes power holders to study by way of anticipation the plural sensitivities of differentiated subjects, thus introducing into the king's court, otherwise little disposed to such measures, a due respect for a multifarious diversity of interests and understandings.

This dignified disobedience, that is to say, civil disobedience, is the dissent of the stubborn. The judges, Montesquieu writes, "never obey better than when they drag their feet," because only then do they "bring into the prince's business the *reflection* that one can hardly expect from the *absence of enlightenment* in the court [of Louis XV]" (*Laws*, V, 10; my emphasis).

The author's picture of French society under monarchy celebrates its sociability and communicative openness to experiments. Its spirit was elsewhere conveyed by his adoption of the pregnant term *commerce*. Commerce, which is a subcategory of the wider concept, 'communication,' referred not only to cross border trade in goods, which was in any event thought to "cure destructive prejudices," encourage "gentle mores," and "lead to peace" (*Laws* XX, 1–2), but to much else besides. Commerce/communication came to mean simultaneously what we call, with a bluntness that might betray the elegance Montesquieu expected from each activity, "free trade," "free speech," and "free love." Its home was apparently French civilization: "If there were in the world a nation which had a sociable humor, an openness of heart, a joy in life, a taste, an ease in communicating its thoughts; which was lively, pleasant, playful, sometimes imprudent, often indiscreet, and which had with all that, courage, generosity, frankness, and a certain point of honor, one should avoid disturbing its manners by laws, in order not to disturb its virtues" (*Laws*, XIX, 5).

Which brings us to free love, Montesquieu's decorously named "private crimes" (*Laws* III, 5). His censorious Jansenist and judicial readers would have had to read selectively to miss the libertarian and epicurean dimensions of the model of monarchy that he advocates. Since so much of the repressive legislation of the classical republic focused on family matters and especially on women, Montesquieu's demonstration that monarchy is more liberal than the republic begins with the demonstration that there is no political reason why one should not simply applaud the greater liberties of women under the monarchy: "One could constrain [French] women, make laws to correct their mores, and limit their luxury, but who knows if one would not lose a certain taste that would be the source of the nation's wealth and a politeness that attracts foreigners to it?" (*Laws*, XIX, 5).

Since the rebellion of Roxanne in Montesquieu's novel the *Persian Letters* (1721), the heroic and also libidinous woman choosing a society of lovers over familial isolation had been his preferred figure of the politically free society. Enlightenment, moreover, requires the free activities made possible from participation in a society beyond the borders of family and tribe. Usbek, the ostensible philosopher in search of enlightenment, learned nothing in France because in imitation of the king—he was an indictment of Louis XIV—he isolated himself in Versailles. Only Usbek's "virtuous" wife, Roxanne, driven into illicit society in rebellion against her jealous husband, proved capable of learning. She exhibited her virtue not as a wife but as a citizen who opted for the open society. Enlightenment and sociability are in this tale mutually implicated intimate allies. Both evidently countenanced personal betrayal with equanimity. In *The Spirit of Laws* Montesquieu generalizes these thoughts into a kind of communication ethics: "[T]he more communicative a people are, the more easily they change their manners." Women are the force behind this potential for disorder: "the society of women spoils mores." This judgment is not, however, a disapproving gesture. Montesquieu thinks only of the benefits of being rid of mores that are too pure: the "society of women" also "forms taste" and improves society (*Laws*, XIX, 8).

The method of this commerce/ communication carries men and women beyond the exchange of goods (free trade), even beyond the exchange of partners (free love) to an exchange and debate about norms (free speech). The latter implicates the very idea of the good, which has now become negotiable and seemingly uncontrollable by any gatekeeper other than the autonomous good sense of the communicating participants. Isaiah Berlin's romantic celebration of diversity allegedly absent from Enlightenment thought is nevertheless already present in this classic text's encomium to the transgressive possibilities, if I may use this postmodern term, of a freely communicating citizenry. Montesquieu does not hesitate to identify these activities as those of a free society. This expanding range of free "communication" produces in free trade an innovation and industriousness in France that stands in invidious contrast with the laziness and poverty of the Spanish (*Laws*, XIX, 10).

The spirit of sociability fostered under French monarchy also contrasts with the conformity of the Chinese where "the rites . . . seem to order everything to be separate [and] as one has seen . . . such separation is generally linked to the spirit of despotism" (*Laws*, XIX, 18). The communicative are enjoying whatever it is they are communicating about; but they are also instructing themselves in how to be free: "[O]ne is less communicative in countries where each man, whether a superior or an inferior, exercises and suffers an arbitrary power, than in those in which liberty reigns in all conditions." There is an invariable sign that marks the presence of arbitrary power: "[W]omen are ordinarily enclosed there and have no tone to give" (*Laws*, XIX, 12).[10]

Monarchy was admirable because it could accommodate heterogeneity. The trade-off was, however, inequality. In addition, monarchy was suitable to large-scale territory, which could not always count upon the citizen homogeneity required in most accounts of republican citizenship. The monarchy anticipates the problems of every large-scale democratic political enterprise. Too unfocused and latitudinarian always to be able to count upon intense citizen commitment, too given to activities that reinforce the desire to distinguish oneself—the ancient activity of honor in new dress—contemporary democracies must recognize the trade-offs implicit in both their size and the heterogeneity of their citizens. If Montesquieu's understanding of the republic was couched in terms of its *overcommitment to public life*, his understanding of monarchy suggests *undercommitment*. The monarchy was generous about the particular "differences" that could be accommodated within its territory, differences that from the republican perspective might detract from public duty. Monarchy was characterized by social differentiation and not moral unity. This was a relatively new theoretical possibility. Honor was a procedure by which communicative agents tested and adjusted their loyalties over time; it lacked a permanent substantive content as it was subject to the changing understandings of divided subcommunities within the nation.

However, Montesquieu's libertarian praise of these multiple freedoms could be misleading. His monarchical political actors were not unencumbered individualists; they possessed far too great a communitarian spirit. This is the larger meaning of a politics of honor. It is filled with reverence for the political community—whose ultimate symbol in monarchy was the throne—on whose behalf one acts: "[A]s [under monarchy] each one has so to speak a larger space, he can exercise those virtues that give the soul not independence, but greatness" (*Laws*, V, 12).

Is this attraction to the noble gesture something that might reconcile liberal individualists to the larger purposes of a historical community? Or does the aesthetic liberalism of the aristocrat seduce its democratic adherents, as it did its monarchical ones, into projects of glory and empire that go beyond what liberals or constitutional democrats should countenance?

Honor is aristocratic care of self. Its only defect is that its possessors are evidently filled with "prejudices" that arise from close attachment to their respective local traditions, habits, and circumstances. A paradox asserts itself.

Attending to the self and its location (pride in family inheritance, for instance) is associated with political liberty (because it promotes pluralist orders where multiple local standards flourish). But it is also associated with blindness and perplexity about how the selves ought to judge their broader situation beyond the standards of locale and location. This is why—though the argument would need to be defended at length—Montesquieu consistently calls honor "false." It is false to genuine self-understanding as measured by the submission of the self to a wider community.

### Third Teaching: In Praise of Overcommitment—Republics Whose Worrisome Solidarity Is Too Little Given to Heterogeneity but Because of This, Possibly Redemptive to the Politics of Drift

Republican virtue is in Montesquieu's works never identified as "false," and it is never associated with "prejudice." What is remarkable about "virtue" is that it is far more demanding than honor. The expectations of "virtue" for republican citizens are genuinely immoderate. Virtue is a "love of the laws and country" (*Laws*, IV, 5) and a "love of equality . . . [and] frugality" (5.3). None of these things is natural. They must be taught. Therefore, virtue calls for "self-renunciation" (*Laws*, III, 5). To establish it in the hearts of citizens, "the full power of education is needed." This "renunciation of oneself is always a very painful thing" (*Laws*, IV, 5).

The republic was different. Its temperament was perfectionist. It depended upon schemes of government surveillance of private life, because as a matter of its basic constitution every republic presupposed its own particular unified understanding of public good and necessarily counted upon all its citizens possessing a suitable character for maintaining this good. Since many of the "corruptions" of character stem from the influences of diverse private lives, republics necessarily have a category of "private crimes," which become matters for the "public" prosecutor. By contrast, surveillance of private life is an eminently dispensable option in the monarchy (*Laws*, III, 5, p. 25).

Republican citizens must learn how not to think of themselves except as agents whose service to public life must be compared to the service of others to the common enterprise. The "distinctions in a democracy arise from the principle of equality, even when equality seems to be erased by successful services or superior talents" (*Laws*, V, 3, p. 43). In reiterating this point, Montesquieu seems to touch upon something like John Rawls' difference principle. "Every inequality in a democracy should be drawn from the nature of democracy and from the principle of equality" (*Laws*, V, 5, p. 47).[11]

The real measure of this immoderate virtue is seen when Montesquieu compares this-worldly republican citizens to the abstemious, perfectionist, other-worldly "monk." Neither the egalitarian republican order nor the monk's order is natural. Both hate as well as love their orders. That is to say, their love for "order" is the side-effect of the hatred they feel for the discipline it imposes upon them. Here is Montesquieu's singular explanation: "Their love comes from the same thing that makes their order intolerable to them. Their rule deprives them of everything upon which ordinary passions rest; what remains therefore, is the passion for the very rule that afflicts them" (V, 2, p. 43).

That Montesquieu does not regard this passage as extreme is suggested by the way in which, after he defines "political virtue" in III, 5—"political virtue is simply "moral virtue in the sense that it points toward the general good"—he calmly adds that "this will be seen in Book 5 chapter 2," which brings us precisely to the abstemious monk. If the ascetic Christian or republican citizen described in V, 2 was extreme or impossible, then, on the above account, any moral virtue that attended to any general good would be similarly extreme or impossible.

Like Weber two centuries later, Montesquieu was tempted by the analogy with Christian forms of discipline. In analogizing the political virtue of the Greek and Roman city-state to the ascetic discipline of the Christian monk, Montesquieu speculated about the required inner life of the priest and democrat much as Weber addressed the inner world of the merchant as a borrowing of Protestant asceticism. Again like Weber, Montesquieu evidently thought that republican "virtue" could also be a credo for individualists. He claims that "the Protestant religion is better adapted to a republic." They are allied practices precisely because they require "a spirit of independence and liberty" (*Laws*, XXIV, 5, p. 463). Only those who know, through ascetic discipline, how to renounce their specific and communal attachments—many of them unreflectively inherited—are capable of being independent persons. Only people who can distinguish between their future possibilities and the claims of their attachments (or roots) have the capacity to act freely.

For Montesquieu, only monarchy privileges attachment and "prejudice." The latter term is never used to describe the republic or its principle of "virtue." However, the republic, like monarchy, depends fundamentally on customs, mores, and manners. The essential point of contrast between monarchy and republic is that the republic relies on "mores" for wholly different purposes. *In monarchy customs attach people to their roots.* They act from within entrenched local understandings and address the general good from partial perspectives. *In a republic customs act upon citizens in order to release them from rooted local understandings so that, in acting, they may adopt perspectives that match the breadth of the public goods they address.* Under monarchy, people are identified with their condition (their roots) and invited to be proud of this fact. Given the facts of honor, everyone is proud for different reasons. Honor is "the prejudice of each person and each condition." Everyone is proud of different things at different times. Honor has, that is so say, "caprices" (III, 8, p. 27). Like its counterpart, a pluralist, multicultural democracy, monarchy has an epistemological problem. There is no agreement on a common standard of virtue. *In Montesquieu's monarchy, customs give people a place even if that place offers each only a partial perspective. In Montesquieu's republic, the pull of custom was justified only to the extent it freed people from a partial perspective.*

Custom has a different purpose in the republic, but that does not mean it is less imposing. What frees people for politics may be customs that are far more of an encumbrance upon the prepolitical condition, that is to say, upon "society," than the relatively relaxed attitude Montesquieu thought it was permissible for the gatekeepers of the monarchical state to have toward society. The republic valorized in the pages of Montesquieu addresses the moment of the purely political or the moment of free judgment and action in which the subpolitical is consistently subordinated to the political. By contrast, Montesquieu's monarchy valorizes what we today call "civil society." Whether the latter is good, indifferent, or rotten—such as a slave-holding democracy—is irrelevant, since upon this perspective no reform is possible that does not begin in civil society.

These distinctions that concern the place of reform divide both political theorists and nations. *Is reform the prerogative of civil society, however unreconstructed?* This is Locke's contract argument and the spirit of Montesquieu's monarchy. *Does reform presuppose a state capable of improving upon the defects of civil society?* This is implicit in Montesquieu's and Rousseau's ideas of the republic. This division also touches upon the differences between America and France or rather between a pluralist democracy that celebrates every form of civil society and a Jacobin, or unitary, democracy that in France once held civil society in suspicion.

During the recent French debate over *laïcité* and the values of republican education aroused by the "affair of the scarves" in public schools, Elizabeth Badinter, Regis Debray, Alan Finkielkraut, Elizabeth de Fontenay, and Catherine Kintzler made the following argument in an open letter to the Minister of Education:

> It is necessary that students have the leisure to be able to forget their community of origin ... If one wants teachers to be able to help them and the school to remain what it is, a place of emancipation, [religious] attachments must not dictate the law to schools ... *The right to difference that is so clear to you is a freedom only if it is matched by the right to be different from one's difference.* In the contrary case, it is a trap ... [E]ach student is constantly identified with his parents, reminded of his condition, tied to his "roots": this is the school of social predestination." (My emphasis)[12]

This passage restates much of the Montesquieu-Rousseau view of the republic whose mores and public policies are required to help release citizens from the partiality of family, religion, or locale. Those who think like the authors of the open letter that the particular habits of scattered and diverse persons makes public transformation more difficult or more unjust will be allied to Montesquieu's understanding of the republic as a project for public self-transformation, albeit in the French case in the form of the secular school as a symbolic icon for an otherwise fading republic.

Does one have a right, even a duty, to learn how to be "different from one's difference?" The way the issue is framed reiterates the old debate between liberals and communitarians. For the liberal Rawls of *A Theory of Justice*—his Jacobin book—the duty of justice requires the detachment of a larger perspective, that is to say, being different from one's difference. For Rawls' communitarian critics, whom he accommodated eventually by writing that celebration of pluralism *Political Liberalism*, being different from one's difference was a recipe for self-alienation, not for justice.[13]

### Fourth Teaching: Montesquieu's Ambivalence about Thought— the Philosopher as Myopic Empire Builder

Even the casual reader notes that everywhere in the *Persian Letters* people are blind, except naturally in the institutions for the blind, where Rica finds the inmates playing cards (letter 32). Vanity and egocentrism (e.g., in letter 52) are the usual causes, but a more deep-rooted incapacity to see is an idea that circulates through the *Letters* as in this exclamation from Usbek: "Our blindness is so great that we do not know when to grieve and when to rejoice. We possess almost nothing but false sorrow and false joy" (letter 40). Although Usbek thinks it is the task of an intellectual detached from illusions to point this out, it is the nature of his own blindness (and of every thinker) that is ultimately at stake in the novel. This points us toward both skepticism as a resource against such blindness and also toward skepticism as the source of this blindness.

In the *Discourse* and *Meditations* Descartes recalls the skeptical moment of his great discovery.[14] Then a soldier, and passing the winter in Germany during the Thirty Years War, isolated, as he says, in his stove, he believed he could find no evidence that would persuade him he was not dreaming. "I shall then suppose ... [that] some evil genius, not less powerful than deceitful, has employed his whole energies in deceiving me."[15] What was left then but unending suspicion and universal doubt? Nothing, it appears, but the slender reed of the cogito, the "I think," which must accompany any thought of being deceived. The cogito establishes the existence of at least one thinking being. On Descartes' account, God and the rest can be resuscitated in minds that had become subjective and detached appraisers of the world rather than irretrievably embedded in it. What had obviously changed with Descartes is that (like a similar assertion in Luther, "here I stand, I can do no other") any claim about the world must pass through each self whose personal cogito of self-authentication is necessarily prior to the authentication of the world.

The *Letters* exhibit the circumstances of self-authenticating minds. Undertaken, one of its main Persian characters Usbek says, out of "a love of knowledge" (letter 1), perhaps also motivated by the need to flee, the voyage of Usbek and Rica recreates the situation of the skeptic. The further removed Usbek is from the Persian capital of Ispahan, the further removed he is from his old absorption in its life, which is now available only indirectly by way of a representation of it, namely, the tangible evidence of the letters (from this epistolary novel) in his hand. The very form of the epistolary novel, which is invented not long after Descartes' discoveries, would seem to have the disadvantage of parceling out time in fragments. The flow of continuous experience, the illusion created by the nineteenth-century novel, is missing. Letters convey fragments of fact and knowledge. They are in effect Cartesian "representations" of situations about which we have no independent confirmation. Each is a theory, concealed as a fact, about how to represent characters or experiences that are otherwise unavailable.

If letters replicate the form that knowledge assumes in its Cartesian manifestation, the content of the *Persian Letters* recalls the catechism of enlightenment. The scientific intelligibility of the Enlightenment is triumphantly touted in letter 97, which is a kind of in-your-face declaration of the superiority of Cartesian science over Muslim superstition—Muslim here codes also as Christian.

When Usbek applies the norms of reason to politics he appears as a Lockean liberal. He commends the English, who believe that only mutual gratitude obliges and only a prince who pursues the happiness of the people should be obeyed. In the face of oppression, "nothing binds them; nothing attaches them to [the prince], and they return to their natural liberty."

Montesquieu thought there was something defective about the model of knowing that he conveyed in his portrait of Usbek as classic Enlightenment intellectual. We start with the fact that Usbek is a classic tyrant, whose despotic character was hidden behind a facade of sweet reasonableness. But whatever else he is, Usbek is also a model of spiritual and intellectual discipline, the picture of a warrior of the Enlightenment mind, inclined and capable of resisting others who stand in the way of its project of making the world safe for its values. While one can see in this figure the possibilities for unjustified aggression that its critics have accused it of harboring, Usbek's Enlightenment virtues are called upon by Montesquieu as those most required for people who must stand in the path of predatory aggression.

The image of Usbek as "virtuous" thinker does not go completely blurry until the very last letter, the suicide note of Roxanne, Usbek's most "virtuous" wife. Throughout the *Letters* Usbek celebrates her beauty, sensitivity, and most of all her sexual "virtue," which, he says, on their wedding night she was too modest to yield. He is subsequently shocked to learn that she was the ringleader of the rebellion, which he and we learn only on these last pages when she announces, "Yes, I deceived you. I seduced your eunuchs, scoffed at your jealousy, and knew how to turn your hideous seraglio into a place of delight and pleasure." Here we have the epicurean as Lockean revolutionary. "I have always been free," she proclaims in her suicide note, "I have amended your laws according to the laws of nature" (letter 161).

The scene causes the reader to reflect on all that has passed before. It recalls the English understanding of obligation in letter 104. Without mutual gratitude and benefits, "nothing unites them . . . and they go back to their natural liberty." We also see now the point of Usbek's chilling defense of suicide in letter 76, which unwittingly justifies his wife's sacrificial rebellion against him. The defense of suicide appears appropriately in the hand of Usbek, the disengaged mind, and not that of Rica, his sociable Persian fellow traveler. Usbek could have restricted his defense of suicide to the Lockian contractual argument. But the letter becomes colder when, in turning to another justification, Usbek's distance from human things becomes greater: "Am I disturbing the order of Providence when I modify the arrangements of matter? . . . I could disrupt the whole of nature at will." It is, of course, eighteenth-century materialist doctrine that Usbek rehearses, despite the cover of references to providence. This manner of speaking, from an enormous distance from any human understanding of the human, illustrates more or less exactly what troubles the critics of disengaged Cartesian reason.

By letter 155 Usbek's rational façade has come crashing down, and he realizes that after nine years of resistance to his fate in which he tried to distance himself from his passions by way of enlightenment, he was still in the grip of jealousy and irrational rage. Apostrophizing the eunuchs, he recognizes in them a common identity based on the absence of love in their lives: "[D]egraded slaves whose hearts are closed forever to any feeling of love, you would no longer bewail your fate if you knew the misery of mine." On this reading, Usbek was condemned to be loveless because of his skepticism, which was now of no use to him except to further alienate him from his world. He was obsessed with knowing the truth about his wives, and this obsession imprisoned him because he had no means of getting at the truth, and the truth would have been useless. He admits, "I shall be surrounded by walls more horrible for me than the women they enclose. My suspicions will remain intact." Usbek forgets that he was not loveless because he had the misfortune to discover a conspiracy against him. As he admitted about his wives to a male friend at the very beginning of his voyage, "It is not, Nessir, that I love them" (letter 6).

Sometime later another friend, Mirza, who is about to ask Usbek to explain the meaning of justice, deplores the fact that Usbek has abandoned Ispahan: "What violence it needs to break the attachments formed by both heart and mind" (letter 10). It is the complaint of the communitarian against the individualist, the complaint of those who see the stress marks in a culture too filled with disengaged minds.

As anti-imperialist in *The Spirit of Laws* as he is in the *Persian Letters*, in the *Laws* Montesquieu contends that despotic government is suitable to empire understood as an effort to govern large territories. In both texts there is a kind of phenomenology of moral distance at work whereby the claim to be able to rule at a distance and to see from afar is distinctive of the despotic personality. It seems to matter less than we think it should that this applies equally: to a king who hides in the palace of Versailles and governs France from across the moral distance as measured by the manners of Versailles versus those of Paris; to an oriental despot governing vast tracts; and to the disengaged philosophical mind, which makes a claim on or about "God's architecture" even as it accepts in its worldly estrangement a self-chosen mutilation. Each of them has departed the human by embarking on a voyage of self-alienation in search of powers that will redeem the sacrifice.

We could go back and pick up almost any expression of discontent from the critics of the Cartesian Enlightenment and find a way in which it is embodied in the action of this peculiar novel. However, it may be that the way of knowing that Usbek embodies—detached and self-alienated, as much prone to illusion as those he criticizes—nevertheless addresses the human condition in a noble and unprecedented manner. Kant insisted that in possession of ourselves, a condition he named "reason," we are free, equal, and self-authenticating, as we always potentially were except for the need to acknowledge the messy business of heteronomous determination. Both Luther and Descartes insist that it all begins inside, in the self, and not with the acceptance of external creation. To allow oneself to be distracted from creation was not originally the vice of narcissism, as is sometimes suggested, but the demanding perfectionist and puritan virtue of abstemiousness. The Cartesian skeptic and the religious puritan have much in common.

Furthermore, Montesquieu's creation, Usbek, reminds the author that as *philosophe*, in possession of a disengaged mind, he has much in common with his fictional double. However commendable his many Cartesian virtues, Usbek is also tempted by the disciplinary procedures of self-estrangement; given to a subsequent overconfidence that amounts to blindness; and too intrigued by the hidden power of the instruments of rationality at his command. Although it is a condition of his learning and theoretical ambition that he can never extricate himself fully from these temptations, nevertheless, at the right moment Montesquieu the man pulls back. In Usbek, the grim puritan and heroic skeptic, whose doubts about an unjust, superstitious world point him to justice, resistance, and egalitarian science, the reader must also deal with what has belatedly been called the "tragedy of enlightenment," this time in the form of a tragic skeptic whose doubts identify him only as out of touch, delusional, or mad with power. The temptation is to separate the tragic from the heroic skeptic by eliminating the former, but like Montesquieu (who was going blind) we may be required to see double. In contemplating the figure of the philosopher, we may be meant to regard both the best hopes of humanity and also a harbinger of its worst possibilities.

## Notes

1. The quote in the title of this chapter is from Montesquieu, *The Spirit of the Laws*, Book XXIV, ch. 7, hereafter abbreviated *Laws*, XXIV, 7, in the body of the text. I follow generally the translation of Anne Cohler, Basia Miller, and Harold Stone (Cambridge: Cambridge University Press, 1989).

An earlier version of this chapter, "Montesquieu in and out of Modernity" was presented at the conference, "Modernity in Question: Montesquieu and His Legacy," University of Toronto, Sept. 9–10, 2005.

2. Hannah Arendt, *Origins of Totalitarianism* (New York: Harcourt, Brace, 1951), which she wrote after an intensive examination of *The Laws*.

3. For more on Burke and Montesquieu, see my "The Skeptic's Burke: Reflections on the Revolution in France, 1790–1990," *Political Theory* 3 (1991): 391–418.

4. "The great privilege enjoyed by Americans is not only to be more enlightened than other nations but also to have the chance to make mistakes that can be retrieved," Alexis de Tocqueville, *Democracy in America*, trans. George Lawrence and ed. J. P. Mayer (New York: HarperCollins, 1988) I, 225.

5. John Rawls, *The Law of Peoples* (Cambridge: Harvard University Press, 1999), 62–70.

6. For a fuller argument see my "The Judgmental Gaze of European Women: Gender, Sexuality, and the Critique of Republican Rule," *Political Theory* 1 (1994): 25–44.

7. "This mixed system of opinion and sentiment had its origins in the ancient chivalry . . . it is this which has given its character to modern Europe." Edmund Burke, *Reflections on the Revolution in France*, ed. John G. A. Pocock (Indianapolis: Hackett, 1987), 67, and more generally 66–70.

8. Pierre Manent, *City of Man*, trans. Marc A. LePain (Princeton: Princeton University Press, 1998), 11–49, 56–67.

9. For more on this episode in French history, see my "Monarchy's Paradox: Honor in the Face of Sovereign Power," in *Montesquieu's Science of Politics: Essays on The Spirit of Laws*, ed. David Carrithers, Michael A. Mosher, and Paul A. Rahe (Lanham, MD: Rowman & Littlefield, 2001), 139–229, especially 192–203.

10. For more on this dimension of Montesquieu's thought, see Mosher, "The Judgmental Gaze of European Women."

11. John Rawls, *A Theory of Justice* (Cambridge: Belknap Press of Harvard University Press, 1971, 2nd edition, 1999). The difference principle reads in its first version, "[S]ocial and economic inequalities are to be arranged so that they are ... to the greatest benefit of the least advantaged and ... attached to offices and positions open to all" (83).

12. Cited in Pierre Birnbaum, *The Idea of France* (New York: Hill & Wang, 2001, original French pub., 1998) translated by M. B. DeBevoise, 228, 341 n.85–86.

13. Rawls, *A Theory of Justice*; John Rawls, *Political Liberalism* (New York: Columbia University Press, 1993, 1996).

14. René Descartes, Discourse part 2 and Meditations 1 in *The Philosophical Works of Descartes*, trans. Elizabeth S. Haldane and G. R. T. Ross (Cambridge: Cambridge University Press, orig. 1911; reprint, 1972).

15. Descartes, Meditations 2, in *The Philosophical Works of Descartes*, I, 148.

Part I

# Morals and Manners in the Work of Montesquieu

## 2

# Morals and Manners in Montesquieu's Analysis of the British System of Liberty

### Cecil Patrick Courtney

In the spring of 1750 the Edinburgh booksellers Hamilton and Balfour published a little pamphlet of thirty pages, costing four pence, with the following title: *Two Chapters of A celebrated French Work, intitled, De l'Esprit des loix, Translated into English. One, Treating Of the Constitution of England; Another, Of the Character and Manners which result from this Constitution.*

This slim publication is of interest for a number of reasons. First, it is the earliest translation into English[1] of *The Spirit of Laws*, not of the complete text, but of those sections that were most likely to be of interest to British readers, anticipating by several months the publication of the full translation of the work by Thomas Nugent and also, one should add, offering, at four pence, good value for money, since Nugent's translation, which was in two volumes, cost ten shillings.[2] Second, the Scottish translation is of interest because it appears that Hume, who was in correspondence with Montesquieu at this time, played some part in its publication, possibly by seeing it through the press.[3] Third—and this is the point that is particularly relevant in the context of the present chapter—this little translation, with its bold title, *Two Chapters of a celebrated French Work*, reminds us that in *The Spirit of Laws* there is more than one chapter on England.

There is a useful lesson here for the modern reader. Everyone knows, or at least knows of, the first of these two chapters (the celebrated chapter 6 of Book XI), which is normally interpreted as a statement of what has become the classical theory of the separation of powers; but there is also, often left unread, the second chapter (chapter 27 of Book XIX), which is devoted to the relation between the English system of government and the morals, manners, and character of the nation. These chapters represent two different, but complementary, perspectives on this topic.[4]

## A Look at Book XI, Chapter 6

These two perspectives correspond to Montesquieu's method in the early books of *The Spirit of Laws*, where, in his typologies of the three different forms of government, he distinguishes between what he calls the "nature" and the "principle" of each. The nature is the formal structure: republic is a form of government where power is in the hands of the many (democracy) or the few (aristocracy); in a monarchy power is in the hands of one person, but there are restraints by intermediary powers and a repository of laws; in despotism power is likewise in the hands of one person, but there are no restraints. As for the principle, or the human passions that make these forms of government function, in the narrowest sense it is virtue in republic, honor in monarchy, and fear in despotism; in a broader sense, and in specific cases, the principle includes the character, morals, and manners of the citizens.

With regard to the English form of government, the formal structure is described in some detail in the first of our two chapters. Before turning to the second, it will be useful to clear up some ambiguity surrounding the status of this description.

Chapter 6 of Book XI is often read as an attempt at an accurate historical account of the English system of government in the early or mid-eighteenth century, and Montesquieu has frequently been taken to task for his alleged inaccuracy.[5] But there is a sentence at the end of the chapter that indicates that historical accuracy is not his aim: " 'Tis not my business to examine, whether the English actually enjoy this liberty or not. 'Tis sufficient for me to say it is established by their laws. I enquire no farther" (XI, 6, section 66). It is clear from this that Montesquieu's purpose is not really to give the kind of literal or factual description that many readers expect. But what, then, is he attempting, and what does he mean when he says that his aim is simply to describe how English liberty is "established by their laws"?

In fact Book XI is closely related to those earlier sections of *The Spirit of Laws* in which we find Montesquieu's definitions of republic, monarchy, and despotism and where he is obviously writing, not as a historian, but as a political philosopher, whose descriptions of different forms of government have the status, not of factual accounts or empirical generalizations, but of abstract models or ideal types.[6] Thus, he writes (III, 11), after describing the "principles" of the three forms of government: "Such are the principles of the three sorts of government: which does not imply, that, in a particular republic, they actually are, but that they ought to be, virtuous: nor does it prove, that, in a particular monarchy, they are actuated by honour; or, in a particular despotic government, by fear; but that they ought to be directed by these principles, otherwise the government is imperfect."

Montesquieu's procedure is, having defined these ideal types, to use them as models, in the light of which he can explain and evaluate existing regimes or those that have existed in the past. What we find in chapter 6 of Book XI is also an idealized model; it is based, not on a description of the practice of the constitution, with all its imperfections, but on certain ideals enshrined in the laws—the laws in question being such constitutional enactments as the Bill of Rights (1689) and the Act of Settlement (1701), interpreted as the foundations of English liberty.

This idealized description will reflect the principles of political liberty: "One nation there is also in the world, that has, for the direct end of its constitution, political liberty. We shall presently examine the principles on which this liberty is founded: if they are sound, liberty will appear in its highest perfection" (XI, 5). Having elaborated the English model, he proceeds, in the chapters that follow, to examine to what extent the principles of political liberty exhibited in this model are to be found in other regimes, for example in those of the ancient world.

His theory is that the English constitution guarantees liberty because it is a highly complex piece of constitutional machinery embodying the principle that, since "every man invested with power is apt to abuse it; [...] to prevent this abuse, it is necessary, from the very nature of things, power should be a check to power" (XI, 4).

This protection of the citizens against the abuse of power is achieved in two ways. The first is by the functional separation of the executive, legislative and judicial powers, a separation which admits of certain clearly defined exceptions,[7] and which in its simplest form is expressed as follows: "All would be lost, if the same man, or the same body, either of Nobles or Commons, at once exercised each of these powers, of legislation, of executing the public resolutions, and of judging in the crimes or the differences of private citizens" (XI, 6, section 6). The second way is by a system of checks and balances within a mixed form of government; this is summarized as follows:

> Such then is the fundamental constitution of the government of which we are speaking. There the legislative body being made up of two parts, they will fetter each other by their cohibitive power, while both are connected by the executive authority, which itself will be so by the legislative.

These three powers should naturally produce repose or inactivity. But as by the necessary movement of affairs they are constrained to act, they will be obliged to act in concert. (XI, 6, section 55–56)

In all this Montesquieu is not entirely original. In fact both the theory of the separation of powers and that of checks and balances within the mixed constitution had been developing in an unsystematic way during the struggle between King and Parliament in the seventeenth century.[8] Elements of these theories, which were eventually assimilated to interpretations of the Revolution Settlement, can be found in such diverse documents as *His Majesties Answer to the XIX Propositions* (1642) and in the works of a multitude of political writers and pamphleteers. References to the balanced constitution of King, Lords and Commons had long been commonplace. As for the theory of the functional separation (or distribution) of powers, this had not been fully developed, but the elements that Montesquieu brought together were already there: the independence of the judiciary (established by the Act of Settlement), the independence of the upper and lower chambers from interference from the monarch who, however, was sole head of the executive and had the various prerogatives, including the right to refuse his assent to bills. Locke had spoken of the separation of the legislative power from the executive but had not mentioned the judiciary as a third element. Montesquieu's real originality was to have made a brilliant synthesis of these dispersed elements. His success in England was immediate, and nobody, not even such an authority as Blackstone,[9] disagreed. David Hume, in a letter to Montesquieu, pointed out a few minor errors but raised no objections to the general picture.[10] Readers had heard all this before, but no one had ever said it quite like this or brought out its full significance.

If we do not go beyond Book XI we have a picture of Montesquieu's analysis of the nature or formal structure of the English system, but nothing that throws light on the underlying principle. Unfortunately there has always been a tendency to concentrate exclusively on the structure and, indeed, we find this tendency, not only in modern legal textbooks, but as early as 1781, when Francis Maseres, the author of a translation of Montesquieu on the English constitution, confined himself to chapter 6 of Book XI.[11] However, to concentrate on the nature, without the principle, to describe the structure without taking account of the morals and manners of the citizens, is to reduce Montesquieu's description of the English forms of government to nothing more than an ingenious piece of impersonal constitutional machinery, a complicated system of separation of powers or checks and balances, without any human dimension. To capture this human dimension it is necessary to read the second of the two chapters.[12]

## The Principle of English Government: Book XIX, Chapter 27

The full title of our second chapter is "How Laws May Contribute to Form the Morals, the Manners, and the Character of a Nation." This comes at the end of Book XIX, which is itself the final section of those books devoted to various physical and moral factors that combine to form the "esprit général" ("general spirit") of any given country. Whereas the earlier books of *The Spirit of Laws* describe three types of government, in practice we do not find republic, monarchy, or despotism in their pure disembodied forms; in the real world they exist in countries where there are wide variations in the general spirit and, in each case, the principle, whether virtue, honor or fear, will be reflected (or refracted) in the character, morals, and manners of the citizens. It is the same with the constitution of liberty; to see how this splendid piece of machinery works, it is necessary to take into account a wide range of factors, particularly the character of the English or, more precisely, the interaction between this character and the principles of their constitution. Thus, we read in the second paragraph: "I have spoken in the 11th book of a free people; I have laid down the principles of their constitution: let us now see the effects which ought to follow [*ont dû suivre*], the character which may be formed, and the manners which result from it."

In the next paragaraph he refers to the influence of climate on the English character, a topic that he had discussed in Book XIV, where he states that the climate is responsible for the high rate of suicide in that country and that it is also responsible for the fact that the English live in a constant state of physical and mental agitation, which, however regrettable, at least has one important advantage, namely, that it makes them intolerant of anything that smacks of tyranny: "This temper, in a free nation, is extremely proper for disconcerting the projects of tyranny, which is always slow and feeble in its commencements, as in the end it is active and lively; which at first stretches out a hand to assist, and exerts afterwards a multitude of arms to oppress. Slavery is ever preceded by sleep. But a people, who find no rest in any situation, who continually explore every part, and feel nothing but pain, can hardly be lulled to sleep" (XIV, 13). However, in the third paragraph of our second chapter Montesquieu states that the importance of climate should not be overestimated: "I don't say, that the climate has not, in a great measure, produced the laws, morals and manners of this nation: but I affirm that the morals and manners of this nation must have [*devroient avoir*] a great relation to their laws."

Montesquieu never mentions England by name in this chapter, and throughout he uses the conditional tense; this is no doubt so that he can present his observations as if they were a series of deductions, showing that there is a logical connection between the form of the constitution, as described in the earlier chapter, and its actual working.

Almost immediately after this, without any further introduction, he gives a rapid description of the relation between the legislative and executive powers, a description in which the abstract model of the earlier book suddenly takes on human characteristics:

> As there must be in this state two visible powers, the legislative and executive, and as every citizen there must have his own will, and according to his own humor must improve his independence; most people will have more affection for one of those powers than for the others, the greatest number not having commonly enough of æquity or sense to regard both with æqual affection.
>
> And as the executive power, disposing of all employments, will be able to raise great expectations, but never to terrify or awe; all those who shall obtain places from it, will have a bias to turn to its side; and it may be attacked by all such as hope for nothing from it. (sections 3–4)

Thus, in practice, an important feature of the beautiful system of separation and balance described in Book XI is a bitter struggle for power between rival parties.[13] However, Montesquieu's reaction to this somewhat unedifying spectacle is not one of disapproval: "All passions, there, being free; hatred, jealousy, an ardor to become rich, and to distinguish one's self, will appear in all their extent: and, if it were otherwise, the state would be like a man overwhelmed with sickness, who has no passions, because he has no strength" (section 5).

Eighteenth-century readers would have seen here a description, somewhat oversimplified, of the confrontation between the different political parties, divided between those who habitually supported and those who opposed the administration of the day. But not everyone would have shared Montesquieu's optimistic views. Numerous French writers of the period regarded the English political scene as nothing more than a fratricidal struggle within Parliament, the outcome of which could only lead to anarchy.[14] Even Rapin de Thoyras who, in his *Dissertation sur les whigs et les torys*,[15] was favorably inclined to England, and who admired the theory of balanced government, was appalled by the existence of parties whose outspoken views, if put into practice, would, he believed, result either in a return to the absolute monarchy of the Stuarts or to a republic. His hope was that, under a wise monarch, party divisions, which he portrays as tainted by parliamentary and electoral corruption, would disappear. However, in his conclusion, he accepts, though reluctantly, that the existing confrontational system was less harmful than domination by any one of the parties.[16]

As for English readers, they would have been aware that Montesquieu was commenting on an important and controversial issue: namely, the proper functioning of the constitution in terms of the relations between King and

Parliament. It was the practice at this time for places and pensions to be distributed by the King or his ministers to a large number of members of the legislature, as a reward or incentive for their support, and this, according to Walpole and later heads of administration, was the only way to avoid the kind of disequilibrium or deadlock that would result if there were a weak executive or no communication between the monarch and Parliament. It was frequently argued that this practice was a form of corruption or influence that increased the power of the Crown and tended to reduce Parliament to a rubber stamp; however, although there certainly was a great deal of nepotism, favoritism, and bribery involved, placemen were never so numerous, or so disciplined, that ministers could always count on an automatic majority vote in favor of government policy, and a serious effort had to be made to obtain the support of those members who had no party allegiance. Winning this support was facilitated by the fact that during this period, before the existence of modern political parties, cabinet government, and ministerial responsibility, most members of Parliament considered organized opposition or unprincipled obstruction of the King's business as not quite respectable.[17]

There were, of course, certain members who formed a more or less permanent opposition, partly from principle (not only those with Tory principles who opposed the Whig government of Walpole, but also a large number of dissident Whigs), partly for personal reasons (including resentment at being excluded from office). The foremost opposition figure was Bolingbroke, and it has been argued that it was mainly from him that Montesquieu derived his leading ideas on the English constitution. Like all opposition politicians of the period, Bolingbroke rings the changes on the theme of the "influence" of the Crown and the practice of offering paid offices to members of Parliament, and he dignifies his condemnation of this practice with a theory that, if taken literally, would have implied a rigid separation of the executive and legislative powers. Montesquieu writes on the same theme, but what is really striking is not the similarity of his views to those of Bolingbroke, but the difference, for Montesquieu never suggests that Parliament should be purged of office-holders[18] and, as has been seen, he considers the struggle between supporters of the Crown and the opposition, not as something to be deplored, but as a sign of health and an essential element in the preservation of liberty.

## Unbridled Self-interest?

Some modern interpreters, taking note of Montesquieu's acceptance of the confrontation of bitterly opposed parties as a sign of vitality and good health in British political life, assume that this supports a theory that the English system functions thanks to the collective selfishness of the citizens and that this competition of selfish factions somehow leads to a balance between the different parts of the constitution.[19] Thus, the principle of the English system of government, or the passions that make it move, must be seen as a form of unbridled self-interest. As for the balance that guarantees liberty, according to a refinement of this interpretation, it is the result of a self-regulating mechanism that can be compared to Mandeville's theory of private vices and public benefits or, indeed, to Adam Smith's invisible hand or Hegel's cunning of reason.[20]

There is, in fact, much in Montesquieu's description of the English character that, at least on a first reading, seems to support this kind of interpretation. In the passages quoted above, he describes how, in the conflict between parties, free rein is given to the passions of hatred, envy, and jealousy, along with an unrestrained desire for wealth and distinction. Again, he writes: "As every particular, always independent, will much follow his own caprices and fancies, people will often change sides; they will abandon one, or they will forsake all their friends, to join another party, in which they will find all their enemies: and often in this nation they will even forget the laws of friendship and resentment" (section 8). However, immediately preceding this passage, there is an important paragraph which gives us pause: "These parties being made up of free men, if the one take too much upon them, the effect of liberty will be, that this very party will be humbled whenever the citizens, as the hands which succour the body, shall come to relieve the other" (section 7).[21] It is clear from this that, in the working of the constitution, more is involved than the mindless opposition of rival parties motivated by caprice, fancy, and various forms of self-interest; to complete the equation one must also take account of the "citizens" who, when necessary, will intervene to preserve the balance of the constitution.[22]

It is interesting to read this paragraph, with its reference to the moderating influence of the "citizens," alongside the following passage from Hume's essay "On the Independency of Parliament" (1741), which explains how the balance of the constitution is preserved thanks to the support, within Parliament, of those public-spirited members who have no fixed party allegiance:

> The Crown has so many offices at its disposal, that, when assisted by the honest and disinterested part of the House, it will always command the resolutions of the whole; so far, at least, as to preserve the ancient constitution from danger. We may, therefore, give to this influence what name we please; we may call it by the invidious appellations of *corruption* and *dependence*; but some degree and some kind of it are inseparable from the very nature of the constitution, and necessary to the preservation of our mixed government.[23]

Hume speaks of "the honest and disinterested part of the House," that is to say, the independent members of Parliament; Montesquieu speaks simply of the "citizens," a term that, in the context must refer likewise to the independents, though it may also include party members who change sides to prevent the collapse of the political system; it may even include public opinion, something that Parliament could never afford to ignore. The metaphor, "as the hands which succour the body" may suggest nothing more than the instinct for self-preservation; but what is to be preserved is a whole set of values associated with the ideal of liberty and for which the citizens are prepared to make sacrifices.[24]

However "citizens" may be interpreted, it is obvious that the same point is made by both writers: that something more than the confrontation between two hostile parties or factions inspired by narrow self-interest is required to preserve the balance of the constitution. If Montesquieu sees animosity between rival parties as a sign of political health, it is because he believes, "As to enjoy liberty it is necessary that every one be allowed to say what he thinks" (section 20),[25] but at the same time he is convinced that their mutual hatred can by itself have no positive outcome and at best can lead only to deadlock: "The hatred betwixt the two parties will remain, because it will always be impotent" (XIX, 27, section 6).[26]

One might ask whether Montesquieu, in writing the second chapter on the English constitution, was influenced by Hume. In theory he could have read Hume's essay, which was first published in 1741, seven years before the publication of *The Spirit of Laws*. However, there is no evidence that he did so, and in any case there can be little doubt that his views on the working of the English constitution owed as much to firsthand experience as to his reading. The most important source for this firsthand experience is the fragmentary *Notes sur l'Angleterre*, in which we find valuable information on Montesquieu's visit to England from 1729 through 1731. Some of the observations in this work seem to give support to the thesis that the English form of government (and indeed, everything else in England) functions in terms of greed, corruption, and the grosser forms of self-interest. Thus, he refers to Scottish members of Parliament who sell their votes for two hundred pounds and, in more general terms, writes that "the English no longer deserve their freedom. They sell it to the King, and, if the King returned it to them, they would sell it to him again."[27]

However, these observations should not blind us to those sections of the *Notes* where Montesquieu expresses a more favorable opinion of England, nor should it be overlooked that he was later to modify his views on the effects of corruption.[28]

Particularly important are the accounts he gives of his presence at two debates in the Houses of Parliament. The first was the debate on the army estimates held on January 28, 1730 when the maverick Tory with Jacobite leanings William Shippen made a violent speech in which he insulted the King by arguing that only tyrants and usurpers had need of a standing army and that England should not be governed by Hanoverian principles. Montesquieu records that the reaction of the House was one of consternation and that, in order to avoid further discussion, the members called for the vote to be put immediately.[29] A contemporary account of the debate informs us that even Shippen's own friends were ashamed of his speech and that the government motion that he was opposing was carried by a huge majority.[30]

The second debate, held on February 27, 1730, was on a motion condemning the government for allegedly conniving at how the French, disregarding the Treaty of Utrecht, had begun restoring the port of Dunkirk. This was one of the most heated and remarkable debates of the period; it lasted from one o'clock in the afternoon until three in the morning and gave Montesquieu the opportunity to hear a large number of speakers. He expressed astonishment at the asperity of the attacks on the French (who were allies of the English at this time) and at the violent language used in the exchanges, particularly between Walpole and Wyndham. He does not record the vote, but, again, it was a majority in favor of the ministry.[31]

It would be surprising if Montesquieu, having attended these debates (and no doubt others), took away nothing but the impression that in Parliament there were no reasoned discussions involving principles or that the British system worked simply because of the interplay between self-interested factions. If Shippen found himself abandoned even by some of his friends, this was because they realized that his speech was an unprincipled attack on the executive and could be interpreted as challenging the constitutional right of the King to be head of the armed forces. As for the debate on Dunkirk, if the motion failed it was no doubt because the majority of the House saw it as a blatant attempt by the opposition to exploit information that certain Tory friends of Bolingbroke had assembled from various sea captains to imply that the government was neglecting British interests abroad. Walpole, in a brilliant speech defending government policy and asking for time to scrutinize the evidence, made a strong reasoned case for a diplomatic approach that would not damage Anglo-French relations; his arguments were accepted by the House.[32]

Toward the end of the *Notes sur l'Angleterre* we find the following extremely favorable description of the English system: "England is at present the freest country in the world, I do not except any republic; I call it free, because the prince does not have power to do any wrong imaginable to anyone, because his power is checked and limited by an act; but if the lower chamber became dominant, its power would be unlimited and dangerous, because it would have at the same time the executive power; whereas at present unlimited power is in parliament and the king, and the executive power in the king, whose power is limited." And Montesquieu concludes: "It follows that a true Englishman (*un bon Anglais*) will seek to defend liberty equally against attempts to subvert it by the Crown and by Parliament."[33]

## Motivations for Political Liberty in England

What is it that motivates a "true Englishman" to defend liberty so that, in spite of the theatricals of self-interested opposition factions or the allure of pensions from the government, the balance of the constitution will be preserved? It is obviously not that puritanical virtue characteristic of republics, which implies a total subordination of the self to the community and which, in the final analysis, is unfavorable to liberty. In fact, in an earlier book of *The Spirit of Laws* Montesquieu described how, in the absence of "virtue," the English attempt at setting up a republic had failed.[34] Nor can we relate the behavior of the English to the principle of honor found in monarchies. In fact, in another earlier section of *The Spirit of Laws* Montesquieu states that the English had abolished intermediary powers and, where there are no intermediary powers, there is no place, at least no central place, for the principle of honor.[35]

Montesquieu, in describing the motives that inspire the true Englishman to defend the constitution, begins with a negative approach, stressing that the English live in constant fear of losing their freedom: "We are afraid to lose a good which we immediately feel, the nature of which we little understand, and which may easily be disguised. Now, as fear always augments objects, the people will be uneasy about their situation, and imagine themselves in danger at a time when they are most secure" (section 10). It is obvious that the fear to which he refers in this passage is not the same as that dumb fear that is the principle of despotism. In despotism the citizen is essentially a slave whose fear leaves him no choice but to obey; in England the citizen enjoys freedom and can take active measures to protect it. In fact, the fear produced by parliamentary debate and political pamphlets is useful: "By so much the more, as those who most keenly oppose the executive power, not daring to confess the interested motives of their opposition, will augment the terrors of the people, who never exactly know whether they be in danger of not. But even this will contribute to make them avoid real dangers to which they may be afterwards exposed" (section 11). However, while the people may be easily misled, there is a stabilizing influence: "[T]he legislative power having the confidence of the people and being better informed than they, will be able to remove the bad impressions which have been given them, and to calm their movements" (section 12). This situation is preferable to that of ancient democracies, where the people were easily stirred up to violence by mob orators; in England there is nothing to fear from such oratory: "Thus, when the terrors with which they have been alarmed shall have no certain object, they will not produce but vain clamours, and scurrilous language; and they will even have this good effect, that they will adjust the springs of government, and make every citizen attentive" (section 14). Nor is the oratory of "those who oppose the executive power" the only danger: "This nation, being of a warm complexion, may be more easily conducted by its passions than by reason, which never produces great effects upon the minds of men; and it may be easy for those who govern, to make it undertake enterprises contrary to its true interest" (section 21).

Eventually, after describing the dangers to the constitution from both sides, Montesquieu reaches the essential point: "This nation will love its liberty prodigiously, because this liberty will be real: and it may happen that, to defend it, people will sacrifice their money, their ease, their interests; that they will burden themselves with taxes the most grievous, and such as a despotic prince would never dare to impose upon his subjects" (section 22). This liberty, which may be endangered by the encroachment of the executive, or by the legislative power becoming tyrannical, can be protected only by citizens who are motivated by something that transcends the narrow self-interest of party and may involve sacrifice. Liberty is the supreme value,[36] but it is not seen as an abstract principle; it is "a good which we immediately feel, the nature of which we little understand, and which may easily be disguised" (section 10, quoted earlier). Thus it is deeply embedded in the natural affections, in the "general spirit" of the English, and in their customs, manners, and traditions. It is not a mere word or a grand political theory, but a way of life and a set of values embodied for the citizens in the kind of government which they know and had emerged from the Revolution Settlement, where liberty means primarily a sense of security and freedom from arbitrary power. The fear of losing this liberty was real, conjuring up images of a return to the absolutism of the Stuarts, to the failed republicanism of the Commonwealth, to the incessant squabbles of factions (Whig, Tory, Jacobite, Protestant and Catholic) or even to civil war.[37]

## Prospects for Political Liberty in England

While in Book XIX Montesquieu gives an optimistic picture of the working of the English system of government, in Book XI he had made a rather gloomy prediction: "As all human institutions have their period, the state we speak of will perish. [. . .] It will perish when the legislative shall become more corrupted than the executive authority." His friend William Domville wrote from London in July 1749, asking him to clarify this statement. Montesquieu's reply, along with a copy or draft, is preserved in the *Pensées*. He writes, expressing views on corruption in England rather different from those earlier views found in the *Notes sur l'Angleterre*: "It seems that you wanted to corrupt your magistrates and your representatives. It is not the same with the general body of the people, and I think I saw a certain spirit of liberty which always lights up and is not ready to be extinguished; and when I think of the spirit of this nation, it seems to me that it appears more enslaved than it really is, because that which is most enslaved shows itself more openly and that which is free less openly."[38] Montesquieu now thinks that the extent and significance of corruption in England have been exaggerated; his considered view is expressed as follows: "I say then that, whilst people of the middle station [*les gens médiocres*] preserve their principles, it will be difficult to subvert your constitution."[39]

Whether this balance could be maintained was in the eighteenth century a matter of speculation. Hume was among those who believed the English system might tip over into absolutism: "Absolute monarchy [. . .] is the easiest death, the true euthanasia of the British constitution."[40] However, Montesquieu believed England would be more successful than most countries in resisting corruption and decline and, indeed, that its example might even retard tyranny elsewhere in Europe. This he says in his reply of July 22, 1749 to Domville: "I think, however, that in Europe, the last sigh of liberty will be heaved by an Englishman" (Je crois pourtant que dans l'Europe le dernier soupir de la liberté sera poussé par un Anglois).[41]

In the little Scottish translation with which we began, Montesquieu offers the reader two different, but complementary, images of England. The first is of a country endowed with a constitution that is a complicated machine where there are weights and counterweights or checks and balances. It is an example of the kind of constitutional engineering of which Montesquieu expresses his admiration when he writes in an earlier book: "To form a moderate government, it is necessary to combine the several powers; to regulate, temper, and set them in motion; to give, as it were, ballast to one, in order to enable it to counterpoise the other. This is a masterpiece of legislation, rarely produced by hazard, and seldom attained by prudence" (V, 14). For Montesquieu the English constitution is one of these masterpieces, in fact the supreme masterpiece, produced no doubt by a mixture of hazard and prudence; it had originated in the woods of Germany[42] but had since evolved and been modified by several centuries of conflict and legislation.

This machine, however expertly constructed, is useless unless it is geared to the character of the citizens and unless they can identify with the values for which it stands and contribute to its working. It will function only if the English take whatever steps are required to preserve the balance of King, Lords, and Commons and resist the accumulation of separate powers by the same person or constituted body. This is a problem common to all constitutions where there is a similar arrangement of balance and division of powers and where the danger to freedom comes from the kind of corruption that fails to arrest the encroachment of one power on another.[43] This can be prevented only if there is a consensus regarding those values on which the whole system is based and that are worth preserving.[44] These values form the "principle" of the English system of government. "Virtue" and "honor" are the simple terms used by Montesquieu to define the principles of republic and monarchy; for

England he has no single term and prefers to refer simply to "liberty" or "the spirit of liberty"[45] which, though less precise, is richer and more suggestive, implying a whole way of life and representing a principled opposition to arbitrary power, along with a public-spiritedness found even in ordinary people and a determination to respect and maintain the political system that followed the Glorious Revolution.

## Notes

1. Announced in *The Scots Magazine*, April 1750. Quotations are from this edition for the *Spirit of Laws* XI, 6, XIX, 27; other quotations from *The Spirit of Laws* are from the translation by Nugent mentioned in the following note; translations from other works are my own.

2. *The Spirit of Laws. Translated from the French of M. de Secondat, Baron de Montesquieu; With Corrections and Additions communicated by the Author*, 2 vols. (London: Printed for J. Nourse and Vaillant in the Strand, 1750). Reviewed among "Books & Pamphlets, published August 1750" in *The Gentleman's Magazine*, August (1750), 384.

3. See Ernest Campbell Mossner, *The Life of David Hume*, 2nd ed. (Oxford: Clarendon Press, 1980), 229, 232; Warren McDougall, "Gavin Hamilton, Bookseller in Edinburgh," *The British Journal for Eighteenth-Century Studies* 1 (1978): 1–19.

4. See C. Courtney, "L'Image de l'Angleterre dans *L'Esprit des lois*," in *Actes du Colloque international tenu à Bordeaux, du 3 au 6 décembre 1998 pour commémorer le 250ème anniversaire de la parution de L'Esprit des lois* (Bordeaux: Académie Montesquieu, 1999), 243–53.

5. On Montesquieu's alleged inaccuracy see, for example, the notes to the most scholarly modern editions: *De l'Esprit des loix*, ed. Jean Brethe de La Gressaye, 4 vols. (Paris: Les Belles Lettres, 1950–1961), and *De l'Esprit des lois*, ed. Robert Derathé, 2 vols. (Paris: Garnier, 1973). For further references, see Courtney, "L'Image," 1999.

6. On Montesquieu and ideal types, see Ernst Cassirer, *The Philosophy of the Enlightenment* (Boston: Beacon Press, 1960, 209–16); see also C. Courtney, "Montesquieu and the Problem of *la diversité*," *Enlightenment Essays in Memory of Robert Shackleton*, ed. Giles Barber and C. Courtney (Oxford: Voltaire Foundation, 1988), 61–81; "Montesquieu and Natural Law," in *Montesquieu's Science of Politics, Essays on the Spirit of Laws*, ed. David W. Carrithers, Michael Mosher, and Paul Rahe (Lanham, MD: Rowman & Littlefield, 2001), 41–68.

7. For example, the role of the Lords and Commons in the impeachment of ministers.

8. For the essential background see the following: W. B. Gwyn, *The Meaning of the Separation of Powers* (New Orleans: Tulane University; The Hague: Nijhoff, 1965); M. J. C. Vile, *Constitutionalism and the Separation of Powers* (Oxford: Clarendon Press, 1967).

9. On Montesquieu and William Blackstone's *Commentaries on the Laws of England* (1765–1769), see F. T. H. Fletcher, *Montesquieu and English Politics (1750–1800)* (London: Arnold, 1939), 119–20.

10. Hume to Montesquieu, April 10, 1749, Montesquieu, *Oeuvres complètes*, ed. André Masson (Paris: Nagel, 1950–1955), III, 1217–1222.

11. *A View of the English Constitution. By the late Baron De Montesquieu. Being A Translation of the Sixth Chapter of the Eleventh Book of his celebrated Treatise, intitled L'Esprit des Loix*. London: Sold by B. White, Horace's Head, Fleet-Street; H. Payne, in Pall-Mall. MDCCLXXXI. [Price One shilling]. 8° [ii], 74.

12. Among modern scholars, a few have taken the later chapter seriously and seen it as a necessary complement to the earlier one, see particularly Thomas Pangle, *Montesquieu's Philosophy of Liberalism* (Chicago: Chicago University Press, 1973). See also, for briefer accounts, J. G. A. Pocock, *The Machiavellian Moment* (Princeton: Princeton University Press, 1975); Keith Michael Baker, *Inventing the French Revolution* (Cambridge: Cambridge University Press, 1990), 173–78. For more recent studies see Paul A. Rahe, "Forms of Government: Structure, Principle, Object and Aim," in *Montesquieu's Science of Politics*, 69–108; Sharon Krause, "The Spirit of Separate Powers in Montesquieu," *The Review of Politics* 62 (2002): 231–65.

13. Robert Shackleton expresses surprise that Montesquieu, in Book XI, ch. 6, does not refers to political parties. However, parties belong to the practice, not to the theory of the constitution: there were no laws defining the composition or activities of political parties. Shackleton, *Montesquieu: A Critical Biography* (Oxford: Oxford University Press, 1961), 291–95.

14. See Gabriel Bonno, *La Constitution britannique devant l'opinion française de Montesquieu à Bonaparte* (Paris: Champion, 1932), 37–43.

15. Published at the Hague in 1717 and translated into English in the same year. On Rapin de Thoyras see Nelly Girard d'Albissin, *Un précurseur de Montesquieu: Rapin Thoyras, premier historien français des institutions anglaises* (Paris: Klincksieck, 1969).

16. "It will always be more advantageous to the State that the people remain divided than if one of the parties should acquire a superiority which would be more harmful to the public than the equality maintained by discord" (*Dissertation*, 183–84). Cf. Girard d'Albissin, 69.

17. There is a vast literature on the working of the eighteenth-century constitution; see particularly Betty Kemp, *King and Commons, 1660–1832* (London: Macmillan, 1957); J. H. Plumb, *The Growth of Political Stability in England, 1675–1725* (London: Macmillan, 1767); W. A. Speck, *Stability and Strife, England 1714–1760* (London: Arnold, 1977); see also Denis Baranger, *Parlementarisme des origines* (Paris: PUF, 1999).

18. On this point one must disagree with Robert Shackleton, who is usually very perceptive on Montesquieu's ideas on government, when he writes, "[Montesquieu] did not understand that there might be some good, even a small, relative or dubious good, to be gained from ministerial exercise of influence; he saw it simply as corruption" (*Montesquieu: A Critical Biography*, 1961, 301).

19. This is, broadly, the interpretation offered by Thomas L. Pangle and Sharon Krause. However, regarding Pangle's interpretation, see note 44 in this chapter.

20. See Sergio Cotta, "L'idée de parti dans la philosophie politiquue de Montesquieu," in *Actes du Congrès Montesquieu réuni à Bordeaux du 23 au 26 mai 1955* (Bordeaux: Delmas, 1955), 257–62; and Céline Spector, *Montesquieu: Pouvoirs, richesses et sociétés* (Paris: PUF, 2004), 193–94.

21. The original text is as follows: "Ces parties étant composés d'hommes libres, si l'un prenoit trop le dessus, l'effet de la liberté feroit que celui-ci seroit abaissé, tandis que les citoyens, comme les mains qui secourent le corps, viendroient relever l'autre."

22. There is an apparent contradiction here: Montesquieu (in section 6, cited earlier), had spoken of the greatest number of citizens as "not having commonly enough of æquity or sense to regard both [the executive and legislative powers] with equal affection." However, in moments when liberty is endangered, the usual loyalties may disintegrate and the citizens (party members and independents) unite in a common cause (to preserve freedom). Cf. section 16, where, in the case of subversion of the fundamental laws, "little interests yielding to those which are more grand all will unite in favor of the executive power."

23. Hume, *Political Essays*, ed. Knud Haakonssen (Cambridge: Cambridge University Press, 1994), 26.

24. See my discussion on pages 41 to 42 of this chapter, as well as Montesquieu's discussion in section 22 of Book XIX, chapter 27.

25. He also states: "In a free nation, it is often all one, whether particulars reason well or ill; it is enough that they reason: from this flows that liberty which prævents the bad effects of this very reasoning" (section 63). This is not a general defence of faulty reasoning; it should be read in the light of the next paragraph, where Montesquieu speaks of the lack of free speech in despotism: "In the same way, in a despotic government, it is æqually pernicious, whether they reason well or ill. Reasoning in any shape is contrary to the principle of their government" (section 64).

26. See also the passage quoted in note 34 of this chapter, in which Montesquieu considers that, when the prevailing parties are unprincipled and "animated by the spirit of faction," the outcome is total instability.

27. Ed. Masson, Montesquieu, *Oeuvres completes*, III, 288.

28. See pages 37ff. of this chapter and notes 38 and 49.

29. Ed. Masson, Montesquieu, *Oeuvres completes*, III, 288

30. Letter of February 3, 1730, from Charles Howard to his father, the earl of Carlisle: "Mr Shippen, in his speech, made use of some expressions so very flagrant and undecent, that I took the words down; he said he hoped he should never see these kingdoms so Germanised as to become military; he went on with giving reasons that such a number of troops were inconsistent with our constitution; then, says he, force and violence are the resort of usurpers and tyrants, whose only security is a standing army. [...] I can but say his own friends were ashamed of him, and it shortened the debate, for we came to a division after that, which was two hundred and forty odd to a hundred and twenty odd" (*The Manuscripts of the Earl of Carlisle* [London, Historical Manuscripts Commission, Fifteenth Report, Appendix, part VI, 1897], 66–67).

31. Masson, Montesquieu, *Oeuvres complètes*, III, 289. For a contemporary account see the *Diary of Viscount Percival, afterwards first Earl of Egmont*, I, 1730–1733 (London, Historical Manuscripts Commission, 1920), 71–74.

32. J. H. Plumb, *Sir Robert Walpole, the King's Minister* (London: Cresset Press, 1960), 210–15.

33. Masson, Montesquieu, *Oeuvres complètes*, III, 292.

34. "A very droll spectacle it was, in the last century, to behold the impotent efforts of the English towards the establishment of democracy. As they, who had a share

in the direction of public affairs, were void of virtue; as their ambition was inflamed by the success of the most daring of their members; as the prevailing parties were successively animated by the spirit of faction; the government was continually changing; the people, amazed at so many revolutions, in vain attempted to erect a commonwealth. At length, when the country had undergone the most violent shocks, they were obliged to have recourse to the very government which they had so wantonly proscribed." (Ed. Masson, Montesquieu, Oeuvres complètes, III, 3).

35. "The English, to favour their liberty, have abolished all the intermediate powers of which their monarchy was composed. They have a great deal of reason to be jealous of this liberty: were they ever to be so unhappy as to lose it, they would be one of the most servile nations upon earth" (Ed. Masson, Montesquieu, Oeuvres complètes, II, 4).

36. Cf. Pensées, n° 1574: "La liberté, ce bien qui fait jouir des autres biens."

37. There is an oblique allusion to the Glorious Revolution in sections 14–18, in which Montesquieu, referring to "a violation of the fundamental laws" and revolutions that "are nothing but a confirmation of liberty," gives an unashamedly Whig interpretation of the events of 1688–1689. This Whig tendency was not lost on the Scottish translator (see note 42).

38. Ed. Masson, Montesquieu, Oeuvres complètes, II, 593.

39. Ibid., 594. For a detailed analysis of the significance of Montesquieu's exchange with Domville, see Lando Landi, L'Inghilterra e il pensiero politico di Montesquieu (Padova: Cedam, 1981), 295–304.

40. "Whether the British Monarchy Inclines More to Absolute Monarchy or to a Republic," Political Essays, 32.

41. Ed. Masson, Montesquieu, Oeuvres complètes, III, 1245.

42. "If we read Tacitus's admirable work on the manners of the Germans, we will see that it is from them the English have taken the idea of their political constitution. This fine system hath been found in the woods" (XI, 6, section 64). To this the Scottish translator added a somewhat imaginative note: "From such imperfect hints as are to be found in this little piece of Tacitus, 'tis not easy to imagine the idea of so perfect a form has been taken. One would rather believe, that the author couched in this mysterious way an opinion a Frenchman dare scarce avow, that this happy establishment was secured at the revolution of 1688, concerted by the lovers of British liberty, and the Prince of Orange, at his house of the Wood, and afterwards completed by the accession of the præsent reigning German family."

43. Sharon Krause, in her Liberalism with Honor (Cambridge: Harvard University Press, 2002), draws attention to the views expressed on this problem in the Federalist by Madison and Hamilton. The former stated that constitutional checks and balances were impotent without the spring of personal motives—motives that were not to be equated with self-interest (Krause, 112); as for Hamilton, he maintained that the British House of Commons, with its reputation for venality, had more virtue than was often thought and that there was "a large proportion of the body which consists of independent and public-spirited men" who are usually able to sustain the separation between the legislative and executive powers (Krause, 113).

44. Cf. the perceptive observation of Pangle, who, though convinced that the English constitution "is based on the collective selfishness of its citizens," writes, "[I]t

still requires a minimal devotion to the whole on the part of each citizen. [...] While Montesquieu thinks that enlightened selfishness can go far in supplying the motive for these restraints, he still thinks it necessary that the principle of self-interest be somewhat muted" (Pangle, Montesquieu's 115–16; see also 147).

45. In his letter to Domville quoted earlier (see note 38) the term "esprit de liberté" is used twice.

# 3

# Honor, Interest, Virtue

## The Affective Foundations of the Political in *The Spirit of Laws*

### Céline Spector

> You could say that it is like the system of the universe, where there is a force constantly repelling all bodies from the center and a force of gravitation attracting them to it. Honor makes all the parts of the body politic move; its very action binds them, and it turns out that each person works for the common good, believing he works for his individual interests.
>
> —*The Spirit of Laws*, III, 7

The notion of the unintended convergence of private interests into the public interest, as it appears in Montesquieu's *The Spirit of Laws*, can strike one as surprising. The nature of honor is to demand preferences and distinctions; it is related to ambition, which, while pernicious in republics and absent from despotic states, gives life to monarchy and constitutes its spring. The analogy to physics[1] justifies the putting in place of a policy conceived of as a regulation of the economy of the passions and not as a prescription of a rational norm: it is fitting to channel the affects rather than to repress them. Human partiality can be taken advantage of; the stability of civil society is dependent on the immanent relations among the forces that constitute it. The "Newton of the moral world,"[2] Montesquieu, whose ambition was to discover in institutions and mores regularities analogous to those that were discovered in the physical world, had, in one of his *Pensées*, already placed the desire to distinguish oneself at the foundation of the social dynamic.³ In the case of honor, the recourse to ambition as a motivating force intervenes also at the moment when the obsolescence of an "austere morality" is announced, a morality imputed to republican regimes whose spring is virtue, linked to good mores. It is a matter of understanding how society can function when the individuals who compose it are no longer moved by love of the fatherland or love of the laws (the subordination of particular interest to the public interest). The definition of honor in *The Spirit of Laws* puts the accent on the result, beneficial to all, of actions motivated by ambition. But the harmony of various particular interests appears to be simply postulated. The invocation of the reader ("you could say") is doubtless revelatory here: can the solidarity of interests be conceived otherwise than in a mode of pure accident ("it turns out that") without having recourse to an authoritarian harmonization on the Hobbesian model? In that case, does the confidence accorded to the social results of actions have to be thought of as an anticipation of the liberal theme of the "invisible hand"?⁴

It appears opportune, in order to answer this question, to take the path suggested by an incidental remark of Albert Hirschman, according to which "the idea of the "invisible hand"—this force that makes men, while pursuing their particular passions, contribute unconsciously to the common good—was formulated by Montesquieu not in relation to love of gain, but love of glory."⁵ If the system of the regulation of the passions present in monarchies permits one to avoid (despotic) coercion as well as the sacrificial subordination of private interest to the common interest (republican virtue), how is the conversion from private vices to public virtues accomplished?

## Theory of the Principles in *The Spirit of Laws*

It will not be possible, in the framework of this chapter, to outline a new characterization of the experimental method employed by Montesquieu in the elaboration of the typology of governments in *The Spirit of Laws*.⁶ Because the laws must first be in relation to the form of the state, the first books of the work return to what had been a commonplace of political philosophy since Antiquity: the classification and the comparison of governments. The return to the ancient tradition, in particular to the Aristotelian tradition, transcends the rupture introduced by the modern philosophers: by putting the plurality of the forms of government in the foreground once again, Montesquieu breaks with the universalist perspective of the sovereignty theorists.⁷ The homage rendered to the genius of Grotius and Pufendorf is associated with a rejection of the abstract rationalism of the jurisconsults.⁸ The political science of *The Spirit of Laws* is comparative: rather than inquiring into the universal conditions of the legitimacy of power, it endeavors to clarify the rationality of the laws and mores proper to each regime. However, the criticism of the sovereignty theorists does not incite Montesquieu to reconcile with the ancient search for the "ideal regime": the highlighting of one figure of the "worst" regime—despotism—is not accompanied by the avowal of a preference for a particular constitution, republican or monarchical.[9] The introduction of a new "type," that of "moderate governments," which subsumes the monarchical and republican regimes by opposition to despotism,[10] translates this rupture with the classical perspective of the "best regime": the good regime can be democratic, aristocratic, or monarchical according to the circumstances. In reaction to modern skepticism, which used the argument of the diversity of laws and mores to deny the existence of a political science,[11] Montesquieu's perspective consists in the suitability to particular circumstances, physical or moral, that define the way of life of peoples: rather than theorizing about the abstract conformity of the political to the universal norms of natural right or outlining the model of a perfect society, "it is better to say that the government most in conformity with nature is the one whose particular disposition best relates to the disposition of the people for whom it is established" (I, 3). In the perspective of their "nature" (what makes them what they are) and their "principle" (what makes them act), the regimes will be compared and evaluated according to their capacity to endure and to preserve the security of the rulers as well as that of the citizens (which constitutes, in the form of the opinion that they have of their security, their liberty); they will be differentiated according to the nature of the solution that they propose to the question of the subjective foundation—the affective foundation—of obedience to political power.

The affirmation of the necessity of a distribution of powers in order to preserve the moderation of governments[12] is, in effect, related in Montesquieu to the importance conferred upon affective motivations that support moderation insofar as mores are concerned. The introduction of the notion of "principle" takes its place at the heart of the typology of governments: while the nature of a regime corresponds to its institutional structure ("what makes it what it is"), its principle resides in the human passions that set it in motion ("what makes it act," III, 1). To every machine of state corresponds a spring capable of setting in motion its internal dynamism. Fear in despotic states, honor in monarchical states, virtue in republican states: the reflection on the conditions of obedience is neither universal nor purely circumstantial; it arises from a plurality of types. The classical contractualist inquiry (why be obedient to political power? under what conditions is it legitimate?) undergoes a major theoretical shift. The question is no longer that of original consent and the reasons that could have induced men to abandon their natural liberty and equality to submit themselves to political authority but rather that of the affective motivations of obedience, once the body politic is instituted. Now the criticism of a regime founded on fear, an inhibiting passion that predominates in despotic states, takes the form of a valuation of the active participation of subjects in the functioning of the institutions, beyond formal consent and external obedience to the laws. The principles determine the affective propensity of individuals to obey certain rules of behavior on which the dynamic of the preservation of states depends. All the people of a given state do not necessarily share the principles, but unless this is the case, "the government is imperfect."[13] The question that now must be posed is critical: will the moderns, generally incapable of virtue,[14] have to content themselves with political regimes contrary to nature or solutions of substitution by default?

## Honor, Fear, Virtue

The importance of honor, the principle of monarchies, is first conceived of in the light of the risk of the corruption of monarchies, which can lead them toward despotism. The determination of the principle is carried out by a deduction starting from the nature of the government: because despotism concentrates powers, and because any procedure of negotiation is foreign to it, power is preserved only by the fear that it inspires.[15] Emerging naturally, in a purely reactive fashion, out of the vision or imagination of punishments, fear has as its effect the suppression of the social passions and the prevention of their expression, which constitutes the reason why it shows itself, in the final analysis, to be contrary to nature. While man is a double being, a sentient and emotive creature, but also, by nature, an intelligent and free being (I, 1), fear reduces the human being to pure animality, governing his behavior as mechanically as the laws of movement that govern bodies. Fear of punishment not only prevents all disobedience, all attempts at insubordination, but it removes the very possibility of political reasoning and deliberation (III, 10). Contrary to virtue or honor, fear—a brute, passive, asocial and apolitical passion—does not rest on any intellectual or moral quality; thus it does not require education (IV, 3). The principle of despotism therefore has as its effect a form of dehumanization tied to the abolition of all liberty and all sociability.

Naturally distinct from fear inasmuch as its glory is to "disdain life,"[16] honor is equally distinct from virtue, the principle of republics. Deducing its necessity from the nature of democracy, Montesquieu redefines this virtue as a political virtue (and not moral or Christian): if virtue is necessary in republics, it is because those who execute the laws know that they themselves will be subject to those same laws, which is not the case in monarchies, where the execution of the laws depends on the will of the prince alone. The specific difficulty of democracy stems from the relation of the citizen to the law: the subject is at the same time the object of the laws. If obedience only requires the "force of the laws" in monarchy, if it only requires brute force in despotism (fear of punishment in case of disobedience to orders), democracy is the regime in which the author of the laws is at the same time the one who must ensure the execution of the laws; in democracy the one who elaborates the laws as a co-legislator is also submitted to the empire of the law as a subject: in a republic, "the one who sees to the execution of the laws feels that he is subject to them himself and that he will bear their weight" (III, 3). Now, virtue, defined as love of the fatherland and love of the laws, makes it possible to overcome this difficulty of self-constraint: only citizens moved by love of the laws are ready to prefer the general interest to their particular interests in order to make the law prevail.[17] By reorienting the selfish social passions (greed, ambition) toward the public (the desire to increase the public treasury, to augment the glory of one's fatherland), virtue furnishes the citizen with the motivation required for the respect of the rules that privilege the common interest over that of individuals (III, 3). In this respect, aristocracy occupies an intermediary position: the nobles who hold power will easily see to the execution of the laws as long as they apply to the people but will constrain themselves with more difficulty; their desire for domination and acquisition must only be tempered. This is why moderation, less exacting than virtue, is the principle of aristocratic regimes (III, 4).

Now, contrary to virtue, the honor that Montesquieu defines is an ambition associated with particular interests rather than the common interest: the glory that it pursues is that of individuals or bodies, not of the state; the desire for reputation that it privileges in commanding "difficult" actions aims at the good of individuals (honors and titles), not the common good.[18] Many of Montesquieu's readers and commentators see in this analysis the sign of the denigration of the monarchical regime and its institutions: either they wish to rehabilitate the figure of a republican philosopher, or they are at least nostalgic for the greatness of ancient virtue,[19] or, in the liberal or Straussian tradition, they intend to put forward a Montesquieu who was a secret partisan of a modern form of republicanism on the model furnished by commercial and free England.[20] The hypothesis of Montesquieu's opposition to the structures of the Ancien Regime could have been reinforced by the portrait of education in monarchy, out of which seems to emerge a satire of the aristocratic ethic, a petty ethic lacking breadth, compared to the authentic nobility of virtue. Does not Montesquieu himself invite this interpretation? "I hasten and I lengthen my steps," he writes, "so that none will believe I satirize monarchical government" (III, 6). Is not the reduction of honor to a prejudice ("the prejudice of each person and each condition") that leads back to ambition (the desire for "preferences and distinctions") evidence of the disdain in which the principle is held? That the particular economy of the feudal ethic can be perceived as a pure and simple imposture from the perspective of the authentic nobility of virtue cannot be doubted. Moved by vanity and cupidity, modern man's horizon is reduced to narrow interests:

It is the love of the fatherland that gave to Greek and Roman histories that nobility that ours lack. It is the continual spring of all actions, and one feels pleasure in finding it everywhere, this virtue dear to all those who have a heart.

When one thinks of the baseness of our motives, of the avarice with which we seek vile rewards, of this ambition so different from the love of glory, one is astonished at the difference of the spectacles; and it seems that, since these two great peoples ceased to exist, men have shrunk by a cubit.[21]

The disjuncture between honor and virtue could not therefore but evoke virulent criticism from the contemporaries and successors of Montesquieu. His definition of honor shocks minds accustomed to seeing honor defined as the "prize of virtue," in continuity with the Aristotelian tradition.[22] In this respect, the study of ecclesiastical criticism that *The Spirit of Laws* was subjected to and the arguments Montesquieu produced in its defense makes it possible to situate the question of the relation between virtue and honor at the heart of the controversy sparked off by the publication of the work.[23] Did not the author affirm that "virtue is not the principle of monarchical government" and that honor "takes the place of virtue and represents it everywhere" to conclude that "in well-regulated monarchies everyone will be almost a good citizen, and one will rarely find someone who is a good man; for, in order to be a good man, one must have the intention of being one" (III, 5–6)? These remarks censured by the faculty of theology of the Sorbonne in 1750 had first struck the attention of Fr. de la Roche, editor of the Jansenist journal *Les Nouvelles ecclésiastiques*. His *Examen critique de "L'Esprit des lois"* takes up the question of the principles using as his point of entry these passages and the opposition between honor and virtue, an opposition which the moderns know only by "hearsay" (III, 5). Is not "false honor," which constitutes the spring of monarchies, founded on selfishness and ambition, irreconcilable with Christian virtue? If the Christian "hates to render men vain," should not she be banned from monarchies, in order to make this type of government perfect?[24] The exclusion of virtue as the principle of monarchies seems to prove that *The Spirit of Laws*, like the *Persian Letters* earlier, had no other end than to topple the church as well as the state in France: in the eyes of the Jansenist, Montesquieu attacked the validity of Catholicism by preaching immorality, and his impious work reduced all the Christians of France to the status of pitiful citizens. The theologians of the Sorbonne insisted even more on the scandal brought upon the monarchy: is not the disjuncture between honor and virtue equally injurious to the nobles as to the people? When, under the pressure brought to bear by the Congregation of the Index, the Faculty increased the number of propositions incriminated in *The Spirit of Laws*, it focused once again on honor, accusing its author of "hatred" of the monarchy, forcing him to respond in an indignant tone[25] and to promise textual modifications. Nevertheless, for Montesquieu, the distinction between the principles (honor and virtue) "is of so great fecundity that they constitute almost my whole book."[26]

This fear of having monarchy denigrated by the contrast established between virtue and honor is largely shared by secular critics of *The Spirit of Laws*. The refusal to dissociate monarchy and virtue is apparent notably in Voltaire, who was desirous to prove that "virtue belongs to all governments and to all conditions."[27] Rousseau became indignant in turn: not having seen that sovereign authority is always the same, this "noble genius" who is Montesquieu did not know that "the same principle ought to apply to every well-constituted State, albeit to a greater or lesser degree according to the form of government."[28] In order to renew the broken bond between honor and virtue, numerous Philosophers wanted to discredit the aristocratic social prejudice—a "false" honor and a barbarous usage—to extol a universal benevolence and an active devotion to civil society.[29] Is it then necessary to deplore the prosecution of Montesquieu's motives and recriminate the misunderstanding relative to the definition of virtue—which is political virtue, and not moral or Christian virtue—as well as of virtue's status? If virtue is not the "principle of monarchies," is it at least not altogether excluded from them?[30]

The alleged compatibility between honor and virtue cannot be maintained when one takes into consideration their respective characterizations. Certainly, the *Persian Letters* traditionally considered honor as the recompense of virtue, understood as love of the fatherland.[31] But *The Spirit of Laws*, in elaborating the notion of "principle," denounces the difference between the recompenses that are adapted to the different regimes: while in monarchies "honor alone reigns" and can only be rewarded by distinctions, in republics virtue is a motive "that suffices in itself and excludes all others" (V, 18). Once the repression of inclinations by fear is ruled out, two solutions present themselves: the interiorization of norms for the common good, which supposes the reorientation of the selfish passions and the education of the citizen; or the putting in place, by dint of honor, of the unintended convergence of particular interests into the public interest: "[I]t turns out that each person works for the common good, believing he works for his individual interests" (III, 7). Contrary to virtue, honor requires neither the orientation of individual intentions toward the common good nor a moral consensus imposed by the state. In the context of laws that support the inequality of conditions, it assures the production of public utility despite the absence of virtuous intentions: "The State continues to exist independently of love of the fatherland, desire for true glory, self-renunciation, sacrifice of one's dearest interests, and all those heroic virtues we find in the ancients and know only by hearsay."[32]

Consequently, the dissociation of honor from virtue is not confined to the political domain, as Montesquieu claimed. The analysis of judgment in the portrait of education in monarchies shows how the principles of the evaluation of honor, are distinct both from religious and moral criteria, considered as vulgar, and the norms of law. In the world, "One judges men's actions here not as good but as noble; not as just but as great; not as reasonable but as extraordinary [...] This eccentric honor shapes the virtues into what it wants and as it wants: on its own it puts rules on everything prescribed to us; according to its fancy, it extends or limits our duties, whether their source be religion, politics or morality" (IV, 2). If Montesquieu begins by making laws the stand-in for virtue in modern monarchies ("The laws replace all these virtues, for which there is no need"), he designates the principle of honor as another stand-in for virtue in the following manner: "Honor, that is, the prejudice of each person and each condition, takes the place of the political virtue of which I have spoken and represents it everywhere."[33] These two elements—the law and the code of honor—are nevertheless in competition with one another: the third supreme rule of honor stipulates that "what honor forbids is more rigorously forbidden when the laws do not agree in proscribing it, and that what honor requires is more strongly required when the laws do not demand it."[34] But in monarchical society, this competition between a regulation by mores and a regulation by laws is not an antagonism: honor "can inspire the noblest actions; joined with the force of the laws, it can lead to the goal of government as does virtue itself" (III, 6). Civil society manifestly needs to be governed by law; but this regulation suffices neither to mobilize individual energies nor to effectively promote the end of the state. Only the concurrence of the hope of rewards and the fear of punishment in case of transgression of the law makes it possible for the political machine to function optimally, by unifying a motivating principle (honor as ambition, desire for honors) with an inhibiting principle: "[I]n monarchies, politics accomplishes great things with as little virtue as it can, just as in the finest machines art employs as few motions, forces and wheels as possible" (III, 5). The mechanistic image translates here, from all that appearances indicate, a transposition of Malebranche's or Leibniz's schema of the simplicity of paths, associated with the fecundity of results: what is minimized is henceforth on the order of constraint of inclinations (what virtue requires); what is maximized depends on "great things" that assure prosperity and political liberty.[35] Without knowing it or wanting to, men, pursuing their personal interest (their desire for glory), produce public utility. Now it is precisely this dissociation between the object of the will of agents and the result of their actions that requires the promotion of a new point of view—that of the social whole or of civil society.[36]

### Honor That Is "False" but Useful to the Public

How then ought one to understand the cunning of reason that presides over the functioning of monarchy? If the folly of the heroic ethic and of conquests of prestige is the object of a definitive denunciation, if heroism is profoundly undermined,[37] if honor is false "philosophically speaking" (III, 7)—it depends on conventions and opinion, proud motivations issuing from the desire to distinguish oneself, which can only produce apparent or vainglorious virtues—the description of honor as an immoral and extravagant prejudice does not in any way end in its invalidation as a political principle: honor, as false as it is, is "useful to the public."[38] In this respect, the theme of the utility of illusion refers to an anthropology in which passion is superior to reason that "never produces great effects on the minds of men" and tends rather to distance them from the requirements of citizenship.[39] Neither the force of the laws nor the rational command of duty creates an obligation comparable to that of honor, which compels one to keep one's word and respect one's promises: "Even in the cases where the laws have strength, they always have less of it than honor. Duty is a considered and cold thing; but honor is an active passion, which moves of itself and, besides, is related to all the others. Say to subjects that they must obey their prince because religion and the laws command it, you will find the people cold. Say to them that they must be faithful to him because they promised it to him, and you will see them enlivened."[40] That honor is a prejudice does not therefore diminish its strength; rather the opposite is true. The Pascalian principle of the reason of effects is reiterated in the following passage: "Singular thing! It is hardly ever reason that does reasonable things, and one hardly ever gets to reason by way of reason."[41] Because "what is founded on healthy reason is very ill founded," it is advisable to count on the folly of the people rather than on the folly of the great: the reason of effects approves the universal reign of the salutary illusion.

The first inversion of "vain" and "healthy" concerns the public use that can be made of symbolic recompenses (honors). In despotic governments, the art of command fails to eradicate disorder[42] to the same extent that it fails to bring about a dynamic order. The fear of punishment can only inhibit all activity, and blind obedience must be passive; coercion is incapable of eliciting initiatives beneficial to the state. Receiving an order and executing it—that is about all subjects can do in the service of their master. "Vile instruments" that the despot can destroy at his pleasure only exist as long as they know how to obey[43] and show themselves to be lethargic in the face of any enterprise from which they can expect no profit.[44] The interiorized norms of honor, in contrast, make it possible to generate the voluntary participation of the subjects, whose dominant passion is called upon—private vices being converted into a public good:

> This happy idea [glory] causes a Frenchman to do with pleasure and inclination what your Sultan obtains from his subjects only by keeping constantly before them punishments and rewards [. . .] The difference between the French troops and yours is this: the latter,

composed of slaves who are naturally cowards, overcome the fear of death only by the fear of punishment, and this produces in the soul a new kind of terror which stupefies it; but the former welcome the blows with pleasure and banish fear by a feeling of satisfaction which is superior to it.[45]

Thus two facets of the political subject correspond to two distinct forms of the art of governing: while the despotic individual reacts instinctively to fear of punishment (and, secondarily, to expectation of a financial reward), the monarchical individual, led by the hope of distinguishing herself rather than by fear of punishment, is capable of comprehending symbolic representations and performing great actions useful to the state by "inclination," particularly in war. In the absence of fear or of the aim of the common good, the desire for distinction and reputation inherent in honor is a source of inspiration to accomplish exploits at the peril of one's life, exploits from which the community, which confers honors in return for services rendered, can benefit. Honor is thus understood as ambition subjected to obligations, and as the desire to prove oneself worthy of one's status and even to distinguish oneself by obtaining new titles; through the desire for glory, honor enables particular interests to contribute to the common interest. Similarly, in *The Spirit of Laws*, monarchical society functions by virtue of the energy mobilized by the desire for preeminence, which makes men "do great things" and prevents certain bad actions—honor playing the role of censor (V, 10)—without offering any other tangible reward.[46]

The substitution of honor for virtue thus carries with it crucial consequences. Whereas despotism can endure only through permanent coercion or threats, and whereas a republic must constantly use constraint to ensure the conversion of the private man into the public man and make judgments concerning the devotion to the common cause, monarchy can enjoy, thanks to honor, an interiorization of social control which liberates the public sphere from continual surveillance and a moral setting in order. Certainly, morality is still under the legitimate jurisdiction of penal laws,[47] but in monarchies, the violence of the republican legislator obliged to combat natural sentiments by sacrificing the man and the citizen to the state is nonetheless avoided,[48] emancipating the sphere of civil society.

## Obedience and Resistance

It remains to identify the political advantage of honor—its contribution to political liberty.[49] As already demonstrated in the *Persian Letters*, honor serves as an agent of resistance to the arbitrary power of monarchs: this "sacred treasure" is "the only one which the sovereign does not control, because to do so would defeat his own interests."[50] By this very fact, the limit of the prince's desire to appropriate and dominate is at the same time the foundation of his power. The regulated use of the principle makes it possible, in the first place, to avoid revolutions, which are characteristic of despotism: threatened on all sides by the passions that it represses, despotic power is constantly vulnerable to a palace revolution analogous to a seraglio insurrection, from the moment a usurper presents himself.[51] In the absence of adherence, submission can only be obtained because the least refusal to obey is punished "without mercy"; only an iron fist can maintain order, an order that is not a real peace but the "silence" of muffled conflicts and captive spirits.[52] In monarchies, by contrast, where powers are shared and the nobles are well treated, sedition does not degenerate into revolution.[53] But in excluding revolution, honor does not by the same token abandon the resources of revolt: the principle must always be the judge and arbiter of the appropriateness of the obedience to superiors as well as to laws, and when the duel is proscribed, "honor, which wishes always to reign, revolts, and regards not the laws."[54] Because his "point of honor" prevents him from obeying dishonorable orders, and because the laws of honor trump all other laws (religious, moral or civil), the gentleman constitutes by his very existence a rampart blocking the extension of royal authority. By publicly defending their status and by desiring to show themselves worthy of their rank, the nobles resist arbitrary actions and abuses of power. Whereas the eunuchs, who believe that the proof of their unconditional fidelity resides in their loyal services, are obliged to obey blindly,[55] the individual moved by honor knows that to enslave oneself to the tyrant never constitutes loyal service. The desire for glory is born with liberty, just as it is a support for liberty: "[I]t may be laid down as a maxim that, in every State, the desire for glory increases and diminishes with the liberty of the subjects: glory is never the companion of slavery."[56]

In *The Spirit of Laws*, this theory does not undergo any significant inflection. The introduction of the nature/principle couple, absent from the *Persian Letters*, simply allows Montesquieu to specify the relation between "compensatory passions" (which subordinate all the other passions to their ends) and "compensatory powers" (which limit royal sovereignty). While fear dominates in despotic States, where no one is "sovereign by right," but only in fact,[57] and while virtue reigns over sovereign citizens, the principle of monarchies is supposed to animate a structure in which sovereign power is limited by the intermediary powers that verify the conformity of royal ordinances to the fundamental laws of the kingdom. Thus the local political bodies (parliamentary, provincial, or municipal powers) are as concerned with the preservation of honor as are the social orders. As a prejudice that "enters into all the modes of thought and all the ways of feeling," honor attaches each individual to the prerogatives of his political body and to the dignity of his order, thereby reconciling the imperative to be loyal to the prince with the independence that directs one to disobey dishonorable orders. All the tension inherent in the code of honor is inscribed in this double movement. Equipped with its own rules that prescribe, authorize, or proscribe, honor must arbitrate between two obligations that circumstances can render incompatible:

> There is nothing in monarchy that laws, religion, and honor prescribe so much as obedience to the will of the prince; but this honor dictates to us that the prince should never prescribe an action that dishonors us because it would make us incapable of serving him [...]
>
> For the nobility, honor prescribes nothing more than serving the prince in war [...] But honor wants to be the arbiter in imposing this law; and if honor has been offended, it permits or requires one to withdraw to one's home.[58]

Thus honor assumes the role of a casuist, prescribing the conduct one is to follow in litigious circumstances; as the arbiter of the obedience one owes to the supreme authority, it can impose courageous resistance to orders whose content is incompatible with its convictions. Resistance, in this sense, is not founded on universal criteria of the just or the good, deduced from a certain conception of the nature of man; neither is it rooted in virtue, in love of the fatherland, or in the desire for the common good. Honor, ambition regulated by principles, is rooted instead in a duty toward oneself, an unconditional obligation to uphold one's code that requires that one refuse to perform degrading actions: "[I]n monarchies, honor, true or false, cannot suffer that which it calls degradation" (V, 19). Now this refusal to accept what would detract from one's idea of one's greatness is what prohibits the will of the monarch from taking effect in all circumstances. The occasional necessity for disobedience is part of the very obligation of obedience: certain actions, because of their baseness, can exempt the subject from the obligation of obedience by making it impossible for him to serve the state worthily. By reconciling the martial honor of the nobility of the sword with the civic honor of the nobility of the robe, Montesquieu highlights the political courage necessary for a state governed by the rule of law, whatever the existing formal guaranties may be. Because the institutions intended to guarantee rights may be transformed into simple walls of paper if no one takes charge of what Machiavelli called the "guard of liberty," it is indispensable to place that responsibility in the hands of officers motivated by the defense of their status, and indirectly, by the defense of fundamental liberties.[59]

Thus the honor defined by Montesquieu provides, in the absence of any authentic contractualist theory, the rule of legitimate obedience; it does not involve taking up arms but formulating a disagreement or retiring to one's home in case of a conflict with the monarch.[60] However, the principle of the "excellence" of monarchical government lies in the possibility of interposing negotiation between the commands of the prince and the "furor" of the people. Not only does this mediation make it possible to avoid the absolutist corruption of monarchy, but it also contributes to the preservation of the power of the prince when confronted with the rebellions of the people. On the one hand, the intermediary powers temper the fervor of the seditious by playing the role of buffer: without repressing popular movements, they channel their ardor and find the reason to prevent the spread of social unrest in their own desire to preserve the established order, within which they occupy an important position. The stability of the regime is thus supported: "[T]he State is more fixed, the constitution more unshakable, and the persons of those who govern more assured."[61] On the other hand, through their remonstrance and resistance, the intermediary bodies prevent the automatic execution of orders. The general and the governor, no more than the member of Parlement, are not simply belts by which power transmits itself mechanically. This is what distinguishes the servile obedience characteristic of despotic states from the obedience present in monarchical and moderate states:

> In despotic states the nature of the government requires extreme obedience, and the prince's will, once known, should produce its effect as infallibly as does one ball thrown against another.
> No tempering, modification, accommodation, terms, alternatives, negotiations, remonstrances, nothing as good or better can be proposed. Man is a creature that obeys a creature that wants. [. . .]
> In monarchical and moderate states, power is limited by that which is its spring; I mean honor, which reigns like a monarch over the prince and the people [. . .]. This results in necessary modifications of obedience; honor is naturally subject to eccentricities, and obedience will follow them all. (III, 10)

Nature and principle are inseparable: the intermediary powers moved by honor constitute instances of authority where the supreme power can be contested without being overturned. The idea of a sphere of public deliberation between the prince and his subjects is in this respect crucial.[62] The parlements, trustees of the fundamental laws, slow the execution of royal legislation by their grievances and petitions, contributing the rationality that one cannot expect either from the court or the councils of the prince (formalities delay the execution of the will of the prince and assure almost involuntarily, its rationality[63]). This takes place when the partial prescriptions of the code of honor are at the source of extraordinary actions, which, by refusing the instrumentation of the will in passive obedience, serve the liberty of all.

The complementary relation between the legality of right and the code of honor can now be identified. Related to the distribution of powers in monarchy, honor contributes to liberty that cannot exist when law is reduced to the command of a superior. The dupe of its own cunning, honor encourages—in spite of itself—the preservation of a regime that the natural inclination of the desire for domination leads toward despotism ("any man who has power is led to abuse it"[64]). Monarchical civil society is thus governed by mores, fundamentally distinct from regulation by laws. But this very independence from law makes it possible in fact for mores to give support to law. Thanks to rules that govern its eccentricities, the principle of monarchy supports the legality of its form of government. The monarch contributes to maintaining the stability of the intermediary bodies, including the Parlements, which act as a "depository of the laws." Honor, like religion in despotic states, has its "laws" ("It has consistent rules and sustains its caprices" [III, 8]) that serve as limits to the arbitrariness of power. The caprices of honor are set against the caprices of monarchs: honor protects the prince from the audacity of the nobles (who must serve him if they wish to obtain the desired distinctions) as well as from his own ambitions (to increase his power).[65]

### Education in Monarchies: The Figure of the *honnête homme*

We must now explore the convergence of interests in monarchies. If the monarchical state can prosper despite the fact that no one is prepared to sacrifice for it; if it can be maintained without all subjects desiring its preservation more than their own, it is because education in this regime has informed the mores that in turn enable the maintenance of its order. The chapter entitled "On education in monarchies" thus provides a description of the logic of appearance and distinction that presides over the formation of the subject of monarchies—whom Montesquieu names the *honnête homme*.[66] The term "education," used throughout Book IV, should be understood broadly: far from being limited to the instruction of children, it also includes the cultivation of men, of their minds as well as their passions. Whereas republican education is dispensed by the family and the state, without full ideological consistency, education in monarchies is divided among parents, schoolmasters, and the world (IV, 4).

The theory of education makes it possible to account for the differentiated political anthropology of *The Spirit of Laws*. Lacking in despotism, where slaves must know nothing and hope for nothing, education is all-powerful in republics, where each must have "the same happiness and the same advantages, must taste the same pleasures, and develop the same hopes" (IV, 3–5). The homogeneity of aspirations is maintained through censorship; mores are linked to a network of subordination (of subjects to magistrates, of young people to old, of women to their husbands, of children to their fathers) and under the control of a domestic tribunal.[67] Corruption arises when public values transmitted by education are no longer sufficient protection against selfish tendencies and when it becomes necessary to "recall" men to the principles of virtue.[68] In monarchies, by contrast, order is effected without the vertical relations of subordination that characterize despotic or republican societies. The school of honor, this "universal master that should everywhere guide us," teaches with the maxim that "one must cultivate a certain nobility in the practice of the virtues, a certain frankness in the mores, and a certain politeness in the manners" (IV, 2). In the first place, the virtues: their logic is not one of benevolence, which brings people together, but rather one of distinction, which separates them. The virtues are selfish; they concern less that which bring subjects toward each other than that which distinguishes them. Normative judgments habitually attribute praise to greatness and distinction and blame to baseness.[69] So the set of criteria for "virtue" in monarchies, as stated by Montesquieu, are reminiscent of aristocratic virtue, if not heroic or chivalrous virtue. Judge or sophist, honor does not know any other criterion than the nobility of actions (noblesse oblige): "One judges men's actions here not as good but as noble; not as just but as great; not as reasonable but as extraordinary." In this way, monarchical education forms subjects capable of "doing all the difficult actions and which require force, with no reward other than the renown of these actions" (III, 7); it provides the criteria of judgment that will motivate their nondeliberate contribution to the common interest.

After the virtues come mores which betray the same distance between motivations and actions. Frankness is not desired for itself but for the appearance of independence that it confers on the one who makes use of it: "One desires [truth] because a man who is accustomed to speaking it appears to be daring and free." For Montesquieu, the man who is frank is none other than the nobleman, who uses the discourse of truth to give himself the appearance of courage and liberty; he is not the man of the people who, if sincere, only wants the truth for itself, intentionally. Once again, imitation in the world teaches men to emphasize a criterion of independence whose public function will be crucial.

Finally, manners also answer to this art of appearances. The propriety that prevents men from "offending" one another, that encourages them to "please one another" and to give one another "credit," must also be attributed to an impure motive: "politeness does not customarily have its origin in such a pure source. It arises from the desire to distinguish oneself. We are polite from pride," flattered to prove thereby that our manners distinguish us from the people who live "in baseness" (IV, 2).

In *The Spirit of Laws*, the portrait of the *honnête homme* educated in monarchies in accordance only with the values of the world contrasts with the perfected figure of the Aristotelian magnanimous man, "a man that judges himself worthy of great things, on the condition that he is in effect worthy of them."[70] Far from proceeding from virtue and from an authentic feeling of value, worldly honor pursues an honorable appearance concentrated in exterior signs of distinction. Its code legislates a purely frivolous art of enjoyment, including gallantry, intrigue, and flattery intended to obtain fortune. The very substance of its seriousness is constituted by "trifles": "[T]he worldly tone consists very much in speaking of trifles as if they were serious things, and of serious things as if they were trifles."[71] The sincerity promoted by honor is factitious, for it proceeds from pride and not from a veritable greatness of soul. The complaisance and deceit it authorizes in order to acquire wealth and power are in opposition to the self-sufficient virtues of the magnanimous man: consisting in ambition and the desire for privileges and distinctions, honor is by nature needy. If the courtier wants to show himself worthy, all he must do is belong to a distinguished elite; he is flattered by his own politeness as much as those toward whom the politeness is directed, because it makes it clear that he belongs to the court, or at least that he is "worthy of belonging to it." Thus Montesquieu appears to bear witness to the degeneration of honor. Being dependent on the honors accorded by the sovereign, the courtier or *honnête homme* is being dependent on reputation and on the hazards of opinion. The contrast with the figure of the magnanimous man or the noble hero is stark: hedonism and the art of pleasing, gallantry, and the empire of taste are central to the life of the *honnête homme*, this perfect subject of monarchies who can easily forego being a virtuous man, a good man, or a Christian. The subversion of the Aristotelian paradigm, reworked by an entire humanist tradition, joins the Jansenist transformation of moral condemnation into the praise of its social effects. The political typology of *The Spirit of Laws* provides the occasion for a resurgence of Augustinian themes from the previous century—the world as the beautiful order of concupiscence or the "beautiful portrait of charity."[72] If Montesquieu transposes the order of grace into the political order of republican virtue, he conserves the idea of a monarchical society governed by the beneficent effects of self-love (*amour-propre*) rather than charity: "It is the desire to please that connects society, and the happiness of the human race was such that this self-love [*amour-propre*], which was supposed to disintegrate society, on the contrary, strengthens it and makes it unshakable."[73]

Honor comes to light as a "worldly science"[74] in each of its three domains—virtues, mores, and manners—or rather, as an art of simulacra, offering to the observer in situ a spectacle of illusion, a staging of shams. On the stage of the world, honor subordinates the desire for domination to an art of pleasing intended to accommodate self-loves. These self-loves constitute the bonds—created not only despite each person's selfish ambition, but because of it—that make monarchy a harmonious system, in which appetites for power are mastered and individual rough edges are smoothed into politeness.[75] What results is an equilibrium within civil society, absent all coercion and external discipline of the inclinations: the ambition that animates men is counterbalanced by the principles that regulate the desire for reputation; pride is tempered by deference and consideration. The metaphor of gravity in Book III becomes clear: the center of the solar system is the monarch who remains the "source of greatness," that is to say, the source of the honors and fortunes that permit the satisfaction of the luxury demanded by distinctions (V, 18). Honor, the motive that presides over people's great actions, is the dynamic principle that sets the elements of the social body in motion. Now this principle of action is at the heart of a double relation.[76] The desire to distinguish oneself separates them (centrifugal force); the politeness by which they must satisfy their desire for greatness brings them together, by inciting them to "please" one another (a centripetal force). Through the mechanical regulation of the desires for domination, the source of the political bond and of the social bond, the stability of civil society is established.

## Societas and Universitas

The theoretical stakes involved in the typology of governments can now be discerned. In the face of despotism, republic and monarchy can be understood as two representations of the state. Following Roman private law, Michael Oakeshott distinguishes *universitas* and *societas*, attempting to apply these categories to the forms of government described by *The Spirit of Laws*. *Universitas* makes reference to a moral person or a corporation composed of persons associated with one another for a defined purpose; its unity results from the concerted action of its members. *Societas*, in contrast, designates for jurists the product of a pact by which individuals agree to recognize the authority of certain conditions of action; it is a formal relationship in terms of rules, rather than substantial relationship in terms of common action—a nomocracy and not a teleocracy.[77] Applied to the political typology presented by Montesquieu, this distinction allows us to elucidate the internal difference between the moderate governments: whereas republican government is confided to each member of the association who aims at a common end and accepts a certain way of life that conforms to it (its principle being virtue), monarchical government only ties men to one another by external norms of behavior—the laws, rules governing the coexistence of liberties. More flexible and more efficient than the republican *universitas*, monarchical *societas*, moved by honor (identified with the personal preferences of the subjects) is, according to Oakeshott, by this very fact, more free.

Because of this, the distinction between the two systems of regulation of the passions and interests capable, according to Montesquieu, of preserving political liberty recalls the distinction between "positive liberty" and "negative liberty," between the political autonomy of the citizen apt to govern herself and the latitude of action offered to the individual who is guaranteed not to be impeded by the intervention of the state or her fellow citizens in the private sphere.[78] The first type of liberty involves people's engagement in the pursuit of certain common ends; the second type, being an opportunity offered rather than the exercise of power, defines itself as the absence of constraints and obstacles preventing the agent from pursuing the ends chosen by free will. A positive conception of liberty must be attributed to the republic as it is conceived of by Montesquieu, and a negative conception of the protection of rights must be reserved for monarchy. The republican harmonization of interests, which requires a certain form of civic existence governed by pure, egalitarian, and frugal mores, is tied to a conception of political liberty understood as participation in power, and by a substantial definition of the public interest. Moreover, the renunciations accepted in the name of the interest of the community are effected in the name of an active conception of citizenship, and the homogeneity of the social body united by love of the fatherland is the guarantor of the command of the community in the face of the risk of corruption by the particularization of interests. In contrast with this restrictive model, which requires the omnipotence of the institution and the total submission of the individual to the law that informs her mores, monarchy appears to provide the site of a flexible harmonization of interests conceived according to the model of the "invisible hand"; the economy of civic virtue opens the possibility of the expansion of the "powers of particularity," as Hegel, a great reader of Montesquieu, had noted.[79] In this way, the abandonment of the monistic conception of a perfect life seems to favor the adoption of a moral pluralism which, even if it is not exempt from disadvantages or protected from corruption, at least guarantees that no one will be, by lack of virtue, "forced to be free."

The temptation of an interpretation justifying liberal historiography by adapting the discourse to the evolution of mores—virtues of the ancients, rights of the moderns—is all the more great given that the caution of Montesquieu is invoked by Benjamin Constant, acknowledged apostle of liberalism, who poses the choice between the two forms of state and the two forms of liberty associated with them. The reference to Montesquieu occurs precisely in the context of the analysis of the error of the French revolutionaries, who got bogged down in the Terror for having presented to men a type of liberty, borrowed from the ancient republics, of which modern commercial peoples were no longer capable. Directly inspired by the analysis in *The Spirit of Laws* of the material and moral conditions of a republic (small territory, equality and frugality, censorship of mores, aptitude for renunciation), Constant proposes a distinction between political liberty and civil liberty. Where the legislator-people accepts to submit itself entirely to the social jurisdiction, to abandon itself to the decisions of the sovereign of which it is a member, political liberty—that of the ancients—is effective. But the situation is entirely different in modern states, in which the majority of the inhabitants do not take an active part in the government, and at the most, men are called to exercise sovereignty by representation, "that is to say, in a fictitious manner."[80] The impossibility of recovering the participatory liberty of the ancients is related to the opposition between virtue and commerce; enjoyment being henceforward procured by one's private existence, the sacrifices required by the imitation of the ancients have become absurd. That is what neither Rousseau nor Mably understood in their neglect of the warnings of *The Spirit of Laws*:

> Montesquieu, who was endowed with a less excitable and therefore more observant mind, did not fall into quite the same errors. He was struck by the differences which I have related, but he did not discover their true cause. The Greek politicians who lived under popular government did not recognize, he says, any other power but virtue. Politicians today talk only of manufactures, commerce, finances, wealth and even luxury. He attributes this difference to the republic and the monarchy; it ought instead to be attributed to the opposed spirit of ancient times and modern times.[81]

The liberal reading thus seems tempting. But the analysis of the unintended convergence of interests defined by honor shows that Montesquieu cannot be reappropriated purely and simply by the tradition of negative liberty that permits each individual to flourish fully in the sphere circumscribed by the law—the sphere of autonomy in which one's private interest can have free reign. Inversely, Montesquieu defines political liberty, whatever the form of government may be, as security or the opinion that one has of one's security; the "right to do everything the laws permit"; exclusive submission to the power of the law.[82] From this point of view, *The Spirit of Laws* does not separate ancient political participation, which prevails in those regimes in which the community is superior to the particular, from liberty under the law, which is supposed to free the individual from all political and social obligations. Montesquieu refuses to choose between these two definitions: his method does not consist in formulating a judgment of the goodness per se of the different regimes but in evaluating the advantages and disadvantages of the institutions in situ and from the point of view of their effects. Preoccupied with the defense of the subject faced with abuses of power, the philosopher remains equally attuned to the dangers of atomization linked to interest, which runs the risk of encouraging despotism and severing the social bond.[83] Correlatively, the modernity whose contours are traced by *The Spirit of Laws* is not exclusively a commercial modernity,[84] to which Constant makes reference, but is to an equal extent a monarchical modernity, governed by honor and not by commercial interest. Hegel, once again, was not mistaken.[85]

What is important therefore is the modern substitution of the paradigm of honor—and not only of interest—for that of virtue. The "liberation of the powers of particularity" that this substitution makes possible is not to be understood as a liberation with respect to any substantial norm. The code of honor is not reducible to a set of procedural rules capable of harboring multiple conceptions of the good. The plurality of values that characterizes, according to Montesquieu, the contemporary universe in which religious beliefs differ from familial values as well as from the values of the "world" (IV, 4) does not give rise, in monarchies, to a legitimate diversity of conceptions of the good life. Far from identifying free society with a pluralist society without a common hierarchy of ends, governed by negative rules of law and in which the collaboration of individuals proceeds only from economic relations of exchange, *The Spirit of Laws* outlines the paradigm of societies moved by the rationality of prestige ("they only tend toward the glory of the citizens, the State and the prince"), governed by rules of irrational and immoral behavior but from which "the spirit of liberty" nevertheless emanates.[86]

## Conclusion

In light of Montesquieu's analyses, the contemporary critique of the concept of honor can be envisaged anew. Bound to the Ancien Régime and to the society of orders, nonegalitarian and exclusive, honor elicits the legitimate mistrust of democratic societies. First, from a political point of view: associated with military rather than civic virtues, honor cannot bring about the pacific stability of the international order. Next, from an ethical point of view: being determined by irrational duties and principles judged iniquitous, honor is normally the object of moral condemnation; the myth of its code is not immune to a critical examination. In short, contemporary political theories are quick to decree the disuse and obsolescence of honor, which died with aristocratic societies and is an absurd valorization of glory, birth, and rank. In modern societies, the central notion, as has been shown by Peter Berger and Charles Taylor, is no longer honor but "dignity."[87] Only a universalist concept, inherent in humanity as such, independent of particular attributes and contingent qualities, independent of heredity especially, can satisfy the love of equality that dominates democratic societies and institutes rights for all. The satisfaction of the desire to distinguish oneself found in the philosophy of Montesquieu has been replaced by an egalitarian politics of recognition and a demand for the status equality of cultures and sexes.

Desirous to justify the egalitarian aspirations of a republican society, this contemporary analysis, however, must face up to a major difficulty. The will to promote the effective equality of civic rights involves, out of concern for social justice, the taking into consideration of the differentiated situations of agents; the universal must be reevaluated in situ. According to Charles Taylor, the defect of the politics of the rights of man and of the concept of dignity on which it rests is two-fold: such a universalist politics permits one neither to conceive of the singularity of individuals in their particular adherences, nor to formulate a positive theory of motivations intended to justify the contribution of citizens to common ends. While the equality of right is not accompanied by an equality in fact, nor even by a real equality of opportunity, the abstract egalitarianism associated with dignity is not very conducive to emulation and to the development of talents. Precisely these difficulties prompt us to return to the philosophy of Montesquieu and to his concept of honor. Often associated with the vestiges of feudalism, with a fixed, hierarchical conception of social relations, honor in reality is not reducible to an aristocratic and reactionary concept; several aspects of its definition make it possible for democratic societies, in which hereditary distinctions have been abolished, to conceive of a theory of motivations that is as removed from ancient civic virtue as it is from interest, which modern liberalism most often leads back to.[88]

Beyond the theoretical alternative between liberals and communitarians, the political anthropology founded on honor makes it possible in effect to surpass certain major difficulties associated with the recourse to interest or the exhortation to virtue. First, there is a defect in interest: the exclusive pursuit of one's personal preferences can lead to a depoliticization of the citizens and a weakening of the social bond. Next, there are the dangers of civic virtue, insofar as the development of a sense of obligation with respect to the community can suppose the imposition by the state of a moral consensus—a tutelage from which modern people, in the context of the pluralism of values, want to emancipate themselves. Now in the framework of the rejection of a single conception of the good life, the philosophy of Montesquieu allows us to conceive of a distinct path for modernity, one that is less demanding than ancient virtue but irreducible to the interest of commercial societies. By exploring the possible virtues of an honor conceived of as the desire for distinction and reputation—its contribution to the social bond and the preservation of rights—political theory can position itself at an equal distance from the monism of republican values and the risk of atomization that interest can ultimately bring about. It can associate a motivating principle (ambition, the desire for prestige and distinction) with a restrictive code of behavior that is not imposed by the state but inspired by mores; it can conceive of a norm immanent in customs, whose effects are productive of liberty, by way of a logic of the nonanticipated consequences of actions. Acting out of honor, individuals who pursue a private end (the valorization of their status) contribute, by the same movement, to public service, to the occasional resistance to abuses of power and, through politeness, to the creation of the social bond. Endowed with certain statutory advantages—which remain privileges—individuals are simultaneously compelled by duties, which they obey independently of any contractual or legal obligation.[89] Under strict conditions, inequalities of prestige and power, distinguished from relations of pure domination, can then benefit the community. The unintended convergence of private interests into the public interest is not reducible to a mystery of the "invisible hand": it is accounted for by the transmission of regulating principles, in the education and formation of manners and mores, which govern the desire for distinction by introducing a hierarchy of goods and a norm of their good use. Prescribing the manner in which it is fitting to make use of wealth, powers, or life, the code of honor can arbitrate obligations by inciting, in addition to the habitual obedience, occasional disobedience to unjust laws or illegitimate orders; it is capable of motivating extraordinary actions that democracy itself may need. The use of honor, for this end, is not incompatible with a theory of rights, and in particular the rights of man; it serves, on the contrary, to protect it from becoming a narrow formalism.

## Notes

1. The reference is not necessarily Newtonian, as has often been said, nor is it Cartesian in the strict sense, despite the apparent proximity to a passage of Descartes' *Le Monde* consecrated to gravity (ch. 11). Montesquieu seems to agree with the more recent research of a certain Bouillet, inspired by Malebranche: the equilibrium of the solar system is the result of gravity's compensation of centrifugal force. Here it is the same force that *moves* and that *binds*; its effects are opposed by a return effect that makes the initial centripetal movement convert itself into gravity. This point was established by Denis de Casabianca in his dissertation entitled "Le sens de l'esprit. Les sciences et les arts. Formation du regard dans 'L'Esprit des lois,'" Université d'Aix-Marseille I (2002), I, 122–24.

2. "Newton discovered the laws of the material world; you have discovered, Sir, the laws of the intellectual world" [Charles Bonnet, letter to Montesquieu dated November 14, 1753, in *Oeuvres complètes* (Oxford: Voltaire Foundation, forthcoming), III, 1478].

3. Montesquieu, *Mes Pensées et le Spicilège*, ed. Louis Desgraves (Paris: Robert Laffont, 1991), 5.

4. On the history of this inquiry, see the author's article, "Cupidité ou charité? L'ordre sans vertu, des moralistes du grand siècle à *L'Esprit des lois* de Montesquieu," *Corpus* 43 (2003): 23–69.

5. Albert O. Hirschman, *Les Passions et les Intérêts*, trans. Andler (Paris: PUF, 1997), 14.

6. The bibliography related to this question is immense. We will limit ourselves to mentioning the most recent works of David Carrithers, "Democratic and Aristocratic Republics: Ancient and Moderns," and Paul Rahe, "Forms of Government: Structure,

Principle, Object and Aim," in *Montesquieu's Science of Politics*, ed. David Carrithers, Michael Mosher, and Paul Rahe (Lanham, Boulder, New York, Oxford: Rowman & Littlefield, 2001), 109–58, 69–108; Céline Spector, *Montesquieu. Pouvoirs, richesses et société* (Paris: PUF, 2004), ch. 1.

7. On the status of sovereignty in the work of Montesquieu, see Jean Ehrard, "La souveraineté," in *L'Esprit des mots* (Genève: Droz, 1998), 146–60; Catherine Larrère, "Montesquieu: L'éclipse de la souveraineté," in *Penser la Souveraineté*, ed. Gian Maria Cazzaniga and Yves-Charles Zarka (Paris: Vrin, 2002), 199–214.

8. "I thank Mr. Grotius and Mr. Pufendorf for having so finely executed what a part of this work demanded of me, with a loftiness of genius that I could not have attained" (*Mes Pensées*, 1863). For a natural law reading of Montesquieu, see Mark H. Waddicor, *Montesquieu and the Philosophy of Natural Law* (La Haye: Martinus Nijhoff, 1970). We cannot comment here on this very controversial interpretation; see in particular Sheila M. Mason, *Montesquieu's Idea of Justice* (La Haye: Martinus Nijhoff, 1975); Francine Markovits, "Montesquieu: L'esprit d'un peuple, Une histoire expérimentale," in *Former un nouveau peuple?* ed. Josiane Boulad-Ayoub (Presses Universitaires de Laval, L'Harmattan, 1996), 207–36; reprinted in *Lectures de L'Esprit des lois*, ed. Céline Spector and Thierry Hoquet (Bordeaux: Presses Universitaires de Bordeaux, 2004), 65–99; Jean-Patrice Courtois, *Inflexions de la rationalité dans "L'Esprit des lois"* (Paris: PUF, 1999); my article "Droit naturel," in *Le Vocabulaire de Montesquieu* (Paris: Ellipses, 2001); and "Quelle justice? Quelle rationalité? La mesure du droit dans L'Esprit des lois," in *Montesquieu en 2005*, ed. C. Volpilhac-Auger (Oxford: Voltaire Foundation, 2005), 219–42.

9. See *Mes Pensées*, 934, 942.

10. See Catherine Larrère, "Les typologies des gouvernements chez Montesquieu," in *Textes et documents* (Publication de la Faculté des lettres et sciences humaines de Clermont-Ferrand, 1979), 87–103, reprinted in the *Revue Montesquieu* 5 (2001): 157–72.

11. See for example the "Dialogue traitant de la politique sceptiquement," by La Mothe le Vayer, *Dialogues faits à l'imitation des anciens, 1630–1631* (Paris: Fayard, 1988).

12. On this notion, essential for Montesquieu, see Bernard Manin, "Montesquieu et la politique moderne," in *Cahiers de Philosophie politique*, Reims, 2–3, OUSIA (1985), 197–229, republished in *Lectures de L'Esprit des lois*, ed. Hoquet et Spector, 171–231.

13. *The Spirit of Laws*, III, 11. The principle has a "supreme influence" over the laws (I, 3), and the laws must first and foremost maintain the principle and preserve it from corruption, for "once the principles of the government are corrupted, the best laws become bad and turn against the State; when their principles are sound, bad laws have the effect of good ones; the force of the principle pulls everything along" (VIII, 11).

14. Of course there exists a new form of virtue in modern commercial republics, but the classical figure of the citizen-soldier disappears henceforth, especially in the face of economic development (*The Spirit of Laws*, III, 3, IV, 4, XX, 1–2). See John G. A. Pocock, *Le Moment Machiavélien*, trans. L. Borot (Paris: PUF, 1997); "Vertu, droits et mœurs," in *Vertu, Commerce et Histoire*, trans. H. Aji (Paris: PUF, 1998), 57–72; "Droit et mœurs chez Montesquieu," *Droits* 19 (1994): 11–22, republished in *Lectures de L'Esprit des lois*, ed. Hoquet and Spector, 233–46.

15. While the subjects of the despot fear him because he can destroy them instantly (*The Spirit of Laws*, III, 9), the despot himself fears his army, revolutions,

and usurpations (V, 11, 14). This is why only the nobles (*les grands*) are threatened by the sovereign: "The people must be judged by the laws, and the important men [*les grands*] by the prince's fancy; the head of the lowest subject must be safe, and the pasha's head always exposed" (III, 9). Despotic violence thus appears as the fruit of a political strategy that aims to preserve power by playing the people against the nobles. Fear, correlatively, acts as an instrument of the repression of the "noble" sociopolitical passions, present in various forms in monarchical and republican regimes: "Therefore, fear must beat down everyone's courage and extinguish even the slightest feeling of ambition" (III, 9).

16. "*Honor* is not the principle of despotic States: as the men in them are all equal, one cannot prefer oneself to others; as men in them are all slaves, one can prefer oneself to nothing" (*The Spirit of Laws*, III, 8).

17. *The Spirit of Laws*, V, 2–3. See Bernard Manin, "Montesquieu, la république et le commerce," *Archives européennes de sociologie* 42.3 (2001), 573–602.

18. *The Spirit of Laws*, III, 5–7. However, the discourse concerning honor sometimes takes advantage of this justification through the aim of the common good. See Rebecca Kingston, "L'Intérêt et le bien public dans le discours du Parlement de Bordeaux," in *Le Temps de Montesquieu*, ed. Catherine Volpilhac-Auger and Michel Porret (Geneva: Droz, 2002), 187–204.

19. Among the recent partisans of this interpratation, see Robert Shackleton, *Montesquieu, Biographie critique*, trans. J. Loiseau (Grenoble: PUG, 1977); Nannerl O. Keohane, "Virtuous Republics and Glorious Monarchies: Two Models in Montesquieu's Political Thought," *Political Studies* 20 (1972): 383–96; "The President's English: Montesquieu in America," *Political Science Reviewer* 6 (1976): 355–87; Elena Russo, "The Youth of Moral Life: The Virtue of the Ancients from Montesquieu to Nietzsche," in *Montesquieu's Spirit of Modernity*, ed. David Carrithers and Patrick Coleman (Oxford: Voltaire Foundation, 2002), 101–23.

20. See David Lowenthal, "Montesquieu," in *Histoire de la philosophie politique*, trans. O. Sedeyn (Paris: PUF, 1994), 563–87; Thomas Pangle, *Montesquieu's Philosophy of Liberalism* (Chicago: University of Chicago Press, 1977), and Pierre Manent, *La Cité de l'homme (1995)* (Paris: Champs Flammarion, 1997), chs. 1–2 (for the Straussian interpretation); Mark Hulliung, *Montesquieu and the Old Regime* (Berkeley: University of California Press, 1976), ch. 2; Judith Shklar, "Montesquieu and the New Republicanism," in *Machiavelli and Republicanism*, ed. Gisela Bock, Quentin Skinner, and Maurizio Viroli (Cambridge: Cambridge University Press, 1990), 265–79.

21. *Mes Pensées*, 221; emphasis added. See *Mes Pensées*, 938, 1256. In monarchies, "everyone wants to live for himself" and seeks pleasures (*Mes Pensées*, 1840); in a word, "in good republics, one says: *We*, and in good monarchies, one says: *Me*" (*Mes Pensées*, 1891).

22. See Giuseppe Cambiano, *Polis. Histoire d'un modèle politique*, trans. S. Fermigier (Paris: Aubier, 2003), ch. 6.

23. See Andrew J. Lynch, "Montesquieu's Ecclesiastical Critics," *Journal of the History of Ideas* 38 (1977): 487–500; Charles-Jacques Beyer, "Montesquieu et la censure religieuse de *L'Esprit des lois*," *Revue des Sciences Humaines* (1953): 105–31.

24. Jacques Fontaine de la Roche, "Examen critique de *L'Esprit des lois*," in *Nouvelles ecclésiastiques* 9 and 16 (1749). He was joined in his opinion by Fr. Joseph

de la Porte in the latter's *Observations sur la littérature moderne* (Amsterdam, 1750, III, art. V, 73–96), which was to be supplemented and published separately, under the title *Observations sur "L'Esprit des lois"* (Amsterdam, 1751).

25. "Even the Inquisition would not make such suppositions. Never a citizen has received from his fatherland such a cruel injury, and, what consoles me, never a citizen has so little deserved it" (*Réponses et explications à la Faculté de Théologie*, in *Œuvres complètes*, I, 661).

26. Ibid., 660.

27. Voltaire, *Supplément au Siècle de Louis XIV* (1753), III, in *Œuvres historiques* (Paris: Gallimard, 1957), 1271; see *Le Siècle de Louis XIV*, 862. In response to Montesquieu, Voltaire affirmed that it is precisely at the Court where least honor is found ("Honneur," in *Questions sur l'Encyclopédie* [Genève, 1774], III, 438). On the relations between Voltaire and Montesquieu, consult Robert Shackleton, "Allies and Enemies: Voltaire and Montesquieu," in *Essays on Montesquieu and the Enlightenment*, ed. David Gilson and Martin Smith (Oxford: Voltaire Foundation, 1988), 153–69; Jean Ehrard, "Le ver et la cochenille," in *L'Esprit des mots, op. cit.*, 195–211; and Domenico Felice, "Voltaire lettore e critico dell' *Esprit des lois*," in *Oppressione e libertà* (Pisa: ETS, 2000), 219–53.

28. Rousseau, *Social Contract*, III, 4; and on the criticism of the decline of honor, *Julie, or the New Héloise*, in *Oeuvres complètes* (Paris: Gallimard, 1964), I, LVII, 152–60. See also Jean Ehrard, "Le fils coupable," in *L'Esprit des mots*, 257–75.

29. See Saint-Lambert's article "Honneur" and Diderot's article "Philosophe" in the *Encyclopédie*, as well as the texts cited by John Pappas, "La campagne des philosophes contre l'honneur," *Voltaire Studies* 205 (1982): 40–43. In the *Système social*, the Baron d'Holbach adds his voice to this line of criticism ([Paris: Fayard, 1994], I, 13), and after the Revolution, Destutt de Tracy returned to the idea of "false honor that seeks out everything that glitters and prides itself on vices and even ridicule, when they are in style," to the point of doubting the seriousness of the president: "[I]s it with seriousness that Montesquieu dared to suggest that veritable vices, or, if one wishes, false virtues, are as useful to monarchy as truly laudable qualities?" (*Commentaire de L'Esprit des lois (1819)* [Caen: Centre de philosophie politique et juridique de l'Université de Caen, 1992], 20). He adds: "Does there not also exist a generous ambition, which desires only to serve one's fellows and win their recognition, and another ambition, which, devoured by the hunger for power and splendor, seeks this end by all means possible?"

30. *The Spirit of Laws*, III, 5. The "Author's Foreword" placed at the beginning of *The Spirit of Laws*, which only appears in the earliest editions, is intended to appease the censors and the critics. This foreword states that political virtue is different from moral virtue and Christian virtue and that these virtues are not excluded from monarchical government.

31. *Persian Letters*, 89. For the sake of convenience, we give the references to the *Persian Letters* in use up until now, that is, those of the 1748 edition. However, the 1721 edition is now taken to be the text of reference; (*Lettres persanes*, in *Oeuvres complètes*, edition directed by J. Ehrard and C. Volpilhac-Auger [Oxford: Voltaire Foundation; Naples: Istituto per gli studi filosofici, 2004], I).

32. *The Spirit of Laws*, III, 5. The opposition is clear between the sacrifice constitutive of love of the fatherland, a renunciation that is always "very painful," and the adhesion to oneself characteristic of honor, which is "favored by the passions and

favors them in turn" (IV, 5). The satire of the courtier attests to this opposition: the "private crime," in the form of vices associated with ambition and with the desire for domination, is authorized in monarchies.

33. *The Spirit of Laws*, III, 5, III, 6 (emphasis added); see *Spicilège*, 601.

34. *The Spirit of Laws*, IV, 2; see VI, 21.

35. The metaphor of the machine appears also in the context of the honors lavished by the monarch: "The kings act like those skillful craftsmen who in executing their works employ always the simplest machines" (*Persian Letters*, 88). In the *Traité de la nature et de la grâce*, Malebranche had praised the wisdom of Providence in establishing a link between theology and politics: "The more machines are simple and their effects different, the more they are spiritual and worthy of esteem. The great number of laws of a State often indicates little penetration and breadth of mind in those who established them" (in *Oeuvres complètes*, Paris: Gallimard, II, 1992, I, 37, 41). According to Leibniz, Providence acting perfectly resembles "a skillful machinist who brings about his effect by the least encumbered path one could choose." In order to create the general harmony of the world, the simplicity of paths was balanced with the richness of effects (*Discours de métaphysique*, trans. G. Le Roy [Paris: Vrin, 1988], sections 5, 40). We do not propose to analyze the differences between these two models, which also led to a transposition of the theological to the political in the conception of the "general will" (see Patrick Riley, *The General Will before Rousseau* [Princeton: Princeton University Press, 1986]).

36. On my use of the concept of 'civil society,' see the author's *Montesquieu. Pouvoirs, richesses et sociétés*. On the transposition of the *Théodicée* into the *Sociodicée* between Leibniz and Mandeville, see Claude Gautier, *L'Invention de la société civile* (Paris: PUF, 1993), ch. 3.

37. See *Mes Pensées*, 760–61: "This spirit of glory and value is being lost little by little among us. Philosophy has gained ground. The ancient ideas of heroism and the new ideas of chivalry have been lost"; *Dialogue de Xantippe et Xénocrate* (*Oeuvres complètes*, III, 123); and *Dialogue de Sylla et d'Eucrate*: "For one man to be above humanity, it costs all the others too much" (*Oeuvres complètes*, I, 560). The duel, in particular, is at the heart of the criticism: do not the rigorous exigencies of the code of honor (to wash offenses in blood) contradict all principles of equality, as is attested by its medieval origin—the judicial combat? A man might show himself to be stronger or more adroit than another; from this it does not follow that he is more reasonable (*Persian Letters*, 90). *The Spirit of Laws*, which gives an account of the usage, nevertheless does not call it equitable (XIV, 14, XXVIII, 17).

38. *Persian Letters*, 80. See my book *Montesquieu, les "Lettres persanes"* (Paris: PUF, 1997), 79–87.

39. *The Spirit of Laws*, XIX, 27. One finds several occurrences of this principle in the work of Montesquieu: "A man, then, who is only guided by reason is always cold in comparison to the one led by zeal" (*Mes Pensées*, 426, see 220); "There is nothing so powerful as a republic in which one observes the laws, not from fear, not from reason, but from passion, as were Rome and Lacedaemon; for then all the strength a faction could have is joined to the wisdom of a good government" (*Considerations on the Causes of the Greatness of the Romans and Their Decline*, IV).

40. *Mes Pensées*, 1856.

41. Ibid., 1951. Pascal, however, used the inversion of "vain" and "healthy" in the name of the imperative of civil peace and in the service of order: to distinguish men by their nobility or goodness, to be offended at receiving a blow or to so yearn for glory are very desirable things from this point of view, "because of the other essential goods that are joined to them" (*Pensées*, ed. Leon Brunschvicg [Paris: Hachette, 1914], 324). See Louis Marin, *Le Portrait du roi* (Paris: Editions de Minuit, 1981), 23–46.

42. See *Persian Letters*, 65, and the final insurrection.

43. Usbek writes to the eunuchs: "And what are you, but vile instruments whom I may destroy at my pleasure; who exist only as long as you know how to obey; who are only in the world to live under my laws or to die when I order it; who breathe only as long as my happiness, my love, even my jealousy, has need of your ignoble service; who, in fine, can have no other lot than submission, no other soul than my will, no other hope than my felicity?" (*Persian Letters*, 21).

44. "I have told you that among us all the slaves are employed in guarding our wives, and in nothing else; that with regard to the state they are in a perpetual lethargy; with the result that industry and agriculture are necessarily confined to a few freemen and heads of families, who apply themselves as little as possible" (*Persian Letters*, 115).

45. *Persian Letters*, 89; see also 24.

46. On the sources of this idea of the salutary illusion of honor, see Montaigne, *Essais*, ed. Pierre Villey (Paris: PUF, 1992), II, 7, 381, II, 16, 628–29; Fontenelle, "Dialogue entre Charles Quint et Erasme," *Dialogues des morts anciens et modernes (1683)* (Paris: Fayard, 1990), 181–82; Pierre Bayle, *Pensées diverses sur la comète*, ed. P. Rétat (Paris: Nizet, 1984), §141–44, 179; Bernard Mandeville, *Recherche sur l'origine de la vertu morale*, in *La Fable des abeilles*, trans. L. Carrive (Paris: Vrin, 1990); and Remark R. On the relations between Montesquieu and Bayle, see my article "Cupidité ou charité? L'ordre sans vertu, des moralistes du grand siècle à *L'Esprit des lois* de Montesquieu," and on Montesquieu and Mandeville, my "Private Vices, Public Virtues: From the *Fable of the Bees* to *The Spirit of the Laws*," in *Montesquieu's Spirit of Modernity*, ed. Carrithers, Mosher, and Rahe, 127–57.

47. *The Spirit of the Laws*, XII, 4. See David Carrithers, "Montesquieu and the Liberal Philosophy of Jurisprudence," in *Montesquieu's Science of Politics*, 291–334.

48. "It is a misfortune of the human condition that legislators are obliged to make laws that oppose even natural feelings; such was the Voconian law. This is because the statutes of legislators regard the society more than the citizen, and the citizen more than the man. The law sacrificed both the citizen and the man and thought only of the Republic" (*The Spirit of Laws*, Book XXVII, only chapter). See also *The Spirit of Laws*, IV, 6.

49. See Louis Althusser, *Montesquieu. La politique et l'histoire*, ch. 4, and the remarkable article of Sharon Krause, "The Politics of Distinction and Disobedience: Honor and the Defense of Liberty in Montesquieu," *Polity* 31.3 (1999): 469–99, and her book *Liberalism with Honor* (Cambridge and London: Harvard University Press, 2002), ch. 2; Mosher, "Monarchy's Paradox: Honor in the Face of Sovereign Power."

50. *Persian Letters*, 65, 89. Montesquieu thus echoes a long tradition, notably conveyed by Blaise de Montluc: "Our lives and our goods belong to our kings. The soul belongs to God and honor belongs to us. For my king is powerless over my honor" (*Commentaires* [Paris, A. Picard, 1911], II, 169). On the invocation of honor in the

discourse of aristocratic resistance to royal power, see Arlette Jouanna, *Le Devoir de révolte* (Paris: Fayard, 1989).

51. *Persian Letters*, 80, 141.
52. Ibid., 64.
53. Ibid., 102.
54. Ibid., 90.
55. The eunuchs must obey the captive women as much as they obey the master and the chief eunuch: "What is necessary in these circumstances is blind obedience and compliance without limits: a refusal from such a man as I am would be a thing unheard of; and if I were to hesitate in obeying them, they could punish me at their discretion" (ibid., 9). See ibid., 34.
56. Ibid., 89.
57. *The Spirit of Laws*, V, 14; see ibid., III, 9.
58. Ibid., IV, 2. See *Mes Pensées*, 1983: "It is necessary to establish the principles of empire and obedience. Are there cases where a subject would be permitted to disobey his prince? He must do nothing for him, and it would be a strange manner of thinking indeed to have so much respect for the orders and so little for the honor of one's prince. It is very dangerous to have subjects that obey him blindly."
59. See Krause, *Liberalism with Honor*, ch. 2. Two historical examples enable Montesquieu to illustrate the modalities of *regulated disobedience* as the supreme recourse against the arbitrariness and abuse of power. In the first case, Crillon refuses the order of the monarch to assassinate the Duke of Guise, while accepting to fight him: far from rejecting the king's demand, Crillon makes another proposition, which requires that the action demonstrate courage (and thus excludes the baseness of the putting to death of an unarmed man taken by surprise), in accordance with honor. In the second case, the viscount of Orte, after Saint Bartholomew's Day, refuses the order of Charles IX to have the Huguenots of his town massacred, for, according to him, there was not among them one executioner, but only good citizens and brave soldiers: " '[T]hus, they and I together beg Your Majesty to use our arms and our lives for things that can be done': this great and generous courage regarded a cowardly action as an impossible thing" (*The Spirit of Laws*, IV, 2). Even if the will to live up to his code of honor required of Orte the refusal of a massacre of innocents, the use of the supplication attests here to the preservation of reverence at the moment of the disobedience to the order judged dishonorable. The exhortation intended to shore up the refusal of the governor attests to the subordination of obedience to the code of honor: the service due to the king concerns only those things "that can be done," not "impossible" things—from the point of view of honor.
60. If honor has been "offended," "it requires or permits one to withdraw to one's home" (*The Spirit of Laws*, IV, 2). Arlette Jouanna has shown that this was in effect a widespread attitude among the nobles, who invoked the wounds to their honor inflicted by the monarch: "[T]heir first act of rupture was often to depart from the court and to withdraw to their domains: a movement from the center toward the periphery which signified threatening consequences for the monarchy" (*Le Devoir de révolte*,108). But the author also describes the veritable revolts that the nobles were associated with or fomented, which Montesquieu does not mention explicitly here.

61. *The Spirit of Laws*, V, 11: "One sees everywhere in the activities of despotic governments that the people, led by themselves, always carry things as far as they can go; all the disorder they commit is extreme; whereas, in monarchies, things are very rarely carried to excess. The leaders fear for themselves; they fear being abandoned; the intermediate dependent powers do not want the people to have the upper hand too much."

62. Montesquieu is sometimes considered to have played a significant role in the development of the concept of 'public opinion.' Even though the expression is absent from his œuvre, it nevertheless constitutes for J. A. W. Gunn the implicit aspect of the concept of 'honor' defined as a prejudice capable of producing resistance to power. Besides, the readers of Montesquieu evoked "the laws of honor and of opinion," and some members of Parlement (such as P.-L. Chaillou in 1760) did not hesitate to invoke this invisible tribunal "that the natural principle of monarchy, honor, suffuses through all the orders of the State; and out of which arises the *public opinion* in their respect of which even the Kings make themselves glorious" (*Queen of the World: Opinion in the Public Life of France from the Renaissance to the Revolution* [Oxford: Voltaire Foundation, 1995], 161).

63. "The bodies that are the depository of the laws never obey better than when they drag their feet and bring into the prince's business the reflection that one can hardly expect from the absence of enlightenment in the Court concerning the laws of the State and the haste of the prince's Council" (*The Spirit of Laws*, V, 10). See II, 4.

64. Ibid., XI, 4. See XXVIII, 41.

65. Althusser, *Montesquieu. La politique et l'histoire*, 80.

66. On the use of this term, see Melvin Richter, "Montesquieu, the Politics of Language, and the Language of Politics," *History of Political Thought* 10 (1989): 71–88.

67. *The Spirit of Laws*, V, 3, V, 7, VII, 9–10.

68. Ibid., III, 3, VII, 2.

69. "As soon as honor can find *something noble* [in actions], it becomes either the judge who renders them legitimate, or the sophist who justifies them. It allows gallantry when gallantry is united with the idea of an attachment of the heart or the idea of conquest; and this is the true reason why mores are never as pure in monarchies as in republican governments. It allows deceit when deceit is *joined to the idea of greatness* of spirit or *greatness* of business, as in politics, whose niceties do not offend it. It forbids adulation only when adulation is separated from the idea of a *great* fortune and is joined only with the feeling of one's own meanness" (ibid., IV, 2; emphasis added). Leibniz had already noted that honor, for the moderns, replaces the love of the fatherland and of the common good that governed the Greeks and the Romans. Now "for the moderns, the mark of the *honnête homme* and the man of honor is merely to not do any base act, as they understand baseness" (*Nouveaux Essais sur l'entendement humain*, [Paris: GF-Glammarion, 1990], IV, XVI, § 4, 365).

70. Aristotle, *Nicomachean Ethics*, trans. J. Tricot (Paris: Vrin, 1987), book IV, ch. 7.

71. *Mes Pensées*, 1244; see 107.

72. Pascal, *Pensées*, Brunschvicg, ed., 402–03. See Spector, "Cupidité ou charité? L'ordre sans vertu, des moralistes du grand siècle à *L'Esprit des lois* de Montesquieu."

73. *Mes Pensées*, 464. One finds another reference to Pierre Nicole on the subject of self-love (*amour-propre*): "Nicole says very rightly that God gave self-love [*amour-propre*] to man just as he gave him the taste for food" (*Mes Pensées*, 2064) and on his method (*Mes Pensées*, 1970). See Keohane, *Philosophy and the State in France*, ch. 14.

74. *Mes Pensées*, 107

75. See Camille Pernot, *La Politesse et sa philosophie* (Paris: PUF, 1996).

76. As we have seen, it is always a conditional submission. This is the reason why Michael Mosher proposes a different interpretation of centrifugal force, which, in his view, represents the tendency to renounce servile obedience and dishonorable temptations ("Monarchy's Paradox: Honor in the Face of Sovereign Power," 205–06).

77. See Michael Oakeshott, *De la conduite humaine*, trans. O. Seyden (Paris: PUF, 1995), 203–05, 246–52.

78. The debate between these two conceptions of liberty dates from the famous article by Isaiah Berlin ("Deux conceptions de la liberté," in *Eloge de la liberté*, trans. J. Carnaud and J. Lahana (Paris: Calmann-Lévy, 1988), 167–218). From a critical perspective, see Quentin Skinner, "The Republican Ideal of Political Liberty," in *Machiavelli and Republicanism*, 293–309; and Jean-Fabien Spitz, *La Liberté politique* (Paris: PUF, 1995), ch. 3. In his article on the liberalism of Montesquieu, Berlin does not, however, attempt to apply this classification, insisting rather on the pluralism of the author of *The Spirit of Laws* ("Montesquieu," in *A contre-courant*, trans. A. Berelowitch [Paris: Albin Michel, 1988], 200–35).

79. Hegel saw in the description of constitutional monarchy in *The Spirit of Laws* the realization of an irreversible evolution that has as its result that "in a more evolved state of society" and "with the development and the liberation of the power of particularity," the virtue of the rulers is no longer sufficient and that "another form of the rational law than that of the disposition of mind becomes necessary, in order for the whole to have the strength to maintain itself and so that one can accord to the developed forces of particularity their positive right and their negative right" (Hegel, *Hegels's Philosophy of Right*, trans. T. M. Knox (Oxford and New York: Oxford University Press, 1967), sections 273, 285).

80. "This liberty [that of the ancients] consisted rather in the active participation in the collective power, than in the peaceable enjoyment of individual independence; and to ensure this participation, it was even necessary that the citizens sacrifice a great part of that enjoyment. But it is absurd to ask for, and impossible to obtain, this sacrifice in the age at which peoples have arrived" (this quote is translated from the original French) (Benjamin Constant, *De l'Esprit de conquête et de l'usurpation dans leurs rapports avec la civilisation européenne* [Paris: GF-Flammarion, 1986], ch. 7, 164). In the same collection, see the speech entitled "On the Liberty of the Ancients Compared with That of the Moderns" (265–91).

81. Constant, "On the Liberty of the Ancients Compared with That of the Moderns," 279–80. See *De l'Esprit de conquête*, 168. Here Constant borrows Montesquieu's formulation (*The Spirit of Laws*, III, 3), already reused by Rousseau, while inversing the polarity: the opposition between virtue and commerce must not call for a renunciation of commerce but for a renunciation of virtue.

82. *The Spirit of Laws*, XI, 3, XI, 6, XXVI, 20, see *Mes Pensées*, 32, 884. On the meaning of the "liberty of the Moderns," see Georges Benrekassa's article "De Montesquieu à Benjamin Constant: La fin des Lumières?" *Dix-Huitième Siècle* 21 (1989): 117–33.

83. *Mes Pensées*, 1253

84. On this commercial modernity, and the models of unintended convergence of interests which are connected to it, see my book *Montesquieu et l'émergence de l'économie politique* (Paris: Champion, 2006).

85. Hegel, *Hegel's Philosophy of Right*, § 273.

86. *The Spirit of Laws*, XI, 7, 5. Rawls rightly perceived this difference in defining the well-ordered society, in which no ultimate end exists that would justify a situation in which individuals have more or less worth for the society and in which, consequently, fundamentally different rights and privileges are attributed to them. "Many past societies have thought otherwise: they pursued as final ends religion and empire, domination and glory; and the rights and status of individuals and classes have depended on their role in gaining those ends" (*Political Liberalism* [New York: Columbia University Press, 1993], 41).

87. Peter Berger, "On the Obsolescence of the Concept of Honor," in *Revisions: Changing Perspectives on Moral Philosophy*, ed. S. Hauerwas and A. MacIntyre (Notre Dame: University of Notre Dame Press, 1983), 172–81; Charles Taylor, *Multiculturalisme. Différence et démocratie*, trans. D.-A. Canal (Paris: Champs Flammarion, 1994), 43–44.

88. In the lines that follow, I have taken inspiration from the excellent discussion of Krause, *Liberalism with Honor*.

89. This political anthropology, evoked here from a normative point of view, is not deprived of an empirical grounding. For a sociological point of view, see Philippe d'Iribane, *La Logique de l'honneur* (Paris: Seuil, 1989), ch. 2 in particular.

# 4

# On the Proper Use of the Stick
## *The Spirit of Laws* and the Chinese Empire

### Catherine Volpillhac-Auger

Quite some time ago, the critical literature focused on the sources of *The Spirit of Laws*, and in particular, travel literature. This task was necessary because it was important to weigh exactly what Montesquieu owed to these sources. The manner in which he perceived and conceived of non-European peoples was directly tributary of them, and it was always thought that from this vast landscape he constructed an anthropology that informed the whole of his œuvre. I would like to demonstrate here to what degree it is necessary to renew the previous work on the subject (all of which dates back at least a half-century), a renewal made possible by new documentation now available in its entirety, namely, the important extant fragments of his reading notes (essentially the *Geographica II*). Furthermore, I would like to show that this documentation allows us to formulate a different conception of Montesquieu's research method, as well as of the role played by these famous travel reports. In reading them, Montesquieu was first concerned with their veracity. He criticized those observers whom he distrusted (the Jesuits first and foremost), in order to discard all but what was irrefutable. Montesquieu was not a "naïve" reader who accumulated his knowledge of humanity in all its breadth while progressively seeking to distinguish, as he went along, the general and specific traits of societies. Rather, as early as the 1730s he revealed his preoccupations and his method of research that formed a basis for his conclusions incorporated into *The Spirit of Laws*.

## At the Sources of the Sources

As early as 1929, Muriel Dodds published a volume that is still useful today, at least in particular instances: *Les Récits de voyages, sources de L'Esprit des lois de Montesquieu*.[1] What remains of current interest in this work is that it brings together a certain number of passages from *The Spirit of Laws* and numerous reports, including *Voyages au Nord*, *Histoire des Tartares*, *Lettres édifiantes et curieuses*, and *Description de la Chine*.[2] The work provides the passages to which Montesquieu himself often refers. Dodds was careful to use the same editions as Montesquieu, to the extent that it was possible to identify and procure them; moreover, she rectifies erroneous references on several occasions, some of which were, however, correct in the first edition of *The Spirit of Laws*[3] or in the working manuscript currently conserved at the Bibliothèque nationale.

However, her intermediary and final conclusions cannot under any circumstances be accepted: her analysis of Montesquieu's ideas themselves remains superficial;[4] her presentation of the "idea of despotism,"[5] which is not supported by any political analysis, is approximate at best and in any case richer in citations and affirmations than in analyses.[6] Dodds' principle is to look for the very foundation of Montesquieu's thought in the travel literature. She suggests that through reading Ricault, Chardin, and Du Cerceau,[7] Montesquieu's conception of despotism was fixed very early on in his intellectual development, a conception that, she argues, he would not change; its essential elements were purportedly contained in the *Persian Letters* (1721).[8] Subsequent work, and notably that of Du Halde, came too late, when his ideas had already been formed. Thus, "he would always be incapable of understanding the enlightened despotism of China." She suggests that because Montesquieu laid down his principles early, he would not be able, for the most part, to overcome the difficulties posed by the testimony of the missionaries. Whenever this testimony was not compatible with his predetermined ideas, Montesquieu had no other recourse than to say "[T]he testimony is false." However, on other occasions when he abandoned his "rigid system" according to which "despotism is always a bad regime," he did decide to follow the conclusions of the Jesuits. For Dodds, "these details [which he is forced to take up at times] carry the mark of sincerity and absolute truth."[9] In effect, according to Dodds, the Jesuit missionaries, very favorable to the Chinese, are infinitely more trustworthy informers than two of their detractors, the admiral Anson (who stayed only four months in the region of Canton) and the Swede Lange, sent by the Russians (and even "agent of the czar"). The Jesuits who had spent their lives in China could not have been poorly informed, nor could they have had any interest whatsoever in disguising the truth.[10] We will come back to this, for Dodds raises a fundamental issue but presents it in an entirely erroneous manner.

There is a last point that requires attention: the intentions that underpin Dodds' inquiry. While criticizing Montesquieu's method as marked by prejudices that drive him to use doubtful information, she also wants to show that, contrary to the affirmations of Voltaire and many other critics, Montesquieu was right to rely on the sources that he quotes, for there could not be better ones; moreover, they were confirmed by the most serious studies carried out later.[11] She carries these assertions far: "As to the veracity of the fact that Shaw reports,[12] I can nowhere find the confirmation of it in a modern author. Nonetheless, in the absence of any contrary assertion to this testimony, and given the fact that all travellers who came after him have a high opinion of its exactitude, I tend to consider the description that he gives of this strange custom as true."[13]

Put another way, Dodds seeks to prove that when Montesquieu relied on the testimony of the Jesuit missionaries and of travelers whose comments she has verified, he was clearly and absolutely right in his conclusions; but otherwise, he erred, and it is possible to retrace his errors by identifying his sources.

## New Readings

We evidently would not have taken pains to expose in detail such a dated method, which showed its limits as early as 1929, if the work had been replaced and if it were not regularly cited and relied upon even today. We can measure the consequences of her approach by considering a reference to the *Description de la Chine*[14] quoted regularly: "The stick governs China, says P. Du Halde" (*The Spirit of Laws*, VIII, 21). Montesquieu's entire chapter here is consecrated to the difficulties posed by the Chinese case, this question being nodal—all the more since Montesquieu exposed the contradictions that he found among his different sources and between the theoretical declarations made by the Jesuit Fathers and the content of their accounts.[15] Dodds considered this idea unfounded and "besides, contrary to the whole spirit of Du Halde" as she could not find this citation in the *Description de la Chine*.[16] She was following Voltaire, who included this phrase in the *Commentaire sur L'Esprit des lois* (1777; chap. 34):[17] "We cannot know China except through authentic elements, furnished locally, brought together by Du Halde, and which are not at all contradicted." More prudent than Dodds was to be, and above all, craftier, Voltaire was satisfied to *suggest* that Du Halde did not say anything of the sort, and thus every reader had to conclude that Montesquieu fabricated citations when he needed to, while still arguing from an irrefutable authority such as that of Du Halde. In fact, as signaled by several editions of *The Spirit of Laws*, that of Laboulaye in the nineteenth century and more recently that of Robert Derathé[18] (the latter even includes the history of this point of criticism, pointing out the precedence of Laboulaye), what Du Halde said was not different from what Montesquieu had claimed: "such that one can say that the Chinese Government hardly subsists other than by the use of the stick" (*Description de la Chine*, II, 134a). Consequently, the hasty generalizations and condescending commentaries concerning the cavalier attitude that supposedly characterized Montesquieu's use of his sources, and especially his use of a guarantor such as Du Halde, cannot be maintained, for often they are not founded on more than one or two examples; they can nevertheless bring any critic inclined to declare openly, "This reference is false, since I have not found it,"[19] to prudence.

It is of particular importance to note that we now have a working instrument of the very first order, whose existence was unknown to Dodds: the seven-hundred-page collection of excerpts entitled *Geographica II*, conserved in the Chateau of La Brède until 1994.[20] Certain excerpts had been reproduced in the edition directed by André Masson,[21] with an excellent introduction by Françoise Weil.[22] But a comprehensive edition of this document,[23] has long been needed.

The first reason for this is that, if we believe Miguel Benítez's very convincing demonstration, the only excerpt reproduced *in extenso* in the Masson edition, entitled "Quelques remarques sur la Chine que j'ay tirées des conversations que j'ay eües avec M. Ouanges" ("Some remarks on China which I extracted from conversations that I had with Mr. Ouanges"), is not the fruit of Montesquieu's "conversations" with Arcadio Hoang, a young Chinese man living in Paris around 1713; rather, Montesquieu contented himself with having the work of one of his friends or relations copied, very likely that of the erudite Nicolas Fréret, much more expert than he in his knowledge of the Chinese language and Chinese customs.[24] In the rest of *Geographica II*, the passages containing original excerpts for purposes of commentary—they are preceded by an asterisk in the manuscript—are far from having been identified in their entirety.[25] The writing of these notes reveals a thought process and suggests a "pre-writing" of *The Spirit of Laws*[26] and merits an in-depth analysis by virtue of this character. Last, the choice of what he retained is by itself extremely revealing: of the four folio volumes of six hundred pages that constitute the *Description de la Chine*, Montesquieu retained approximately 3 percent; of the twenty-five small volumes of the *Lettres édifiantes*, each of which contains approximately four hundred pages, Montesquieu retained one one-hundredth. It is essential to study the *Geographica*, if only to find the litigious sentence about the "stick that governs China." And in effect, these lines appear there: "One hardly imposes punishments, except for fines, which are not preceded or followed [by a beating], such that the Chinese government hardly subsists except by the stick,"[27] at the end of an entire page consecrated to the immoderate use of this punishment. A reading of this collection of excerpts would have sufficed to remove all uncertainty, by showing how Montesquieu remains faithful to Du Halde's text, the formulation of which he did not modify except in writing *The Spirit of Laws*.[28] It even explains the origin of the critics' confusion: in *The Spirit of Laws*, the note does not include the page reference; in fact, in the *Geographica II*, the secretary who copied the text (or Montesquieu himself in writing his notes) omitted the page number. Small causes, big effects.

In general, the collection *Geographica II*, while it contains only one part of the documentation used by Montesquieu,[29] is of great strategic importance, for it includes nearly all of his readings on the Orient, in particular China and Tartary,[30] except for two volumes of the *Lettres édifiantes* (XXI, XXII) which were in the *Geographica I*. Because it dates prior to 1742 (the first excerpts can go back as far as the 1710s; the majority date from 1730 to 1740), it allows us to discover the manner in which Montesquieu treats his information from a perspective that is not necessarily that of *The Spirit of Laws* but one that comes close or perhaps one that puts Montesquieu on the path of what would become *The Spirit of Laws*. Now we see clearly in the *Geographica II* what could not be brought out in the succinct presentation given in the Masson edition: Montesquieu did not in any way abandon himself to a "naïve" reading, letting himself be led by his curiosity or by the intrinsic interest in the works from which he extracted excerpts. His attention was attracted very early on by the dubious character of the idyllic portrait that the Jesuits present of China. Put another way, he was far from believing in the possibility of objective informers capable of depicting a radically foreign world without deforming it through their own interests and prejudices: he recognized the need to seek information beyond the informers. Confronting the *Anciennes relations* and the *Description*, he followed the path cleared by "Quelques remarques sur [mes] conversations avec M. Ouanges," which doubtless constitute one of the oldest parts of the *Geographica II*:[31] "I believe that the Chinese would suffer infinite losses in becoming known" (f. 83); in effect, they are cruel, superstitious, even barbarian. The author of "Quelques remarques" desired to denounce the "Chinese myth" that the Jesuits were beginning to propagate.

But Montesquieu was not influenced by this text to the point of following blindly such an accusation.[32] It is said there, "The ceremonies of the Chinese people seem to have been invented to make foreigners laugh" (f. 96v), while Montesquieu, for his part, made Chinese manners and civility the keystone of their empire (*The Spirit of Laws*, XIX, 4, 10, 13, 16), drawing his inspiration this time from the *Description de la Chine*. He read with particular attention another passage of volume II of this work, whose page reference he indicated this time (page 97 and following).[33] "One believes that the attention to duties and ceremonies is very capable of inspiring gentleness, good order, and subordination. [...] These ceremonies are therefore regarded as important for the stability of the state It is a study, it is a science, it becomes subsequently as if natural. Artisans, villagers observe the formalities of politeness. They are gentle and honest" says the *Geographica II* (f. 193–94), in which Montesquieu was nevertheless careful not to draw inspiration from Du Halde's long, banal considerations concerning the relativity of mores and usages, except to retain a forceful idea from an observation made by the Jesuit (but whose consequence—that "gentleness," "good order," "subordination" are connected—he did not discover): civility produces tranquility, which requires mutual respect and dependence, without which the immense and contradictory Chinese Empire would collapse (*The Spirit of Laws*, XIX, 16).

We can immediately see the degree to which traditional questions used to study Montesquieu's use of sources have been inadequate: Is Montesquieu faithful to his sources? Does he generalize an isolated case? Did he "borrow" such and such an idea?[34] It is of more import to consider Montesquieu as the political analyst and observer that he was and above all to define the status of the latter. The importance of studying Montesquieu's "sources" resides in uncovering this complex relation to the information and to its guarantor. It is not possible in the framework of this chapter to review the question treated precisely by Etiemble:[35] what was Montesquieu's position on the Chinese Rites Controversy?[36] If his attitude appears to be clear on the whole (and in conformity with Etiemble's analysis, that is to say, hostile to that of the Jesuits), it seems nevertheless necessary to question what is surely an overly simple idea, that he owed this "prejudice" to the influence of Msgr. Fouquet, as it appears in the *Spicilège*:[37] the reading of the *Lettres édifiantes* and especially of the *Description de la Chine* could only reinforce convictions with different origins. In the portrait of China that Montesquieu constructs—by gathering first of all the prior reflections of Fénelon or Malebranche,[38] and subsequently being "informed" rather than "prejudiced" by the adversaries[39] of the Jesuits—the imprudence and the excesses of the latter played a capital role.

## Montesquieu, Reader of Jesuit Sources: The Return of the Stick

It is not an accident that Montesquieu retained from Du Halde the famous sentence concerning the stick "that governs China." The publication of the *Description de la Chine* in 1735, even though the work was a compilation of the *Lettres édifiantes et curieuses*, with which a vast public was already familiar, conferred upon the "Chinese matter" a dignity that it did not enjoy previously.[40] Despite his ignorance of the Chinese language and his "never having left Paris," as is remarked by Voltaire in a notice added in 1756 to the "Catalogue [of] French writers who were published in the century of Louis XIV," Du Halde penned a monumental work, which constituted a turning point in Europe's knowledge of China. He did not conceal the origin of his information and the name of his "contributors,"[41] and persons such as Fréret admitted their disappointment at not having discovered anything in it that they had not already read.[42] Still, he accomplished a masterful feat: starting from the volumes of the *Lettres édifiantes et curieuses* in which the information was dispersed, he elaborated a superb, methodically organized work. The fragmentary, personal, "missionary," not to mention "edifying and curious" character of the "letters" addressed to the Superiors of the Order or to important personalities, was reconfigured to become testimony, and even a veritable whole, as intended by the title in its entirety: "Historical, Chronological, Political and Physical Description of the Empire of China and of Chinese Tartary."

Du Halde is therefore an "authority." Montesquieu was attuned to the biased nature of his assertions, which in this respect are no different from those of his predecessors and the "contributors" to the *Description*. This was partially concealed in the excerpts of the *Geographica* of the Masson edition, which omitted a number of Montesquieu's caustic remarks. For example, the province of Kiang Nan, whose wealth Du Halde praises, collected taxes said to total as much as 32 million taels (f. 112v). This figure provoked the following ironic comment: "Since the tael is worth seven pounds ten sols in our currency it would follow that this province renders 240 million not counting the duties on merchandise which would be one third or one quarter more than what the Kingdom of France gives, which shows that it is a boast [*une gasconnade*]." Later (f. 178r), he again takes up the question of the Emperor's revenues in a double commentary: "If one converts these revenues to France's currency he [the author] brings them to one billion which would be five times more than what France gives." This time the remark is not accompanied by any qualifier, but it is no less clear that Montesquieu denounces another exaggeration: how could a country in which some people starve to death furnish such a tribute? So two of the commentaries reproduced by the Masson edition, concerning the "exaggerations" relative to the number of inhabitants of Canton and the "enthusiasm" of the Jesuit priests for China (f. 117 et 118), are not in any way accidental or isolated. They even illustrate a significant tendency characteristic of these commentaries: Montesquieu is skeptical regarding all of the estimations that make China into a land of plenty overflowing with agricultural and commercial activity.[43] *Major e longinquo reverentia* ("from afar one inspires more respect"): such was the motto, the origin of which was Tacitus, carried by the catalog of the library of La Brède and the *Pensées* to characterize the Chinese.[44] The reality appeared to him to have been much less gleaming than that which Du Halde depicts. Concerning the figures indicated by these data, the prejudice of the Jesuits seemed to him to be flagrant.

It is but one of the characteristics of the Jesuits, who, to satisfy the needs of their cause, sought to present the beliefs of the Chinese as conforming perfectly to the spirit of Christianity and their political system as a model of stability. At the time when Montesquieu was having his notes on Du Halde transcribed (between 1735 and the beginning of 1739, according to the identification of the secretary's handwriting), the Chinese Rites Controversy was not over: Du Halde, without taking a position, at least in appearance, was in fact a firm partisan of the compatibility of the Roman religion with Chinese culture, as one could have expected. One will find, in the new edition of this notebook, the most significant passages (many of which are indicated in the Masson edition) in which Montesquieu denounces the ideological and religious prejudices of Du Halde: "the intention of the said Father is to muddle their ideas and to make objections and not to explain their doctrine," says Montesquieu of the savants (f. 232); and to speak of "Tien" as of the "Lord of the Sky" (f. 121), to ignore that they are in fact idolaters (f. 233), to present their doctrine as admirable even though there are numerous examples of their superstitious practices.[45] As a result, even if Du Halde reports how the savants refute the doctrine of an atheist, "We do not know if we can trust the Jesuits in this seeing their system of the sanctity of the Chinese" (f. 147r, omitted in the Masson edition).

As for Chinese political and judicial institutions, they are formidably complex; therefore Montesquieu avoids applying simple ideas to them. In fact he sets up a veritable dialogue with his different sources; through this very process, contradictions erupt, which need to be resolved. Not every confrontation is to the disadvantage of the Jesuits: as we mentioned previously, having read the *Lettres édifiantes* and the *Description*, the accusation of cannibalism made in the *Anciennes relations* appears to him to be, in the final analysis, unfounded, and the Chinese "ceremonies" have nothing ridiculous about them in his view, as they appeared to have in "Quelques remarques sur [mes] conversations avec M. Ouanges." The avowed principle of Montesquieu is the following: "[L]et us look in P. Du Halde for what is not at all in the interest of the Jesuits to hide from us or disguise" (f. 232v). And in fact, when he evokes the *Description de la Chine* (sometimes referred to as the *Histoire de la Chine*), it is not because he believes it to be irrefutable; rather, it is because those who flatter the Chinese can say nothing against Du Halde, on whom they rely for the most part. This is why it is so important for Montesquieu to produce his sources, including even the page numbers, as a general rule, while many of his contemporaries were far from demonstrating an equal degree of precision: it is a matter of showing that he did not systematically seek out sources unfavorable to the Chinese.

Such is Montesquieu's operating rule: all information provided by the Jesuits is not to be condemned a priori as suspect, but is to be accepted on the basis of partial knowledge. Does this mean, as Dodds would have it, that having established certain principles beforehand, he could not accept what came into contradiction with them? The "dialogue" that we have mentioned shows precisely the opposite.[46] The *Geographica II* exposes this dialogue in action: missionaries and merchants do not make the same judgment regarding the good faith of the Chinese: "I would be able to reconcile what the Muscovites say in their reports about the mandarins' harassment and pillaging of the merchants[47] and what Du Halde says about their punctuality and the order they maintain[:] as much as they fear doing something that exposes them to punishment like not obeying the tribunals or the emperor not putting order among the peoples they are as ardent in pillaging themselves which is tolerated because of the confiscations" (f. 120). Montesquieu does not "choose" Lange (the envoy of the Muscovites that Dodds judged severely) against the Jesuits; rather, he opposes the judgment of someone who has no interest in presenting the Chinese in a favorable light. But above all, far from denouncing the one by means of the other, he shows that each of them saw a different aspect, or rather two sides, of the same phenomenon. And when Du Halde himself suggests that one cannot trust the Chinese, the consequences are highly significant, as suggested by *The Spirit of Laws* (XIX, 10): "The precariousness of their lives makes them so prodigiously active and so excessively desirous of gain that no commercial nation can trust them. This acknowledged unfaithfulness has preserved Japanese commerce for the Chinese; no European trader has dared undertake it in their name, however easy this might have been for their maritime provinces in the north." A reference to "Du Halde, Vol. II" allows us to consult the following passage: "If one could count on the faithfulness of the Chinese, it would be easy for Europeans to have commerce with Japan via the Chinese: but this is as if impossible, unless we can accompany them, be master of its effects, & have the power in hand to prevent their insults" (171b–72a).[48]

Who would presume to contest an "acknowledged unfaithfulness" after having read this reference, not only because it is henceforth an integral part of the received notions about the Chinese (one can in effect understand the expression in this way) but especially because it is attested by a guarantor hardly to be suspected of severity toward them? The manuscript of *The Spirit of Laws*[49] also allows one to observe an interesting phenomenon: this remark dates only from 1746 or 1747 and replaces a long note that dates from five years earlier, taken from Lange's journal, removed in 1743 or 1744.[50] Montesquieu preferred to refer to Du Halde rather than to the enemy of the Chinese, Lange: his statement thus became irrefutable.

However, are there not contradictions in Montesquieu's consideration of despotism? He was the first to acknowledge its existence, for despotism is by its essence contradictory and literally *unthinkable*: an excess of power and powerlessness at the same time, it seems to be pure corruption even when it is at the apogee of its strength. It can only at the best survive, for the despotic regime is on the verge of collapse, so much is it loath to reason and human nature;[51] and nevertheless it is resistant thanks to "particular causes,"[52] like in the case of the Eastern Roman Empire, which lasted for ten centuries in Constantinople, or the Chinese Empire, which saw twenty-two dynasties succeed one another in four thousand years. A "violent" regime, therefore supposed to be unstable, it is at the same time the easiest regime to establish and maintain, for it rests on "simple ideas." Can one account for such a difficulty when one has as a mental model that of a religious order that demands above all submission to the Superior? "Could it not be that the missionaries [...] were struck by that continuous exercise of the will of one alone by which they themselves are governed?" says the chapter of *The Spirit of Laws* (VIII, 21) that gives an account of this contradiction.

The same could be said in the cases where the Jesuits themselves contradict themselves without realizing it, as is shown by the same chapter of *The Spirit of Laws*: complacently evoking the persecution that was unleashed against the neophyte princes of the blood in the eighteenth collection of the *Lettres édifiantes*,[53] P. Parrenin thought he was writing the apology of the martyrs of the faith; above all, he attacked the Chinese system of justice and the emperor, who was without pity for the princes "who had displeased him," which reveals "a tyrannical plan consistently followed" (VIII, 21). One thus has a better understanding of how the stick mentioned by Du Halde could have had so much importance, and in fact, one sees it return in Book XVII: "The peoples [in Asia] are governed by the cudgel; the Tartar peoples, by long whips" (ch. 5). How can one write *ad majorem gloriam* of the Chinese Empire and consider the role that force plays there to be negligible? How can one speak of honor and the cudgel at the same time? The Jesuits themselves were caught in a contradiction that they had never perceived. They are therefore at worst the defenders of an untenable position, which makes them see spirituality where there is only idolatry, or at best near-sighted observers of a reality that escapes them due to the absence of a minimal political analysis; they are neither impartial, "naïve" (in the sense used in the eighteenth century), nor clairvoyant. However, their works exist; they are indispensable and recognized as such. Montesquieu's art consists therefore in preserving what he could from their accounts, within their limits, which he acknowledges. Taking these works as guarantors of severe judgments is not only to produce an authority; it is also to show that even the Jesuits could not conceal the true nature of this monstrous regime that is despotism, one of the ruses of which is to adopt contradictory appearances. If even the Jesuits come to recognize that the Emperor is naked, who will dare to praise his silk clothes?

We are thus very far from the image of a Montesquieu collecting his information according to the whim of his curiosity, or continuing for all of his life to apply principles forged in his youth. The travel reports and other sources of information about foreign peoples do not offer him a mass of information ready to constitute his anthropological or sociological vision progressively and cumulatively; rather, they themselves are sifted out. For Montesquieu, there is no reading that is not a critical reading, which we have a tendency to forget, so far removed from us is this documentation and so much does it coalesce into an indistinct mass. The geographical distance of the realities described tends to occlude the fact that the questions considered are for Montesquieu perfectly contemporaneous. When he met Msgr. Fouquet in Rome in 1729 (which is attested to in the *Spicilège*), he was by virtue of that meeting at the heart of the recent negotiations between the Pontifical Court and the Chinese Empire; when he read the *Description de la Chine*, the Chinese Rites Controversy had not yet been resolved. The entire Chinese case thus must be considered with infinite precaution.

To help us proceed in this manner, the collection of the *Geographica II* is of immense value: one cannot turn two consecutive pages without happening upon a formulation that appears familiar to the reader of Montesquieu. And in effect, it turns out to be a first approach, or an explanation of a fact or an idea that will appear either in a summary or allusive manner, or on the contrary in a largely developed manner, in *The Spirit of Laws* or the *Pensées*. The *Geographica II* constituted an indispensable step in Montesquieu's intellectual formation and information-gathering; for the critics of today, the same is true.

## Notes

1. Muriel Dodds, *Les Récits de voyages, sources de L'Esprit des lois de Montesquieu* (Paris: Honoré Champion, 1929).

2. Abu'l Ghazi, *Histoire généalogique des Tatars traduite du Manuscript Tartare d'Abulgasi Bayadur Chan*, par D*** [i.e., Bentinck] (Leyde: Abraham Kallewier, 1726); Jean Frédéric Bernard, *Recueil des Voyages au Nord contenant divers mémoires très utiles au commerce et à la navigation* (Paris: J. F. Bernard, 1725–1738); Jean Baptiste Du Halde, ed., *Lettres édifiantes et curieuses écrites des missions étrangères par quelques missionnaires de la Compagnie de Jesus* (Paris: s.n., 1703); and Jean Baptiste Du Halde, *Description de la Chine* (Paris: G. Lemercier, 1735).

3. Montesquieu, *L'Esprit des lois* (Geneva: Barrillot, 1748).

4. She especially deplores the fact that Montesquieu took little interest in the destiny of the peoples of America conquered by the Portuguese and the Spanish; as to slavery, he dedicated an entire book to the subject in vain: "[H]e does not conclude": "[H]e seems to say that [slavery] is an evil, but a necessary evil, which nonetheless carries with it some attenuations," an attitude for which we cannot but reproach him, according to Dodds, even if such an attitude represents "in itself an advancement" at that time (*Les Récits*, 120–24, particularly 123). We will not spend time here to point out the weaknesses of this interpretation.

5. *Les Récits*, part II, ch. 1, 136–49.

6. An example of this can be found in a passage of *The Spirit of Laws* (XXII, 1), which evokes the use of salt or gold as currency in Africa: "It is therefore most natural

that, citing Shaw [*Voyage du Levant*, 1743, the French translation of *Travels or Observations relating to several parts of Barbary and the Levant*, 1738] from memory, he spoke of the salt trade in Niger and not of the different goods of which Shaw speaks. The passage of *The Spirit of Laws* is similar enough to that of Shaw that we can see in it a reminder of the work of the English savant" (67). Montesquieu attests to reading Shaw only in the posthumous edition of 1757 (with the addition to Book XXVI, 6); questions remain as to whether Montesquieu even consulted the text prior to 1748 and whether there really is an affinity between the two texts, given that the only similarity is the question of salt—something that, in our opinion, is not sufficient to prove her point.

7. Paul Ricault, *État présent de l'Empire ottoman* (Paris: S. Mabre-Crmoisy, 1670); Jean Chardin, *Voyages de Mr. le Chevalier Chardin, en Perse, et autres lieux de l'Orient* (Amsterdam: Delorme, 1711); Jean Antoine Du Cerceau, *Histoire de la dernière revolution en Perse* (Paris: Briasson, 1728).

8. *Les Récits*, 148–49.

9. Ibid., 97.

10. Ibid.

11. As an authority she cites Raynal, *Histoire philosophique et politique des [. . .] deux Indes*, (Geneva, 1870). The very nature of this reference (the book was originally published almost a hundred years earlier) suggests that she was not primarily concerned with consulting original texts and that she was not careful in choosing her sources of validation, given that Raynal consulted Montesquieu's text for his own work.

12. See note 4 in this chapter.

13. *Les Récits*, 67. We will not elaborate on the final merit that she attributes to Montesquieu, that of having *portrayed* the Orient better than the travelers, thanks "to the magic of his epigrammatic style" that permitted him to "synthesize" and "make come alive" the passages he cited, while these travelers do not "show anything of India as it is in reality" (*Les Récits*, 89). One could continue the citation: "[T]hey do not show us the gilded pagodas, the priests in yellow robes, the women in their brightly-coloured veils walking with the slow sway of Oriental women," but is it worth the trouble to show to what degree this perspective is futile?

14. See note 2 in this chapter.

15. Montesquieu provided an opening that Dodds valiantly seized: "Our missionaries speak of the vast empire of China as of an admirable government [. . .]. I have therefore made an empty distinction in establishing the principles of the three governments." (*The Spirit of Laws*, VIII, 21).

16. *Les Récits*, 95.

17. Moland, XXX, 434. Cf. *Commentaire sur le livre* Des délits et des peines (1766), ch. 11 (Moland, XXV, 556–57). E. Carcassonne, "La Chine dans *L'Esprit des lois*," *Revue d'histoire littéraire de la France* (April–June 1924): 193–205, admitted to being unable to find it as well.

18. (Paris: Classiques Garnier, 1973, 2 vols.).

19. Dodds was better advised when she admitted to not having found the origin of a reference "in this muddle that is the *Recueil des voyages qui ont servi à l'établissement de la compagnie des Indes*," the edition used by Montesquieu being particularly difficult to find (p. 79). Whoever has spent hours searching in vain for a reference, only to find it later by accident, will feel an intimate sympathy for Dodds.

20. Thanks to the dating carried out by Mme de Chabannes, this manuscript has been assigned the call number 2507. See L. Desgraves, *Inventaire des documents manuscrits des fonds Montesquieu de la bibliothèque municipale de Bordeaux* (Geneva: Droz, 1998), 28–30; C. Volpilhac-Auger, with the collaboration of Hélène de Bellaigue, *Les plus belles pages des manuscrits de Montesquieu confiés à la bibliothèque municipale de Bordeaux par Jacqueline de Chabannes* (Bordeaux: William Blake, 2005), especially 20–25 (with reproductions of pages of the manuscrpit).

21. (Paris: Nagel, 1955), III, 923–63.

22. F. Weil corrected a certain number of Dodds' remarks and above all worked in an entirely different spirit.

23. To be completed shortly (2007), in the new edition of the *Œuvres complètes* of Montesquieu (XVI).

24. See M. Benítez, "Montesquieu, Fréret et les remarques tirées des entretiens avec Hoangh," *Actes du colloque de Bordeaux (1998)* (Bordeaux: Académie nationale des sciences, belles-lettres et arts de Bordeaux, 1999), 111–26; republished in the new edition of the *Geographica* (*Œuvres complètes*).

25. For the *Description de la Chine*, we count fewer than forty passages in the Masson edition; we have identified more than eighty in the manuscript.

26. Catherine Volpilhac-Auger, "Du bon usage des *Geographica*," *Revue Montesquieu* 3 (1999): 169–78, and "L'ombre d'une bibliothèque. La bibliothèque manuscrite de Montesquieu," *Lire, copier, écrire. Les bibliothèques manuscrites et leurs usages au XVIIIe siècle*, ed. É. Décultot (Paris: CNRS Editions, 2003), 79–90.

27. *Geographica*, f. 198 r–v.

28. In the manuscript of *The Spirit of Laws*, this sentence is transcribed by secretary H (1741–1742).

29. Volume I has disappeared; the publication to come out shortly (*Œuvres complètes*, XVI) will provide a summary of this text, to the extent that it will have been able to be reconstituted.

30. Notably a work that Dodds hardly mentions, the *Anciennes relations des Indes et de la Chine de deux voyageurs mahométans, qui y allèrent dans le neuvième siècle*, published in 1718 by Fr. Renaudot (forty pages in the *Geographica*); the work is contested by Montesquieu himself on several occasions, but his first reading of it had impressed him enough that he cited it on several occasions in *The Spirit of Laws*. "Quelques remarques sur [mes] conversations avec M. Ouanges" occupy forty pages as well; but the majority is constituted by the *Description de la Chine* (three hundred pages, nearly half of the entire volume) and by excerpts of the *Lettres édifiantes et curieuses* (nearly one hundred pages but not all of which are devoted to China): these are the Jesuit sources that are predominant. Apart from the *Voyages en Perse* by Chardin, the *Historia imperii japonici* by Engelbert Kaempfer (La Haye: P. Gosse et J. Neaulme 1729), and the *Nouvelle relation de l'Égypte* by Johann Michael Wansleben (Paris: Compagnie des librairies associés, 1698), which figured in the *Geographica I* (but were far from occupying the totality of the volume), the *Geographica II* contains the majority of all of the documentation on the Orient used by Montesquieu, including the notes on La Loubère's *Du royaume de Siam* (Paris: Coignard, 1691), William Dampier, *New Voyage around the World* (London: J. Knapton, 1699), François Bernier's *Voyages* (Amsterdam: Paul Marret, 1710), and the *Histoire généalogique des Tartares*. The *Geographica II* (and

perhaps the two *Geographica* together) could be titled *Sinica* (as suggested by Françoise Weil), or *Despotica*, if Montesquieu had wanted to give them an appellation that in fact only appeared retrospectively (it seems that the denomination *Politica II*, to designate le *Geographica II*, which one could infer from a passage of the *Pensées* citing Du Halde [No. 1880], derives from a material error on the part of the secretary).

31. It seems that "Quelques remarques" were used in the *Éloge de la sincérité* (1717): see the *Œuvres complètes*, VIII, 143, note 16.

32. Similarly, the *Anciennes relations* treated cannibalism as a widespread practice in China, which was in no way unusual, at any rate; Montesquieu returns to this point on several occasions, in the margin of his notes as well as in the *Pensées* and in the manuscript of *The Spirit of Laws*, concluding in the final analysis in favor of the Jesuits' account, against the assertion made in the *Anciennes relations*; our edition of this text will go into this issue in detail.

33. This work is due to Sylviane Albertan-Coppola, who contributed to the editing of the *Description de la Chine* for the publication of vol. XVI.

34. In the same vein is the question whether Montesquieu is "Sinophobe," as opposed to a "Sinophile" Voltaire, to which the relation between these two philosophers and one of their common objects of study is often reduced.

35. René Etiemble, *Les Jésuites en Chine. La querelle des rites (1552–1772)* (Paris: R. Julliard, 1966).

36. That is to say, what was his position on the question of the compatibility of Chinese rites and ceremonies that owe their origin to Confucius, the Emperor, and the ancestors, with the Christian religion, and in general, on the question of the compatibility of Chinese thought and customs with Christianity; and on the problem of the "religion" of the Chinese people, whom the Jesuits' adversaries identified as being, in fact, atheists (and in particular on the translation of the notion of *Tien*, or "Sky").

37. Etiemble, *Les Jésuites en Chine*, 178: "All the same, to understand the chapters of *The Spirit of Laws* which deal with China, it is necessary to put them back in the heart of the Chinese Rites Controversy, and to know that they were inspired by the resentments of a Jesuit at war with his Company" (i.e., Fouquet). To these adversaries, it is doubtless necessary to add Fr. Ripa, evoked by Michele Fatica, "Le fonti orali della sinofobia di Ch.-L. Secondat de Montesquieu," *L'Europe de Montesquieu*, *Cahiers Montesquieu*, ed. M. G. Bottaro Palumbo and A. Postigliola (Napoli-Oxford: Liguori-Voltaire Foundation, 1995), IV, 395–409 . As M. Fatica suggests, it is most certainly to Fr. Ripa that the name *Rota* refers (even if it was Montesquieu himself who transcribed the name) in the *Spicilège* (no. 484).

38. It is certainly necessary to reconsider the contribution of these two authors, especially of the first one, whose "Dialogue between Confucius and Socrates," in the *Dialogues des morts*, could have played a crucial role.

39. Who ought to be considered with tenacious disdain, it seems: Dodds, who manifestly could not speak ill of the Jesuits, testifies to this, but so does even Etiemble, who, a priori, prefers them to "the merchants who, quite ignorant of Chinese mores and thought, saw no farther than the debit and the credit" and who reproaches Montesquieu for having privileged their reports (*Les Jésuites en Chine*, 174). Now Montesquieu's openness to commerce is one of the most original aspects of his thought, and this is true even well before *The Spirit of Laws*: "[T]he reflection on international affairs was

displaced from the diplomatic and military domain to that of the examination of commercial relations" (C. Larrère, "Introduction to the *Réflexions sur la monarchie universelle* (1734)," *Œuvres complètes* (Oxford: Voltaire Foundation, 2000), II, 335.

40. On the work of Du Halde, who was first the editor of the *Lettres édifiantes*, see Isabelle Landry-Deron, *La Preuve par la Chine. La Description de J.-B. Du Halde, Jésuite, 1735* (Paris: Éditions de l'EHESS, 2002).

41. I. Landry-Deron devoted herself to determining which information can be traced back to the contributors and which to Du Halde.

42. Letter from Fréret to Fr. Gaubil, cited by I. Landry-Deron, *La Preuve par la Chine*, 380–81.

43. See in particular his remark on Du Halde's estimate of internal commerce in China, which would make it superior to that of all of Europe (*Description*, II, 169; *Geographica II*, f. 203r): "*He is mistaken. European external commerce greatly increases the internal." This becomes more diplomatic in *The Spirit of Laws* (XXI, 21): "This might be, if our external commerce did not increase our internal commerce."

44. Catalog manuscript, 555 (*Le Catalogue de la bibliothèque de Montesquieu à La Brède* in collaboration with F. Weil and L. Desgraves), *Cahiers Montesquieu*, 1999, IV, 392); *Pensées*, no. 1656.

45. Montesquieu does not fail to point out every instance in which an emperor is hoaxed by a charlatan purveying a concoction that guarantees immortality. When one retains 3 percent of a work, to regularly choose this trait reveals a very precise intention.

46. Moreover, contrary to what Dodds thought, the publication date of the texts that Montesquieu consulted has no relation to the date at which they were read (even if it is true that Montesquieu read Du Halde less than four years after its publication).

47. In the "Journal of Sr. Lange concerning his negotiations at the court of China in 1721 and 1722," in vol. VIII of the *Voyages au Nord*, of which Montesquieu provides an excerpt in the *Geographica II* (f. 22–30). Cf. *The Spirit of Laws*, XIII, 10–11, VIII, 21: "[O]ne can consult them [the merchants] about the banditry of the mandarins." The *Geographica II* (f. 26) reveals that this lapidary judgment issues from a much more nuanced reflection. Also see note 34 in this chapter.

48. The *Geographica II* shows an "intermediate" stage of the formulation: "[O]ne could have commerce with Japan via the Chinese, but their unfaithfulness in commerce prevents it" (f. 203v).

49. Bibliothèque nationale de France, n.a.fr. 12835, f. 124r. All of my remarks concerning dating rely on the study "Une nouvelle 'chaîne secrète' de *L'Esprit des lois*: l'histoire du texte," in *Montesquieu en 2005*, directed by C. Volpilhac-Auger (Oxford: Voltaire Foundation, 2005), 83–216.

50. The note was in fact transferred at this time to chapter 20, f. 149r–v.

51. See Catherine Larrère, *Actualité de Montesquieu* (Paris: Presses de Sciences-Po, 1999), 87–89: "The paradox of despotism is that it subsists."

52. "Particular causes" applies to the Eastern Roman Empire in the *Considérations sur les causes de la grandeur des Romains et de leur décadence*; in *The Spirit of Laws*, Montesquieu speaks of "particular, and perhaps unique, circumstances" in reference to China (VIII, 21).

53. *Geographica II*, f. 330r.

# 5

# Montesquieu on Power
## Beyond Checks and Balances

### Brian C. J. Singer

This chapter proposes to examine Montesquieu's understanding of power. Montesquieu's one indisputable legacy is, arguably, the idea of checks and balances. In a first movement, this chapter proposes to examine the understanding of power that underlies this idea. Here the claim will be that Montesquieu separates power from the law and, more generally, from the symbolic. The result is that power, by itself, stripped of all encumbrances, is reduced to force alone, with no end other than its own indefinite extension, thus the need to divide power against itself, balancing force against force, in order to impede power from realizing its despotic vocation. Such a conception, it will be argued, reflects a uniquely modern conception of power; it is also, one must add, potentially highly reductive. In Montesquieu, however, neither judgments nor concepts are simple. Thus, in a second movement, the chapter will claim that one can, to a degree, find the resources to combat such reductionism, as the symbolic (if not the law) returns to power but, as it were, through the back door of the passions. With the partial exception of despotism, this can be demonstrated for all the regime types, including the "English regime," the home of the division of powers. A word of caution before continuing: Montesquieu's thought has been described as being systematic without being systemic; however, within the limited space allotted me, his ideas will have to be presented not just systemically, but schematically.

In order to understand Montesquieu's conception of power, one must begin with his distinction among the three types: despotic, monarchic, and republican regimes. This distinction replaces an earlier one that originates in the ancients and speaks of monarchy, aristocracy, and "democracy," as well as their "shadow regimes": tyranny, oligarchy, and "anarchy."[1] This older typology not only distinguishes between the rule of the one, the several, and the many; it also suggests that each form of rule bears its own law, in accord with different ideas of the good. When a power no longer upholds its law, it is not just the law that is corrupted but power itself. Thus tyranny is not a form of power; it is a corruption of the form monarchic power. Power, by its definition, supposes the law that gives it its form and attaches it to its ends.

Now Montesquieu not only collapses the rule of the few and the many into a single rubric, republicanism, but he also divides the rule of the one into two, distinguishing monarchy from despotism, according to whether the one rules with or without the law. Consider for a moment the inclusion of despotism in this typology. Previously despotism referred to the private, domestic realm and the relation between master and slave. When one spoke of despotism with regards to the public realm, one was suggesting a type of rule that was not political properly considered.[2] The tyrant could still be considered a political animal; for he maintains, if only by the fact of usurpation, a reference to the law he seeks to corrupt. With the despot there is no law to corrupt, everyone and everything having been reduced to his personal property.[3] Montesquieu, then, by claiming despotism as one of the three basic political regimes, is stating that political power does not require the idea of law. There is, after all, a regime where power is essentially lawless, yet whose form, by virtue of its regularities, still bears a certain coherence and intelligibility.[4] This is not to suggest that, for Montesquieu, the law and, by extension, all normative concerns have no place in political life or its comprehension. On the contrary, he distinguishes the different regime types according to the relations power establishes with law. If in despotism power is lawless, in democratic republics—and I am simplifying tremendously—power and law tend to fuse, with the sovereign people upholding and internalizing the law; while in monarchies law and power are related without being equivalent, as the monarch rules by law, but the law exists independently, in its own "*dépôt*."

Nonetheless, if one wants to understand how Montesquieu sees power in its pure state, disencumbered of the law, one must look to despotic power. Here power is, in principle, unlimited; it would encounter no obstacle to the realization of its will, which is itself unlimited, capable of doing anything it pleases, whenever and however it pleases. Such a power can only belong to one person, as sharing power can only limit power. And if power, in its nakedness, bears a "law" in its lawlessness, it is the tendency toward the maximization of the will and of the force required for the realization of that will. Such force need not, in principle, entail violence, but less forceful means of power, like persuasion, appear as a brake on the despotic will, as they suppose the recognition of the needs and concerns of others. In Montesquieu, to an extent not found in the ancients, despotic power is associated with fear. Indeed, the figure of despotism haunts the entire political field, being the simplest, most spontaneous, most widespread form of regime (V, 14). It exists not just in points east, or in hot climes; it existed in the West, notably with imperial Rome[5] and casts its shadow, under the sign of absolutism, over the governments of his own time. Wherever there is society, there is power, and wherever there is power, despotic rule is always possible.[6]

I am not saying that Montesquieu invented this conception of power—power as will, and power as force, where power, will, and force all seek their maximum expansion. He does, however, bring this conception, which is a peculiarly modern conception, into particular relief. Power had often been attached, directly or indirectly, to a single will, most often with reference to the divine will, in order to guarantee the establishment of an orderly, meaningful, and just world in common. Similarly force was seen as necessary to the exercise of power but always as a secondary instrument in the service of the law that articulates the ends of power. Here, however, separated from the law, power becomes its own end or better, becomes the means in the exercise of a will that is its own end, as it exults in a claim to unhindered autonomy.[7] And if force appears the ultimate instrument of this will to power, one is tempted to refer it to the newly developed science of mechanics, with its rhetorical and epistemological prestige. Some would find such a vision of power, with its promise of endless mastery, exhilarating. Many, including Montesquieu (at least in matters political), found it disturbing. There had always been an awareness of the possible equation of power, will, and force; but the identification of this equation with the very essence of power explains a uniquely modern suspicion of government.[8] When thinking of Montesquieu's understanding of power, one is reminded of Lord Acton's famous dictum: "[P]ower corrupts, and absolute power corrupts absolutely." Note: where once power was an object in danger of being corrupted, it is now power that is dangerous, being the agent of corruption. With this shift in grammatical position, the problem is no longer how to construct a good power (let alone how to maximize power in view of the good); the problem is how to limit power, whatever its coloration. This is a key reason why Montesquieu is generally considered a liberal, even though he lacks such key conceptual credentials as, for example, a well-developed idea of human rights.[9]

It is this view of power that sets the stage for the characterization of the English regime in terms of checks and balances, as opposed to the earlier conception of mixed government.[10] The earlier conception had claimed to blunt the tendency, relative to any of the three types of power taken individually, to become corrupt. The idea was that, if each type, in the face of its seemingly inevitable degeneration, tended to be replaced by a new type, then a regime that included elements of all three types would be able to avoid political cycles and their revolutions. The theory of checks and balances, by contrast, wants to limit, not so much the corruption of power, as power itself.[11] And it does so by rejigging the separation of powers (with which it is often confused) in a way that sets power against power.[12] One must not think, however, that checks and balances are the only way to limit power. Every regime that is not despotic has, by definition, found a means to limit power. The system of checks and balances is certainly one means, the means most appropriate to the establishment of what Montesquieu, at one point, calls "extreme political liberty."[13] It is also the means most befitting a "mechanical" understanding of power, one that sees power in terms of opposing relations of force.

My argument, so far, claims that, by separating power from the law, Montesquieu presents what appears as power's essential defining characteristics. As evidenced by his association of power in its unhindered state with despotism, he renders the limitation of power imperative. His examination of despotism reveals that a regime based on power alone is not simply brutal and unjust; absolute power is ultimately self-defeating as it threatens to destroy itself and everything around it (V, 14). Despotism, in effect, reduces history to the proverbial "tale told by an idiot, full of sound and fury signifying nothing."[14] As such despotic power suggests a separation not just from the law, but from what is implied by the law, the larger symbolic order, by which I understand the establishment of an orderly, meaningful world in common.

Now to make this latter claim is to raise two questions. First, how is a symbolic order to be established, once one judges what were the two most likely candidates—law and religion (both previously deemed inseparable from power)—insufficient, even deficient?[15] The second question asks if power, as conceived here, must always and necessarily be cut off from the symbolic? I cannot respond here, at least not directly, to the first question, which is far too large, even as it touches on what I consider to be decisive in Montesquieu, the movement from a juridically based power to the "spirit" beneath the laws, to the mores and manners, from, in short, a political to a more properly social analysis. This chapter seeks to respond to the second question alone: it asks whether, within Montesquieu, one can situate the symbolic not just at the social, but at a political level, within the action of power, despite its apparent definition as force. And the response to this question will be double. There is something very reductive about Montesquieu's understanding of power, as is most evident, it will be argued, when he speaks about the monarch. For he goes on at considerable length about what in monarchy limits the monarch's power but has almost nothing to say about that power itself, particularly as regards its symbolic dimension (symbolic here understood in a more restrictive sense, referring to his "representational" role). Yet the relation of power to the symbolic (in both the general and the restricted sense) does appear and appears where one would least expect it, through a discussion of what, at first, seems to exclude it—desire or, more broadly, the passions. And in truth, desire in despotism bears more of a relation, to borrow the vocabulary of Jacques Lacan, to the imaginary than the symbolic.

Despotic power originates in the despot's desire: he desires to do what he wants, whenever and however he wants. And who does not, somewhere deep down, have the same desire? Despotic desire is, for Montesquieu, a fantasy, a fantasy of power. This is not to say that despotism is not real. Yet, if one thinks that the despot is the supreme master and commander of all he surveys, that everything that happens is a product of his will, that the physiognomy of his regime is contoured in accord with his genius—this is very much a fantasy. Never mind that this is how the absolute monarch, Louis XIV, for example, represented his power.[16] The truth is that the despot, according to Montesquieu, tends to impotence. Often he is sexually impotent (and despotism, as practiced in the seraglio, is very much a sexual fantasy).[17] And he is impotent in that he is the "weakest man" in his regime—not that he does not strike fear into the heart of all and sundry but in the sense that he is weak-willed, as well as weak headed (II, 5, IV, 3, V, 14, XVI, 6). His weakness is due precisely to the fact that all his desires are met. Only when desire is frustrated does it find the interior strength, not to mention the "intelligence," necessary to overcome the obstacles in its way. In truth, the despot has neither will nor reason; instead of will he knows only caprice, and instead of reason, only blind passion. In order for desire to become will, it must give itself its own law, thereby doubling the limits it encounters without, with limits it imposes within. If there can be unlimited desire and unlimited power, there can be no unlimited will that would mediate the two terms to produce something lasting. The idea of an "unlimited will" is an oxymoron; a strong will positions itself in relation to limits. This is why the idea of "enlightened despotism" would have appeared nonsensical to Montesquieu; the very premise of despotism negates the possibility.[18] With free reign given to the despot's desire, the place of power is emptied of will, reason, and, ultimately, power itself; no wonder that it is the most ruinous of regimes.

Now if despotism originates in the despot's desire, that is, his desire to have all his desires satisfied, what can we say about passions of the other two regimes? Here a quotation from a book by Alain Grosrichard proves most helpful:

> [O]ne has not sufficiently stressed that the three seemingly quite heterogeneous principles (virtue, honour and fear) actually form three modalities of a single passion that can be called either love or fear, depending on whether one refers to its root or expression. Thus virtue is based on *amour de la patrie*; honour on *amour-propre*; and fear on *amour de soi* which corresponds to the vital instinct of self-preservation. But fear too is inscribed, in one form or another,

in the principle of each of the governments. In despotism it is a question of the fear of death, in monarchy, the fear of opinion, and in the republics, fear of the law. (my translation)[19]

Each of the passions corresponding to the three regimes supposes a different relation to the self, and in consequence, a different relation to others, and to that set of others that forms a collectivity. Borrowing Rousseauist terminology for very non-Rousseauist purposes, Alain Grosrichard distinguishes *amour de soi*, the form of love associated with despotism, from *amour propre*, associated with monarchic honor. What I want to draw from this distinction is the implicit claim that despotic desire is essentially narcissistic: it refuses to recognize that others have desires of their own, treating them instead as instruments for its own satisfaction. *Amour propre* supposes one loves not so much oneself, as an idea of oneself that one then upholds. Thus one acts in relation to others, their perceptions, their desires; and one acts in relation to one's self-image because one has internalized the perspective of the other. This is to say that with *amour-propre* one has given a law to one's passions, such that, in contrast to *amour de soi*, desire is mediated by the symbolic. "One needs only passions to establish despotism" writes Montesquieu (V, 14); in the other regimes, there are passions, but they are not unlimited, blind passions, for they incorporate what lies outside the self and its desire. In monarchy—and here I deviate somewhat from Grosrichard—one's sense of self is formed in relation to a particular group of others (e.g., the nobility and their idea of what is right), and in democracy in relation to the general other as supposed by equality. Only in despotism can one speak of passions outside of any symbolic order. The implication is that, once one leaves despotism, one can speak of a symbolic order without yet having to speak of juridical law. The question is, with juridical law separated from power, can one relate power to the symbolic, at least in the regimes other than despotism? In an attempt to address this question, I want to examine, if only briefly, the three regime types in terms of two topics: first, language—more particularly, the language of power; and second, the bond that ties ruler to the ruled.

In principle, fear, unlike honor or virtue, does not require language. Nonetheless, one cannot really say that there is no speech under despotism (just as one cannot really say that there is no law).[20] Yet the despot does not tie his subjects to himself through his words, as he is too enamored of the pleasures of the seraglio to address his subjects in a consistent manner. When he gives commands, they come like bolts of lightning out of the blue. In truth, they are more signaletic than semantic, there being nothing to negotiate, interpret, or even understand; blind obedience alone is countenanced (III, 10). The despot's word demands total allegiance, but as the despot does not keep his word, the content of his speech is ultimately of little significance. It is the name of the despot alone that underwrites the continuity of despotic rule and whose utterance is enough to incite fear.[21] The name of the despot is a pure signifier, enabling the sign to function without being attached to anything meaningful. Only in the other regime types are the signs of power articulated in the terms of a coherent discourse. This is true particularly of democracy, where the language of power fuses with that of the law and with the language of patriotism that defends the community and its law. As regards monarchies, to give one's word already implies the language of honor, though it is not certain that the latter is the language of power. For honor, if it ties one to the monarch, does so on its own terms, which is to say, at a distance from and, if offended, in opposition to monarchic power and law.[22] And what about the language of the monarch? Montesquieu has little to say about monarchic speech: from the contrast with despotism, we know that it is neither unreasonable nor inaccessible[23]; ideally it is both virtuous and honorable.[24] What he does insist on, however, is that the closer language comes to the monarch, the more degraded it is likely to become. The language of the court is a degenerate language, a language of flattery that reduces the distance established by the code of honor, as the courtier's sense of self is made to depend on the regard of the king rather than a self-regard rooted in the opinions of his peers (III, 5, IV, 2, XII, 28).

Turn now to the second question, that of the political bond. Power binds, but in different ways in different regimes. It would be too simple to say that in despotism people are bound together by fear alone. Following Grosrichard, *amour de soi* has to be added to the equation. Despotism can be said to construct a chain where everyone except, arguably, those at the very top and bottom are linked by fear to those above and *amour de soi* to those below.[25] Almost everyone, from the vizier down to the humble family head, is simultaneously master and slave, granted absolute power over those below by the one above to whose capricious power he is enchained. One is, as it were, seduced by a fantasy of power that threatens one's destruction. Such a chain, however, cannot be very strong. Not simply because there is, arguably, little love lost for the one who tyrannizes you, but because, each link being structurally similar to every other link, there can be no strong identifications based on position, place, or person. Hence the links, particularly the upper ones, easily fall away. One thinks of the nomads of the eastern steppes—the Tartars being, in Montesquieu's mind, the most despotic of peoples (with the possible exception of the Japanese)—who band together to form hordes that rapidly expand into world empires, only to disperse, a few generations later, and often miles from their original homeland, into their original clan-based components.

There is no real need to speak about the character of the political bond in the democratic republic. As power is not really separated from law, and the law is largely internalized,[26] the relation of power to a symbolic order is evident. The more interesting case is presented by monarchy. Codes of honor do form bonds. Montesquieu presents honor as based on identifications with position and place and not with persons. This becomes evident in the last book where he speaks of the importance for the establishment of monarchy properly considered with the development of feudal law at the beginnings of Capetian rule.[27] Feudal law attaches the noble to his lineage and his lineage to landed property, independent of the will of the monarch; this in contrast to the previous period, when title and demesne still remained very much at the monarch's discretion. Thus a properly feudal nobility serves the monarch out of a sense of honor and not out of personal loyalty or with an eye to the future distribution of rewards. Honor, in effect, supposes (feudal) law separated from (monarchic) power; indeed, feudal law emerges when the monarchy, in a sense, was without a monarch, the first Capetian's power barely extending beyond his own demesne (XXXI, 32). With feudal law each link in the chain, being released from its immediate dependence on the monarchic will, appears differentiated (distinguished according to position and place), durable (rooted in blood and soil), and autonomous. In this manner, Montesquieu constructs a certain image of aristocratic liberty and of monarchy as a stable, complex institutional order that functions largely independent of the sovereign will. It should be pointed out that, in explaining monarchy in terms of the spirit of honor, horizontal bonds must be played up at the expense of vertical ones. Thus, in stark contrast to earlier advocates and later opponents of aristocratic liberty, the latter is not made to depend on the absence of liberty among the aristocrat's inferiors, as though the noble's sense of honor depended on his peers alone. What is even more striking is the unwillingness to speak of the passion that ties the monarch to his subjects. Most of Montesquieu's contemporaries would have contrasted fear of the despot with love for the monarch; they would have claimed that, through the love of and identification with the monarch, one is able to rise above one's own narrow sphere, acquire an elevated identity, curb one's egoism, and enter the stage of world history (if not some more sacred stage).[28] With Montesquieu love of the monarch is mentioned only in passing (VIII, 6, XII, 27), lest the door be opened to personal dependence and, eventually, despotism. One is tempted to say that the relation between the monarch and his subjects appears curiously "spiritless." That such a relation must exist, however, is demonstrated by the metaphors he chooses to describe the monarchy's institutional functioning. When likening the monarchy to a solar system, how can the monarch not be compared to the sun whose invisible force prevents all centrifugal movements (III, 7)? Or when comparing the monarchy to an irrigation system, how can the king not appear as the ultimate source, the river from which all the lesser channels draw their water?[29] These metaphors, whatever their author's intentions, cannot but underline the strictly symbolic importance of the monarch in holding things together. Moreover, Montesquieu implicitly admits an identification with the monarch, when speaking of the English regime where, precisely, such an identification is deemed to be largely absent.

Montesquieu speaks of England not just in Book XI, chapter 6, which analyzes its constitution in terms of checks and balances, but notably in Book XIX, chapter 27, which examines the "general spirit" corresponding to the English constitution. In Book XIX, the spirit turns "national," detached not just from the commanding logic of the three regimes but from a close articulation with power. Much of the book is given over to an analysis of China, the least despotic of despotisms, where the social bond is constantly being reconstructed from the bottom up, at the level of family manners and village ritual, repairing the effects of despotic rule and even rendering it "super-structural." In England, which can be considered the least monarchic of monarchies,[30] one can also speak, if in much more dynamic terms, of a split between power and society. Where power is divided between two opposing branches of government, its hold is both diminished and decentered, even as it comes to depend on forces outside the orbits of governance. The kingdom cannot be held together through an identification with the monarch when, at any given moment, the majority of the populace may support the country over the court party. One cannot apply to the English case metaphors that suggest a single focal point, calibrated degrees of distance, and stable lines of communication. If one must have a metaphor, think instead of a rather singular ship of state with two captains, one on the starboard, the other the port side: when power becomes too concentrated, the ship lists to one side, at which point increasing numbers of people become alarmed, clamor about their liberty being in danger, and begin to shift to the other side, until the ship lists in the opposite direction, the process repeating itself indefinitely in a tacking motion. In effect, the checks and balances in government are underwritten by dueling parties, themselves the reflection of the competing forces of a changeable, agonistic civil society.[31]

Now the question is whether one can still speak of power in relation to the symbolic under the English system, where power's empire appears so reduced. An affirmative response is possible, but once again only by following the paths of indirection. For Montesquieu provides, if somewhat scantily, the materials relative to the English system required to engage in the same lines of questioning as sketched above in relation to the more generic regime types. He has tantalizing things to say here concerning the language of politics, the national bond, and the sense of self as revealed in the relation to the other. Though, when taking up these topics with regard to the English system, one sees the effects of the articulation of the symbolic relative, not so much to power, as to the division of power. Consider first the question of language.

The language of politics is a language of argumentation and thus a language of passion, sometimes verging on paranoia—hardly Habermas' communicative reason.[32] The English can "reason well or badly" (332), but they are more likely to reason, and reason well, when reasoning alone, outside politics and outside society (332–33). The polarities implicit here find an echo in his description of the socio-political bond. The English are simultaneously the most and least patriotic of peoples. In the face of foreign threats to their liberty, they are willing to make sacrifices that the most absolute despot would not dare impose (327). But Montesquieu also says that, in contrast to republics properly considered, Englishmen relate to each other more as confederates than fellow citizens (332).[33] Thus they find it relatively easy to leave their country and not always to spread English mores to English colonies. Sometimes they seek easy fortunes, "even in the countries of servitude" (328), where the desire to avoid hard work and "excessive imposts" trumps the advantages of liberty. Obviously one is facing here the phenomenon of English individualism, which the division of power both supposes and renders possible: if one is to choose (or refuse to choose) between powers, one must bear, as an individual, a certain independence from the collectivity and the power that claims to embody it. There can be no such independence, however, if one's sense of self is tied to one's identification with that power.

How then is one to describe this individual sense of self? Montesquieu says that the object of the English system is (extreme) "liberty"; but the object is not the same as the "spirit," understood as the "passion" that sets the system "in motion" (III, 1). In truth, he never directly tells us what the "spirit" of the English is. But he does say that in England "all the passions are free" to manifest themselves to their full extent (325). And he suggests that, if not all the passions are political, in their freedom they resemble the political system by their continuous agitation. The English are impatient (XIV, 13) and restless, constantly searching out new projects for enriching and distinguishing themselves. If in monarchies *amour propre* suggests a sense of self defined in relation to a particular group, and in democracies in relation to the general community, how is one to understand the *amour propre* of the English?[34] The individualist sense of self appears too general to suggest honor (loyalties shift too easily to become closely tied to particular groups) yet too distant from and even indifferent to one's co-citizens to suggest virtue. A different author might have been tempted to claim that the presence of actual others carries less weight, because the perspective of the virtual "general other" has been so internalized as to fuse with the Englishman's sense of self, such that he orients himself in terms of either the substantive rationality of inner conscience or the more instrumental mode of self-interest. Montesquieu, however, does not pursue such paths. He does not oppose the passions to the interests and claim that in England the latter have triumphed—at least, *pace* Albert Hirschman, outside matters commercial.[35] Nor does he view English restlessness in terms of some moral or religious inner quest as suggested by the more rigorous forms of Protestantism.[36] His emphasis is on the troubled character of the relations between self and other, as manifested by tendencies towards excessive pride, personal eccentricity, even misanthropy (332).[37] Moreover, if the relation of self to other is troubled, the same is also true of the relation of self to itself. In an earlier book Montesquieu speaks of a disease peculiar to Englishmen: their "resolve to kill themselves when one can imagine no reason for their decisions" (XIV, 12). In this book, senseless suicide appears truly a disease, caused by "a failure in the filtering of the nervous juice" and attributed, in some unspecified way, to the English climate. Yet this "repugnance for all things [including] that of life" (XIV, 12) reappears in Book XIX, 27, the chapter under discussion here, when he speaks of a "disdain or disgust for everything" (332). In the earlier book Montesquieu claims the English government is particularly well suited to a potentially melancholic population.[38] And in the later chapter this *tedium vitae* can be considered the underside of the English spirit. It is what happens when an inflated individual sense of self deflates, when the general restlessness can no longer find the energy to become a principle of action, when the dissatisfaction that accompanies the constant agitation of the passions is converted into a sense of futility. Montesquieu may be an admirer of the English constitution; he also finds the English rather depressing. And the problem is that the two phenomena are not entirely unrelated.

Now I have not said this simply to dampen the portrayal of Montesquieu's anglophilia. As a Frenchman he may well have preferred French sociability and *joie de vivre* to the English lack thereof.[39] Nor am I simply seeking to trade in national stereotypes, particularly now that *la fatigue d'être soi* must also be considered a French disease.[40] A general rule when reading Montesquieu is to treat the different "nationalities" that populate his text less as "real" populations about which truth claims are being made than as conceptual "alibis" for the interrogation of sociopolitical life in all its potential variety. There are many reasons to read Montesquieu. There are the reasons his work has been read, his legacies, the most important of which is the idea of checks and balances. And there are reasons to reread his texts, that is, to read them not just as landmarks of intellectual history but as living texts that can be made to speak to the present. This chapter has sought to develop such a reading, though in its own particular mode.

Montesquieu is a modern, as opposed to the ancients. He is, however, not a very modern modern, both in the sense that he must be situated at the very threshold of the modern democratic revolution and in the sense that he was more attached to the complex institutional geography of the Ancien Regime than the militants of Enlightenment reason. There is, consequently, something very familiar about his way of thinking (as demonstrated in this chapter by the idea of force) but also something quite unfamiliar. Sometimes it is where he is most unfamiliar that he speaks most to us, because it is there that he is most challenging. Ultimately, one continues to read an author because one is attracted to his way of thinking. On this note I wish to conclude by pointing to three elements of his thought that I find most attractive and thought provoking. First, there is the relation between the political and the social. I have argued elsewhere, though I am hardly the first to do so, that, in certain decisive respects, Montesquieu was the first to discover the social. However, even as the social begins to separate from the political, the two domains do not appear autonomous. One is tempted to use such metaphors as the *chiasmus* or the *Moebius strip* to describe their relationship. In a sense, this chapter, with its introduction of the idea of the symbolic, has sought, from the perspective of power, to suggest the different ways this relationship can be articulated. Second, within Montesquieu one finds what could be called a differential political sociology of the passions. One finds little talk of passions today, particularly in political theory. Instead, as there is still the need to speak of what holds the social/political bond together, one finds weak substitute terms, quasi-universalized, quasi-naturalized—the liberal notion of interest, the communitarian idea of virtue, or some limp concept of identity formation.[41] Not only are Montesquieu's passions more psychologically acute, but they are posed, not in terms of the polarities of mind and body, reason and unreason, but as potentially mediating terms, the bearers of a particularizing reason, as giving force to sense. Last, there is the question of the "liberty of the moderns." Montesquieu recognizes that such liberty is not "natural"; the liberty of the English is far more singular and strange than its absence in other, more exotic climes. Modern liberty, particularly in its extreme English form, but also its more moderate monarchic form, is a genuine if not irreversible accomplishment of European development. Nonetheless, once situated within the play of passions, which must itself be situated in the larger tangle of laws, powers, and moeurs, the suggestion is that such liberty is not without its costs. In short, when one reads Montesquieu, one can still question our time, as he questioned his.

## Notes

1. I have put the twin "democracy-anarchy" in scare quotes because sometimes demagogy is the "shadow regime"; sometimes, as in Aristotle, it is democracy, with the "politeia" providing the more respectable twin (Aristotle, *The Politics*, trans. and ed. Ernest Barker [London: Oxford University Press, 1958], 113–15).

2. This is independent of whether slaves submitted to the despot voluntarily, being born "slavish." In Aristotle, for example, one only has a political existence (as a citizen) if one shares, directly or indirectly, in judicial and deliberative office (Aristotle, *The Politics*, 96–97). What is true is that "kingship among some uncivilized people," which is deemed despotic, has a constitutional form (Ibid., 138); in this regard, it should be contrasted to the absolute type of kingship (*pambasileia*), which also "corresponds to paternal rule over a household," but where the king, being sovereign in all matters,

is not beholden to any law. That Aristotle is willing to justify this latter form of rule when one person is vastly superior to the rest (one thinks of Alexander?) is only possible where the law (*nomos*), being conventional, is separable from order-giving form (*eidos*). In a Christian civilization such a superman would be either a monster or the living expression of a divine law (ibid, 137–49).

3. Montesquieu does, on occasion, speak of tyranny. It would appear synonymous with despotism except for the context, which is always with regard to the decline of democratic republics, and almost always with regard to the ancients—as though it represented a shift between regime types, rather than a shift within a regime type. (III, 3, VIII, 2, XII, 18, and, above all, XIV, 3). As there are several editions of *The Spirit of Laws*, references are to the book and chapter, with the exception of the long chapter at the end of Book XIX. In the latter case page numbers are taken from the Cambridge edition (Montesquieu, *The Spirit of Laws*, tran. and ed. Anne M. Coehler, Basia Carolyn Miller, and Harold Samuel Stone [Cambridge: Cambridge University Press, 1989; originally published in 1748]); all English translations are drawn from the same edition.

4. Behind this apparent paradox lies a different understanding of the relation between positive law and, for want of a better term, "natural" law. To simplify tremendously, where previous thinkers speak of a translation of "natural" law into positive law, Montesquieu speaks of the division between and interference by different types of law. Thus a "form" can be established without reference to positive law and without the reference of the latter to a higher law, the ultimate guarantor of its "sense."

5. This is a claim that immediately prevents Montesquieu from siding with the Romanists against the Germanists.

6. Society, Montesquieu suggests, is born in violence, and power, even as it prolongs that violence, is necessary to respond to it (I, 2).

7. Max Weber's definition of power presents a banal version of such a vision: "Power is the probability that one actor within a social relationship will be in a position to carry out his will despite resistance" (Max Weber, *Economy and Society* [Berkeley: University of California Press, 1978], I). Such a definition instrumentalizes power even as it tacitly admits that power is without substantial rationality.

8. Why is this the case? I am suggesting "epistemological" reasons. There may be more "mundane" reasons, for example, the increasing use of mercenary armies. (I wish to thank Ed Andrew for this suggestion).

9. One must not confuse Montesquieu with the writings of the Anglo-Scots of the same period. It is not just that *The Spirit of Laws* is not a normative work, or that it seeks to induce norms from circumstances rather than deduce them from principles. For Montesquieu an orderly, meaningful, collective existence—something that excludes despotism—is formed of the relations between power and (positive) law (as they interact with a host of other factors). For the Anglo-Scots, the basis of a meaningful collective order is always already given, largely independent of power and positive law. Thus the purpose of the latter is not to give form to that order but to maintain it against all threats. On an exploration of these differences see my article (Brian Singer, "Montesquieu, Adam Smith and the Discovery of the Social," *Journal of Classical Sociology* 4 [2004], 31–57).

10. This movement from mixed government to checks and balances was, one suspects, decisive for the writing of the American Constitution; it allowed the founding

fathers to find functional substitutes for monarchy and aristocracy without having to conjure up actual aristocrats or a monarch.

11. Montesquieu certainly speaks of the corruption of republics and monarchies, but within a different "economy" of corruption. The problem is that despotism, being already corrupted, is incorruptible; as such the cycle of regime types is halted, with despotism becoming the "degree zero" of political life.

12. The separation of powers distinguishes between powers on an essentially functional basis (legislative as head, executive as hand) in order to uphold the generality of the law in the face of its application to particulars. Checks and balances, while still maintaining the generality of the law, must begin to undo the separation of powers, for one power cannot check another if their fields of action do not, at least minimally, overlap. The French revolutionaries were, generally, very much in favor of the separation of powers; it promised the maximum expansion of a just power. For this reason they tended to oppose checks and balances.

13. XI, 6 (second last paragraph). That a declared moderate would use such an expression should give one pause when considering his Anglophilia.

14. If Montesquieu has no general theory of history, it is because each regime type tends to institute time in its own manner. Democratic republics tend to freeze time; monarchies alone have a history, understood as a meaningful accumulation of events.

15. Law not only requires power if it is to have force, but by itself is powerless in the face of a power's desire to overcome all limits.

16. Louis Marin, *The Portrait of the King* (Minneapolis: University of Minnesota Press, 1988). That the monarch represented himself in such a manner suggests why Montesquieu was loath to speak of his symbolic power.

17. Diana J. Schaub, *Erotic Liberalism: Women and Revolution in Montesquieu's Persian Letters* (Lanham, MD: Rowman & Littlefield, 1995).

18. I want to thank Melvin Richter for pointing out in a personal communication that the term "enlightened despotism" would not have been familiar to Montesquieu.

19. Alain Grosrichard, *Structure du sérail. La fiction du despotisme asiatique dans l'Occident classique* (Paris: Seuil, 1979), 45–46.

20. Montesquieu defines despotism as having no law (II, 1) but also says, "Despotic states, which prefer simple laws, make much use of the *law of retaliation* (*loi de talion*)" (VI, 19).

21. "[M]en in these countries.... need only a name to govern them" (V, 14). And he goes on to suggest that behind the name there need not be a person, just a boot!

22. Note that for Montesquieu honor is not articulated to any law (IV, 2).

23. "A monarchy is ruined when a prince ... is more enamoured of what he fancies than of what he wills [*plus amoureux de ses fantaisies que de ses volontés*]" (VIII, 6).

24. Such a speech is discussed in Book XII, 27, 28. Honorable because the monarch sees men of merit as his equals; virtuous because he subordinates his will to the common good. In effect, there is nothing that distinguishes the monarch's speech from the patriot and aristocrat.

25. Arguably at the top the despot himself is afraid of being deposed. And at the bottom? One may well argue that if "no one is a tyrant there without at the same time being a slave" (IV, 3), one can easily be a slave without being a tyrant. But then the "pure" slave may still dream of being a tyrant.

26. Sometimes to the point of becoming a fetish: one loves the law because it is the law and seeks to subordinate oneself to ever more and ever more detailed laws.

27. For this reason, Montesquieu cannot really be considered a Germanist. Whatever he might say about German liberty, the safeguards against despotism that define monarchic rule did not come into place until long after the original barbarian invasions.

28. Thus in contrast to Montesquieu's claim that the nobles limit the monarch's will, the Abbé Bossuet claims that it is love for the monarch, a living saint, that causes the nobles to limit their their natural egoism (Luc Boltanski and Laurent Thévenot, *De la justification. Les économies de la grandeur* [Paris: Gallimard, 1991]).

29. Already in II, 4 he speaks of "mediate channels through which power flows."

30. Montesquieu, at one point refers to the English system as "a republic [that] hides under the form a monarchy" (V, 19), but given his insistence on its origins in the forests of Germany (XI, 6), one might ask if it is not rather a monarchy disguised as a republic.

31. This was a lesson that the American founding fathers did not draw from Montesquieu, though they were, in a sense, to experience it. See Richard Hofstadter, *The Idea of a Party System. The Rise of Legitimate Opposition in the United States, 1780–1840* (Berkeley: University of California Press, 1969).

32. "This nation, always heated, could more easily be led by its passions than by reason, which never produces great effects on the spirits of men" (327).

33. The implication of this passage is that each Englishman, seeing himself as equal to his peers before the law, instead of subordinating himself to the law under the sign of the people, "regard[s] himself as the monarch."

34. One cannot speak of *amour de soi* when restlessness suggests a desire to confront (as well as overcome) limits.

35. Albert Hirschman, *The Passions and the Interests* (Princeton: Princeton University Press, 1977).

36. One might recall that William Penn and his Quakers is one of the only modern examples of a democratic republic that he provides.

37. This troubled character is particularly true as regards sexual relations. English women are *"timides"*; English men lack "gallantry" (that is, women are afraid to interact with men, and men do not know how to interact with women), the result being that the men "throw themselves into a debauchery that would leave them their liberty as well as their leisure" (332).

38. "In a nation where the soul is so affected by an illness of climate that it could carry the repugnance for all things to include that of life, one sees that the most suitable government for people to whom everything can be intolerable would be the one in which they could not blame any one person for causing their sorrows" (XIV, 13). The argument, admittedly, is difficult to follow. Note that it then segues into a discussion of the uses and abuses of "impatience."

39. There are several implicit references to French sociability, particularly as it affects relations between the sexes. His favorable attitude toward the latter is suggested, for example, in XIX, 5.

40. Alain Ehrenberg, *La fatigue d'être soi* (Paris: Odile Jacob, 1998).

41. I owe this idea to Mark Blackell who argues (without reference to Montesquieu) that there is a specifically French tradition of political theory (he speaks of Rousseau, Constant, and Tocqueville) that thematizes the passions. Mark Blackell, *Symptoms of Democracy: Ambivalence and Its Limits in Modern Liberal Conceptions of the Liberal Democratic Bond* (Toronto: York University, 2004).

Part II

# Montesquieu's Legacy in Eighteenth- and Nineteenth-Century Political Thought

# 6

# Montesquieu's Constitutional Legacies

## Jacob T. Levy

There is greater continuity than has often been recognized between the "ancient constitutionalism" of medieval institutions that could check early-modern monarchs, of particular liberties and jurisdictional patchworks, and the ostensibly rationalistic, uniform, and contractarian modern constitutionalism of written constitutional texts and judicial review. In this chapter I dispute both the idea of a radical intellectual break between constitutionalism before and after the period of the 1770s through the 1790s, and the tightly related claim that modern constitutions themselves necessarily represent radical institutional and legal breaks from their societies' pasts, the claim that all that comes before a written constitution's enactment ought to be understood as so much prehistoric state-of-nature detritus. In this transition from ancient constitutionalism to modern—or, more precisely, in the transmission of ancient constitutionalism into modern—Montesquieu is the pivotal figure. In its reorganization and restatement of ancient constitutionalism, making it intellectually available to and respectable in an age of rationalist philosophes, in its account of the freedom available in modern commercial monarchies if only they remain moderate, and in its argument about what is needed to keep them moderate, *The Spirit of Laws* makes a powerful if implicit normative argument about constitutionalism. Bringing this argument out into the open can help us to understand much about the constitutionalism that has been with us since the last quarter of the eighteenth century, much that is obscured by an overemphasis on modern constitutionalism's modernity, its rationalism, and its contractarianism.

Charles McIlwain (among others) long ago noted the 1780s British and American understanding of a discontinuity between the two societies' understandings of what a constitution is, between "the new conception of the conscious formulation by a people of its fundamental law, the new definition of "constitution"; and the older traditional view in which the word was applied only to the substantive principles to be deduced from a nation's actual institutions and their development."[1]

More recently James Tully has influentially refocused attention on the discontinuity between the respect for pluralism and diversity found in ancient constitutionalism and the rationalism and monism of modern constitutionalism, derived from Enlightenment contractarianism and resulting in an "empire of uniformity."[2] Much contemporary American constitutional theory relies on just such a strongly rationalist and contractarian understanding of constitutionalism. The position described by McIlwain and that embraced by contemporary American constitutional theory are closely linked. They run together in Stanley Katz's concise account of eighteenth-century American constitutionalism, "a consciously contrived mechanism for yoking limitations on government to the will of the people in a dynamic, geographically distributed manner. American constitutionalism was thus distinguishable at the time of the American Revolution from the organic and taxonomic British notion of a constitution as little more than a historical description of the proper functions of a government."[3] And indeed something like this picture—modern, American constitutionalism as rationalist and contractarian and, therefore, constraining on the state, as against ancient, British constitutionalism that was customary and, therefore, descriptive rather than normative—is, I think, pretty common in the American academy, when ancient constitutionalism is noticed at all.

This slippage between contractarianism and constitutionalism is not necessary. When Locke developed his contractarian theory and deployed it as a critical tool, he did not have any particular English constitutional moment that he could equate to entering into the contract nor any charter (not even Magna Carta) that he read as literally enacting the contract. But the slippage has become routine.

Contractarian constitutionalism can emphasize a kind of democratic positivism, relying on the constitution that a people in fact did agree to ordain and establish. Or it can emphasize the kind of rights theory that derives from hypothetical contractarianism; a constitution is understood as protecting those rights that free, equal, and rational persons would have agreed to under some counterfactual set of circumstances. And one does see disagreements about whether the positivist kind of contractarianism is the more important strand or whether, as Walter Murphy would have it, the rationally discoverable objective values of individual rights and equality before the law are the essence of modern constitutionalism, taking priority over any pedigree.[4] This position allows Murphy and others to identify Britain as (modern) constitutionalist, because of its adherence in practice to the relevant values; from positivist contractarians one hears instead the claim that Britain has no constitution.

But what is most striking is that the British "ancient" constitution does not enter into either picture at all; the supposed discontinuity between ancient and modern constitutionalism is so stark that the former does not even come up in discussions of the latter.[5]

The continuities between ancient and modern constitutionalism run both backward and forward. The ostensibly distinctive features of modern constitutionalism were present in ancient constitutionalism; and the ancient constitutionalist legacy was not so decisively abandoned during the late 1700s as has sometimes been thought. Four continuities are noteworthy, though only the third can be examined at length here.

First, ancient constitutionalism had, by the eighteenth century, developed a very clear sense that a state's constitution provided binding normative constraints on state action, that is, constraints on what ought to be considered legal. This has been obscured by the anomalous British case, with its doctrine of absolute parliamentary sovereignty. The tug of war between the parlements and the Crown in France was certainly not modern judicial review; but it shows a very clear sense on the parlementaire side that France's ancient constitution constrained what could be understood as legal. And ancient-constitutionalist theory had contained the idea of limitations on the state enforceable through the state's own legal system for many generations before the development of modern judicial review in early America. The theory of customary-legal and ancient-constitutional limitations on state power enforceable by the judiciary, evident from both Coke and Mornay, was brought into the eighteenth century by Montesquieu, married to a doctrine of the status of the judicial function, and transmitted to America.

Second, the understanding of a constitution as established by written documents, contracts, or covenants at a particular moment in historical time was not new to the late eighteenth century. Especially through the "constitutions" of free cities, but also through those of intermediate bodies including guilds and the Freemasons, and through the covenantal tradition among dissenting churches, ostensibly modern constitutions had been a component of complex ancient constitutionalism for centuries. That is to say, the most distinctive formal traits of constitutionalism as developed in late eighteenth-century America and France had been components of Europe's complex constitutional patchwork of institutional foundations for many centuries. Written documents deliberately enacted and understood in contractarian terms were not the whole of ancient constitutionalism, but neither were they alien to it.

Third, and most centrally for this chapter, important constitutional theorists of the late eighteenth and early nineteenth centuries such as Madison and Constant show strong ongoing influences from Montesquieu and ancient constitutionalism. Such theorists are more representative of modern constitutionalism than are purely rationalistic contractarians. The radical dichotomization of ancient and modern constitutionalism can only be sustained by disregarding both Montesquieu, who provided ancient constitutionalism with its culminating statement, and his successors, who attempted to adapt it to post-revolutionary and republican societies.

Fourth, modern constitutionalist practice was not so consistently rationalist-contractarian as it has been made out to be. The French revolutionary abolition of feudalism makes for a dramatic synecdoche for constitutional founding moments. But the American constitution of the 1780s, like most liberal democratic constitutions since then, did not treat the constitution's enactment as a complete abolition of preexisting political institutions or social distinctions. France was unusual in consigning its prefounding state and society to the state of nature. More typical have been federations that incorporated, and entrenched, pre-existing states or provinces and constitutional orders that recognized, protected, and even relied upon the continuity of ethnic or linguistic cleavages in society. Pre-founding social and political facts are typically built into the new constitutional order, not wished away.

If there is continuity to be had from before the American founding and the French Revolution to after, we will find it in the transition from Montesquieu to the generation of Madison and Constant. Some readers will find this insistence on the importance of Montesquieu an overemphasis of the obvious. But Montesquieu is surprisingly and strangely absent from many discussions of the break between ancient and modern constitutionalism; or if he is present at all, it is only in the context of the American appropriation of the idea of a separation of powers, with no attention paid to the defense of urban and provincial liberties, the parlementaire cause, or institutional and legal pluralism.[6]

## Ancient Constitutions as Legal Limits

The idea that a polity's constitution could be invoked as placing normative and, eventually, legal limitations on the exercise of state power is much older than its American instantiation.[7] The idea of constitutionalism as it developed in early modernity turned the descriptive into the normative. During those centuries, references to the "ancient constitutions"—and, later, "the ancient [or medieval, or Gothic] constitution," singular—of a European polity ceased to mean purely a sociological description of the laws and statutes of the realm. "Ancient constitution" came to denote the fundamental governing arrangements of the polity, innovation against which—in particular by centralizing monarchs—was understood as illegal. The question of what could be done about such illegality met with a variety of responses. But the basic doctrine that even the most powerful actor or body in the polity was constrained, not only by natural law or religious duty but also by the obligation to respect the ancient constitution, was the unifying theme of ancient constitutionalism. If the phrase was characteristically English, the underlying doctrines were common throughout Western Europe.[8] "[I]t entails no anachronism to describe as 'constitutionalist' [fifteenth- and sixteenth-century] ideas to the effect that power ought to be exercised within institutionally determined limits."[9]

Ancient constitutionalism has been the subject of much criticism as a set of legal or historical claims, above all by Pocock; it incorporated stories about medieval pasts that were often simply false. But this should not lead us to overlook the centrality of ancient constitutionalism to early modern political and legal theory.[10]

The supposed "ancient constitution" of European polities typically included some version of the estates or orders of the realm (the Estates General, the English Parliament) and the "ancient liberties" of self-governing cities, provinces, and other regional jurisdictions. Often these more local units in turn had internal constitutional requirements involving the local Estates; this remained true for some French provinces until the Revolution. In the "composite kingdoms" of the early modern era each province was understood to be under the monarch's jurisdiction somewhat independently—as indeed remains the case to this day in a handful of jurisdictions, such as the Isle of Man and the Channel Islands—and to have a right to its autonomy and distinctive traditions. Even after the Act of Union of 1707 Scotland retained its own legal system, separate and in important respects different from the English, though 1707 is generally and reasonably taken to mark the final transition away from composite monarchy on the island of Great Britain. (The eighteenth-century disputes about the constitution of the composite kingdom centered on Ireland, and later on the North American colonies.)[11]

The privileges of merchant and craft guilds, and sometimes of the locally appropriate established church, were also sometimes understood to have a kind of constitutional, guaranteed standing. Early modern common law judges in England were understood to occupy a constitutional office. And in France, the parlements—judicial bodies of predominantly aristocratic makeup that had the traditional role of registering royal edicts but could refuse to do so and remonstrate against them if they viewed those edicts as unconstitutional, the most important of which was in Paris but which also existed in a number of the provinces—were the final pillar of ancient constitutionalism. Readers of Bodin or Hobbes, the great intellectual opponents of ancient constitutionalism, will recognize each of these institutions and the idea that they might have rights and powers that limit those of the monarch, from the caricature and attack to which they are subjected by those authors. But it is important always to remember that Bodin and Hobbes were not fencing with phantoms; they were engaging with very real ancient constitutionalist beliefs.

It is true that by the 1770s the British constitution did not include any legal limitations on the legislative authority of Parliament. But the equation of "the British constitution" with parliamentary absolutism was a post-1688 innovation. "The idea of an ancient constitution" in Britain "would ultimately yield to the theory of parliamentary sovereignty."[12] Nowhere else did the estates gain such a decisive victory over the monarchy; nowhere else did the defense of the estates' rights evolve into the doctrine that the estates were all-powerful. Sixteenth- and seventeenth-century Whiggish ancient constitutionalism was much like ancient constitutionalism as a general European school of thought, unlike its Blackstonian successor. And the American intellectual climate of the 1770s and 80s, in which the new constitutionalism took shape owed more to seventeenth-century Whiggism than to eighteenth-century Blackstonianism.

Pocock's emphasis on the literal insularity of the common law mind has had tremendous influence and has also obscured some of the continuities between English and continental ancient constitutionalisms.[13] Ancient constitutionalism did take a distinctive form in England, and by the late eighteenth century had mutated into a unique form. But for most of the preceding two centuries, ancient constitutionalism provided a partially shared and mutually influencing vocabulary for politics and law across much of Europe. When Burke appealed to the French revolutionaries to return to the ancient constitution of Europe, of which the English constitution was merely the surviving exemplar, he was repeating an old trope.[14]

The eighteenth-century Whig Molesworth translated Hotman's *Francogallia*, one of the manifestoes of French Huguenot ancient constitutionalism, into English under the telling description *Franco-Gallia or an account of the ancient free state of France and most other parts of Europe, before the loss of their liberties*. Molesworth's lengthy preface explicitly linked Whiggism with "Gothick" constitutionalism, and discussed "our just Rights and Liberties, together with the solid Foundations of our Constitution: Which, in truth, is not ours only, but that of almost all Europe besides."[15] "This Book," Molesworth maintains, "gives an Account of the Ancient Free States of above Three Parts in Four of Europe,"[16] and the defense of the theory of such governments would be an aid to Whiggish defenders of the ostensibly restorative Glorious Revolution. "My Notion of a Whig," Molesworth continued, "I mean of a real Whig [...] is, That he is one who is exactly for keeping up to the Strictness of the true old Gothick Constituion [...] A true Whig is of the Opinion, that the Executive Power has as just a Title to the Allegiance and Obedience of the Subject, according to the Rules of known Laws enacted by the Legislative, as the Subject has to Protection, Liberty, and Property; and so on the contrary [i.e., 'and vice-versa']."[17]

The preface quickly becomes a treatise on this "true Whiggism," this defense of the old British, and old European, constitution. Whiggism supports resistance to arbitrary rule; the rule of law, and the subjection of the king to law; and religious toleration, including the extension of civil rights to persons of whatever religion (including Catholicism) who will affirm loyalty to the principles of the Revolution. Molesworth insists on the need for parliamentary elections every three years at the most and annual meetings of Parliament; short durations on tax and expenditure bills; union with Scotland and Ireland "on equal terms" rather than governing "by Force" (Molesworth was a longtime opponent of Parliament's claim to legislate for and rule over Ireland); electoral reform and the abolition of rotten boroughs; and vigilance against standing armies. The political agenda is that of eighteenth-century Whiggism; the intellectual justification offered is that of sixteenth-century French ancient constitutionalism. The two are treated as seamlessly continuous.

As Ernest Barker has shown, *Franco-Gallia*'s rival as the major text of French Huguenot ancient constitutionalism, the *Vindiciae Contra Tyrannos*—printed in England during both the Civil War and the Glorious Revolution—may have played its own part in shaping Whig thought, both directly and indirectly through its influence on seventeenth-century Dutch thought. Barker makes a case for Locke having learned directly from the *Vindiciae*, for the ancient-constitutionalist doctrine of resistance informing the modern contractarian one.[18] The Amsterdam Locke fled to and wrote in had earlier served as refuge for many of the Huguenots exiles. And the Whiggism exemplified by Molesworth and theorized by Locke was, of course, one of the major intellectual inheritances of the American revolutionaries.

## Montesquieu's Constitutionalism

We need not trace the path from ancient constitutionalism to early America from the Huegenots through Locke or Molesworth. A much more certain and direct path is to be found through Montesquieu.[19]

The constitutionalism of *The Spirit of Laws* goes well beyond the elements most familiar to American readers, the separation of powers (and the rule of law and independent judiciary that are tied up with it), and the theory of republican confederation. In thinking about Montesquieu's constitutionalism, it helps to begin with a few explicit reminders. At least, to French readers and to Montesquieu scholars these will be reminders; but some of these points remain little appreciated by Anglophone and particularly American readers, even those well versed in the history of political ideas.

First, Montesquieu was not a republican. The American founding generation (and some French revolutionaries) sometimes willfully and sometimes ignorantly failed to appreciate this, and some strands of Anglophone Montesquieu commentary have persisted in the misreading.[20] Montesquieu's analysis of republics as states oriented toward virtue and the resistance of luxury was an indictment of republicanism as being hopelessly anachronistic for an age of large commercial monarchies. Americans under the influence of English commonwealth and Whig traditions took the equation of republics with virtue as praise for the former. But Montesquieu was too persuaded of the merits of modern liberty, commerce, and refinement in arts and manners to have much affection for Spartan, monastic virtue. Nor was he impressed by attempts to combine republican forms of government with modernity and commerce. The Netherlands and Venice embraced commerce at the expense of virtue and thus failed at republicanism, falling into corruption.[21] Finally, republicanism as such was certainly no guarantor of freedom. "In the Italian republics, where the three powers are united, there is less liberty than in our [i.e., the Western European moderate] monarchies."[22]

This should affect how we read Montesquieu's famous discussion of England (particularly in XI, 6, which is too often taken in isolation). When he refers to England as a "republic [that] hides under the form of a monarchy,"[23] he does not mean that the monarchical form is unimportant. That form makes it possible to sustain some of the advantages of republican liberty in a state that is both too large and too commercial to actually survive as a republic. Cromwell's republican experiment is discussed with derision, and the memory of it shadows the discussion in XI, 6 of what would happen if the executive power were not properly separated from the legislative by entrusting it to an independent king. The lesson of the English devotion to freedom is not to turn to republicanism but to see that large modern commercial monarchies can be liberty's truest political home.

This reminder also serves to correct the view, common in the debates of the American founding generation, that Montesquieu's ideal constitution was the confederated republic described in IX, 1–3.[24] It is true that he held that confederation was the best option for republics, since it allowed them to gain the defensive advantages of size while still remaining small enough to remain republics. Small, virtuous, and noncommercial republics could maintain their independence by banding together; the Swiss had followed this route. But Switzerland does not displace England as the primary object of Montesquieu's constitutional admiration; it was anachronistic and of no real interest to moderns. A large monarchy, not a large confederation of republics, was the proper locus for modern freedom.

Second, even with the first reminder in mind, Montesquieu's admiration for the English constitution was not unqualified. In II, 4, a tremendously important chapter for understanding Montesquieu's constitutionalism (along with its companion chapters, VIII, 6–9), he insists on the tight relationships among moderate lawful (i.e., nondespotic) monarchy, the rights and liberties of intermediate bodies, and respect for the ancient constitution and fundamental laws. "Intermediate, subordinate, and dependent powers constitute the nature of monarchical government, that is, of the government in which one alone governs by fundamental laws."²⁵ And, since the English Civil War, an increasingly centralized England has lost these powers. "If you abolish the prerogatives of the lords, clergy, nobility, and towns in a monarchy, you will soon have a popular state or else a despotic state [. . .] In order to favor liberty, the English have removed all the intermediate powers that formed their monarchy. They are quite right to preserve that liberty," he sardonically concludes; "if they were to lose it, they would be one of the most enslaved peoples on earth" because of their abolition of intermediate powers.²⁶ This perilous state of affairs dates from the days of Cromwell: "the English nobility was buried with Charles I in the debris of the throne."²⁷

This ancient constitutionalism—the commitment to the liberties of cities and provinces, ecclesiastical rights, the privileges of the nobility, the authority of the estates—is the context for Montesquieu's genuinely central preoccupation with the separation of powers and the theory of an independent judiciary and the rule of law with which it is inextricably tied up. There are few themes in the whole work on which Montesquieu offers such a clear, explicit, and unambiguous normative position as the need for executive, legislative, and judicial powers to be separated for a government to be moderate and its citizens to be free. The emphasis on when and how a person can be punished by the state, on criminal and judicial questions, and on the despotic possibility that persons might be subjected to lawless despotic punishment pervades the work.

Montesquieu infelicitously defined freedom as the right to do what the laws permit, an idea that, taken out of context, allowed no less than Isaiah Berlin to misidentify him as a theorist of positive freedom.²⁸ But these words in the context of *The Spirit of Laws* mean something quite different from what they would mean coming from, say, Rousseau. Their importance is negative: to insist that a person who has obeyed the promulgated law cannot be arbitrarily arrested or punished. "The laws" here does not mean the body of commands of the sovereign, and individual freedom is very far from being equated with absorption into a sovereign general will. Montesquieu has little sense of laws as deliberate creations or acts of will. He respects the role of careful legislation, but that role is one of incremental reform of the body of known, inherited law. The freedom to do what the laws permit is the freedom to live according to traditional liberties and settled understandings, secure in one's sense of security from the possibility of arrest, imprisonment, torture, execution, confiscation, and so on—and this is the meaning of the equation elsewhere, also easily misunderstood, of freedom with security.

And this freedom depends on the separation of powers, which is to say on the denial of judicial capacities (trial, conviction, punishment) to either a legislature passing what we would call "bills of attainder" or to an executive imprisoning or punishing enemies without benefit of trial. But the usual understanding of Montesquieu on the separation of powers, the rule of law, and the independence of the judiciary underemphasizes his statements on the judiciary in general at the expense of his discussion of that in England. In particular, it loses sight of his recurrent characterization of the judiciary as the depository of the laws.[29]

Of all the ancient-constitutional institutions defended by Montesquieu, it is the French parlements, lying at the intersection of fundamental laws, provincial autonomy, noble authority, and judicial independence, that most fully exemplify his approach. The parlements were the judicial depositories of the laws, including the customary laws of the various provinces, as well as, on their own self-understanding, the fundamental and constitutional law of the kingdom as a whole. Between the Bourbon triumph of the Fronde and the final, successful, parlementaire insistence that the Estates General be summoned at the beginning of the Revolution, the parlements engaged in a sometimes-interrupted but never-abandoned struggle with the Crown, both over the limits of royal authority and over the limits of the parlements' rights to refuse to register royal edicts and so to deny them the force of law. The parlements stood as the independent judiciary in Montesquieu's theory, but independent not only because the fundamental law said so. Kings who innovated against the ancient constitution could innovate against the judiciary as well. They were independent in large part because they rested on an independent social base of authority, the nobility, and in some part because they embodied provincial autonomy, where the provinces were understood to be genuinely differentiated from the center with their own laws and liberties. The fundamental law was protected by vesting it in the judiciary; the judicial power and provincial autonomy were protected by vesting them in the nobility. "The nobility should be hereditary. In the first place, it is so by its nature; and, besides, it must have a great interest in preserving its prerogatives, odious in themselves, and which, in a free state, must always be endangered."[30] This is a constitutionalism that does not deny the reality of social cleavages and distinctions outside the formal law. Indeed it is a constitutionalism that seeks to make use of those cleavages and distinctions—even when "odious"—to bolster the fundamental law that keeps kings in check and citizens free. It is ancient constitutionalism in the service of ends that are recognizable to modern jurists.

## Responding to Montesquieu

An image of modern constitutionalism as rationalist, contractarian, and radically discontinuous with ancient constitutionalism requires thinking that Montesquieu was decisively rejected or completely forgotten by the two generations that followed him, the generations in which modern constitutional theory and practice took shape. In fact Montesquieu's ancient constitutionalism received a complex variety of responses among liberal and constitutional theorists of the late eighteenth and early nineteenth centuries, including the theorists of the American and French revolutionary and constitutional experiences. Decisive rejection was not the typical modern constitutionalist stance. Rather there was a deliberate attempt to incorporate elements and insights from Montesquieu's theory, to simulate the desirable effects of ancient constitutionalism even after its traditional forms became anachronistic.

Montesquieu's constitutional theory suggested that a large, institutionally complex and diverse kingdom might offer its subjects more freedom than other forms of government, provided that intermediate powers and bodies were respected and not suppressed, and that uniformity of law was no great virtue in a free society, typically aimed at by men of system who would suppress liberty for its sake. Freedom was best to be protected by a combination of the rule of law and a constitution in which provincial or cultural diversity, institutional variety, and a range of degrees of privileges and immunities could check the tendencies of a monarch to centralize and self-aggrandize—something like a reformed French constitution, with the parlements and the provinces restored to their proper status and much of the Bourbon centralization undone.

In the years leading up to the Revolution, intellectual movements for constitutional reform pulled in two opposed directions. On one side were the physiocrats, whose priorities were rationalization and centralization, with a concomitant increase in royal authority. They understood the traditional constraints to hopelessly complicate the task of creating a reasonable fiscal order; hence, Turgot's famous complaint that the French "nation has absolutely no constitution; it is a society made up of diverse orders only badly united."[31] The parliamentarians and their supporters, by contrast, sought to reinvigorate and reassert provincial and urban liberties, parliamentary privileges, and eventually, the rights of the Estates.

"In the second half of the eighteenth century, the Parlement [of Paris] became far more militant. It was certainly inspired by Montesquieu's *The Spirit of Laws*—the so-called 'Grand Remonstances' of 1753 contained much of Montesquieu's own language and vocabulary—but, in addition, the magistrates had clearly lost their sense of awe for the king's authority."[32] From the 1750s until the summoning of the Estates General, the parlements fitfully came to embrace a constitutional theory of parliamentary solidarity, holding that the various parlements had the right and the obligation to defend one another, that they were tied to one another horizontally and not only each tied vertically to the crown. This doctrine justified remonstrances and strikes by the provincial parlements in support of the Parisian body in its especially frequent conflicts with the Bourbons. It likewise made the important Parisian parlement an advocate for provincial liberties and an opponent of the power of royally appointed Intendants to rule the provinces.

This avowedly constitutionalist and sometimes self-consciously Montesquieian movement was of course not the whole of the conflict between king and parlement during the pre-Revolutionary crisis. But even some of those who were hostile to aristocratic privileges as such, including Lafayette, rallied to the parlementaire cause when that was associated with the rule of law, provincial liberties, and the Estates.[33] And during the final crisis, the parlements articulated this constitutional theory to justify their continued resistance and, ultimately, the summoning of the Estates. The remonstrances of 1787–88 were filled with the ideas of parlementaire solidarity and provincial liberty, of the partly contractual and partly traditional right of the provinces to be governed according to their customs and by their own Estates. Uniformity was unjust; parlements and Estates were the right of each of the nations and provinces that made up the kingdom. The provincial parlements declared the provinces to be nations bound to the crown by treaties "independent and sovereign countries united only to the Crown of France under express and formal complete reservations of their privileges, their rights, their liberties, and their traditions."[34] And their Parisian counterpart agreed.

> [T]he Parlement of Paris persisted in classifying among the fundamental laws of the French kingdom the traditions of the provinces. "By a sacred oath," it declared it in its Remonstrances of April 30, 1788, "is all of France bound to the sovereign; but the King does not reign in all the provinces on the same basis: in Normandy, in Brittany, in Guienne, in Languedoc, in Provence, in Dauphiné, in Alsace, in Burgundy, in Franche-Comté, in the conquered countries, in the allied countries, various conditions regulate obedience. In Béarn, the first article of the traditional constitution is an oath of the king to respect its privileges. [. . .] The will of the King, to be right, must thus vary according to the provinces. It is not the courts that so constrain him, but principles. What fortunate constraints! That secure the foundations of legitimate power! Each province requires a Parlement for the defense of its particular rights. These rights are not mere figments, these Parlements are not vain institutions; without them the king could say to Brittany, I deny you your Estates; to Guyenne, I abrogate your treaty; to the people of Béarn, I will no longer take your oath [. . .]; to all the provinces [. . .] I abolish your freedoms, I destroy your Parlements. [. . .] For your Parlement, these principles, or rather, Lord, those principles of the state which are entrusted to it, are immutable." On the eve of the Revolution, there was thus a right of the provinces. The Parlement

proclaimed it constitutional, and maintained that it remained so even where its exercise had been suspended.[35]

The parlementaire tradition of ancient constitutionalism, mixing contract with custom and emphasizing the evils of uniformity, centralization, and royal power, remained closely associated with Montesquieu. Responses to him were often in part responses to it, and vice versa.

Destutt de Tracy (1754–1836) was one of the primary intellectual forces in the group of rationalist radical liberals who came to be known as ideologues.[36] Tracy's book-length *Commentary and Review* of Montesquieu's *The Spirit of Laws*, a work translated into English and lavishly praised by no less than Thomas Jefferson, offers one extreme of the reception of Montesquieu. The *Commentary* offers a book-by-book critique and reconstruction of *The Spirit of Laws*, sometimes going through a chapter almost line-by-line, sometimes critiquing an entire book in a few pages.[37] Often through the work Tracy purports to derive the essential truths from Montesquieu's notoriously chaotic presentation, but these "truths" are inevitably republican and libertarian truths, recognizing only the sovereignty of the people on one hand and the liberty of persons on the other. Whenever Montesquieu's views are unambiguously on the side of complexity, diversity, intermediate bodies, and balances of power, Tracy attacks them. "This system of balancing," for example, "I consider as erroneous and indefensible; it originates in imperfect combinations, which confer powers of defense on particular personages, under the idea of protecting them from the general interest." (117)

The portions of *The Spirit of Laws* that were most influential in the debates about ancient liberties, centralization, and diversity include Book XIX and the chapter "Of Ideas of Uniformity" from Book XXIX, as well as the defense of intermediate powers under monarchies in Books XI and XII. About intermediate powers Tracy says much the same that he does about balances of powers or interests: if sovereignty vests in the people, then an intermediate body with rights to resist (whether hereditary or not) is necessarily an illegitimate partial interest. From Book XIX Tracy claims that only one good principle can be extracted—that "for the best laws it is necessary that the mind should first be prepared by cultivation," a principle that (unsurprisingly) dictates representative democracy so that the laws will not be out of step with the "general disposition of the nation" (203). Montesquieu's other arguments for legislative caution, for leaving habits and manners alone, for not seeking to correct all errors, are rapidly dismissed.

In lieu of an extended commentary of his own on Book XXIX, Tracy appends a previously unpublished essay by Condorcet, "Observations on the Twenty-Ninth Book of *The Spirit of the Laws*." In discussing the chapter "Of the spirit of the legislator," Condorcet simply observes that "the spirit of a legislator ought to be justice ... It is not by the spirit of moderation, but by the spirit of justice, that criminal laws should be mild, that civil laws should tend to equality, and the laws of the municipal administration to liberty and prosperity"—a distinction that fairly sums up much of what divided Montesquieu from the philosophes.

Condorcet's greatest criticism is reserved for the chapter on uniformity. "Uniformity in laws may be established without trouble, and without producing any evil effects by the change." (274) "As truth, reason, justice, the rights of man, the interests of property, of liberty, of security, are in all places the same; we cannot discover why all the provinces of a state, or even all states, should not have the same civil and criminal laws, and the same laws relative to commerce. A good law should be good for all men. A true proposition is true every where" (274). This is the crux of the argument for uniformity and, necessarily, an indictment of decentralized institutions that might come to different conclusions and of the idea that morally desirable liberty could be found in a patchwork of such institutions.

The transition from Montesquieu to Tracy would seem to bear out the radical dichotomy between ancient and modern constitutionalism. The ideologue's constitutionalism is grounded in a radically individualistic social contract theory, envisions the deliberate creation of political institutions on a rational basis, and leaves no room for institutional plurality of the ancient constitutionalist sort. But Tracy's was not the only attempt to come to terms with Montesquieu's legacy during and after the age of revolutions.

Tracy is all but forgotten today; his friend Benjamin Constant is hailed as one of the progenitors of liberal constitutionalism. And Constant's understanding of constitutions, even long after the French Revolution, was neither rationalist nor contractarian. "Constitutions are seldom made by the will of men. Time makes them. They are introduced gradually and in an almost imperceptible way. Yet there are circumstances in which it becomes indispensible to make a constitution. But then do only what is indispensible. Leave room for time and experience, so that these two reforming powers may direct your already constituted powers in the improvement of what has been done and the completion of what is still to be done."[38]

The *Commentary*'s antipathy toward Bonaparte is one of its few points of agreement with the great anti-Napoleonic work written by Constant, *The Spirit of Conquest and Usurpation* (1814). In that work's criticism of the centralization and rationalization of political life under the Empire, of the Napoleonic Code and the suppression of local loyalties and culture, Constant modestly suggests that there is little point in adding to Montesquieu's own writings on uniformity. But his two chapters on the subject surpass Montesquieu's brief pages in their clarity and the quality of their argument. Stripped of Montesquieu's obscure references (and of Burke's rhetorical excesses), and explicitly normative in a way that Tocqueville's *Old Regime* was not to be, they provide what may be the liberal canon's most powerful defense of institutional diversity, cultural variety, and local autonomy. Tracy's implicit critique of Bonaparte consisted primarily of defenses of democracy and commercial freedom, but Constant's attacked the imperial apotheosis of Bourbon and Jacobin centralization.

Constant's criticism of centralization and uniformity was a careful one and all the more effective for that. While he gives weight to people's attachments to custom and tradition, he insists that time can never help to sanctify abuses such as slavery. He freely admits that some kinds of local diversity may be irrational on their face and would never be constructed deliberately. But he maintains that this is not an appropriate standard of evaluation when deciding what to do with already-existing diversity. He argues both against the spirit of system that accompanies and initiates governors' desire to rationalize, and in defense of the sentiments that attach people to their local traditions and rules. He embraces the idea of change and progress but insists that it should be allowed to come in its own time and by free choice. The doors of abbeys and convents should be opened, rather than shutting the institutions down; an irrational winding road might prompt the construction of a competing straight one, but there is no need for a ban on the use of the former. Constant here makes explicit an argument against the spirit of system that Smith had made[39] but Montesquieu and Burke did not (though both clearly believed it; it lies under Montesquieu's mention of the desire to emulate Charlemagne). The desire to create order and rationality in society need not be destructive in itself; but it is too easily joined with force. The emphasis on men of system or the spirit of uniformity rather than on system or uniformity themselves emphasizes this worry about temperament and temptation.[40]

Montesquieu's example was much on Constant's mind as he composed his work in exile—the *Fragments . . . on the Possibility of a Republican Constitution in a Large Country* as well as the work that would become the *Principes de Politique* of 1806–1810, which together provide the substance (and most of the words) of Constant's later political writings. (The two were originally envisioned as one *The Spirit of Laws*–style opus.) As he read Montesquieu while trying to write his own work, he wrote in his journal, "What a keen and profound eye! All that he said, even in the smallest things, proves true every day."[41] The influence on the work during that era was so profound that de Staël noticed it much later; upon the publication of *Conquest and Usurpation* (mostly adapted from the *Fragments* and *Principes*) she complimented the work but asked whether the style "à la Montesquieu" was really suited to the times.

When Constant advised Bonaparte on the creation of a new constitution during the Hundred Days, he argued in favor of a hereditary aristocracy, which was "indispensable" for a constitutional monarchy. Looking back on this episode in his *Mémoires sur les Cent-Jours*, Constant changed his mind. He said that he, like Montesquieu, had been "seduced" by the example of the British constitution. Here Constant himself criticizes the creation of a new, imperial, aristocracy but not on rationalist or egalitarian grounds. Instead, he maintains that "nothing is created by artifice" in politics (317). "The creative force in politics, like the vital force in the physical world, cannot be supplemented by any act of will or by any act of law"; rather, the spirit of the age and of a people would in some important way shape political developments and institutions. This is a Montesquieuian critique of the Montesquieuian emphasis on an aristocracy and returned Constant to one of the themes of *Conquest and Usurpation*: Bonaparte's status as a usurper, the inability to create new bloodlines and institutions and traditions from scratch that would have the same perceived legitimacy as those that had come before. Moreover, it recalls the comment that it would be irrational to deliberately create the diversity in local laws, weights, measures, and so on that Constant defended in his chapter on uniformity.

In other words, Constant was torn between two Montesquieuian impulses. He perceived the need for an intermediate and independent body of aristocrats to balance the Emperor; but such a body would be a deliberate and artificial creation, out of keeping with the spirit of the nation and of the age. In his later writings and political work under the Restoration it seems to me that we can see the same dynamic. The social background, the spirit of the society in which Constant lived, was one that had been shaped by the Revolution and what followed it. Counterrevolution no more appealed to him in the 1820s than it had in the 1790s;[42] he always held that counterrevolution would be at odds with changes in social character that had taken place. The argument in *Conquest and Usurpation* that political reforms should not outpace social change and that customs should be allowed to evolve freely meshes perfectly with the view that political reactions should not attempt to undo social change that has already taken place. Indeed it meshes with the account of the importance of social change over time in "Liberty of the Ancients and Moderns." Constant's constitutional project was one of trying to simulate or recreate the benefits of a Montesquieuian ancient constitution in an age when that constitution's social bases were lost and anachronistic.

For Constant, it was perfectly possible to perceive freedom in the ancient constitution—whether that of France or that of the more pluralistic, more decentralized Holy Roman Empire[43]—without hoping for its resurrection, to see aristocratic privileges and particular liberties as having helped to protect liberty from monarchs without proposing that they be restored. But he, unlike Tracy, thought there were crucial lessons to be learned from the ancient constitution and that there was a need to undo the excesses of revolutionary/ Bonapartist centralization and rationalization. Institutions that might not have been rationally justifiable from first principles could nonetheless provide desirable constitutional counterbalances to the concentration of power. For Tracy, the rational unjustifiability of the institutions was all that was needed to condemn them. But Constant understood that such institutions could not be recreated or replaced at will; their desirable effects stemmed in part from their appearance of permanence and from the sentiments of attachment that had developed around them. New protections of diversity, new kinds of decentralized power, would be necessary for an age in which the ancient constitution had been swept away. These themes would persist a generation later, in Tocqueville's famous lament for the lost possibility of building modern constitutionalism on France's and Europe's ancient constitutionalist foundations.[44]

In the early United States, too, older views left too great a legacy on the most important constitutional theories for the "modern" constitutionalism developed in the 1770s and 80s to be considered a radical break. The most interesting and the best-known disagreement between Jefferson and Madison highlights the latter's Montesquieuianism, his ongoing desire to simulate the desirable effects of ancient constitutionalism. In Federalist 49, against Jefferson's argument (in the *Notes on the State of Virginia*) in favor of frequent recourse to constitutional conventions, Madison argues that

> frequent appeals would in great measure deprive the government of that veneration, which time bestows on every thing, and without which perhaps the wisest and freest governments would not possess the requisite stability. [. . .] When the examples, which fortify opinion, are antient as well as numerous, they are known to have a double effect. In a nation of philosophers, this consideration ought to be disregarded. A reverence for the laws, would be sufficiently inculcated by the voice of an enlightened reason. But a nation of philosophers is as little to be expected as the philosophical race of kings wished for by Plato. And in every other nation, the most rational government will not find it a superfluous advantage, to have the prejudices of the community on its side.

In correspondence, Jefferson subsequently argued that the dead having no rights, and the earth belonging in usufruct to the living, it was illegitimate for one generation to legislate for another.[45] This was the opportunity for Jefferson's famous proposal that all laws, debts, and constitutions be canceled every generation. Madison dryly responded that Jefferson's doctrine might not be "in all respects compatible with the course of human affairs."[46] With regard to constitutions in particular, however powerful Jefferson's theoretical point might be, it "seems liable in practice to some very powerful objections. Would not a Government so often revised become too mutable to retain those prejudices in its favor which antiquity inspires, and which are perhaps a salutary aid to the most rational Government in the most enlightened age?" Madison placed little faith in the pure enlightened rationalism Jefferson looked toward. Ancient constitutionalism was in part a result of institutions acquiring normative force simply in virtue of their age; and that was a real advantage of ancient constitutionalism. Jefferson's idea would prevent the American constitution from gradually acquiring the same advantage, and so Madison politely but firmly dissented.

James Tully treats Paine as exemplary of the modern turn in American constitutional thought and *The Rights of Man* as a definitive statement of modern constitutionalism. But Paine was far from typical in his enthusiasm for radical, and institutionally simple, democracy. (He was closely associated with the first constitution of independent Pennsylvania, an outlier among the early state constitutions, with a unicameral legislature that was effectively unconstrained by other branches.) At the other extreme was John Adams—the openly Montesquieuian Anglophile with both unconcealed contempt for Paine and an interpretation of the state constitutions as squarely within the mixed, balanced, ancient-constitutional tradition. But if anyone is to be understood as representing the mainstream of early American constitutional thought, it must surely be neither Paine nor Adams but Madison. And Madison's constitutionalism, like Constant's, represented an ongoing attempt to apply Montesquieuian and ancient-constitutionalist ideas to new social and political realities. Jefferson, Paine, and Tracy represent a strand of modern constitutional thought, but we cannot allow them to stand in for the whole of it.

## Continuities and Otherwise

None of this is to deny that something changed in the second half of the eighteenth century. Written contractarian or covenantal constitutions, enacted at a particular moment in time and subject to deliberate alteration, were by 1800 not simply a component of constitutionalism. They were predominant. Henceforth, ancient-constitutionalist inheritances would at most find their place in the authoritative written constitutional document. Moreover, the longstanding idea that a constitution set legal limits on all branches of the state, and the theory of judicial authority that this implied, finally coalesced into a fairly fully worked out account of judicial review of legislation, not only of executive and police activity. And, with the American development of the constitutional convention, traditional paradoxes involving how a constitution could be not only stable and constraining but also changeable were finally resolved. This in turn reinforced both the turn to constitutional texts and the development of judicial review, since the constitutional convention or constituting power must approve something—always, it turns out, some document—all at once; and the supremacy of that something to any and all branches of the constituted government is no longer so difficult to understand. The predominance of written and enacted constitutional documents, the emergence of full-fledged judicial review, and the innovation of constitutional conventions left constitutionalism a much changed theory and practice.

Indeed, the variant of modern constitutionalism that took hold among many French republicans and their admirers—think of Sièyes—left no or almost no space for ancient constitutional inheritances; and the radical French republican tradition was of course tremendously influential throughout Europe and beyond. Constant's writings were widely read by liberal-republican revolutionaries in Europe and Latin America in the years leading up to 1848; but so were Tracy's. The influence of Bentham and his followers grew over time as well, and their constitutionalism often veered toward rationalist constructions.

In the wake of the Enlightenment and the age of revolutions, the idea that institutions could be altered by deliberate design, and that leaving them in place therefore demanded rational justification, became all but irresistible. And those who saw advantages in not calling every institution into constant question had to offer rationally accessible arguments about that, in the fashion of Constant and Madison.[47] There is always something difficult about defending the second-order rule in the face of an attack on the first-order case. The intellectual pull toward democratic rationalist contractarianism became especially powerful during that era. And the process of trying to deliberately create pluralism and complexity if it is not already present—of trying to create a federation out of a centralized state without traditional provinces, of simulating the effects of Houses of Lords or parlements when nobility by birth comes to be seen as absurd and abandoned—always risks a certain kind of foolishness, as Constant came to think about his abortive attempt to create a new aristocracy under Napoleon during the Hundred Days.

Still, much of the ancient-constitutionalist, Montesquieuian theory of limits on absolute monarchs remains present in the modern-constitutionalist theory of limits on sovereign democratic legislatures, just as Hobbes and Bodin remain present in Blackstone and Dicey. The idea that within the fundamental political order of a polity there are constraints on political actors—constraints internal to the polity's own normative legal structure—has persisted. So has the concomitant emphasis on the rule of law. So, too, has the emphasis on diversity, jurisdictional complexity, and institutional plurality. It is less prominent now than it was then, and it has sometimes been overlooked entirely, but it has never been absent.

## Notes

Portions and/or previous drafts of this chapter were presented at the 2002 annual meeting of the American Political Science Association, the McGill-University of Montreal

Political Theory Workshop, the University of Chicago Political Theory Workshop, and the conference that prompted this volume. I am grateful to participants in those sessions and to Bernard Yack, Charles Larmore, Zubin Khambatta, Melvin Schut, Deborah Boucyanis, and Lyman Stebbins for their comments and to Emily Nacol for valuable research assistance.

1. Charles Howard McIlwain, *Constitutionalism Ancient and Modern* (Ithaca: Cornell University Press, 1947).

2. James Tully, *Strange Multiplicity: Constitutionalism in an Age of Diversity* (Cambridge: Cambridge University Press, 1995).

3. Stanley Katz, *Common Knowledge* 2 (2002): 288–89.

4. Walter Murphy, "Constitutions, Constitutionalism, and Democracy," in *Constitutionalism and Democracy*, ed. Jon Elster and Rune Slagstad (Cambridge: Cambridge University Press, 1993). See also his "Civil Law, Common Law, and Constitutional Democracy," *Louisiana Law Review* 52 (1991): 91.

5. Compare also with Wil Waluchow's entry on "Constitutionalism" in the *Stanford Encyclopedia of Philosophy*. Ancient constitutionalism as such is neither discussed nor mentioned, and the debates surveyed are fundamentally those among various emphases in rationalist and enacted-contractarian constitutionalism. Tellingly, the entry mentions Montesquieu only in the context of the separation-of-powers doctrine of *The Federalist* and U.S.-style judicial review. <http://plato.stanford.edu/entries/constitutionalism/>.

6. Two fine exceptions to the neglect of Montesquieu in recent theorizing about the emergence of modern constitutionalism are Michael Zuckert, "Natural Rights and Modern Constitutionalism," *Northwestern Journal of International Human Rights* 2 (2004); and Paul Carrese, *The Cloaking of Power: Montesquieu, Blackstone, and the Rise of Judicial Activism* (Chicago: University of Chicago Press, 2003). But they are mainly concerned with the separation of powers and the argument for judicial independence. An understanding of Montesquieu as committed ancient constitutionalist, *parlementaire*, and moderate monarchist—that is, the French rather than the Anglo-American Montesquieu—is apparent in the work of Michael Mosher, e.g., "Monarchy's Paradox: Honor in the Face of Sovereign Power," in *Montesquieu's Science of Politics: Essays on The Spirit of the Laws*, ed. David Carrithers, Michael Mosher, and Paul Rahe (New York: Rowman & Littlefield 2001); and Rebecca Kingston, *Montesquieu and the Parlement of Bordeaux* (Geneva: Librairie Droz, 1996).

7. As was of course emphasized by Edward Corwin, "The 'Higher Law' Background of American Constitutional Law," *Harvard Law Review* 42 (1928–29): 149–85, 365–409; but Corwin's emphasis was on the constraints set by natural rights against arbitrary state action, whereas in what follows I emphasize the constraints on such *institutional* innovations as centralization and the diminution of the traditional rights of the Estates.

8. See John G. A. Pocock, *The Ancient Constitution and the Feudal Law* (Cambridge: Cambridge University Press, 1957). See also Quentin Skinner, *The Foundations of Modern Political Thought*, vol. 2, *The Age of Reformation* (Cambridge: Cambridge University Press, 1978), chs. 4–9; and Robert Kingdon, "Calvinism and Resistance Theory, 1550–1580"; J. H. M. Salmon, "Catholic Resistance Theory, Ultramontanism, and the Royalist Response, 1580–1620"; Howell A. Lloyd, "Constitutionalism"; Julian H. Franklin, "Sovereignty and the Mixed Constitution: Bodin and His Critics"; J. P. Somerville, "Absolutism and Royalism"; Corinne Weston, "England: Ancient

Constitution and Common Law"; and David Wootton, "Leveller Democracy and the Puritan Revolution"; in *The Cambridge History of Political Thought 1450–1700*, ed. J. H. Burns (Cambridge: Cambridge University Press, 1991).

9. Lloyd, "Constitutionalism," 256

10. This has been a recurring theme in the work of John Philip Reid; see, e.g., *The Ancient Constitution and the Origins of Anglo-American Liberty* (DeKalb: Northern Illinois University Press, 2005).

11. Charles Howard McIlwain, *The American Revolution: A Constitutional Interpretation* (New York: Macmillan, 1923); John Adams, *Novanglus, or a History of Dispute with America* (1774).

12. Howard Nenner, "The Later Stuart Age," in *The Varieties of British Political Thought, 1500–1800*, ed. John G. A. Pocock (Cambridge: Cambridge University Press, 1993), 206.

13. Pocock, *The Ancient Constitution and the Feudal Law*. It seems to me that Pocock's more recent commentaries on ancient constitutionalism are more balanced in this regard. See volumes II and III of his *Barbarism and Religion* (Cambridge: Cambridge University Press, 2001–2003), where he continues to disparage the historical claims made by ancient constitutionalists but seems to treat English and continental ancient or "Gothic" constitutionalism as comparable and similar. (He does stress that Scotland lay outside the traditional narrative of ancient constitutionalism.)

14. Edmund Burke, *Reflections on the Revolution in France* (1790).

15. Robert Molesworth, "Translator's Preface," in *Franco-Gallia, or, an account of the ancient free state of France, and most other parts of Europe, before the loss of their liberties*, by Francis Hotman, trans. Molesworth (London: Edward Valentine, 1721 [1574]), i. The preface was later reprinted as a standalone pamphlet, *The Principles of a Real Whig* (London: J. Williams, 1775). The translation was not Molesworth's first engagement with the question of preserving European "Gothick" constitutions or to link that question with domestic English concerns; while serving as the British ambassador to Denmark, he caused considerable offense by publishing a pamphlet (*An Account of Denmark, as it was in the year 1692*), accusing the Danish crown of tending toward absolutism and the subversion of Denmark's traditional constitution.

16. Ibid., iii.

17. Ibid., vii.

18. Ernest Barker, "A Huguenot Theory of Politics," in *Church, State, and Study* (London: Methuen, 1930), 96, 98–99.

19. For Montesquieu's constitutionalism see especially *The Spirit of Laws*, Books XI, XII, XIX, XXIX. See also *Mes Pensées*, III, xviii; III, xxi–xxii; VI, xvi; VII; VIII. See also Daniel Roche, *France in the Enlightenment*, trans. A. Goldhammer (Cambridge: Harvard University Press, 1998); James Stoner, *Common Law and Liberal Theory: Coke, Hobbes, and The Origins of American Constitutionalism* (Lawrence: University Press of Kansas, 1992), ch. 9.

20. On the partial reading of Montesquieu by the American founding generation, see Mark Hulliung, *The Social Contract in America* (Lawrence: University Press of Kansas, 2007), 34–35, 51–52.

21. See David Carrithers, "Not So Virtuous Republics: Montesquieu, Venice, and the Theory of Aristocratic Republicanism," *Journal of the History of Ideas* 52 (1991): 245–68.

22. Ibid. XI, 6, 157.
23. *The Spirit of Laws* V, 19, 70.
24. In an important article that appeared after the present chapter was written, Lee Ward has offered a rebalanced understanding of federalism and Montesquieu's constitutionalism, one that deemphasizes the theory of republican confederation and reemphasizes the provincial pluralism of constitutional and moderate monarchies. Lee Ward, "Montesquieu on Federalism and Anglo-Gothic Constitutionalism," *Publius* 37(2007): 551–77. I mean my argument in this chapter to be compatible with Ward's.
25. *The Spirit of Laws*, II, 4, 17.
26. Ibid., II, 4, 18–19
27. Ibid., VIII, 9, 118.
28. Berlin, "Two Concepts of Liberty." Reprinted in *Liberty* (Oxford: Oxford University Press, 2002).
29. *The Spirit of Laws* II, 4, XXVIII, 45.
30. Ibid., XI, 6, 160–61; emphasis added.
31. Turgot, "Mémoire sur les municipalities," 1775.
32. J. H. Sheehan, *The Parlement of Paris* (Bodmin: Sutton, 1998), 308.
33. Sylvia Neely, *Lafayette and the Liberal Ideal, 1814–1824* (Carbondale: Southern Illinois University Press, 1991), 13.
34. Declaration of the Parlement of Navarre, June 21, 1788.
35. Charles Berlet, *Les Provinces au XVIIIe siècle et leur division en departments* (Paris: Bloud, 1913), 16–17; translation is my own.
36. For the biographical and historical information in the following paragraphs I am indebted to Cheryl B. Welch, *Liberty and Utility: The French Ideologues and the Transformation of Liberalism* (New York: Columbia University Press, 1984); Gilbert Chinard, *Jefferson et les Ideologues* (Paris: Les Presses Universitaires de France, 1925).
37. Destutt de Tracy, *A Commentary and Review of Montesquieu's* The Spirit of the Laws (henceforth *Commentary*), trans. Thomas Jefferson (New York: Burt Franklin 1969 [1811]), 12–14. All further quotations will be from the Jefferson translation. The Franklin edition is a reproduction of the 1811 Duane printing, so pagination remains the same.
38. Benjamin Constant, *Réflexions sur les constitutions* (1814). In *Political Writings*, trans. Biancamaria Fontana (Cambridge: Cambridge University Press, 1988), 172 fn 1.
39. See Smith's famous discussion of the "man of system," in the sixth edition of the *Theory of Moral Sentiments*. See Adam Smith, *Theory of Moral Sentiments*, ed. D. D. Raphael and A. L. Macfie (Indianapolis: Liberty Fund, 1982), 233.
40. Compare James Scott, *Seeing like a State* (New Haven: Yale University Press, 1997).
41. Benjamin Constant, "Journaux Intimes January 28 1804," in *Oeuvres*, ed. Alfred Roulin (Paris: Gallimard, 1957).
42. See "Des réactions politiques," in *Oeuvres*.
43. Benjamin Constant, "Mélanges de Littérature et de Politique," in *Oeuvres*, 895.
44. Alexis de Tocqueville, *The Old Regime and the Revolution*, trans. Alan Kahan and ed. François Furet and Françoise Mélonio (Chicago: University of Chicago Press, 1998), 249–56.

45. Thomas Jefferson, letter to James Madison, 6 September 1789, in *The Republic of Letters: The Correspondence between Thomas Jefferson and James Madison*, 3 vols., ed. James M. Smith (New York: W. W. Norton, 1985).

46. James Madison, letter to Thomas Jefferson, February 4, 1790, in ibid.

47. This is something that I think Hayek understood and Oakeshott did not, or else Oakeshott rejected for reasons that remain opaque to me. When Hayek offered second-order arguments in favor of tacit knowledge, inherited institutions, and the like, Oakeshott accused him of being excessively rationalist and instrumentalizing.

# 7

# Montesquieu's *Humanité* and Rousseau's *Pitié*

## Clifford Orwin

Having spent much effort on studying Rousseau, I am really just a novice in turning to his great teacher, so it is an honor for me to appear in this volume with so many distinguished experts on Montesquieu. Deferring to those republican virtues of equality and simplicity stressed by both masters, I will keep this contribution brief.

Was the eighteenth century an age of the softening of morals? Montesquieu followed most philosophers in taking one side of this quarrel, while Rousseau took the other. Which of the two had the better of it can still offer matter for quarrel today.

This disagreement found expression even in their respective terms of preference for the *douceur* to be coveted. Montesquieu extols *humanité*; Rousseau, *pitié*. Neither resorts very often to the term of choice for the other.

True, in his *Discours sur les origines de l'inégalité*, Rousseau too promotes the virtue of *l'humanité*. He specifies, however, that it is merely one (if the most comprehensive) application of *pitié*—*pitié* applied to the human race in general. Similarly Book IV of *Emile* raises the question of whether the passions dominant in the character of that lucky youth will be "humane and gentle or cruel and malignant." Again, however, the context discloses that the relevant variable is the tutor's success at cultivating against long odds the elusive natural gift of *pitié*. Nothing afoot in the broader society will support him in this project.

Emile's education in humanity, then, like his education generally, is not one in the ways of the eighteenth century. It is not a variety of acculturation; rather it is countercultural. It depends not on his exposure to the greater world but on his isolation from it. True, he must eventually enter that world, so he is being educated to that end. Yet he will enter it only to live on its fringes, in the hopes that his marginality will help preserve him from its corruption.

According to Rousseau the corruption of the society of his day is to be ascribed above all to its inequality, from which no relief is in sight. Inequality stifles the gentler virtues as surely as it does the manly ones. The extinction of pity by inequality is a rhetorical mainstay of both the *Discours sur l'inégalité* and *Emile*, and the countermeasures to be taken occupy many pages of the latter.

As always Rousseau's searing rhetoric masks a treatment of daunting complexity. His theme is the weakness of pity in a world in which inequality differentiates and thereby divides human beings. The distinctions of inequality are as invidious here as elsewhere: inequality makes men pitiless. If you were to posit (or lament, or fulminate) that the rebirth of a compassionate sensibility would have to await some wholly unforeseeable restoration of equality among the peoples of Europe, you would seem to have grasped Rousseau's point.

In fact, though, you would not quite have grasped it. For it is clear from the melodramatic prominence of Rousseau's rhetoric of compassion that he anticipates a receptive audience for it. At the very least he expects his readers to regret what they have been missing. That his writings fostered a cult of compassion in Europe was anything but an unintended consequence.

There are two possible interpretations of Rousseau's rhetorical reliance on a sentiment he presents as virtually extinct. The first is that nature has not been as wholly submerged by the many centuries of ascendant inequality as Rousseau sometimes pretends. The other is that the reigning *moeurs* in Europe, *moeurs* of inequality though they be, are not as hostile to compassion as he pretends. If the first of these views informs Rousseau's position, it remains opposed to that of Montesquieu. If in fact he holds the second, then he is closer to his great teacher even on this issue than it serves his purposes to admit.

A substantial historical and sociological literature links the rise of a humanitarian sensibility in the West to the birth and dissemination of modern market institutions. A recent scholar has put it as follows: "By defining a universal field of others with whom contracts and exchanges can be made, market perspectives also extend the field of moral concern, however unintentionally."[1] Tocqueville's argument for the broader sway of compassion within democracy represents a variant of this claim.[2] There is little doubt, however, that Tocqueville's position is an adaptation of Montesquieu's, with the homogeneity of equality of condition replacing (and radicalizing) that which Montesquieu had ascribed to commerce.

It is possible, then, to define two basic approaches to the rise of humane or compassionate sensibilities in the West. One view, the major strand in Rousseau's thought and subsequently (and more dogmatically) in Marxism, presents the history of Europe as one of ever-growing inequality and hence of pitilessness among men. From this perspective, the transition from the Ancien Régime to bourgeois liberalism mattered little, since inequalities of wealth simply supplanted those of inherited class as barriers to mutual sympathy. That this was Rousseau's standard line no less than Marx's explains why he consistently treats emergent liberalism not as a subversive alternative to the Ancien Régime but as just another variation on its theme.

Rousseau offers no optimistic scenario for the restoration of relations of mutual sympathy; for him it is only those rarest of creatures, the "great cosmopolitan souls" of the Discours sur l'inégalité (and, to a lesser extent, the fictional Emile) who "surmount the imaginary barriers that separate Peoples and who, following the example of the sovereign Being who created them, include the whole human Race in their benevolence." Marx was to offer the Revolution, the survivors of which, having murdered so many of their fellows, would live thereafter as one big happy universal class.

Liberalism shares with Marxism over and against Rousseau the conviction that the historical process is tending toward the eventual triumph of mutual sympathy. It opposes Marxism in denying the necessity of a violent rupture in order to realize this promise. By this criterion at least Montesquieu would seem to qualify as liberal.

Commerce makes men more alike, even as it multiplies inequalities of wealth among them. Montesquieu seized on the first of these facts as more salient in the present context; Rousseau on the second of them. Montesquieu held differences of nation, sect, and caste the worst stumbling blocks to mutual sympathy; and these commerce eroded. Rousseau, by contrast, deemed inequalities of wealth the most pernicious, so could find nothing good to say for commerce.

For both thinkers, as for their contemporaries, the elephant in the tent, too big and malodorous to be ignored, was Christianity. What was its relation to Montesquieu's humanité or to Rousseau's pitié? Both men followed the common early modern practice of appropriating Christianity to buttress their respective projects, including therefore humanité and pitié. Each claimed that authentic Christianity, rescued from the clammy grip of priests, was of just the same mind as they were. Neither made this claim in good faith. Not without cause did both incur the wrath of the guardians of Christian orthodoxy.[3] Protest if you wish the sincerity of their professions of Christian faith; as a scholar in a free country, it is your right. Just do not waste your breath protesting it to me.

Both men viewed dogmatic Christianity as a barrier to the softening of moeurs. Here there was substantial agreement between them: otherworldliness, asceticism, the hypocritical striving for power that inevitably besets any supposedly spiritual authority, asceticism (which makes men harsh rather than gentle), sectarianism (which makes them fanatical)—their indictment does not lack for counts.

What, however, of Christianity in a more diffuse but more extended sense? If the Christianity of the eighteenth century remained complicit in intolerance and vindictiveness, did it not also hold some promise of combating these?

This is one of the hardest nuts to crack in the interpretation of Rousseau's thought. His most garrulous champion of Christianity, the Savoyard vicar of Book IV of *Emile*, is a Christian only after a manner of speaking if at all. Neither, however, is he or his outlook conceivable without Christianity. He is post-Christian,[4] and designedly so: Rousseau's whole religion of a mythically beneficent nature is his intended substitute for a dying but still pernicious Christianity.

Much of this myth of a beneficent nature turns on pity. Insofar as it is conceived as natural, *pitié* comes to light not as an outcome of a process of historical evolution but rather as a casualty of this process. Its recovery depends on our casting off the burden of a repressive history. By the same token, *pitié* is not a matter of *moeurs*. For these are as such not natural but artificial and contingent. *Pitié* pertains to a stratum of our common humanity prior to and more primal than *moeurs*, while subject to burial beneath them. Rousseau casts the *moeurs* of civilized man as fatal to pity. Hence the mostly prophylactic character of the education of Emile, of whom it is always so much easier to say what he is not supposed to be than what he is.

What Montesquieu means by *humanité*, by contrast, falls firmly within the camp of *moeurs*. Consider his initial and most schematic treatment of this virtue, in chapter 15 of the *Considérations*. If even that one of the Roman emperors *qui étoit d'un naturel doux* (the reference is to Claudius) became bloodthirsty through frequenting the arena, this *fait bien voir que l'éducation de son temps étoit différente de la nôtre*. Montesquieu thus suggests that he and his contemporaries possess the virtue the Romans lacked and that consists, stated negatively, of the absence of that cruelty that the Romans possessed. And, considering that the pagan Romans had lived many centuries before him, Montesquieu appears to suggest that this virtue and the education to which we owe it are historical outcomes. Where Rousseau suggests regress, Montesquieu implies progress.

It would be odd if Montesquieu's original readers did not assume that the chief agent of this progress in gentleness was Christianity. In the paragraph that follows Montesquieu duly expounds the reasons for the Romans' ignorance of *cette vertu que nous appelons humanité*. He makes no mention of their paganism, however. Rather their habituation to the practice of slavery is fingered as the source of their harshness. And by way of confirmation of this hypothesis he offers "cette férocité que nous trouvons dans les habitants de nos colonies.... Lorsqu'on est cruel dans l'état civil, que peut-on attendre de la douceur et de la justice naturelle?" It is the slavery that unites the French *colons* with the ancient Romans, not the Christianity that distinguishes them from them, that Montesquieu offers as decisive here.

In the third and final paragraph of this sequence Montesquieu takes up the practice of proscription by the Roman emperors, and here he does ascribe the rarity of this practice in his own day to *des moeurs plus douces, et une religion plus réprimante*. At last a bouquet to Christianity—which, however, soon withers, the victim of its arid context. For we learn that another consideration explains the dearth of proscriptions in Christian times: namely, a scarcity of private fortunes so immense as to attract the cupidity of kings. And in a footnote, Montesquieu cites a notable exception. "Le duc de Bragance avoit des biens immenses dans le Portugal: lorsqu'il se révolta, on félicita le roi d'Espagne de la riche confiscation qu'il alloit avoir." Handshakes all around at the court of the Catholic king: so much for *moeurs douces et une religion plus réprimante*.

To be sure there are many passages friendly to Christianity in Montesquieu (such as that in *The Spirit of Laws*, XXIV, 3, which credits it for that progress "both ... in governance [in] a certain political right and in war [in] a certain right of nations, for which human nature can never be too thankful." Yet such comments are counterbalanced by his incessant critiques of Christian asceticism, hypocrisy, fanaticism, celibacy, and indifference to the exigencies of earthly prosperity. Besides which are those passages no less emphatic than XXIV, 3 that ascribe the significant progress in the *douceur* of *moeurs* in Europe to the rise of commerce—commerce, not Christianity; commerce, the modern European epoch of which emerged from under the shadow of Christianity and has remained very much at loggerheads with it.

The relevant point for us remains that Montesquieu swells the philosophic choir of his day in proclaiming a new era of *douceur*, while Rousseau insists in singing out of key. Montesquieu is aware, of course, that there is still much work to be done as well as novel threats to be met. Yet he does regard at least the enlightened parts of Europe as gentler than they were, and this as a result of a secular tendency in which Christianity and commerce have played conflicting but complementary roles.

Montesquieuian *humanité* resists both clear definition and intensive analysis precisely because of its participation in *moeurs*. It is to a large extent negative rather than positive, the obverse of the decline of fanaticism and simultaneous rise of commerce. As so frequently with Montesquieu, its situation in history is clearer than its relation to nature.[5] Just what are we to take to be its natural basis? We could point of course to *The Spirit of Laws*, I, 2 and Montesquieu's refutation of Hobbes's claim that man is naturally ferocious, but that argument falls far short of establishing that man is naturally humane. (Indeed insofar as we deem *humanité* a social virtue, its naturalness thereby stands refuted by just the same token as Hobbes's ferocity.) It seems that the strongest claim of *humanité* to naturalness is negative: namely, that fanaticism is not so. Yet what Montesquieu means by *humanité* did not precede the rise of Christian fanaticism, even if it has ensued from its decline. For all these reasons it seems safest to regard it as a fortunate historical accident.

Rousseauian *pitié*, however, is avowedly transhistorical, and indeed he assigns its greatest flourishing to the epoch of the prehistoric. Elsewhere I have offered reasons for taking this claim (like so many others of Rousseau) with the largest grain of salt obtainable.[6] And even if *pitié* is allegedly natural in the rawest, least ambiguous sense of that term (which in Rousseau as in Hobbes means present at the origin), the virtue of *humanité* is not. For like the other "applications" of pity described in the *Discours sur l'inégalité*, it depends on the presence of reason. To apply one must distinguish, and distinction is the work of reason. The nicest and most precise distinctions would require the most perfected reason.

The opposition between nature and history is so rich in rhetorical value that we could hardly expect Rousseau to abandon it. It also serves to pose the central problem of his theoretical enterprise. In the end, however, the notion of the intended efflorescence of pity as a recovery of our original nature will not stand up to scrutiny. Neither, however, in Rousseau's view, will the notion of any kind of redemption through history: no new era of mildness can be expected to follow from the progress of commerce and enlightenment. This difference at least remains between him and Montesquieu. While the latter is at least hopeful that the facts on the ground are accomplishing the work of "humanization" for him, Rousseau faces the daunting task of bringing it about against the grain of his time so almost all by himself.

Or does he? This returns us to the question posed earlier as to whether Rousseau's rhetorical practice does not at least in some measure undermine the persuasiveness of his claim that never society had offered more arid ground for compassion than Europe of the ancien régime. Would so careful a writer persist in throwing good rhetoric after bad?[7] Clearly Rousseau harbored some hope (which is to say also some strategy) for snatching victory from the jaws of defeat. Discussion of this strategy, however, would carry us beyond the modest bounds of this chapter.

In his trenchant comments on the conference version of this chpater, Ronald Beiner suggested that in my contrast between the two thinkers I had exaggerated Montesquieu's emphasis on the historical dimensions of *humanité* as opposed to its natural ones. "I want to suggest that there may be more of an appeal to the notion of natural boundaries of our humanity than we get in Orwin's critique of Montesquieu's historicism. My idea is that *part* of what Montesquieu intended in his invocation of *humanité* is that we should renounce the ambition to be super-human [an ambition that Beiner proceeds to associate with the heroic politics of classical antiquity]."

Without denying that Montesquieu understands the virtue of *humanité* as a historical and therefore contingent development, Beiner nonetheless takes its name to suggest that it represents our achievement of maturity as human beings. As he stated in the passage cited and proceeded to elaborate, we evince this maturity above all by renouncing a *more than human*, that is to say, heroic life such as both Montesquieu and Rousseau ascribed to the ancient citizen.

Professor Beiner has called attention to what was indeed a crucial defect of my original presentation, namely, that I failed to account for why Montesquieu should describe what I portrayed as an accident of history by a name that casts it as an expression of our human essence and thereby of our nature. One might argue that Montesquieu's usage of *humanité* is (like many usages of Spinoza, for example) both obfuscatory and provocative. As such it does not contradict but rather emphasizes Montesquieu's claim that we are to understand the quality that more than any other defines what we moderns mean by humanity as a fact not of nature but of history and culture—very simply, that humanity has evolved through history to become what it is today, and so is not to be understood as a realization of our nature.

However, we might argue that for Montesquieu as for his great student Tocqueville, we are to understand the historical process as culminating however accidentally in a kind of naturalization of man. This would seem to be Beiner's view, and it is certainly a possible interpretation of Montesquieu's somewhat ambiguous position.

Be this as it may, I do think that Beiner hit the nail on the head in suggesting that the ultimate significance of Montesquieu's choice of '*l'humanité*' lies in its implicit yet emphatic rejection of a superhuman standard for man, which as much also looms as a supernatural one. Yet it also seems to me that having hammered that first nail so squarely Beiner has fanned on the next one. I find implausible his suggestion that Montesquieu's primary target here is the larger-than-life heroic model of the ancient citizen. Is it not rather the literally superhuman and supernatural one of Jesus Christ?

What Montesquieu means by '*humanité*' is a highly complex phenomenon. We could perhaps understand it in terms of Nietzsche's *Sittlichkeit der Sitte* ("morality of mores"): as the result of Christianity's centuries of work upon the soul of Western man and of centuries of commerce, the most and best of these still to come, purging Christian mildness of that otherworldliness that left it so liable to fits of extreme harshness. That *humanité* is at the same time at the furthest remove from the very different harshness of the pagans is undeniable. That the eighteenth century (precisely inasmuch as it was moving away from Christianity) displayed some nostalgia for paganism is equally so. Yet we must not forget that the main debate in the eighteenth century was not between modernity and paganism but between modernity and Christianity.

That Montesquieu understood *humanité* as in some sense a "secularization" of Christianity I do not mean to deny. Yet in "secularizing" Christianity, the new dispensation rejected it, of which we could hope for no clearer token than that the gentler virtues that are avowedly owed in part to Christianity should be reconceived in terms of humanity which (as its name so clearly proclaims) is merely human, rather than in terms of charity which is divine.

## Notes

1. Natan Sznaider, *The Compassionate Temperament: Care and Cruelty in Modern Society* (Lanham, MD: Rowman & Littlefield, 1994), 11 (cf. 9–20). Cf. John Radner, "The Art of Sympathy in Eighteenth-Century British Moral Thought," *Studies in Eighteenth-Century Culture* 9 (1979): 189–210; Thomas Haskell, "Capitalism and the Origins of the Humanitarian Sensibility," *American Historical Review* 90 (1985): 339–61, 547–66; John Ashworth, "The Relation Between Capitalism and Humanitarianism," *American Historical Review* 92 (1987): 813–28; Allan Silver, "Friendship in Commercial Society: Eighteenth Century Social Theory and Modern Society," *American Journal of Sociology* 95.6 (1990): 1474–1504; Claudine Hochard, "La Compassion comme amour social et politique de l'autre au XVIIIe siècle," in Jacques Chevallier et al., *La Solidarité: Un sentiment républicain?* (Paris: PUF, 1992), 11–25; Vic A. C. Gatrell, *The Hanging Tree: Execution and the English People, 1770–1868* (Oxford: Oxford University Press, 1994). I am grateful to Professor Silver for his guidance in this domain.

2. Alexis de Tocqueville, *De la Démocratie en Amérique* (Paris: Charles Gosselin, 1836), II, iii, 1, 2. See Clifford Orwin, "Compassion and the Softening of *Mores*," *Journal of Democracy*, Tenth Anniversary Issue (*Democracy in the World: Tocqueville Reconsidered*), 11.1 (2000): 142–48.

3. On Montesquieu's treatment of Christianity, see especially Thomas L. Pangle, *Montesquieu's Philosophy of Liberalism* (Chicago: University of Chicago Press, 1975); Pierre Manent, *La Cité de l'homme* (Paris: Fayard, 1995); Diana Schaub, *Erotic Liberalism: Women and Revolution in Montesquieu's Persian Letters* (Lanham, MD: Rowman & Littlefield, 1997); Robert C. Bartlett, *The Idea of Enlightenment: A Post-mortem* (Toronto: University of Toronto Press, 2001), 13–44. On the immediate historical context and the stances Montesquieu adopted within it see Rebecca Kingston, "Montesquieu on religion and on the question of toleration," in *Montesquieu's Science of Politics: Essays on the Spirit of Laws*, ed. David W. Carrithers, Michael A. Mosher, and Paul A. Rahe (Lanham, MD: Rowman & Littlefield, 2001), 375–408.

4. Allan Bloom, *Love and Friendship* (New York: Simon & Schuster, 1993), 71–86; Arthur Melzer, "The Origin of the Counter-Enlightenment: Rousseau and the New Religion of Sincerity," *American Political Science Review* 90 (1996): 344–60.

5. For a sophisticated argument that Montesquieu is the pivotal thinker of modernity in his development of this ambiguity see Manent, *La Cité de l'homme*. Manent may overstate Montesquieu's deprecation of nature, but his book remains the most challenging recent interpretation of Montesquieu.

6. See my "Rousseau and the Discovery of Political Compassion," in Clifford Orwin and Nathan Tarcov, ed. *The Legacy of Rousseau* (Chicago: University of Chicago Press, 1997), 296–320.

7. On Rousseau's masterfulness as a writer, see now the wonderful book of Christopher Kelly, *Rousseau as Author: Consecrating One's Life to the Truth* (Chicago: University of Chicago Press, 2003).

# 8

# Montesquieu and Tocqueville as Philosophical Historians
## Liberty, Determinism, and the Prospects for Freedom

### David W. Carrithers

Only very rarely did Tocqueville speak of the inspiration he derived from any of his predecessors.[1] In a letter written in November 1836 to Louis de Kergorlay he confided, "There are three men with whom I spend time every day, Pascal, Montesquieu, and Rousseau."[2] Many years later, again writing to Kergorlay, he singled out Montesquieu's history of Rome as the best example of how "philosophical history" should be written.[3] Not long thereafter, in a conversation with Nassau Senior, he once again mentioned Montesquieu as an influence—this time also referring to Voltaire, Rousseau, and Buffon.[4] Montesquieu's name also surfaced only infrequently in Tocqueville's published works. In *Democracy in America* (1835–40) he alluded to Montesquieu's views on despotism, on transitions from republics to empires, and on the need for citizen involvement in republican regimes.[5] In *The Old Regime and the Revolution* (1856) he cited Montesquieu's views on Paris' influence over the rest of France, on freedom contributing more to land productivity than soil fertility, and on the uniqueness of England.[6] One encounters, then, only fleeting glimpses in Tocqueville's works and correspondence of how much guidance he may have derived from reading the works of his illustrious French predecessors, including Montesquieu.[7]

The intellectual kinship between Montesquieu and Tocqueville was nonetheless quite apparent to the first generation of readers of *Democracy in America*. When the first volume of that work appeared in 1835, the prominent Doctrinaire politician and Tocqueville mentor, Pierre Paul Royer-Collard, opined, "Since Montesquieu there has been nothing like it."[8] He also remarked to a friend that "to find a work to compare it with, you have to go back to Aristotle's *Politics* and [Montesquieu's] *Spirit of the Laws*."[9] Some among Tocqueville's contemporaries felt he remained very much in Montesquieu's shadow. The editors of the periodical *L'univers*, for example, reacting negatively to what they regarded as the excessive abstraction in the second volume of *Democracy in America*, remarked in their October 11, 1840 issue: "The difference between Montesquieu and Tocqueville is that the former was gifted with historical feeling and poetical feeling to an eminent degree, whereas the second seems to be lacking in any. It is these two feelings that cause one to appreciate in the life of nations the enduring power of traditions and prior events, the influence of race, the land, the climate."[10]

Whatever their respective merits, Montesquieu and Tocqueville developed quite different understandings of such key concepts as 'democracy' and 'equality.' Certainly there was no counterpart in Montesquieu's thought to Tocqueville's conviction that democracy was a "Providential" force sweeping away the remnants of aristocratic society. For Tocqueville, democracy was much more than an exhibit in a historical museum, much more than a mandatory category in every political philosopher's typology of governmental forms. By his day democracy was recognizable as a veritable "social state" (*l'état social*) destined to replace aristocracy as an organizing principle. Above all, it was the French Revolution that separated the intellectual worlds of these two writers. Montesquieu died in 1755, fifteen years prior to the assault on the French parlements during the Maupeou crisis of 1771, which many, including Tocqueville, have seen as a rehearsal for the Revolution,[11] and seven years before Rousseau published his *Social Contract* (1762), the work that so greatly inspired democratic sentiments once the Revolution commenced. Tocqueville, in contrast, would be unrecognizable apart from his life-long preoccupation with the Revolution and its aftermath—an interest served even by his journey to America since he used his observations in the New World to better forecast the probable effects of democracy in France.

If Montesquieu and Tocqueville were exposed to quite different events and developments, there were nonetheless striking similarities in their methodological assumptions and political perspectives. Both adopted the comparative method,[12] often reasoned deductively,[13] divided causes into physical and moral components, constructed ideal types, and displayed a penchant for generalizing from particulars.[14] Both investigated types of societies rather than just types of government, and both regarded the separation of powers and the presence of an aristocratic class and other intermediary powers as instrumental to achieving liberty. In addition, both were pluralists when it came to regime choice, and both prioritized liberty over equality, concluding that an excess of the latter prejudices the former. Moreover, they shared a belief in the importance of tradition and a conviction that societies are governed by a single principle, or general spirit that contributes greatly to regime stability. In addition, both warned that commerce and materialism incline citizens to withdraw from politics, and both alerted their contemporaries to the twin dangers of political despotism and administrative uniformity.[15] Each regarded religion as the best means for eliciting moral behavior from the masses, while also considering the character, mores, and customs of a people even more important to regime success than laws or institutions. Moreover, both Montesquieu and Tocqueville concluded that geography and climate substantially influence human behavior—but certainly not in a determinist manner. And finally, coming to the focus of this essay, they both wrote "philosophical history" while denigrating purely factual, narrative history that ignores questions of causality.

## The Genre of Philosophical History

The key question for philosophical historians is whether there are general causes predetermining historical outcomes, or whether the decisive role belongs to human agents and unpredictable contingencies. Over time, three sorts of responses have been developed to this basic question. A determinist position posits that whatever the precise historical moment, there are always present an array of general causes sweeping historical events along in a necessitous direction. A diametrically opposed position posits that underlying causal forces are never so strong as to displace the primacy of the unpredictable decisions made by kings, statesmen, legislative assemblies—and sometimes crowds. A third position blending the two others suggests that historical outcomes are sometimes the result of underlying general causes, sometimes the consequence of the unpredictable actions of human beings, and sometimes the combined result of the two.

Montesquieu and Tocqueville both adopted versions of the third position. Their viewpoints were far from identical, however. Montesquieu seems to have been untroubled by his determinist conclusions regarding Rome's collapse into empire being pre-ordained by the very circumstances that had initially produced Roman freedom. Tocqueville, however, for whom the French Revolution was the key historical event to be explained, while also fully convinced of the determining power of general causes, and while penning several passages asserting that the causes of the French Revolution had been brewing for centuries and that the revolution was preordained,[16] wanted very much to believe that the main responsibility for how events unfold nonetheless rests with human agents. There was a palpable tension in Tocqueville's thought between his determinist conclusions and his voluntarist predilections. In spite of his findings regarding the inevitability of the replacement in the modern era of the social condition of aristocracy by democracy,[17] he abhorred fatalistic theories suggesting the impotence of human beings.[18] Thus, while in the very first chapter of *The Old Regime* he characterized the French Revolution as fully prepared by underlying causes that made its outbreak well nigh inevitable,[19] he nonetheless took great pains, both in that work and in its unfinished sequel, to explore whether more skillful kings could have navigated the French ship of state through less troubled waters. Montesquieu did not adopt a similarly hedged position in delineating the fate of the Roman republic. Instead he forthrightly identified general causes so strong that Roman leaders were reduced to acting out roles dictated by underlying circumstances.

## Montesquieu and Tocqueville as Philosophical Historians

Montesquieu's skills as a practitioner of philosophical history are well known, and it is not at all surprising that Edward Gibbon studied his history of Rome before embarking on his own Herculean efforts.[20] As for Tocqueville, he expressed his understanding of the goals of this type of history in a long letter to Louis de Kergorlay written shortly after embarking on what he originally projected as a study of Napoleon Bonaparte's empire, but which evolved instead into *The Old Regime*. "What I have been most successful with until now," he remarked, "is to judge the facts rather than narrate them in a history properly speaking." Intending to use that same approach in analyzing "the birth, development, decline, and fall" of the empire of Napoleon, he remarked to Kergorlay, "I would not write a history of the Empire, strictly speaking, but a combination of reflections and judgments on its history. I would no doubt indicate the facts and follow their thread, but my main objective would not be to narrate them; I would try to make the reader understand the principal facts and see the diverse causes that produced them and the consequences that flowed from them."[21]

A similar focus on causal explanation had earlier guided Tocqueville's efforts in *Democracy in America*. A key purpose of that work had been to elucidate the underlying causes of American freedom. Thus he asserted, "It is not due to idle curiosity that I seek the predominance of the causes which allow peoples to be free."[22] And one of the headings he prepared for the index of his papers reads: "Causes which maintain the present form of government in America."[23] Moreover, an entry in one of the notebooks he kept while in America suggests that the goal of the philosophical historian should be to "understand the reasons why a particular people move in a particular direction . . . the chief criterion for success being whether that people have attained "real, effective liberty."[24] Normally, he explained, the complexity of unraveling causal factors precludes full understanding, but he considered America a "special" case since Americans "have been able to build their social edifice from a clean start."[25] Ever the philosophical historian, Tocqueville would again seek to unravel causes when, in the 1850s, he turned his attention to French history. After his English translator, Henry Reeve, proposed as the title for the English edition of *L'Ancien régime et la revolution*, "On the State of Society before the Revolution of 1789," Tocqueville insisted on adding "and on the causes which led to that event."[26]

There is certainly every reason to believe that Tocqueville's understanding of the practice of philosophical history was influenced by Montesquieu. Explaining to Kergorlay what he considered the difficulties of this method of doing history, he candidly remarked, "The one that troubles me most comes from the mixing of history, properly speaking, with philosophical history ... The inimitable model of this genre is Montesquieu's book on the greatness and decline of the Romans."[27] Tocqueville asserted that he greatly admired Montesquieu's ability to provide just enough facts about Roman events to make the philosophical discussion of causation intelligible, and he wondered whether he would be able to live up to those high standards.[28]

## Montesquieu's Philosophical History of the Romans

Tocqueville left no account of precisely what it was about Montesquieu's book on the Romans that so greatly appealed to him, but surely he must have paid attention to the work's central theme, which was expressed as follows: "It is not chance that rules the world. Ask the Romans, who had a continuous sequence of successes when they were guided by a certain plan, and an uninterrupted sequence of disasters when they followed another. There are general causes, moral and physical, which act in every monarchy, elevating it, maintaining it, or hurling it to the ground."[29] Roman history, on Montesquieu's reading, far from being one chance event randomly following another, evolved according to a pattern reflecting the influence of general causes beyond the power of individual Roman statesmen and generals to control. He did not mean to suggest that the presence of "general causes" altogether eliminates the role of unpredictable contingencies, but he concluded that general causes control the effects of such historical accidents: "All accidents are controlled by these causes, which clearly channel the paths within which accidents or contingencies can work their effect. If the chance of one battle has brought a state to ruin, some general cause made it necessary for that state to perish from a single battle. In a word, the main trend draws with it all particular accidents."[30]

As the general cause of the collapse of Roman liberty, Montesquieu identified the relentless expansion of Roman territory. Unbeknownst to the

Romans witnessing victory after victory, their conquests set in motion a course of events that doomed the republic.[31] Since the spirit of civic virtue can only be maintained when there is intense citizen involvement in politics, and since the Romans inevitably lost the spirit of self-sacrificing, republican virtue as their conquests turned the original republic into a vast empire, it was inevitable that Roman generals would one day compete among themselves to gain dominion over the spoils of empire.[32] Thus the history of Rome embodied a great paradox. The more successful the Romans were in subduing others, the weaker their republican institutions became. By the first century B.C.E. Rome had become too large to be ruled as a republic, and internecine conflict rose to such a level that instead of being a constructive support of liberty, tensions exploded into civil war. Nor was there any potential to stem the flow of predetermined events. Thus, after describing Caesar's victories in Rome's civil wars, Montesquieu asserted that, had there been no Caesar, "the republic, destined to perish, would have been dragged to the precipice by another hand."[33] Similarly, he remarked, in summing up the damage Sulla had done during his brief period of control prior to Caesar's dominance, "Since the republic necessarily had to perish, it was only a question of how, and by whom, it was to be overthrown."[34]

Clearly, then, Montesquieu stressed the influence of underlying general causes rather than the chance actions of key Roman protagonists in explaining Roman historical outcomes. Roman expansion dissipated unity and rendered portions of the population subservient to different generals, each of whom was eager to abuse the Roman constitution in order to augment his personal power. Thus it became not a matter of *whether* but *when* the republic would fall. Roman militarism ultimately doomed her republican prospects and made imperial government necessary. He well summed up the causes of both Roman greatness and Roman decline as follows: "Here, in a word, is the history of the Romans. By means of their maxims they conquered all peoples, but when they had succeeded in doing so, their republic could not endure. It was necessary to change the government, and contrary maxims employed by the new government made their greatness collapse."[35]

## The Role of Human Agency in Roman History

Although historical determinism was the main theme of Montesquieu's history of Rome, he did not turn a blind eye to contingent factors involving human agency that shaped some of the nuances of Roman historical evolution. He attributed substantial weight, for example, to the wise maxims of the senate that were the product of shrewd political thinking rather than being dictated by underlying general causes. He considered the decision that the Roman consuls should serve annual terms a stroke of genius. This augmented their war-making ambition since they needed to achieve glory before their terms expired. Contributing also to Roman propensity for war was the decision to divide lands equally, which gave everyone an equal interest in defending the country. Similarly helpful in ensuring Roman self-aggrandizement was the decision to allow the aristocratic senate "to direct public affairs," as compared to Carthage where popular control was excessive.[36] "Rome," Montesquieu concluded, "was a marvel of constancy.... The reason is that the senate never departed from its old maxims."[37]

The wisdom of the senate became the predominant theme of a chapter Montesquieu entitled "The Conduct the Romans Pursued to Subjugate All People." The main point was that "the senate always acted with the same profundity."[38] For example, the senate always gave part of the land they conquered to Rome's allies while at the same time making ruthless use of these very same allies, first employing them in making war and then destroying them. In addition, when Rome was faced with two enemies simultaneously, her policy was to make peace with the weakest. Moreover, the Romans "never made peace in good faith" and always specified terms that ruined the other side. Moreover, should a foreign people ever rebel against their prince, the Romans immediately came to their assistance. At other times, they fomented factions while allowing "a city to remain free," knowing that in the end the pro-Roman faction would prevail.[39]

Nor did these stratagems exhaust Roman ingenuity. They made frequent use of succession struggles in other lands as pretexts for taking over those countries and also made it their policy to overrun states exhausted by conquest. Moreover the Romans always sought allies in the vicinity of the wars they were fighting and always kept a backup army near the conflict. In addition, if the Roman senate did not like the terms of peace one of their generals had signed, they simply ignored the agreement. Also characteristic of Roman practice was not imposing the same form of government on all conquered peoples since obedience—not uniformity—was the goal, and the imposition of similar laws could contribute to co-operation among conquered peoples. And, finally, the Romans knew how to divide and conquer by splitting up leagues of states and returning each of them to their local laws to ensure that centralized power would collapse.[40] For the most part, Montesquieu recounted these Roman maxims without interjecting moral judgments into the discussion. His disdain for the ruthless tactics of Rome, however, became transparent in his comment that "not even the justice of brigands, who bring a certain honesty to the practice of crime, was to be found among the Romans.[41]

In addition to stressing the influence on Rome's progress toward empire of strategic principles and maxims, Montesquieu also acknowledged that there had been certain turning points in Roman history that were shaped by human agency rather than by underlying causes. He suggested, for example, how pivotal it had been for Caesar to be awarded the rule of both Transalpine Gaul, covering what is today southern France, and Cisalpine Gaul, including the area in present day Italy from the Rubicon to the Alps. This gave him control of a western province for waging nearly continuous wars that transformed his troops into seasoned veterans while at the same time providing him with a strategic position in the eastern province, thereby preventing Pompey from heading him off at the Alpine pass before he could cross the Rubicon.[42] Presumably, then, if Caesar had not been awarded command of both provinces, Pompey might have been able to prevent his march on Rome. Moreover, Montesquieu suggested that Pompey only suffered defeat at the hands of Caesar's armies at the battle of Pharsalus in Greece because he listened too sympathetically to the pleadings of the Roman senators in his entourage to hasten the conflict so that they could return home and "eat the figs of Tusculum."[43] Pompey's own preference had been not to engage the troops of Caesar until they had been more thoroughly weakened by poor logistical support from Rome, but he wrongly followed the wishes of his advisers. Perhaps, then, if Pompey had kept his own counsel and had delayed the battle, he would have prevailed over Caesar in Greece.

Montesquieu also pointed to events following Caesar's assassination to demonstrate the role of human agency in shaping events along unpredictable lines. He noted that the conspirators had not properly planned for the aftermath of the assassination. Therefore, Anthony, as consul, was able to assume the mantle of Caesar's power, and he began using vast sums of money as bribes to gain supporters. Moreover, by not throwing Caesar's body into the Tiber, the conspirators set the stage for a funeral, and Anthony so inflamed the people in his oration that they set fire to the houses of the conspirators. When the Senate finally met, "it was too late." Nor did it help that another "accident was involved" in exalting Caesar's memory. During the games to honor him, a comet was seen in the sky for seven days, and "the people believed his soul had been admitted into heaven."[44]

It is important to emphasize that Montesquieu did not believe that his observations on the role of human agency in shaping the details of Roman history undermined his main contention that general causes destined the Roman republic to perish by some general's hand. He retained the view that the main reason why republicanism could not be revived, even after the assassination of Caesar, was that the same general causes that had brought the republic to the point of civil war—imperial expansion dissipating the republican spirit and tempting generals to seek personal dominion—were still present.[45] Montesquieu's discussions of the role of human agency and contingency, however, do reveal his awareness that even if the end result of the loss of Roman liberty was determined by deep structural causes, human actions were influential in shaping the exact path Rome took on her downward spiral from republic to empire.

## Was Rome a Special Case of Historical Determinism?

In assessing Montesquieu's philosophy of history it is important to ask whether he regarded Rome as a special case where the influence of inexorable, general causes was unique? Did he believe that in other historical settings human agency might play a much greater role? He had pondered this matter deeply while composing *De la politique*, a brief fragment originally written as the concluding portion of the now lost *Traité des devoirs* (1725).[46] In that short composition he turned his attention to human agency and historical contingency, acknowledging, for example, that the expulsion of the Huguenots from France in 1685 by Louis XIV "was tied to accidents they could not foresee." And he noted that no one could have predicted the enormous influence on European affairs in the seventeenth century of Gustavus Adolfus, who was just an obscure Swedish king until his armies invented new tactics to tip the balance to the Protestant side in the Thirty Years' War. Moreover, he portrayed the life and career of Mohammed as an even more striking example of the influence of unpredictable human agency, remarking that neither Byzantine nor Persian kings, as they engaged in their intense rivalry, could have foreseen that their kingdoms soon would be eclipsed by the followers of a once obscure religious prophet.[47]

However interested Montesquieu was in explaining the role of human agency in producing historical change in some situations, he clearly believed that in many settings it is general causes that prevail. Thus in *De la politique* he highlighted the determining influence of general causes in producing the English Revolution of the 1640's whose roots he traced back a century to the English Reformation. Henry VIII believed he was substantially increasing the crown's power by severing ties with Rome and creating England's own national church, but in freeing English souls from the Papal yoke he was opening the doors to the religious enthusiasm and frenzy destined to overthrow the monarchy a century later.[48] Hence the fate of Charles I was pre-determined:

> In all societies, which are really groupings of minds, a common character takes shape. This collective soul takes on a manner of thinking which is the effect of a chain of infinite causes that multiply and combine from century to century. Once the tone is set and has permeated the society, it alone governs and all that sovereigns, magistrates, and peoples are able to do or plan, whether they seem to go against this tone or follow it, is always in relation to it; and it dominates until the society is totally destroyed.[49]

Once the tone of religious enthusiasm took hold following Henry Tudor's break with Roman orthodoxy, its influence proved irreversible:

This tone was such under Charles I that, however he acted, his power was sure to be diminished. Prudence was of no value amidst such fanaticism and universal frenzy. If this king hadn't offended his subjects in one way, he would have offended them in another. It was fated by the order of causes that he would be in the wrong.[50]

As another example of the determinist grip a dominant tone can exercise on events, Montesquieu cited developments in France during the Regency of Louis XV (1715–1723). What enabled France to get through this difficult period following the death of Louis XIV in 1714, Montesquieu concluded, was a spirit of obedience that rendered the French tolerant of the policy decisions of the regent, the Duke of Orleans:

> One could say that there has never been a more unusual government and that from the first day to the last, France was in the grip of extraordinary events. However, someone who had done the opposite of what was done, and who had made decisions just the opposite of those adopted, would have finished his regency quite as felicitously as this regent completed his. If, one by one, fifty others princes had taken up the government in their own way, they would also have completed this regency successfully. Minds, circumstances, situations, and respective interests were such that the end result would have been the same, whatever the cause or power at work.[51]

This determinist line of thought prompted Montesquieu to make the following remarkable statement about the insignificance of human agency under many circumstances:

> The prudence of man actually amounts to practically nothing. In most situations, deliberation is useless, because, except where major disadvantages are immediately obvious, all the courses of action one might adopt are equally good.[52]

Clearly Montesquieu's interest in historical determinism was well developed by the mid-1720s when he wrote *De la politique* and well prepared him to discern determinist currents swirling beneath the surface of Roman political developments when he turned his attention to composition of his history of Rome.[53]

## Tocqueville on Historical Inevitability

Like Montesquieu before him, Tocqueville gave serious thought to the relative weight of irreversible general causes and human agency in shaping historical outcomes. He devoted a whole chapter of *Democracy in America* to explaining how the "social state"—whether aristocratic or democratic—will substantially affect a historian's viewpoint regarding the relative weight of vast impersonal forces as compared to human agency.[54] Since equality has a leveling influence on society that reduces the influence of great leaders, historians residing in democratic societies will be prone to exaggerating the importance of general causes. "Historians who live in democratic ages," he asserted, wrongly resort to such invented causes as "an inflexible Providence or to some blind necessity."[55] He considered this a very dangerous tendency since it inclines men toward fatalism. What is at stake is nothing less than a proper appreciation for freedom. In fact, he concluded, if the "doctrine of necessity" should become widespread, "it will soon paralyze the activity of modern society and reduce Christians to the level of the Turks."[56] Thus, he considered it crucial to recognize that historical outcomes are sometimes the effect of general causes beyond the power of individuals to control and sometimes the result of the impact of the unpredictable actions of key individuals:

> For myself, I am of the opinion that, at all times, one great portion of the events of this world are attributable to very general facts and another to special influences. These two kinds of cause are always in operation; only their proportion varies. General facts serve to explain more things in democratic than in aristocratic ages, and fewer things are then assignable to individual influences. During periods of aristocracy the reverse takes place: special influences are stronger, general causes weaker.[57]

Thus he chose to conclude that neither general causes nor "individual influences" will ever completely dominate. Historians in democratic societies, he wrote, are correct "in assigning much to general causes ... but they are wrong in wholly denying the special influence of individuals because they cannot easily trace or follow it."[58] Historians must guard against concluding that because historical causes move "millions of men at once" and seem "sufficiently strong to bend all them together in the same direction, they should be judged irresistible."[59] And yet, all too often, historians in democratic societies seek to shorten their labors by focusing only on general causes:

> M. de Lafayette says somewhere in his *Memoirs* that the exaggerated system of general causes affords surprising consolations to second-rate statesmen. I will add that its effects are not less consolatory to second-rate historians; it can always furnish a few mighty reasons to extricate them from the most difficult part of their work, and it indulges the indolence or incapacity of their minds while it confers upon them the honors of deep thinking.[60]

In composing *Democracy in America* Tocqueville resisted determinist conclusions. He pointedly rejected climate, geography and race as general causes capable of explaining American achievements.[61] After pondering whether climatological explanations could account for the differences between the French in Canada and the French in Louisiana, he rejected all such explanations as misguided materialism.[62] "The idée-mère of this book," he asserted in an undated draft text now among the papers housed at Yale University, "is directly the contrary, since I started invincibly from this point: whatever the tendencies of the social condition [whether democratic or aristocratic], men can always modify them and avert the bad while adapting to the good."[63] In *Democracy in America*, Tocqueville wanted very much to conclude that human agency is ultimately more determinative of historical outcomes than the social and material causes beyond man's control. Thus he inserted at the very end of the second volume a text suggesting that, within certain limits dictated by underlying causes, human beings are free to fashion their own destinies:

> I am aware that many of my contemporaries think that nations on earth are never their own masters and that they are bound to obey some insuperable and unthinking power, the product of pre-existing facts, of race, or soil, or climate. These are false and cowardly doctrines which can only produce feeble men and pusillanimous nations.... Providence did not make mankind entirely free or completely enslaved. Providence has, in truth, drawn a predestined circle around each man beyond which he cannot pass; but within those vast limits man is strong and free, and so are peoples.[64]

No more than Montesquieu, however, did Tocqueville believe that literally everything is within the power of law makers to achieve. To accurately assess his philosophy of history, due weight must also be given to the following text from the first volume of *Democracy in America*, which inclines more in the direction of historical determinism:

> When, after many efforts, a legislator succeeds in exercising an indirect influence upon the destiny of nations, his genius is lauded by mankind, while, in point of fact, the geographical position of the country, which he is unable to change, a social condition which arose without his co-operation, customs and opinions which he cannot trace to their source, and an origin with which he is unacquainted exercise so irresistible an influence over the courses of society that he is himself borne away by the current after an ineffectual resistance. Like the navigator, he may direct the vessel

which bears him, but he can neither change its structure, nor raise the winds, nor lull the waters that swell beneath him.[65]

Clearly Tocqueville found sorting out the balance between determinism and freedom a complex matter. He certainly believed that general causes set limits to the efficacy of human action. This recognition of human limits, however, never evolved into fatalism. In fact, in a letter to Francisque de Corcelle, he pointedly criticized Hegel for preaching a doctrine that was too prone to accepting what history has dictated and too pessimistic regarding the potential for ameliorative change. "Hegel," he lamented, "wanted people to submit to the old and still existing fact of the established powers of his time, which he declared legitimate as a consequence of their existence." And he went on in this same letter to criticize the German government for supporting "the Hegelian school . . . because its doctrine in its political consequences established that all facts are respectable and legitimated by their existence and deserve obedience."[66] Clearly, then, however much he believed that "Providence did not make mankind entirely free," Tocqueville nonetheless wanted very much to believe that the existing nature of things, fashioned by many complex and interacting influences, is not entirely fixed and may be altered and improved by human effort and ingenuity.

## Tocqueville's Philosophical History of the French Revolution

As insightful as were Tocqueville's comments in *Democracy in America* on historical causation, the key texts for analyzing his philosophy of history are in *The Old Regime* and in its unfinished sequel.[67] In studying the Revolution he was intrigued by the same basic question that had preoccupied Montesquieu regarding Rome: was that cataclysmic event the product of general, irreversible causes, or could different decisions by French kings have averted it? True to the formula he had previously worked out in *Democracy in America*, he considered both types of explanations. In the end, however, he adopted a determinist explanation of the Revolution. Given the presence in France of a deep-seated conflict between the principles of equality and privilege, and given the development of bureaucratic, paternalistic centralization rendering French subjects at the same time dependent on and resentful of the monarchy, it was inevitable, he concluded, that the political structure of the old regime would one day collapse.[68] Thus he remarked in the very first chapter of *The Old Regime*, "The Revolution was least of all an accident. True, it took the world by surprise, and yet it was the result of a very long process, the sudden and violent climax of a task to which ten generations had contributed."[69]

Tocqueville portrayed the Revolution as the preordained result of ineradicable general causes rooted in grievances that gave rise to deep discontent. "Many contemporaries, unable to fathom the general causes attributed it to the action of secret societies," but the "secret societies were assuredly not the cause of the Revolution." Rather, he noted, they were simply "one of the most obvious signs of its approach."[70]

Tocqueville boldly announced his thesis of the historical inevitability of the Revolution in the very first paragraph of *The Old Regime*, remarking "[n]ever was such a great event, with such ancient causes, so well prepared and so little foreseen."[71] The general causes of the Revolution, he concluded, were so deeply rooted in long-term trends and so inexorable as to deserve the label "providential."[72] He believed a centuries-old push for equality and democracy functioned as the general cause of the Revolution. Adopting very much the *longue durée* view, he concluded that a transformation from aristocracy to democracy had been under way in France since the eleventh century. Moreover, he portrayed the Third Estate as coming on the scene as early as the twelfth century with the result that "the subsequent history of Europe could be seen as the historical quest of this Third Estate for liberty and power."[73] Thus the fiscal crisis of the eighteenth-century that led to the calling of the Estates General in 1789 was only a secondary cause of the Revolution. The general cause was the inexorable force exerted by a relentless quest for equality that rendered inevitable, in one form or another, the clash between the privileged orders and the third estate of France.[74]

Tocqueville found it striking that French monarchs "could have maintained the ridiculous and senseless inequality [between France's three orders] which existed in France at the time of the Revolution," and he believed that "the slightest contact with 'self-government' would have profoundly changed and rapidly transformed or destroyed it."[75] Such was the power monopoly of French kings, however, that with the exception of Brittany and Languedoc not since the fourteenth century had the nobility and the Third Estate worked together effectively either in the Estates General or in provincial assemblies. Thus, unlike the different classes in England that found it necessary to work together to solve real problems, the three orders in France were denied such opportunities, and this greatly contributed to the class suspicions and intense animosities that fueled the Revolution. Privileged noblemen deprived of political power snubbed members of the middle and lower classes since, having ceased to rule, they no longer needed such individuals to help them govern.[76] Moreover, French aristocrats made their caste status all the more obnoxious by consoling themselves for their loss of "real power' by flaunting "conspicuous privileges" that had long ceased to be the reward for political or military service.[77] And adding still more fuel to the fires of class conflict was unequal taxation. "[F]rom the moment when the two classes were no longer equally subject to taxation, they had almost no further reason to meet together again, no more reason to experience common needs and feelings." In short, "the motive and desire to act together had been taken from them."[78] This isolation of classes in France, Tocqueville pointed out, contrasted sharply with the situation in England where still vibrant political liberty worked to produce class harmony. In England, "freedom always forced them all to stay in touch with one another, in order to be able to reach an understanding when necessary."[79] In France class suspicions were exacerbated by the absence of common goals achieved in concert.

As a philosopher of history, Tocqueville concluded that it is not surface events but rather underlying conditions and structural aspects of society—in the case of France deeply entrenched class differences between the three orders and a culture of paternalistic centralization destroying local liberties—that serve as the general causes of epochal events. The deeply felt commitment in France to the principle of equality necessarily gave rise to revolutionary sentiments since it took root in the context of a regime based on privilege.[80] Thus while conducting his research leading to *The Old Regime* Tocqueville explained to George Cornewall Lewis that it was in public opinion that he hoped to find the causes of the Revolution. And in a letter to A. de Circourt he explained that what he was seeking to identify was "the state of mind out of which the Revolution came," or "the general spirit of the time."[81] Without going quite so far as to assert, "*C'est la faute à Rousseau*," Tocqueville identified the French *philosophes* as "the real chiefs of the great party which intended to overthrow all the social and political institutions of the country."[82] Equality became the driving passion of all these French writers who elevated reason above "old things and tradition," and allowed "pure theory" to guide their "literary politics." The end result was that "[e]very public passion was thus wrapped up in philosophy; political life was violently driven back into literature, and writers, taking in hand the direction of opinion, found themselves for a moment taking the place that party leaders usually hold in free countries."[83] French intellectuals displayed intense hostility toward the status quo. Instead of expressing "instinctive love, or almost involuntary respect . . . for their own institutions, their traditional customs, or the wisdom or virtue of their fathers," French theorists were uncompromisingly critical of the status quo. "Everywhere the talk was of the inadequacy, incoherence, and ridiculous features of institutions, the vices of contemporaries, the corruption and rottenness of society."[84]

Tocqueville considered the physiocrats just as much to blame as the *lumières*. In fact, he noted that "the institutions that the Revolution was going to permanently abolish had been the particular objects of the physiocrats' attacks." Even more than the *philosophes*, the physiocrats displayed "the democratic and revolutionary temperament we know so well," including "limitless contempt" for the past. In fact, "there was no institution too old, too well-founded, for them not to demand its abolition." Moreover, Tocquevile remarked that the physiocrats "adore[d] equality even in servitude" and were "hostile to deliberative assemblies, to local and secondary powers, and in general to all counterweights which had been established . . . to balance the central power." In short, they advocated "democratic despotism" with "[n]o more hierarchy within society, no more classes, no more fixed ranks." They envisioned "a people composed of almost identical and entirely equal individuals" led by "a single individual, charged with doing everything in its name, without consulting it."[85]

There was also present, as part of the pre-Revolutionary landscape of France, according to Tocqueville, a naive and dangerous susceptibility to starry-eyed utopian innovation. Everywhere innovators with dreams of reforming humanity were listened to intently. "There was no enthusiasm that could not pass for science, no dreamer who could not get himself heard, no imposter who could not be beloved." Europe—and above all France—was beset by a "malady" that consisted of "the troubled agitation of the human mind . . . running this way and that like a hurried traveler who cannot find his way and also sometimes abruptly retraces his steps instead of going forward."[86] With the exception of a very few writers—chiefly Montesquieu whose ideas on the balance of powers he singled out for praise—Tocqueville blamed French intellectuals of the eighteenth century for pedaling false and dangerous ideas suggesting that existing imperfections could only be remedied by wiping the historical slate entirely clean. Amid such uncompromising radicalism, all appreciation for the complexity of politics vanished. "[P]olitics was reduced to a question of arithmetic. The notion of government was simplified. Numbers alone became the basis for law and right" as the Third Estate pushed for representation equal to the other two orders combined.[87]

Gone was all respect for tradition. Even pamphlets by such supposed moderates as Lacretelle and Roederer had "no perception of the past or of old influences and interests." There was "nobody upholding [historical] principles," Tocqueville lamented. "Thirty years before, there would have been. Montesquieu had defended or at least noted them. No one in 1788 understands them, not even the interested parties; or from political expediency they dare not maintain them. The ideas of Rousseau are a flood submerging for a moment all this part of the human mind and human knowledge."[88] What no one seems to have understood "is that there should exist different orders with a mutual veto." This bit of Montesquieuian wisdom was summarily dismissed. "The very idea of a temperate and prudent government, that is, of a government in which the different classes forming society and the different interests that divide it act as counterweights to one another" was "replaced by the idea of a crowd of similar elements represented by deputies, who represent number rather than interests or persons."[89] In sum, it was the "underlying basis of thinking," which was in turn a reflection of the centuries old quest for equality, that made the revolution "in advance" and which always "produces the final result of revolutions."[90] Tocqueville was convinced that the Revolution in thought preceded the Revolution in action so that the actual events of 1789 were a foregone conclusion, a working out in practice of a move to equality that had already taken place in the minds of the French people.[91]

## Tocqueville's Reflections on the Role of Human Agency in the Revolution

Although he focused primarily on the deterministic role of underlying general causes in producing the Revolution, Tocqueville by no means ignored the potential influence of human agency. There are passages in both *The Old Regime* and in the chapters and stray notes of its unfinished sequel, where he pondered whether different policies employed by Louis XV or Louis XVI could have moderated—or possibly even have averted—the revolution. He concluded that Louis XVI had tragically blundered in not stipulating by executive fiat all the procedures that would govern the meeting of the Estates General. This resulted in a dangerous vacuum that class conflict quickly filled. Beyond deciding that the number of representatives of the Third Estate should be doubled, Louis should have imposed voting by head in a common assembly. This "would doubtless have been to make a revolution, but a revolution from above," which "while ruining the old institutions of the country, would have softened their fall." [92] Moreover, "[t]he upper classes would have adjusted in advance to an unavoidable destiny," and "[i]nstead of madly fighting to preserve everything, they would have fought not to lose all." By leaving the mode of voting unspecified, Louis gave "the two classes" five months "to refresh and ripen their old hatreds," thereby ensuring that the conflict of orders would reach "the point of frenzy."[93] So momentous did Tocqueville consider this failure of Louis to take control of legislative events that in his unfinished sequel to *The Old Regime* he referred to it as marking nothing less than "the king's abdication of the regal power." Once the door had been opened for historical debates regarding the Estates General, discussions promptly expanded to encompass the very nature of power and who should wield it:

> At first they talked only of a better balance of powers, a better adjustment between classes; soon they walked, they ran, they threw themselves on the idea of pure democracy. At first it was Montesquieu who was quoted and commented on; in the end, it was only Rousseau. Rousseau became and was to remain the sole teacher of the Revolution in its first stage.[94]

If Louis XVI came in for pointed criticism, so, too, did Louis XV. What the French people had desired at mid-century, Tocqueville asserted, were "reforms" rather than "rights." Thus a more reform-minded monarch could perhaps have set changes in motion that would have quelled public discontent. "[I]f there had been found on the throne a ruler of the stature and disposition of Frederick the Great," Tocqueville asserted, "I do not at all doubt that he would have accomplished in society and government several of the great changes that the Revolution made, not only without losing his crown, but greatly increasing his power." Twenty years later, however, this opportunity to avert revolution had passed. "[T]he image of political freedom had presented itself to the French mind, and became more and more attractive to it every day."[95]

Tocqueville's assertions regarding the ineptness of French kings are certainly useful in reminding us that, as convinced as he was of the inexorable influence of general causes, he was also aware of the shaping influence of human agency in certain settings. His final judgment, however, about the coming of the French Revolution was determinist. Louis XVI's actions, he ultimately concluded, were entirely peripheral compared to the deep-seated general causes of the Revolution. Speaking in a summary fashion of Louis' missteps at the time of the convening of the Estates General, he remarked: "But we must not attribute too much importance to these procedural details. Human affairs are determined by human ideas and passions, not by machinery of the laws. It is always in the depths of the mind that facts are molded as they are then produced in the outside world."[96] In the final analysis, then, Tocqueville believed that Louis' decisions did not play a very significant role in unleashing what was to come. "Whatever decision had been taken on the form and regulation for these assemblies of the nation, it must be supposed that the war between classes would have nonetheless broken out violently. Class hatreds were already too inflamed to make common action possible, and the royal power was too far weakened to restrain them."[97] In short, the monarchy's fate was sealed by underlying general causes, just as the fate of the Roman republic had been dictated, according to Montesquieu, by the general causes associated with imperial expansion. Thus we may conclude that both Montesquieu and Tocqueville were convinced that there are certain historical moments when human beings are in the grip of dominant ideas and passions traceable to deep structural causes, and it is in those historical moments that the influence of human agency is at its nadir.

## Conclusion

We have seen that Montesquieu's exploration of Rome's decline into empire and Tocqueville's reflections on the French Revolution may be read as extended dialogues on whether those events were the result of the influence of general causes beyond the power of individual historical agents to control. Ultimately they both opted for the thesis of historical determinism. Tocqueville grew nearly as convinced of the power of general causes as Montesquieu had been. "Chance," he acknowledged in his *Recollections*, his personal memoir of the Revolution of 1848, is "a very important element" in historical change, but "chance can do nothing unless the ground has been prepared in advance" by more general causes.[98] In a similar vein he wrote to Beaumont a half decade later, "general causes ... always end up dominating through particular accidents."[99] It is difficult to imagine assertions any closer in spirit to the determinist conclusions Montesquieu had earlier reached as a result of his investigations of the demise of Roman republicanism. Tocqueville was willing to qualify his argument only to the extent of asserting that "[i]f it [the Revolution] had not taken place, the old social structure would nevertheless have collapsed everywhere, here sooner, there later, with the only difference that it would have continued to fall apart piece by piece instead of collapsing all at once."[100]

Montesquieu's and Tocqueville's historical determinism must not be conflated with fatalism. They were not fatalists believing that the underlying causes at work in producing the events they described were somehow predestined and could not have taken any different form. Their viewpoint, rather, was that given the nature of the causal factors that were present in the Roman republic and in the Old Regime—attributable in large part to choices made by free agents rather than to vast impersonal forces beyond human control—the collapse of Roman republicanism and the coming of the French Revolution became, at a certain point, inevitable. Tocqueville was careful to differentiate his position of historical determinism, stressing that things happen as a result of discernible causes, from fatalism. He remarked in his *Recollections*, "For my part I hate all those absolute systems that make all the events of history depend on great first causes linked together by the chain of fate." Such systems, he lamented, "succeed, so to speak, in banishing men from the history of the human race."[101] It had been free human beings who had been responsible for the centuries long quest for equality that Tocqueville regarded as the general cause of the Revolution. Although he labeled the force of this inexorable egalitarian tide "Providential," he did not actually mean to imply that human beings were merely acting as necessitous agents of an external force exerted by the deity.[102] As for Montesquieu, he never implied that the Roman republic was somehow predestined to expand to the point where republican sentiments were eclipsed and republican institutions became unworkable. Rather his argument was that given the decisions taken by Roman politicians to embark on aggressive expansionism, the transition from republicanism to empire became at a certain point inevitable.

Far from being fatalists convinced that human beings have no influence on what transpires, both Montesquieu and Tocqueville believed in the capacity of human beings to achieve liberty. It is true that Gilbert Chinard once labeled Montesquieu a "historical pessimist"[103] and that Montesquieu even predicted the demise of English liberty "when legislative power is more corrupt than executive power."[104] But certainly Montesquieu was far from pessimistic regarding the prospects for liberty in the modern world. In Book X of *The Spirit of Laws* he focused on confederate republics, such as Holland and Switzerland, as vehicles for combining republicanism with larger territory so that republican states based on civic virtue could be made compatible with the geographical situation of modern times. Moreover he believed that liberty was sustainable even in a large monarchy such as France if the parlements were allowed to moderate the king's power through their historic right to register the crown's edicts before they became law. Eschewing thoughts of reconvening the Estates General, Montesquieu considered the parlements as both the legitimate representatives of the nation and effective shields against despotism, and he became their foremost apologist prior to the writings of Louis Adrien Le Paige.[105] Montesquieu well understood that despotism arises quite naturally from human instincts for power,[106] and he also knew that the achievement of liberty requires great ingenuity in devising complex constitutional structures to counteract excessive concentrations of power. And yet he never took the position that human prospects for liberty might one day be extinguished.

As for Tocqueville, he was similarly aware that the prospects for liberty are by no means guaranteed. If he judged the progress of equality inexorable, he considered liberty a different matter. Liberty, he believed, is more fragile and requires constant nurturing. Moreover liberty can be compromised by the excessive pursuit of equality. But Tocqueville nonetheless clung to the hope, even during the dark years following the *coup d'état* of Napoleon III, that French liberty could be revived. Thus he sharply disagreed with that notorious author of racist theories, Arthur de Gobineau, that modern man was doomed to servitude and that we might just as well accept "government of the sword and even of the whip. . . . To me," he explained to Gobineau, "human societies, like persons, become something worth while only through their use of liberty. I have always said that it is more difficult to stabilize and to maintain liberty in our new democratic societies than in certain aristocratic societies of the past. But I shall never dare to think it impossible."[107]

Tocqueville did not abandon hope that human beings would prove capable of freedom—whatever the odds. "Some may accuse me," Tocqueville remarked in the "Preface" to *The Old Regime*, "of displaying too strong a taste for freedom."[108] Not so, he responded. "Only freedom can tear people from the worship of Mammon and the petty daily concerns of their personal affairs and . . . create the atmosphere which allows one to see and judge human vices and virtues."[109] Montesquieu displayed a similarly high regard for liberty, remarking in one of his *Pensées*, "Liberty [is] that good that renders us capable of enjoying other goods."[110] He had written his first published work, the *Persian Letters* (1721), in part to warn of the dangers of despotism in France, and he had traced out the fundamentals of the English political system in *The Spirit of Laws* to show how one modern nation had resolved to make liberty its "direct object."

Arguably, Tocqueville's faith in liberty was more sorely tested by the return of Bonapartism to France in the 1850s than Montesquieu's had been by any acts of earlier Bourbon absolutism.[111] Nonetheless, following the *coup d'état* on December 2, 1851 creating France's Second Empire, Tocqueville did not conclude that political liberty could not be restored. In spite of periodic expressions of pessimism, as in his remark in a January 21, 1855 letter to Pierre Freslon that Napoleon's *coup* "destroyed the liberties of France in a way that seems permanent," he managed to remain hopeful.[112] In a letter to Gustave de Beaumont, for example, he rejected any analogy to "the vices of the Roman Empire" that might suggest France would go down the same road from freedom to servitude. "We are not yet ripe," he concluded, "for the regular and definitive establishment of despotism." Should authoritarianism be pushed too far, he believed, the government would "find a layer of Frondeurs" that would join with the French people to overthrow despotism and re-establish liberty. Hence Tocqueville remained convinced that the current authoritarian government, whose authority rested on a plebiscite passed by a passive citizenry lulled to sleep by a desire for security and material comfort, would one day be rejected.[113] This would take time and would require substantial effort, but eventually freedom would be restored. Of that, Tocqueville remained convinced, though he did not live to savor the republican moment when parliamentary liberty was finally restored with the advent of the Third Republic.

## Notes

During the composition of this essay I have had the pleasure of sharing my thoughts with the following scholars who have offered useful advice and counsel: Roger Boesche, Hank Clark, Susan Dunn, Arthur Goldhammer, Daniel Gordon, Thomas Kaiser, Rebecca Kingston, Sharon Krause, Melvin Richter, Jay Smith, Steven Smith, Jennifer Thompson, Stephen Vincent, and Kent Wright.

1. Regarding Tocqueville's reluctance to reveal his sources, François Furet has remarked, "there is no reliable way of reconstructing what he read as an adolescent. Tocqueville was remarkably discreet about his reading not only during the process of his studies but indeed throughout his life, as can be seen from his correspondence. His was a mind convinced of, not to say obsessed by, its own originality. Even in places in his main works when he clearly drew on one or another of his predecessors, he generally remained silent about what he was up to." In fact, Furet concluded, Tocqueville's "discretion is so thoroughgoing that even a question as simple as whether Tocqueville read a lot or a little in his youth or late life is hard to answer unequivocally." See

François Furet, "The Intellectual Origins of Tocqueville's Thought," in *The Tocqueville Review/La Revue Tocqueville*, Vol. XXVI, No. 1 (2005), pp. 121–22.

2. Tocqueville to Kergorlay, Nov. 1836, in *Œuvres complètes*, ed. J.-P. Mayer, (Paris: Gallimard, 1951– ), XIII (1), p. 418, cited in Sheldon Wolin, *Tocqueville between Two Worlds. The Making of a Political and Theoretical Life* (Princeton: Princeton University Pres, 2001), p. 171.

3. Tocqueville to Kergorlay, December 15, 1850, in R.R. Palmer, ed. and trans., *The Two Tocquevilles. Father and Son. Hervé and Alexis de Tocqueville on the Coming of the French Revolution* (Princeton: Princeton University Press, 1987), p. 228. Hereafter cited as Palmer.

4. This conversation took place in February, 1851. See *Œuvres complètes*, ed. J.-P. Mayer, (Paris: Gallimard, 1951– ), VI (2), p. 346.

5. Harvey Mansfield and Delba Winthrop note that in *Democracy in America* Tocqueville "refers to Montesquieu three times directly (I, 1.5; I, 2.6; I, 2.10) and twice indirectly (II, 3.11; II, 3.18)." See Alexis de Tocqueville, *Democracy in America*, translated, edited, and with an introduction by Harvey C. Mansfield and Delba Winthrop (Chicago: University of Chicago Press, 2000), p. xxxiii, footnote 33. Hereafter cited as Mansfield.

6. See Alexis de Tocqueville, *The Old Regime and the Revolution*, ed. François Furet and Françoise Mélonio and trans. Alan S. Kahan (Chicago: University of Chicago Press, 1998), pp. 145, 153, and 182. Hereafter cited as *Old Regime*, trans. Kahan. Tocqueville's source for Montesquieu's comment on Paris' dominance over the rest of France was a letter written by Montesquieu to Abbé Nicolini on March 6, 1740 that had been printed in editions of his *Familiar Letters*. On land productivity, Tocqueville provided no citation, but the text to which he refers is in Book XVIII, chapter 3 of *The Spirit of Laws*. The reference to Montesquieu's views on England includes no source citation, but Tocqueville appears to have been referring to a letter written by Montesquieu from England, which Tocqueville wrongly dated 1739 instead of 1729. The translation of *The Old Regime* by Alan Kahan is far superior to the excessively free translation by Stuart Gilbert (Anchor Books, 1955), which often reads as a paraphrase of Tocqueville's text.

7. The same problem exists for exploring the Guizot/Tocqueville connection. There are no footnotes to Guizot in *The Old Regime*, but Guizot's influence is apparent, as Aurelian Craiutu and Robert Gannet have recently shown. See Aurelian Craiutu, *Liberalism under Siege. The Political Thought of the French Doctrinaires* (Lanham, MD: Lexington Books, 2003) and Robert T. Gannett Jr., *Tocqueville Unveiled. The Historian and His Sources for The Old Regime and the Revolution* (Chicago: University of Chicago Press, 2003). Gannet (p. 19) reports that Tocqueville produced "polished résumés of seventeen of Guizot's lectures, laced with his personal interjections" and that Tocqueville read "the greatest part" of Guizot's works during the summer of 1829. For Guizot's influence on Tocqueville, see also François Furet, *Interpreting the French Revolution* (Cambridge: Cambridge University Press, 1981), pp. 135–39. Hereafter cited as *Interpreting the French Revolution*.

8. See Seymour Dresher, "Foreward," p. x, in Françoise Mélonio, *Tocqueville and the French*, translated by Beth G. Raps (Charlottesville: University Press of Virginia, 1998). Hereafter cited as Mélonio.

9. Mansfield, p. xxxiii, citing Jean-Claude Lambert, *Tocqueville and the Two Democracies*, trans. A. Goldhammer (Cambridge, MA: Harvard University Press, 1989), p. 122.

10. Dresher, p. x, in Mélonio, ibid., p. x.

11. *The Old Regime*, trans. Kahan, p. 215.

12. See Melvin Richter, "Comparative Political Analysis in Montesquieu and Tocqueville," *Comparative Politics* (January, 1969), pp. 129–60 for a comprehensive survey of the grounds for concluding that Tocqueville may be regarded as "Montesquieu's greatest disciple." (p. 130). See also Melvin Richter, "The Uses of Theory: Tocqueville's Adaptation of Montesquieu," in *Essays in Theory and History. An Approach to the Social Sciences*, ed. Melvin Richter (Cambridge, MA: Harvard University Press, 1970), pp. 74–102.

13. In the essay cited in footnote one, François Furet suggested that Tocqueville utilized a "hypothetico-deductive method." (p. 122) On Tocqueville's deductive method, see also Roger Boesche, "Why Could Tocqueville Predict So Well?" *Political Theory*, XI, 1 (Feb. 1983), pp. 79–103. On Montesquieu's use of deductive method, see David Wallace Carrithers, ed. *The Spirit of Laws by Montesquieu. A Compendium of the First English Edition* (Berkeley: University of California Press, 1977), "Introduction," pp. 40–44. Hereafter cited as *Spirit of Laws*, ed. Carrithers.

14. Tocqueville expressed concern regarding his tendency to generalize, remarking to John Stuart Mill following the publication of Volume 1 of *Democracy in America*, "I have a too pronounced penchant for general ideas." See Wolin, p. 114.

15. For Montesquieu's strictures against uniformity, see Book XXIX, chapter 18 of *The Spirit of Laws*. For an interesting example of Tocqueville's well-known disdain for uniformity, see his pleas for pluralism and respect for local difference in his *Second Letter on Algeria* (August, 1837) in Alexis de Tocqueville, *Writings on Empire and Slavery*, edited and translated by Jennifer Pitts (Baltimore: Johns Hopkins University Press, 2001), p. 23.

16. For passages stressing general causes as preparing the ground for the Revolution, see *Old Regime*, trans. Kahan, I, 1, p. 93; I, 5, p. 106; II, 3, p. 215.

17. For Tocqueville's stress on the irresistible force of this transformation, see the lengthy discussion of "the principle of equality" as "a providential fact" that is "universal" and "lasting" and "constantly eludes all human interference" while "all events as well as all men contribute to its progress" in his Introduction to *Democracy in America. The Henry Reeve Text as Revised by Francis Bowen Now Further Corrected and Edited with a Historical Essay, Editorial Notes, and Bibliography by Phillips Bradley*, 2 vols. (New York: Vintage Books, 1945), I, pp. 3–7. Hereafter cited as *Democracy*, ed. Bradley. See also *Old Regime*, trans. Kahan, p. 87 for reference to democracy as a "force" which we cannot "defeat" and "which sometimes gently urges and sometimes shoves us towards the destruction of aristocracy."

18. This abhorrence of fatalism is particularly apparent in chapter XX of Volume II, Book One of *Democracy in America*, which Tocqueville entitled "Some Characteristics of Historians in Democratic Times." Tocqueville was later intrigued by John Stuart Mill's comment in his *A System of Logic* (1843), "When we say that all human actions take place of necessity, we only mean that they will certainly happen if nothing prevents." This assisted Tocqueville in distinguishing between necessity, which stems from causes

that may be altered, and fatalism, which implies irresistible forces beyond human control. It would certainly seem, however, that he regarded the relentless pursuit of an equality of social conditions leading to democracy as an irreversible tide that finally washed over France in the Revolution. In his Introduction to *Democracy in America* he explained that "the whole book ... has been written under the influence of a kind of religious awe produced in the author's mind by the view of that irresistible revolution which has advanced for centuries in spite of every obstacle and which is still advancing in the midst of the ruins it has caused." (*Democracy*, ed. Bradley, p. 7). For the exchange with Mill, see Tocqueville to Mill, October 25, 1843, cited in Harvey Mitchell, *Individual Choice and the Structures of History. Alexis de Tocqueville as Historian Reappraised* (Cambridge: Cambridge, University Press, 2005), p. 45. Hereafter cited as Mitchell.

19. "Never was such a great event," he wrote, "with such ancient causes, so well prepared and so little foreseen." (*Old Regime*, trans. Kahan, p. 93)

20. See Edward Gibbon, *An Essay on the Study of Literature. Written originally in French* (London, 1762), p. 111–13, cited in David Carrithers, "Montesquieu's Philosophy of History," *Journal of the History of Ideas*, XLVII, Number 1 (January–March 1986), pp. 61–80.

21. Tocqueville to Kergorlay, Dec. 15, 1850, in Palmer, p. 228.

22. Drafts, Yale, CVh, Paquet 3, cahier 4, p. 48, cited in James T. Schleifer, *The Making of Tocqueville's Democracy in America* (Chapel Hill: the University of North Carolina Press, 1980), p. 58. Hereafter cited as Schleifer.

23. "Sources manuscrites," Yale, CIIc, cited in ibid., p. 58.

24. Pocket Notebooks Numbers 4 and 5, 13th January (1832), in Alexis de Tocqueville, *Journey to America*, trans. George Lawrence, ed. J.P. Mayer (New Haven, CT: Yale University Press, 1960), p. 177.

25. Ibid., p. 177.

26. Tocqueville to Reeve, Feb. 6, 1856, in Palmer, p. 230.

27. Tocqueville to Kergorlay, Dec. 15, 1850, in Palmer, p. 228.

28. Alexis de Tocqueville, *Selected Letters on Politics and Society*, trans. James Toupin and Roger Boesche, ed. Roger Boesche (Berkeley: University of California Press, 1985), p. 257.

29. *Considerations on the Causes of the Greatness of the Romans and Their Decline*, translated with notes and an introduction by David Lowenthal (Ithaca: Cornell University Press, 1965), p. 169. Hereafter cited as *Considerations*.

30. Ibid., p. 169.

31. For the extent of Montesquieu's animosity toward Roman militarism and imperialism, see, in particular, Jean Ehrard, "'Rome enfin que je hais' ... ?" In *L'Esprit des mots. Montesquieu en lui-même et parmi les siens* (Geneva: Droz, 1998), pp. 55–65 and Paul Rahe, "The Book that Never Was: Montesquieu's *Considerations on the Romans* in Historical Context," *History of Political Thought*, XXVI, (2005), pp. 43–89.

32. On the theme of self-destructive conquest, Montesquieu later asserted that "an immense conquest presupposes despotism" since the prince needs to be "always ready to assail the part of the empire that may waver." (See Book X, chapter 16 of *The Spirit of the Laws*, trans. and ed. Anne Cohler et al. (Cambridge: Cambridge University Press, 1989), p. 152. Hereafter cited as *Laws*, trans. Cohler.

33. *Considerations*, p. 108.

34. Ibid., p. 102.
35. Ibid., p. 169.
36. Ibid., pp. 26–27, 40, 50.
37. Ibid., p. 50.
38. Ibid., p. 67.
39. Ibid., pp. 67–70.
40. Ibid., pp. 70–73, 75.
41. Ibid., p. 74.
42. Ibid., pp. 105–06.
43. Ibid., p. 106.
44. Ibid., pp. 114–15.
45. Ibid., p. 13.
46. This work was not, of course, part of what Tocqueville could have read since it was not published until the late nineteenth century.
47. *De la politique*, in *Œuvres complètes de Montesquieu*, ed. Roger Caillois, 2 vols. (Paris: Bibliothèque de la Pléiade, 1949–1951), I, p. 113. Hereafter cited as Pléiade.
48. Ibid., in Pléiade, I, pp. 112–13.
49. Ibid., in Pléiade, I, p. 114.
50. Ibid., in Pléiade, I, p. 115.
51. Ibid., in Pléiade, I, p. 114. Clearly this spirit of obedience had vanished completely by the time of the calling of the Estates General in 1789. For commentary on Montesquieu's views on revolution in general and interesting speculation as to how he might have reacted to that event, see C.P. Courtney, "Montesquieu and Revolution," in *Lectures de Montesquieu. Actes du Colloque de Wolfenbüttel* (26–28 octobre 1989) réunis par Edgar Mass et Alberto Postigliola (Naples, Paris, Oxford, 1993), pp. 41–62.
52. Ibid., in Pléiade, I, p. 114.
53. Turning to more recent events, Montesquieu assessed the victory of Sweden over Denmark as also the result of root causes that pre-determined that outcome. (*Considerations*, p. 74) And later, in *The Spirit of Laws* (1748), he cited the defeat of Charles XII by the Russians at Pultova as another example of an historically determined event, remarking that "if he had not been destroyed at that place, he would have been destroyed at another. Accidents of fortune are easily rectified; one cannot avert events that continuously arise from the nature of things." (*Laws*, trans. Cohler, Book X, chapter 13, p. 147).
54. *Democracy*, ed. Bradley, II, pp. 90–93.
55. Ibid., II, pp. 92–93.
56. Ibid., II, 93.
57. Ibid., II, p. 91.
58. Ibid., II, pp. 91–92.
59. Ibid., II, p. 92.
60. Ibid., II, p. 91.
61. For his thinking on this subject during the 1840's, see his lengthy correspondence with Gobineau, in Alexis de Tocqueville, *"The European Revolution" & Correspondence with Gobineau*, introduced, edited and translated by John Lukacs (Gloucester, Mass.: Peter Smith, 1968). Hereafter cited as Lukacs.
62. Schleifer, p. 68.

63. Undated; Drafts, Yale CVk, Paquet 7, cahier 1, p. 37, in Schleifer, p. 68.

64. Cited in Schleifer, p. 69. For Montesquieu's views on the predominance of moral causes over physical causes, see the translation of his *Essay on Causes Affecting Minds and Characters* (1736–1743) in *Spirit of Laws*, ed. Carrithers, p. 443.

65. *Democracy*, ed. Bradley, I, p. 171.

66. Tocqueville to Corcelle, July 22, 1834, in *The Tocqueville Reader. A Life in Letters and Politics*, ed. Olivier Zunz and Alan S. Kahan (Oxford: Blackwell Publishing, 2002), pp. 270–71.

67. Tocqueville originally planned two volumes as sequels, enabling him to cover the events of the Revolution and the rise of Bonaparte. A portion of these materials was first assembled by Gustave de Beaumont for use in the first edition of Tocqueville's works. Much later André Jardin gathered together a larger portion of this manuscript material, which he published as Volume Two, Part II of Alexis de Tocqueville, *Oeuvres complètes*, ed. J. P. Mayer, 17 vols. (Paris: Gallimard (1951– ). To date, there have been three English translations of portions of these materials. The most complete is volume two of Alexis de Tocqueville, *The Old Regime and Revolution*, ed. François Furet and Françoise Mélonio and trans. Alan S. Kahan, 2 vols. (Chicago: University of Chicago Press, 1998–2001). The first translation of a portion of these materials was incorporated into Lukacs (see note 51). Another translation of the seven chapters that Tocqueville completed, plus a few of his miscellaneous notes and observations, was presented in Palmer.

68. *Old Regime*, trans. Kahan, pp. 138–45. For the view that Tocqueville exaggerated the extent of bureaucratic centralization in the old regime, see Furet, *Interpreting the French Revolution*, pp. 144–45.

69. Ibid., p. 106.

70. Palmer, p. 158.

71. *Old Regime*, trans. Kahan, p. 93.

72. This conviction of the Providential force of the principle of equality had been firm ever since he composed the first volume of *Democracy in America* wherein he had remarked: "In running over the pages of our history, we should scarcely find a single great event of the last seven hundred years that has not promoted equality of condition.... The gradual development of the principle of equality is, therefore, a providential fact. It has all the chief characteristics of such a fact: it is universal, it is lasting, it constantly eludes all human interference, and all events as well as all men contribute to its progress." (*Democracy*, ed. Bradley, I, p. 5–6)

73. Alexis de Tocqueville, *Journeys to England and Ireland*, edited Jacob-Peter Mayer (Garden City, New York, 1968), p. 5, cited in Roger Boesche, "Why did Tocqueville Think a Successful Revolution was Impossible?" in *Liberty, Equality, Democracy*, ed. Eduardo Nolla (New York: New York University Press, 1992), pp. 167, 174. In his Introduction to *Democracy in America*, Tocqueville spelled out his thesis regarding the centuries-old push for equality in France, remarking that "the clergy opened their ranks to all classes" at a very early date, and "the kings have always been the most constant of levelers for no less than seven hundred years." Moreover, the demise of feudal land tenures in France had enabled the serfs to enrich themselves well beyond the norm in other countries where inequality was much more prevalent. (See *Democracy*, ed. Bradley, I, pp. 3–5)

74. *Old Regime*, trans. Kahan, pp. 93, 106; Palmer, p. 212.

75. *Old Regime*, trans. Kahan, footnote 26, p. 283. The phrase "self-government" appears in English in this passage.

76. Ibid., pp. 155, 158.

77. Ibid., p. 158. For Tocqueville's treatment of Brittany and Languedoc, see the Appendix in ibid., pp. 249–56.

78. Ibid., p. 157. Tocqueville also remarked on this subject of taxation that "from the day when the nation . . . permitted the kings to establish a general tax without its consent, and when the nobility had the cowardice to allow the Third Estate to be taxed provided that the nobility itself was exempted, on that day was planted the seed for almost all the vices and abuses which affected the old regime for the rest of its life, and finally caused its violent death." (Ibid., p. 164)

79. Ibid., p. 163.

80. Thus Roger Boesche has suggested in the essay cited in note 73 (p. 172) that Tocqueville identified two basic factors as the chief underlying causes of the Revolution: "class needs and the role of ideas." As evidence of Tocqueville's keen appreciation for the role of classes, we have his trenchant remark, "I speak of classes, they alone ought to interest history." (*Old Regime*, trans. Kahan, p. 181)

81. Tocqueville to George Cornewall Lewis, October 6, 1856; Tocqueville to A. de Circourt, March 11, 1857, in Palmer, pp. 232, 236. In a note for a projected chapter on events from the fall of the Bastille to the end of the Constituent Assembly Tocqueville wrote: "*The French Revolution was made by a system of general ideas*, forming a single body of doctrine, a kind of political gospel where every idea resembles a dogma. Its aims not only inspired enthusiasm but also proselytism and propaganda. Its secular doctrines were not only believed but ardently preached, an entirely new thing in history." (Lukacs, pp. 101–02; italics in original.) For a comprehensive appraisal of Tocqueville's views on the influence of public opinion, see Mitchell, pp. 228–53 and particularly his conclusion (p. 241) that "Tocqueville laid down as a general law that all revolutions, not only the French, owed their force to the cumulative effect of public opinion."

82. *Old Regime*, trans. Kahan, p., 204. Referring to the decades prior to the French Revolution, Tocqueville wrote Beaumont on February 1, 1857, "There are times when books are political acts." (Palmer, p. 237)

83. *Old Regime*, trans. Kahan, pp. 197–98.

84. Palmer, p. 153. Tocqueville did not restrict his comments about the spirit of intense hostility to the status quo to France alone. He included the rest of Europe as well.

85. *Old Regime*, trans. Kahan, pp. 209–10, 213.

86. Palmer, pp. 157–58.

87. Ibid., p. 204.

88. Ibid., p. 213

89. Ibid., pp. 212–13.

90. Ibid., p. 212. Tocqueville considered the content of the *cahiers de doléances* of 1788 ample evidence that the revolution had already taken place in the minds of men. "I carefully read the cahiers. . . . I realize with a kind of terror that what is demanded is the simultaneous and systematic abolition of all the laws and all the customs in use in the country. . . . Poor fools! They had even forgotten that . . . '*by demanding too much freedom one gets too much slavery.*' " (*Old Regime*, trans. Kahan, p. 199 italics in original)

91. Thus François Furet could conclude, "Tocqueville suggests that the Revolution was above all a transformation in values and patterns of thought." (*Interpreting the French Revolution*, p. 157).

92. Palmer, p. 202.

93. Ibid., pp. 209–11.

94. Ibid., pp. 203–04.

95. *Old Regime*, trans. Kahan, p. 214.

96. Palmer, p. 210.

97. Ibid., pp. 210–11.

98. Alexis de Tocqueville, *Recollections*. A New Translation by George Lawrence, ed. by J. P. Mayer and A. P. Kerr (Garden City: Doubleday, 1970), p. 62. Hereafter cited as *Recollections*.

99. Tocqueville to Beaumont, March 25, 1855, in *Correspondance d'Alexis de Tocqueville et de Gustave de Beaumont*, André Jardin, ed., in *Œuvres complètes* ed. by Mayer, VIII, p. 290, cited in Roger Boesche, "Why did Tocqueville Think a Successful Revolution was Impossible?" p. 171.

100. *Old Regime*, trans. Kahan, p. 106.

101. *Recollections*, p. 62.

102. Thus Edward Gargan once asserted that "even when Tocqueville sought the sacred support of Providence to give force to his observations, the test that he employed was a profane one: the presence in any historical process of that which is constant and cumulative in impact, the extensive evidence that a process in history was unfolding towards an ascertainable present and dimly known future." See Edward Gargan, *De Tocqueville* (New York: Hillary House, 1965), p. 46. See also footnote 18 above for the distinction Tocqueville drew between necessity, or determinism, and fatalism.

103. Gilbert Chinard, "Montesquieu's Historical Pessimism," in *Studies in the History of Culture* (Menasha, Wisconsin, 1942), pp. 161–72.

104. *The Spirit of the Laws*, trans. Anne Cohler et. al., XI, 6, p. 166.

105. On the contents and influence of Le Paige's *Lettres historiques sur les fonctions essentielles du parlement, sur le droit des pairs, et sur les loix fondamentales du royaume*, 2 vols. (Amsterdam, 1753–54), see Dale Van Kley, *The Religious Origins of the French Revolution. From Calvin to the Civil Constitution, 1560–1791* (New Haven: Yale University Press, 1996), pp. 203–10.

106. *The Spirit of the Laws*, trans. Anne Cohler, V, 14, p. 63.

107. Tocqueville to Gobineau, January 24, 1857, in Lukacs, p. 309. Richard Herr has pointed out that Tocqueville had earlier remarked to Gobineau in a letter dated Dec. 20, 1853: "Perhaps you are right, but you have seized on the thesis that has always seemed to me the most dangerous possible to uphold in our day." And in a letter written on January 8, 1856 Tocqueville had said to Gobineau: "A work which tries to prove that in this world man obeys his *constitution* and can scarcely affect his destiny by his own free will is like opium given to a sick man whose heart is already slowing down." (italics in original) See Richard Herr, *Tocqueville and the Old Regime* (Princeton: Princeton University Press, 1962), p. 93. Hereafter cited as Herr.

108. *Old Regime*, trans. Kahan, p. 86.

109. Ibid., p. 88.

110. *Pensée* 1797 in Pléiade (1949–1951), I, p. 1430.

111. For Tocqueville's attitude toward the two Bonapartes, see Melvin Richter, "Tocqueville and French Nineteenth-Century Conceptualizations of the Two Bonapartes and Their Empires," in *Dictatorship in History and Theory. Bonapartism, Caesarism, and Totalitarianism*, ed. Peter Baehr and Melvin Richter (Cambridge: Cambridge University Press, 2004), pp. 83–102.

112. Herr, p. 87.

113. Tocqueville to Gustave de Beaumont, February 27, 1858, in Alexis de Tocqueville, *Selected Letters*, ed. Boesche, 366–68. The French text of this letter is in *Œuvres complètes*, edited by Gustave de Beaumont, 9 vols. (Paris, 1864–1866), VIII, 543–44.

# 9

# Montesquieu and the Scottish Enlightenment

## James Moore

In the judgment of virtually all of the major thinkers of the Scottish Enlightenment, the publication of *The Spirit of Laws* in 1748 was an event of historic importance. David Hume, Robert Wallace, Henry Home, Adam Smith, Adam Ferguson, John Millar, Dugald Stewart were all of them impressed by what they took to be Montesquieu's genius. And every one was influenced in his thinking by one aspect or another of Montesquieu's great work. This impression is confirmed by knowledgeable scholars among our contemporaries. Robert Wokler wrote that: "the *Esprit des Lois* towers over the Enlightenment in Scotland like a colossus in whose shadow so many of her leading thinkers stood in awe";[1] and Richard Sher considered that "no individual—including even... Francis Hutcheson—exerted a greater influence upon Scottish inquiry into these [social and political] questions than Montesquieu."[2]

The canonical account of the reception of Montesquieu's work in Scotland appears in Dugald Stewart's "Dissertation: Exhibiting the Progress of Metaphysical, Ethical and Political Philosophy since the Revival of Letters in Europe" (1814). There, as Stewart explained it, the significance of *The Spirit of Laws* was that it marked the beginning of the end of natural jurisprudence or the systematic study of natural rights. "The well-merited popularity of *The Spirit of the Laws* gave the first fatal blow to the study of natural jurisprudence: partly by the proofs which, in every page, the work afforded of the absurdity of all schemes of Universal Legislation; and partly by the attractions which it possessed, in point of elegance and taste, when contrasted with the insupportable dullness of the systems then in possession of the schools."[3] Following the publication of *The Spirit of Laws*, moral philosophers, jurists, and historians redirected their studies to "the natural or theoretical history of society in all its various aspects: to the history of languages, of the arts, of the sciences, of laws, of government, of manners, and of religion."[4] And in another place, Stewart wrote that

> the greater part of politicians before the time of Montesquieu having contented themselves with an historical statement of facts, and with a vague reference of laws to the wisdom of particular legislators, or to accidental circumstances, which it is now impossible to ascertain. Montesquieu, on the contrary, considered laws as originating chiefly from the circumstances of society, and attempted to account, from the changes in the condition of mankind, which takes place in the different stages of their progress, for the corresponding alterations which their institutions undergo.... The advances made in this line of inquiry since Montesquieu's time have been great. Lord Kames, in his *Historical Law Tracts*, had given us many excellent specimens of it ... and many ingenious speculations of the same kind occur in the works of Mr. Millar.[5]

Stewart's account of the reception Montesquieu's work was considered authoritative in nineteenth-century Scotland. He had an influential following not only of academics but also of significant figures in public life, including the authors of *The Edinburgh Review*, his former pupils.[6] His "Dissertation" was reprinted in the *Encyclopedia Britannica* when that work was published in 1820. Stewart was himself a man of encyclopedic learning, an impression reinforced by the publication of his collected writings in 1854. His biographies of Adam Smith, Thomas Reid, and William Robertson provided more detailed corroboration of the outline of his history. His very presence in nineteenth-century Scotland was monumental in both the literary and literal senses of the term: his tombstone continues to dominate the skyline above the city of Edinburgh.

There are, however, a number of problems in his telling of the story. Perhaps the most serious deficiency in his narrative is that it creates an impression of uniformity among Scottish intellectuals, that they formed somehow a school, a "Scottish school," a term employed by Sir William Hamilton in his edition of *The Collected Works of Dugald Stewart*. This description of intellectual life in Scotland in the eighteenth century is profoundly misleading; nothing is gained in intelligibility by reifying their thinking in this way. In fact the distinguishing feature of the Scottish Enlightenment was not the agreement or consensus among its leading philosophers and jurists. It was the more stimulating ambience of intellectual disagreement on the most fundamental questions of morals and politics. Nor were they passive followers and celebrators of the genius of Montesquieu. Indeed it is highly likely that Montesquieu would have found cause to regret some of the ways in which his ideas were put to use by

Scottish thinkers. It is no doubt the case that an author never exercises exactly the influence he would have wished. Elisabeth Labrousse put the matter very well in her study of the life and work of Pierre Bayle: "jamais un auteur n'exerce exactement l'influence qu'il eut souhaitee et quant aux lecteurs, ils ne sont pas des miroirs passifs, ils reagissent devant les textes et les trient selon une perspective conforme a leurs preventions.[7]

In this chapter, I will examine three episodes or moments in the reception of Montesquieu's work in eighteenth-century Scotland. I will review first the manner in which *The Spirit of Laws* was read by David Hume and consider what effect that reading may have had on Hume's own political thought. Second, I will turn to the work of Adam Ferguson, the political thinker in eighteenth-century Scotland who was most directly and profoundly influenced by Montesquieu. Finally, I will look at the succession of Scottish jurists who practiced what Stewart called "theoretical history" or the "history of stages of society" and consider not only their indebtedness to Montesquieu but also their own reasons for undertaking those studies and for differing in crucial respects with the spirit and the letter of Montesquieu's work.

## Montesquieu and Hume

Any history of the reception of *The Spirit of Laws* in Scotland must begin with David Hume, who read Montesquieu's work in 1748 during diplomatic travels in Europe. He later described this period in his life, in the late 1740s, as the only years in which he neglected his studies; but this recollection is not strictly true: he was reading Montesquieu and reading him with great admiration. He said as much in a long reflective letter of April 10, 1749, which was delivered to Montesquieu by Hume's friend, the Edinburgh wine merchant, John Stewart, who had occasion to travel frequently to Bordeaux.[8] Hume's compliments on that occasion were not merely formal niceties; he would help arrange for the publication, in Edinburgh, in 1750, of an edition of *L'Esprit des Lois; avec les derniers corrections et illustrations de l'auteur.*[9] And in "An Enquiry concerning the Principles of Morals" published in 1751, Hume would describe Montesquieu as the author of "the best system of political knowledge that perhaps has ever yet been communicated to the world."[10]

This is remarkable praise, coming from Hume, who had his own science of politics, outlined in *Essays, Moral and Political* (1741, 1742, 1748), which were in turn based upon *A Treatise of Human Nature* (1739, 1840), which contained a theory of the understanding of the passions and of morals, which was at variance in many respects with Montesquieu's science of politics. Hume did not think that moral and political principles could be derived by reason from the nature of things. He argued that the relations of things had no relevance at all for moral distinctions, which must be made by a sentiment informed by judgment concerning the usefulness and agreeableness of qualities of character and forms of conduct. Hume's theory of justice and of political life rested moreover upon the assumption that human nature remains the same in all times and places. Men in general and politicians in particular are motivated by avarice and ambition, by what they take to be the interest of themselves and the interests of the persons closest to them. Hume did not share Montesquieu's view that the laws in different forms of government are inspired by different principles and that forms of government must become corrupted when they cease to be inspired by the relevant principle. In Hume's view, political life is unavoidably corrupt, and the best constitutions are those that make provision for corruption and also restrain it by arrangements that ensure that the venality of public men will be checked by the venality of other public men.[11] This theory may inform a remark made late in his letter to Montesquieu that if simple governments are subject to abuse because they lack any counterweights, mixed governments are subject to a different kind of disorder by the clash and opposition of parties. Hume, unlike Bolingbroke, did not approve the independence or separation of Parliament from the Crown in the British constitution.[12] He favored a degree of influence or corruption sufficient to enable the Crown to govern but not so much that all opposition must cease. Montesquieu would seem to have endorsed a similar qualification (in Book XIX) to his theory of the separation of powers set out in Book XI, chapter 6.

Notwithstanding his generally different understanding of political life, Hume found much to agree with in *The Spirit of Laws*. He agreed with Montesquieu that the loss of the hereditary powers of the nobility in England had made the liberty of British subjects more precarious. Hume even explained the abolition of the hereditary jurisdictions of the Highland lairds in Scotland, following the Jacobite rebellion of 1745, as a decision made in England by public men who considered Scotland insufficiently republican.[13] Hume's position (and Montesquieu's) that the nobility was important as a bulwark against despotism was not shared, however, by most of Hume's contemporaries in the Scottish Enlightenment; as we will see. Hume also found Montesquieu's views on the purchase of judicial office consistent with his own sentiments on the subject. If the appointment of judges depended entirely on the favor of the court, judges would not enjoy the independence required to make equitable decisions.

Hume's first encounter with Montesquieu's work is revealing not only for their disagreements and agreements on political subjects, but his reading of *The Spirit of Laws*, particularly of Books XX, XXI, XXII, and XXIII, appears to have provided a focus for his thinking on economic subjects. This is not to say that Hume's economic reading began at this time; there are manuscript jottings of Hume's that appear to date from the early or mid-1740's,[14] which indicate that he had been reading some of the same *economistes* and *financiers* whom Montesquieu (and Voltaire) had also read: notably, John Law, the Scots financial adviser who persuaded the Regent of France to undertake the highly speculative Mississippi scheme; Melon, a critic of Law and the author of a defence of commerce and luxury; Dutot, a defender of Law; and Paris Duvernay, author of a rejoinder to Dutot.[15] But it appears to have been Montesquieu's presentation of these subjects that suggested to Hume the order in which economic subjects are treated in his *Political Discourses* of 1752. There, discussions of commerce and luxury are followed by discourses on money, the balance of trade, interest, taxes, public credit, and the populousness of ancient nations, as in Books XX to XXIII of *The Spirit of Laws*.[16] Moreover Montesquieu's remarks on money and the balance of trade provided the occasion for the first articulation by Hume of his theory that money and trade will always remain in equilibrium in relation to the wages of labor and the prices of commodities. As wages and prices rise, money will flow to neighboring nations to purchase less expensive goods and services; as wages and prices fall, money and the balance of trade will return. Both men were ultimately in agreement on the vexed topic of public credit or investment in government stock. Montesquieu was very clear in Book XXII, chapter 18, that no benefits whatever would follow from investment of this kind.[17] Hume in his letter intimated that some benefit to commerce might follow from investment by manufactures and merchants in public stocks. The fixed income received from such stock might allow them to lower prices on products and commodities. But in his published essay on the subject of public credit and through the later years of his life, Hume became increasingly alarmed by this practice, particularly when he perceived that the national debt had doubled during the Seven Years War (1756–63) and increased still further as Britain struggled to maintain, mistakenly in Hume's view, its overseas empire in America.[18]

In the years following this initial exchange, Hume corresponded with Montesquieu on other subjects. Montesquieu read Hume's essay "Of National Characters," where Hume criticized the theory of the Abbé DuBos and others that physical causes, the climate, the soil, are more important than moral causes in the determination of the character of nations.[19] Montesquieu is famous, of course, for having explained various aspects of political and domestic life by reference to physical causes; he expressed nevertheless his agreement with Hume on this matter.[20] They disagreed, however, on another subject: the populousness of ancient nations. Robert Wallace, a moderate Presbyterian clergyman, a friend of Hume, had written a dissertation on the subject in which he supported the opinion of Montesquieu, that the quality of life in the ancient world must be conducive to population growth as long as citizens retained something of the virtue and the love of equality that must inspire the laws in republics.[21] Hume recognized the merits of the position taken by Montesquieu and by Wallace, but he countered that the endless factions, the disorders, the generally tumultuous politics of the ancient world, combined with the inhuman institution of slavery, must have had a limiting effect on the numbers of people at that time.[22] Hume and Wallace reviewed each other's texts before publication. Montesquieu was aware of this friendly disagreement and was charmed by it.[23] It was indeed one of the most commendable features of the Scottish Enlightenment that disagreement generally occurred in this spirit; not always, to be sure. Hume and Hutcheson (as I read their relationship); Hume and Kames; Hume and Rousseau—as unpleasant an altercation as one can readily bring to mind between great men—may be considered exceptions to the bonhomie that generally prevailed among the philosophers of the Scottish Enlightenment. One of these philosophers was Adam Ferguson, the moral and political philosopher who was perhaps most directly influenced and affected by the work of Montesquieu.

## Montesquieu and Adam Ferguson

In *An Essay on the History of Civil Society* (1767), Ferguson wrote, "When I recollect what the President Montesquieu has written, I am at a loss to tell why I should treat of human affairs." He excused himself for proceeding with his *Essay* on the grounds that his thoughts were "more to the comprehension of ordinary capacities, because I am more on the level of ordinary men."[24]

It was pleasant of Ferguson to have put the matter in this way, but in fact Ferguson was a subtle and an original thinker. His moral philosophy was quite unlike Hume's, which was based on the principle of utility, or Adam Smith's, which was based on sympathy. He also imparted to the term *moral sense* a signification very different from the meaning given it by Hutcheson and modified by Lord Kames. Ferguson proposed a theory of moral estimation that supposed that man is an intelligent and an active creature, capable of forming an idea of perfection, which he finds in contemplation of his Creator. The world appeared to him to be a graded system of creatures, more or less excellent; but in man alone one finds intelligence, and with it a capacity for improvement or progression. As he put it in his *Principles of Moral and Political Science* (1792), "Perfection is no where to be found short of the infinite mind; but progression is the gift of God to all his intelligent creatures. . . . And as far as wisdom depends upon a just conception of familiar objects, it is the nature of created mind in the course of experience and observation to improve its sagacity and to make continual approach to the highest measure of intellectual ability of which it is susceptible."[25]

Ferguson's distinctive theory of moral estimation had implications for his differences with those among his contemporaries who continued to subscribe to the hypothesis of the state of nature. Ferguson had no use for this idea: "If the palace be unnatural, the cottage is so no less. . . . In what situation of the human race are the footsteps of art unknown?"[26] His understanding of moral estimation and "the principle of progression" also had implications for the manner in which he read Montesquieu. He was entirely content, in his *Essay*, to rehearse Montesquieu's description of the nature of republican, monarchical, and despotic governments and the principles of virtue, honor, and fear that inspire or should inspire the laws and the policies of those governments. He was happy to endorse Montesquieu's distinction between democratic republics inspired by love of equality and aristocratic republics inspired by moderation. But even in the most democratic republics, the claims of active and intelligent minds will always merit recognition: "The most perfect equality of rights can never exclude the ascendant of superior minds, nor the assemblies of a collective body govern without the direction of select councils."[27] Whereas Montesquieu's scrupulous distinctions among the natures and principles of government generated a theory of corruption in which the laws of every one of the forms of government considered severally would become corrupt when they ceased to be inspired by their respective principles, Ferguson maintained that we find these distinctions, "in reality, both in respect to the principle and the form, various blended together." We find, that is to say, in the history of mankind, as it moves from savage societies (like that of the American Indians) to rude or barbaric societies (like that of the Tartars, but also the ancient Greeks and the Romans of the early republic) to more refined and polished societies, like the societies of London, Paris, and Edinburgh, a continuous need to reconcile the virtues of rude societies with the sense of honor of polished or refined societies. It is entirely appropriate that in polite societies everyone should enjoy a sense of pride or honor in her fulfilment of the duties of her station and in the polite manner in which she relates to her fellow citizens. But if the same polite citizens of a civil society ever lose sight of or neglect the virtues, characteristic of more rude societies, they will succumb to moral and intellectual corruption and to the fearful manners of despotic regimes.[28]

Hume had read with pleasure an early draft of Ferguson's *Essay* in 1759 (it was then entitled "A Treatise on Refinement.") When Hume read it again in 1766, he had come to a different estimation: "I have perus'd Ferguson's Papers more than once . . . [and] I am sorry to say it. . . . I do not think them fit to be given to the Public, neither on account of the Style nor the Reasoning, the Form nor the Matter. . . . It is needless to enter into a Detail, where almost everything seems to me exceptionable."[29] Hume's opinion had not changed a year later. He told William Robertson: "Ferguson's book goes on here [in London] with great success. A few days ago I saw Mrs. Montague, who had just finished it with great pleasure: I mean, she was sorry to finish it, but had read it with great pleasure."[30] Hume now connected his advice to Ferguson that he should not publish, with the advice given Montesquieu by his friends.

"Helvetius & Saurin both told me at Paris, that they had been consulted by Montesquieu about his *De l'Esprit des loix*: They used the Freedom to tell him as their fixed Opinion, that he ought to suppress the Book; which, they foresaw, would very much injure his Reputation.... Helvetius and Saurin assured me that this Freedom of theirs never lost them anything of Montesquieu's Friendship: I believe the like would be my case; but it is better not to put it to a Trial."[31] In fact Hume and Ferguson remained the closest of friends to the end of Hume's life, in August 1776. Hume had now also revised his estimate of Montesquieu's work; it had now sunk in public estimation, he said, and was likely to sink still further. Whatever value Hume's belated estimate may have—and he did say that he hoped he would be proved wrong in both cases—his fellow countrymen did not for the most part share his opinion. Indeed by the end of the eighteenth century, Montesquieu's work was judged to have marked the beginning of a new phase in Scottish higher education; it marked a turn away from natural law or natural jurisprudence as it had been traditionally understood to the history of stages of society.

## Montesquieu and Theories of History in the Scottish Enlightenment

There are at least two places in *The Spirit of Laws* where Montesquieu undertook to relate laws to the circumstances of society. In Book XVIII, "Of Laws in the Relation They Bear to the Nature of the Soil," Montesquieu remarked that the laws of commercial nations must be more extensive than for nations devoted to the culture of the earth. The laws of agricultural nations will be more complex than in nations of herdsmen. And societies of hunters and fisherman have fewer laws than any of the other three.[32] Here then, in embryo, are the four stages of society as they would be distinguished and explored by philosophers and historians of the Scottish Enlightenment. There is another section of Montesquieu's work that caught the attention of Scottish jurists and historians. It was Montesquieu's discussion of feudal laws and government in Books XXX and XXI. When these two seemingly unconnected sections of Montesquieu's work were brought together, a remarkable sequence of exercises in historical jurisprudence followed. As we shall also see, Scottish writers had their own very immediate practical political concerns that led them to situate laws relating to feudal property in the context of stages of society.

The first publication in the English language that explained changes in the laws by reference to the four stages of society was by a Scottish advocate, Sir John Dalrymple. *An Essay towards a General History of Feudal Property in Great Britain* was published in 1757. The author's indebtedness to Montesquieu was advertised on the title page in an epigraph taken from *The Spirit of*

*Laws*: "C'est un beau spectacle que celuy des Loix Feudales, Un chene antique s'eleve," ["The feudal laws form a very beautiful prospect, A venerable old oak raises its lofty head to the skies."][33] Dalrymple also advised the reader in this dedication of his work to "Lord Kaims," that many of his thoughts had been "revised by the greatest genius of our age, President Montesquieu." And in the preface, he remarks that he has attempted to emulate Montesquieu's style: "The spirit of laws first suggested in France, and the considerations upon forfeiture first suggested in England, that it was possible to unite philosophy and history with jurisprudence, and to write even upon a law subject like a scholar and a gentleman."[34] And much of Dalrymple's *Essay* was written in the epigrammatic, eminently quotable style of Montesquieu himself. The other author referred to by Dalrymple was Charles Yorke (1722–1770) who had written *Some Considerations on the law of forfeiture for high treason* (1749). Yorke had corresponded with Montesquieu and had visited him in Paris.[35] It is very likely that it was through Yorke that Dalrymple had entered into correspondence with Montesquieu on the subject of feudal property.

Dalrymple also professed his debt to Montesquieu on matters of substance, particularly in the early part of his work. Montesquieu had maintained that the German nations—the Burgundians, the Franks, and the Visigoths—did not take possession of all the conquered lands for themselves. They had no need to; they were a martial people, "fond of hunting and of pastoral life"; they grazed their herds on fallow pasture land, leaving the Romans to cultivate the more arable land: "the Burgundians' flocks fattened the Romans' fields."[36] Dalrymple took over this distinction and applied it to the Saxon conquest of Britain.

The Saxons claimed only some of the land for themselves; that land was distributed to their chieftains or *thanes*. The remaining land continued to be farmed by free men under their *sherrifs* or *reeves*. This was the source of the distinction between thane land or boc land and reeve land or folk land. Dalrymple was aware that "[t]his account of the distinction between Folkland and Bocland is different from the various accounts given of it by modern historians, and lawyers, and antiquarians; but I appeal to the nature of the German conquests, to the analogy of law in neighbouring nations at the time and to a general view of the surest guides in this question, the Saxon laws themselves."[37]

All of this changed to be sure following the Norman Conquest in England, and the reign of Malcolm III in the late eleventh century in Scotland. The effect of the feudal law was to further transform folk land into feudal land or land held in leasehold or tenancy as a benefit conferred upon a vassal by a lord. Dalrymple had now taken his story beyond Montesquieu into mediaeval Scotland. At this point in Dalrymple's history it is appropriate to link his narrative with the work of Henry Home, Lord Kames, the man to whom Dalrymple's work was dedicated, whose unpublished papers were open to

Dalrymple, and who is said, by Dalrymple, to have directed his thoughts on the subject of feudal property.

Kames was not a man given to praising overly the abilities of others. Indeed David Hume was said (by Boswell) to have told Adam Smith that "when one says of another man he is the most arrogant Man in the world, it is only to say that he is very arrogant. But when one says it of Lord Kames, it is an absolute truth."[38] Kames permitted himself in his late work, *Sketches of the History of Man*, to describe Montesquieu as "the greatest genius of the present age."[39] He was quick to follow this compliment by observing that Montesquieu was badly misinformed about the government of Mexico (it was not despotism as Montesquieu supposed)[40] and about the reasons for the barbarian invasions of the Roman Empire. (It was not that these nations had been pushed into northern Europe by the Roman legions in the early centuries of the empire and then returned when the empire had become weak. It was rather that the barbarians needed pasture land for their herds and flocks: "[I]t has quite escaped him [Montesquieu] that men cannot, like water, be dam'd up without being fed.")[41]

Kames's interest in the history of feudal property antedated publication of *The Spirit of Laws*. In 1747, Kames published *Essays upon Several Subjects concerning British Antiquities*, in which he described the introduction of the feudal law into Scotland. It happened in Scotland no earlier than the eleventh century, in imitation of English practice and in order to consolidate power over land and vassals in the person of the king. At that time Scottish thanes surrendered their lands to the king in return for feudal titles to the land and a guarantee that their fiefs would continue in their families by the principle of primogeniture or the indefeasible right of succession of the eldest son. This was the most disastrous consequence of the feudal law of property in the minds of both Kames and Dalrymple. For, as Kames put it, "Primogeniture, tis certain, is not a Right of the Law of Nature, but a consequence of the Feudal Law. Hence it is a Principle embraced by the gravest writers, that all Mankind are born free and independent of one another."[42] Later, in *Historical Law Tracts* (1758), the text that was open to Dalrymple as he wrote, Kames described the feudal system as "[a] violent and unnatural system, which could not be long supported in contradiction to love of independence and property, the most steady and industrious of all human appetites."[43] Feudalism in Scotland had declined through the sixteenth and seventeenth centuries, as lords disposed of their lands for their own advantage. But this natural course of human affairs had been arrested by an act of the Parliament of Scotland in 1685, which permitted landlords to *entail* their estates, thereby making it impossible for their heirs to ever sell the land. The effect of this act was to withdraw land from commerce and ensure that it remained in the possession of Scottish lairds with their tenants and their clansmen and retainers.

Kames and Dalrymple were writing in the aftermath of the Jacobite rebellion of 1745. The Jacobite armies had taken over most of Scotland. They occupied the city of Edinburgh from August 1745 to June 1746, before the rebellion was brutally crushed at the battle of Culloden by an army sent up from England consisting largely of Hanoverian mercenaries. The Jacobites were relentlessly pursued; their estates were forfeited or confiscated.[44] Kames was himself in the 1760s the commissioner for the forfeited estates. This was the immediate historical background in which Kames, Dalrymple, and earlier, Charles Yorke, had written. And it gave all of them an appreciably different perspective on the nobility and their landed estates than that of Montesquieu. In his description of the nature of monarchical government, Montesquieu had argued that it was the presence of the independent and subordinate jurisdiction of the nobility that distinguished monarchy from other forms of government, notably from despotisms. He told Charles Yorke, in 1749, that he considered seigniorial rights "a barrier against the Crown, to prevent monarchy from running into despotism." This was not how Yorke perceived it; those hereditary rights of the nobility might have merit in France where they might limit the power of the king. But, in England, and certainly in Scotland, "all private rights, which encroached on the legal authority of the Crown, tended to erect tyrants at the expense of the people's liberty."[45] Dalrymple thought that the law permitting entailment of land in Scotland must soon lapse and disappear altogether. Kames was less sanguine: he thought that the Parliament of Great Britain must act at once to repeal the practice of entailment, that failure to act would be subversive not only of industry and commerce but also of that "liberty and independence, to which all men aspire, with respect to their passions as well as their persons."[46]

There were then urgent practical political considerations that prompted the turn to historical jurisprudence in Scotland. Kames, Dalrymple, and Yorke were all concerned primarily to amend the law that sanctioned the perpetuation of hereditary estates by the entailment in perpetuity of feudal land. They sought to forestall yet another uprising of the highland lairds by removing the economic and social conditions that had fostered highland unrest in the past: hence the emphasis upon the unnatural condition of feudal property. It deprived men of their independence, of their natural right to own property and transfer or alienate their land, as they would any other species of goods. The mobility of property was its natural condition. The theoretical framework in which their legal arguments were cast was still very much the natural rights tradition of Grotius, Pufendorf, and especially, Locke, cast now in the temporal sequence of states of society. In societies of hunters and fishermen, and in the second stage of society, pastoral societies of shepherds and cattlemen, property was clearly mobile. It became immobile only in the third stage of society, the agricultural stage, and then, only in an extreme form, in feudal societies where land was excluded entirely from trade and commerce by the practice of entailment of hereditary estates. The challenge for Scottish jurists was to articulate a principle that would explain why it was natural for men to trade or transfer property by consent. The recognition and elaboration of such a principle was of course the distinctive and memorable contribution of Adam Smith.

It was John Millar's view that Smith followed, in his lectures on jurisprudence, "the plan that seems to be suggested by Montesquieu; endeavouring to trace the gradual progress of jurisprudence . . . from the rudest to the most refined ages."[47] Millar attended Smith's lectures in the first year of Smith's professorship of moral philosophy at Glasgow, in 1751–52. And it is entirely possible that Smith may have followed Montesquieu's exposition more closely in those years than in the record of his *Lectures on Jurisprudence,* which is now available to us, which dates from the years 1762–63 and was discovered only in the 1950s and published for the first time in 1978.[48] In those lectures, as in *The Theory of Moral Sentiments,* published in 1759, Smith's point of departure appears rather to have been an idea of justice and its application to stages of society that he would have found in *The Historical Law Tracts* of Lord Kames. There is also to be sure the possibility that Kames had heard it all first from Smith (in Edinburgh, where Smith had lectured, before his appointment in Glasgow) and that he then repeated Smith's story without acknowledgment, a conviction shared by more than one student of their writings. Both at any rate took the position that justice is "a sense of merited punishment and dread of its being inflicted upon us."[49] As Kames explained it, the sense of justice was one of a number of natural or instinctive senses implanted in us by divine providence. Smith arrived at the same theory by a more indirect route.

We sympathize, Smith thought, with the resentment of a possessor, that something has been "wrongfully wrested out of his hands."[50] But the occasion for this resentment must vary depending upon the stage or condition of society. In a society of hunters, a spectator would sympathize with another, only if the animal or fish he had caught was snatched violently from his hands. In a society of shepherds, the spectator's sympathy would be aroused only if the animal bore some mark distinguishing it as belonging to the owner. It was at this stage that property came to be distinguished from possession. Here Smith was again on common ground with Kames and Dalrymple. But in his observations on the third stage of society, Smith's denunciation of feudal property exceeded, if anything, the warmth of the language used by his fellow jurists. It was "the tyranny of the feudal government and the inclination men have to extort all they can from their inferiors"[51] that had removed land from individual proprietorship. His most bitter comments were reserved for primogeniture—a "method of succession, contrary to nature, to reason and to justice"—and the so-called right of entailment:

This right is not only absurd in the highest degree but is also extremely prejudicial to the community, as it excludes land entirely from commerce. The interest of the state requires that lands should be as much in commerce as any other goods [. . .] I shall hereafter show more fully, only hinting at it now, that the right of primogeniture and the power of making entails have been the causes of the almost totally bad husbandry that prevails in those countrys where they are in use.[52]

Smith's exposition of the impolitic character of primogeniture and entailment was reserved for discussion under that section of his lectures on jurisprudence that he called "political economy." It was in this section of his lectures, explored more fully in *An Inquiry into the Nature and Causes of the Wealth of Nations* (1776) that Smith would explain how the great feudal estates of England had been dissolved. It was not (as Bacon, Harrington, and Hume had proposed) by legislation passed during the reign of Henry VII; it was not by recognition of the inconsistency of these practices with the natural right to own private property and transfer it to others, as Kames and Dalrymple had declared. It was rather the disposition of the great feudal magnates to trade away their lands for things, commodities, which they would not have to share, even indirectly, with others. "All for ourselves, and nothing for other people, seems, in every age of the world, to have been the vile maxim of the masters of mankind . . . and thus, for the gratification of the most childish, the meanest and the most sordid of all vanities, they gradually bartered their whole power and authority."[53] It was the natural disposition to truck, barter, and exchange that had brought about the transition in England from the third stage of society to the fourth stage, the stage of commercial society. Smith traced this disposition to a still more basic propensity to persuade others to be of one's own sentiment or feeling. This was the theme of Smith's lectures on rhetoric and belle lettres, which he introduced at Glasgow in 1750 as a more appropriate training for students than the study of logic and metaphysics. And the disposition to be of the same sentiments as others lies also behind Smith's theory of sympathy in *The Theory of Moral Sentiments*. The underlying coherence of Smith's system of thought may have been what Millar had in mind when he called Smith the "Newton" of moral philosophy: "the great Montesquieu pointed out the road. He was the Lord Bacon in this branch of philosophy. Dr. Smith is the Newton."[54]

Smith, like Newton, had a principle that could account for a wide variety of moral and political phenomena. Montesquieu, in Millar's mind, was the writer who opened up the historical world for Smith. And it appears from Millar's own *Observations concerning the Distinction of Ranks in Society* (1771) that he followed Montesquieu's account of the advent of feudal laws and government more closely perhaps than any of the Scottish jurists who preceded him. And it was Millar's recollection of his studies with Smith that prompted Dugald Stewart to make Montesquieu's *The Spirit of Laws* the turning point in Scottish higher education. Before Montesquieu, it was the study of sterile schemes of universal jurisprudence. After Montesquieu, the study of moral and political philosophy became the study of the natural or conjectural history of social and political institutions. As we have seen, the story was more complicated than Stewart's sweeping generalizations would lead one to believe. In fact the study of natural jurisprudence continued in Scottish universities up to the time of Stewart himself, the end of the eighteenth century and the beginning of the nineteenth. Thomas Reid at Glasgow and Adam Ferguson at Edinburgh continued to lecture on natural jurisprudence in the classroom. It was in works published for a more general readership that they and others wrote in the language of manners or moeurs.

But Stewart appears to have had another reason for claiming that the natural rights tradition had become a dead letter. Stewart was appalled by the French Revolution and by the defence of that revolution in England by the friends of John Locke. The great fallacy of the promoters of those "mistaken notions concerning Political Liberty which have been so widely disseminated in Europe by the writings of Mr. Locke" was the idea that the people are capable of forming correct notions of their rights or of the policies that would be conducive to their happiness.[55] Stewart thought, as John Stuart Mill would later think, that "the progressive happiness and improvement of mankind" depended upon knowledge of the "systematic and enlightened principles of Political Economy."[56] "I do not think that in the present state of the world Democratic constitutions in any form which it is possible to give them are favourable to the establishment of those systematic and enlightened principles of Political Economy which are subservient to the progressive happiness and improvement of mankind."[57]

We have seen that the legacy of Montesquieu's work to the jurists and the philosophers of the Scottish Enlightenment was as diverse as it was generous. His thinking on economic subjects almost certainly shaped the structure and some of the substance of David Hume's *Political Discourses*, as much as it provided matter for Hume's skepticism on particular subjects, such as the populousness of ancient nations. Montesquieu's analysis of the principles that inspire the laws in republican, monarchical, and despotic governments seemed to Ferguson a set of insights that could not be improved upon. But Ferguson also transformed Montesquieu's analysis by transposing it to the history of societies as they pass from rude and barbarous to polished and refined nations. Scottish jurists found in Montesquieu's account of the relation of laws to land or the soil and the application of that account to the feudal laws a part at least of the historical narrative that would become the four-stages theory of society. In every case their reading of Montesquieu's work was informed by critical appreciation of his theories as they applied to social and political problems peculiar to themselves. This appears to have been the spirit—critical, appreciative, nuanced—in which the work of Montesquieu became an integral part of the Scottish Enlightenment.

## Notes

1. Robert Wokler, "Apes and Races in the Scottish Enlightenment: Monboddo and Kames on the Nature of Man," in *Philosophy and Science in the Scottish Enlightenment*, ed. P. Jones (Edinburgh: John Donald, 1988), 162. I should like to record my indebtedness to the writings and conversation of Robert Wokler, whose early death (2006) is a great loss to the world of scholarship on the Enlightenment.

2. Richard B. Sher, "From Troglodytes to Americans: Montesquieu and the Scottish Enlightenment on Liberty, Virtue and Commerce," in *Republicanism, Liberty and Commercial Society, 1694–1776*, ed. D. Wootton (Stanford: Stanford University Press, 1994), 169.

3. *The Collected Works of Dugald Stewart*, ed. Sir William Hamilton (Edinburgh: Thomas Constable, 1854), I, 193.

4. Ibid., 69.

5. Ibid., X, 35.

6. Donald Winch, "The System of the North: Dugald Stewart and His Pupils," In *That Noble Science of Politics: A Study in Nineteenth-Century Intellectual History*, ed. Stefan Collini, Donald Winch, and John Burrow (Cambridge: Cambridge University Press: 1983), ch. 1. See also Knud Haakonssen, "Dugald Stewart and the Science of a Legislator," in *Natural Law and Moral Philosophy: From Grotius to the Scottish Enlightenment* (Cambridge: Cambridge University Press: 1996), ch. 7.

7. Elisabeth Labrousse, *Pierre Bayle: Heterodoxie et Rigorisme* (The Hague: Martinus Nijhoff, 1964), Avant-propos, ix.

8. Hume to President de Montesquieu, Londres, 10 avril, 1749, in *The Letters of David Hume*, ed. J. Y. T. Greig (Oxford: Clarendon Press, 1932), I, 133–38.

9. John Hill Burton, *The Life and Correspondence of David Hume* (Edinburgh, 1846), I, 304.

10. Hume, "An Enquiry concerning the Principles of Morals," in *David Hume: The Philosophical Works*, ed. T. H. Green and T. H. Grose (London: 1882), IV, 190 n. 1. This was how Hume phrased it in the first (1751) and second editions (1753). See also *An Enquiry concerning the Principles of Morals*, ed. Tom L. Beauchamp (Oxford: 1998), 220.

11. See my article, "Hume's Political Science and the Classical Republican Tradition," In *Canadian Journal of Political Science* 10 (1977): 809–39.

12. Robert Shackleton, "Montesquieu, Bolingbroke and the Separation of Powers," *French Studies* (1948).

13. Hume to Montesquieu, April 10, 1749. *Letters of David Hume*, I, 134.

14. M. A. Stewart, "The Dating of Hume's Manuscripts," in *The Scottish Enlightenment*, ed. P. Wood (Rochester: University of Rochester Press, 2000), 267–314.

15. See Catherine Larrère, "Montesquieu on Economics and Commerce," in *Montesquieu's Science of Politics*, ed. David Carrithers, Michael Mosher, and Paul Rahe (Lanham, MD: Rowman & Littlefield, 2001), 335–75.

16. *The Spirit of Laws*, trans. T. Nugent, intro. by Franz Neumann (New York: Hafner, 1949), I, 316ff.

17. Ibid., 384.

18. See John G. A. Pocock, "The Dying Thoughts of a North Briton," in *Virtue, Commerce and History* (Cambridge: Cambridge University Press, 1988).

19. See Peter Jones, *Hume's Sentiments: Their Ciceronian and French Context* (Edinburgh: Edinburgh University Press, 1982), 93 ff.

20. "Montesquieu to Hume, 19 May 1749," in J. H. Burton, *Life and Correspondence of David Hume*, 456–57.

21. Robert Wallace, *A Dissertation on the Numbers of Mankind in Ancient and Modern Times* (Edinburgh: G. Hamilton & J. Balfour, 1753).

22. Hume, "Of the Populousness of Ancient Nations," in *Political Discourses* (1752).

23. "Montesquieu to Hume, 13 July, 1753," in Burton, *Life and Correspondence of David Hume*, 457–58.

24. Adam Ferguson, *An Essay on the History of Civil Society* (1767), ed. D. Forbes (Edinburgh: Edinburgh University Press, 1966), 65.

25. Adam Ferguson, *Principles of Moral and Political Science* (Edinburgh, W. Creech, 1792), II, 403.

26. Ferguson, *An Essay*, 8.

27. Ibid., 67.

28. Ibid., 71

29. "Hume to the Rev. Hugh Blair, 11 February, 1766," *Letters of David Hume*, II, 133.

30. "Hume to William Robertson, 19 March, 1767," *Letters of David Hume*, II, 131.

31. "Hume to Blair, 11 February 1766," *Letters of David Hume*, II, 133.

32. *The Spirit of Laws*, XVIII, 8, 275. See also Ronald Meek, *Social Science and the Ignoble Savage* (Cambridge: Cambridge University Press, 1976), 32–35.

33. *The Spirit of Laws*, XXX, 1, vol. II, 171.

34. John Dalrymple, *An Essay towards a General History of Feudal Property in Great Britain* (London: A. Millar, 1757), preface, vii.

35. Robert Shackleton, *Montesquieu: A Critical Biography* (Oxford: Oxford University Press, 1961), 383–84.

36. *The Spirit of Laws*, XXX, 8, vol. II, 176.

37. Dalrymple, *An Essay*, 14.

38. *Boswell Papers*, XV, 12; cited by Ian Ross in *Lord Kames and the Scotland of His Day* (Oxford: Clarendon Press, 1972), 349.

39. Henry Home, Lord Kames, *Sketches of the History of Man* (London and Edinburgh: W. Strahan & T. Cadell, 1774), II, 2.

40. Ibid., III, 110–11.

41. Ibid., I, 53 n.

42. Henry Home, Lord Kames, *Essays upon Several Subjects concerning British Antiquities* (Edinburgh: A. Kincaid, 1747), 193.

43. Henry Home, Lord Kames, *Historical Law Tracts* (1758) (Edinburgh: A. Kincaid, 1792, 4th edition), 141.

44. A. J. Youngson, *After the Forty-Five* (Edinburgh: Edinburgh University Press, 1973).

45. Shackleton, *Montesquieu*, 287–88, n. 5.

46. Kames, *Historical Law Tracts* (1792), 156.

47. John Millar to Dugald Stewart [1790?] and cited by Stewart in his "Account of the Life and Writings of Adam Smith," in *Biographical Memoirs of Adam Smith, William Robertson, Thomas Reid* (Edinburgh: George Ramsay & Company, 1811).

48. Adam Smith, *Lectures on Jurisprudence*, ed. R. L. Meek, D. D. Raphael, and P. G. Stein (Oxford: Clarendon Press, 1978).

49. Henry Home, Lord Kames, *Essays on the Principles of Morality and Natural Religion* (Edinburgh: R. Fleming for A. Kincaid, 1751), 64.

50. Smith, *Lectures on Jurisprudence*, 17; and *The Theory of Moral Sentiments*, ed., D. D. Raphael and A. L. Macfie (Indianapolis: Liberty Classics, 1982), 83.

51. Smith, *Lectures on Jurisprudence*, 23.

52. Ibid., 70.

53. Adam Smith, *An Inquiry into the Nature and Causes of the Wealth of Nations* (1776) (Indianapolis: Liberty Classics, 1979), I, 418–19.

54. John Millar, *Historical View of the English Government* (1803) II, 429, cited in William Lehmann, *John Millar of Glasgow* (Cambridge: Cambridge University Press: 1960), 363 n.

55. *The Collected Works of Dugald Stewart*, VIII, 23.

56. Ibid.

57. Ibid., IX, 376.

# Part III

# Montesquieu and Comparative Constitutional Law

# 10

# Montesquieu and the Renaissance of Comparative Public Law

## Ran Hirschl

The publication of Montesquieu's monumental *The Spirit of Laws* (1748) is undisputedly a—if not the—defining moment in the history of comparative law. Montesquieu's foundational approach of unearthing links between law and society across cultures has inspired an impressive tradition of comparative scholarship. It has also led to a curiously different genealogy in the social sciences scholarship than in legal scholarship. This chapter compares the extent to which Montesquieu's thought continues to resonate in three different genres of comparative public law scholarship: (1) comparative social science studies of legal transformation; (2) comparative social science studies that treat courts as political institutions; and (3) comparative constitutional law scholarship produced by legal academics. I use Montesquieu's comparative sociolegal work as a benchmark against which we can assess the epistemology, methodology, and thematic framework of later generations of comparative public law scholarship.

I begin by briefly surveying the main comparative sociolegal aspects of *The Spirit of Laws*. Next, I examine the influence of Montesquieu's work on two later generations of comparative scholarship in the area of legal transformation: the evolutionist pioneers (Henry Maine, L. H. Morgan, and Emile Durkheim); and functionalist institutional economics (from Max Weber to Douglas North). In the third part, I examine recent comparative works that challenge Montesquieu's notion of judicial independence by highlighting the political origins of judicial review and judicial behavior. Whereas this thread of scholarship accepts Montesquieu's basic understanding of law as derivative of nonlegal factors, it identifies a critical missing link in Montesquieu's thought—the political construction of law. I conclude by contrasting the resonance Montesquieu's ideas have with comparative social science studies of constitutional law, and among legal academics studying the same sets of phenomena. The former type of scholarship treats Montesquieu's work either as the bedrock of comparative sociolegal inquiry or as a benchmark against which to develop novel theses concerning the political nature of the courts. Comparative constitutional lawyers, in contrast, have simply adopted Montesquieu's "least dangerous" view of the judiciary and, alas, some anachronistic epistemological and methodological elements of his comparative work in the process. Too little has changed from the time of Montesquieu's *The Spirit of Laws* to the early twenty-first century in respect of the ability of legal scholarship to draw upon comparative research to trace causal links among pertinent variables, and more generally, in the way comparative constitutional lawyers conceptualize and pursue their research. This is a compliment to Montesquieu's foundational scholarship; but, at the same time, it also reflects the blurred epistemological matrix of modern-day comparative constitutional law.

## Montesquieu as a "Comparativist"

Montesquieu's contribution as forerunner, if not founder, of modern sociology and anthropology was acknowledged by pioneers of these disciplines, from Auguste Comte to Emile Durkheim and Edward Evans-Pritchard. Latter sociological giants such as Max Weber, Alfred Radcliffe-Brown, Raymond Aron, and Louis Althusser have all emphasized the scientific nature of Montesquieu's scholarship. Likewise, Montesquieu may be considered the first master of modern comparative law. His attempt, tentative as it was, to draw upon comparative research to trace causal links between a polity's material, demographic, and cultural characteristics and the nature and organization of that polity's legal and political institutions was a major leap forward in the evolution of comparative law as a method, discipline, and science.

At the outset of *The Spirit of Laws*, Montesquieu defines laws as "the necessary relations deriving from the nature of things"[1] and states that the purpose of the work is to "examine all these relations."[2] With this monumental task before him, he analyzes and classifies the different types of laws and governments, describing how they connect to, and are affected by, a range of factors. He argues that out of the different types of government he examines—monarchy, republic, and despotism—monarchy is the most preferable.

In the book's first part, Montesquieu describes these three basic forms of government in topological form and with reference to Aristotle's *Politeia*. This approach involves developing an extensive taxonomy—classifying laws and governments according to their distinguishing characteristics. He sets out several types of laws: invariable (the laws of God and the physical world) and variable (the laws of human creation); moral, civil, and political laws; and finally natural laws (which derive from the human constitution) and positive laws (of human creation). Man is similarly classified into states: the "state of nature" (a timid, solitary creature) being fundamentally different from the "man in society" (after the introduction of property and inequality, which creates a state of war that, in turn, laws can remedy by providing him with liberty). Another series of key classifications are the divisions that he sees between the three types of government societal man can form: republics (in which all or part of the people rule, with two subclasses of democracy and aristocracy); monarchies (in which one alone governs by fixed and established laws); and despotisms (in which one alone governs according to her own will without fixed laws).

The Spirit of Laws is resplendent with distinctions. The most important aspect of the theme of "separation" is Montesquieu's argument in favor of separation of powers. The most successful government is the one that provides the highest degree of political liberty (security). This is best achieved when the legislative, executive, and judicial branches operate independently of one another. "When legislative power is united with executive power in a single person or in a single body of the magistry, there is no liberty, because one can fear that the same monarch or senate that makes tyrannical laws will execute them tyrannically."[3] Montesquieu argues that this separation of powers can only occur in a monarchy because the constitution of such a regime demands that countervailing powers exist to check the power of the prince. Such divisions of power do not exist in either republics or despotisms, Montesquieu suggests, because of the fundamentally egalitarian nature (albeit in different ways) of those governments. So for these reasons, monarchy must be considered the best form of government.

Having identified the three types of government, Montesquieu connects each type to a principle, which functions as both a goal and an animating force. In monarchies, the principle is honor; in republics, it is civic virtue; and in despotism, it is fear. The structure of the government and its principle is connected to the type of laws it should have to function most effectively. Montesquieu then outlines the manner in which laws in each type of government should and do govern areas of social interaction: education, inheritance, civil and criminal laws, sumptuary laws, luxury, the condition of women, defense, religion, and commerce. In a typical descriptive/prescriptive paragraph he suggests, "Laws should be so specific to the people for whom they are made, that it is a great coincidence if those of one nation can suit another. They should be relative to the physical qualities of the country; to its frozen, burning, or temperate climate; to the quality, location, and size of the territory; to the mode of livelihood of the people, farmers, hunters, or pastoralists; they should relate to the degree of liberty which the constitution can admit, to the religion of the inhabitants, to their inclinations, to their wealth, to their numbers, to their commerce, to their mores, to their manners."[4]

Following his exploration of the nature of government, Montesquieu turns to the second theme of his work: not only do laws affect a wide variety of issues, but laws are themselves affected and dictated by various environmental, societal, and cultural factors. The second part of *The Spirit of Laws* deals with the effect of material factors, such as climate and soil quality, on the structure of human societies, their traditions, and organizations. The book's third part focuses on the significance of social and economic factors, such as trade and commerce, demographic conditions, and religiosity, for the traditions and laws of various societies and their political institutions. The last section of the book illustrates the arguments put forth in parts 2 and 3 by comparing the laws of ancient Rome and medieval feudal society, mainly in France. It is here that Montesquieu's comparative mastery and theory of the mutual cause-and-effect relationship between law and society are best exemplified.

Montesquieu's arguments in *The Spirit of Laws* are supported by hundreds of comparative examples, cast in an inductive form of argumentation. "History and our laws would have said . . . 'we shall testify for you' " he exclaims.[5] The book features 667 citations, 204 of which are drawn from ancient Rome (primarily Tacitus, Livy, and Denis of Halicarnassus). Remarkably for his time, no fewer than 213 citations, approximately one-third of all citations, refer to the non-European world. Of these citations, the vast majority (165 citations) concern Asia (primarily China, Turkey and Persia, India, and Japan). Sources on the Americas are cited 18 times, and sources on Africa are cited merely 8 times. Asian "despotism" in particular provides Montesquieu with a useful antithesis of Europe.[6] The "great princes of the east" and their laws serve as cautionary tales against laws that are too severe, the corruption of monarchy, and other perils of despotism.[7] Native North American, West Indies, and African "savagery" help Montesquieu demonstrate principles of natural law. The governmental structure of England, a constitutional monarchy, figures prominently in *The Spirit of Laws* as an ideal regime type, one that has been able to adopt the type of government that is in accordance with its nature, and the "one government in modern Europe that made freedom the aim of its constitution and policies."[8]

Montesquieu's methodology in *The Spirit of Laws* is not unproblematic. Crude taxonomy serves alongside his genuine quest for determining causal links between pertinent factors.[9] His choice of comparative examples is biased: he cites either situation in which a government or law succeeded because it followed the approach Montesquieu advocates or in which a government or law failed presumably because the Montesquieu formula was not applied. This normatively driven selection of supposedly prototypical cases highlights the dual nature of *The Spirit of Laws* as both descriptive (comparative examples illustrate the taxonomy of regime types and their characteristics) and prescriptive (particular examples are brought to further Montesquieu's own arguments for effective means of governance). His information-gathering methods are best described as "armchair" constitutional ethnography. His analysis of non-European societies is haphazard and relies exclusively on secondary sources, primarily travel literature, Jesuit missionary propaganda, and biased reports by French and Dutch merchants.[10] And, like many authors after him, Montesquieu was quite willing to overlook the attitude of authors he cited when it did not suit his purpose.[11]

Notwithstanding these deficiencies, however, the portrayal of Montesquieu as one of the founding fathers of comparative law seems apt. Few authors before him (and, alas, too few after him) drew so knowledgeably and extensively upon comparative law materials for the illustrative backbone of their sociolegal work. Although Montesquieu's comparative scholarship is primarily taxonomic, at the same time it treats law as an indicator, cause, and outcome of society's development. It is descriptive, prescriptive, and explanatory. One can hardly ask for more from the first serious work in comparative public law.

## Two Branches of Post-Montesquieu Comparative Sociolegal Scholarship

### Evolutionist Theories of Legal Change

Evolutionist theories of legal transformation suggest that legal development is linked to a society's passage from one socioeconomic stage to another.[12] Thinkers such as Adam Smith argued that development of genuine contract and property concepts could only occur alongside agricultural development. However, it was not until the second half of the nineteenth century that comparative law and evolutionist views of social progress (primarily in the works of Herbert Spencer) were organized into a coherent theory. This emphasized organic societal evolution and variations in legal development as an important indicator of differences in societal and political development.

The first classic book with a social science orientation that advanced such a theory is Sir Henry Maine's *Ancient Law*.[13] Comparing ancient Rome, rural communities in India, and nineteenth-century British society, Maine traced movement in human organization from the centrality of the family in ancient society to the individual in modern society. This has been accompanied by an evolution in the orientation of law from the centrality of status in ancient societies to contract in modern societies. One of the implications of this development is the evolution of correctional justice: whereas in so-called primitive societies, a sinner's punishment may be exacted on her children, kinfolk, or tribesmen, in a modern society, the offender alone is held accountable for her wrongdoing.

Lewis Henry Morgan's *Ancient Society* (1877) continued to develop an even more encompassing theory of the social evolution of mankind (his title in fact intentionally recalls Maine's work). Unlike Maine (who was concerned with societal transformation and the corresponding evolution of law) Morgan's interest was in organic societal evolution. He envisaged progress from clan organization to the establishment of political society, through to changes in territory, property, and kinship lineage rules (which, unlike most twentieth-century anthropologists, he saw mainly in juridical terms). Following Montesquieu, Morgan identified three stages of societal organization—savagery, barbarism, and civilization. His emphasis on the "art of subsistence" provided a mechanism for the evolution of societies through these stages. This became foundational in modern archeology, as well as in ethnographical distinctions between hunters and gatherers, sedentary agriculturalists, and urban dwellers.[14]

The impact of Montesquieu's sociolegal thought on Emile Durkheim—a prominent figure in late-nineteenth-century comparative sociolegal studies—is well documented. In his Latin dissertation on *Montesquieu's Contribution to the Rise of Social Science*, Durkheim suggests that "it was he, who, in *The Spirit of the Laws*, laid down the principles of the new science of sociology."[15] In his own major work, *The Division of Labor in Society* (1893), Durkheim draws upon comparative examination of "primitive" and "advanced" societies to develop Maine's "from status to contract" thesis. Durkheim sees law as reflecting the evolving division of labor and interpersonal solidarity within a society. In primitive societies the division of labor among people was less developed, and social bonds were typically stronger. Hence, formal law was not required. In more developed societies, there is an increased specialization and clearer division of labor among people, accompanied by lower social cohesiveness. Contract, rather than status or barter has become the major form of exchange among people. The state apparatus now assures the fulfillment of the contract and establishes the external conditions for its use. A special class—lawyers—arose to negotiate and litigate the more complex and ever-increasing contractual relationships.[16]

These four thinkers—Montesquieu, Maine, Morgan, and Durkheim—all draw on comparative examples, analogies, and dissimilarities between laws and societal institutions of different polities to illustrate and substantiate their arguments. A central theme is the historical development of law; more precisely, they consider the various factors that influence the formation and evolution of laws, and, in turn, how laws influence society. Montesquieu, Maine, and Durkheim all understand the mores and ethos of a society having a central effect on its legal organization. At the same time, law is also an important indicator of societal and political development.

There are at least three features that distinguish these nineteenth-century evolutionary theorists from Montesquieu. First, the work of Maine, Morgan, and Durkheim is more methodologically rigorous. While they may still be considered "armchair anthropologists," their collection and analysis of data are more systematic (and less biased) than that of Montesquieu. The evolutionary theorists pay more attention to controlling their comparisons, as well as to basic principles of inference-oriented case selection. A second and related difference is that the more scientific (or empirical) orientation leads them to debunk earlier philosophical notions about presocietal man, the state of nature, and natural law. As Tom Pangle argues, Montesquieu accepts a type of natural law theory to which laws and governments should conform, regardless of whether not adhering to these laws produces good effects.[17] So although comparative illustrations form the backbone of Montesquieu's argument, the historical record is not the sole means by which a law or government is deemed to be just or effective. Unlike Montesquieu, the nineteenth-century thinkers treat law as being purely man made. Variance in legal development, for Maine or Durkheim, reflects nothing more than variance in social progress. A third difference, and probably the most important, is the attempt by the nineteenth-century thinkers to build a coherent theory of social and legal change. The "uniform development thesis" and its emphasis on organic societal change goes beyond Montesquieu's taxonomy to offer a parsimonious explanation—not merely description—of the evolutionary dynamic of social and legal transformation.[18] Montesquieu's despotic Asian polities lack the necessary conditions to develop into successful republics. Unlike Montesquieu's static depiction of fundamentally different types of legal and governmental systems, evolutionists argue that all societies progress through a uniform series of developmental stages; different societies may be at differing stages of social or legal development, but all are essentially on the same trajectory.

*Functionalist Theories of Legal Change*

A second branch of comparative sociolegal studies advances a functionalist view of law and legal institutions.[19] Like Montesquieu and the evolutionist pioneers, the early functionalists (most notably Max Weber) engaged in extensive typology, especially the framing of comparative debate around "legal families," "legal traditions," and so on. Like the evolutionists, functionalists often see legal transformation as an organic response to pressures within the political system itself. Such explanations accept the ineluctability embedded in any legal progress. However, they also recognize particular ways in which legal innovations can follow from, and provide solutions to, demonstrated systemic social need.

A simple illustration of the functionalist logic of legal change is provided by Alan Watson's writings on legal transplants. Watson challenges the Montesquieu view that law is a local phenomenon linked to the living conditions of a given society. In most cases, legal rules are not peculiarly reflective of the particular society in which they operate. Legal borrowings (or "transplants") of rules, institutions, or doctrines—not living conditions in a given polity—account for most legal change in most systems. Borrowing occurs primarily because existing law in a given polity is not in touch or in concert with current social or economic needs. As systemic needs evolve, critical gaps in existing laws call for completion, more often than not through borrowing.[20]

Arguably the best-known functionalist explanations for legal change focus on increases in systemic efficiency as the products of such change. Some institutional economists, for example, posit a systemic efficiency-driven process of legal transformation, in which inefficient legal rules would more likely be litigated while new efficient rules would persist once established.[21] Equivalent arguments have been made for legal changes in tort law and contract law, and even in the legal organization of a society to allow for modes of production that increase the rate of return on capital. Douglass North and Robert Thomas' analysis of the demise of feudalism in Europe illustrates the logic of this argument. During the Middle Ages, feudalism remained stable as long as land remained the scarce resource. Although lords could offer more rights to laboring serfs, it was not in their interests to do so. Following the Black Death, however, it was labor that became the scarce resource. Lords facing competition for labor for the first time attempted to lure workers by offering them more attractive working conditions. In turn, this stimulated labor force mobility, thus destroying feudalism in Western Europe.[22]

Whereas evolutionist approaches treat legal arrangement mainly as indicators of social progress, functionalist sociolegal studies see law and legal institutions as important determinants, even necessary preconditions, of social and economic development. Max Weber's comparative law project, as it is reflected in *Economy and Society*, for example, attempts to explain the ascendancy of the West by drawing causal links between law (mainly as an independent variable) and social and economic development (mainly as a dependent variable) across societies.[23] His attention to comparative law develops alongside his well-known efforts to explain the origins of European capitalism and modernism in terms of the unique religious formation and ethic of Calvinist Protestantism. From a legal standpoint, the West had a key advantage in the early development in European societies of formal-rational legal systems juxtaposed with rational systems of political authority. Such a constellation of formal and rational structures and norms provided fertile ground for the development of capitalism.

A closely related functionalist approach—the institutional economics-derived theory of constitutional transformation—sees the development of constitutions and judicial review as mechanisms to mitigate systemic collective-action concerns such as commitment, enforcement, and information problems.

One such explanation sees the development of constitutions and independent judiciaries as an efficient institutional answer to the problem of "credible commitments."[24] Political leaders of any independent unit want to promote sustainable long-term economic growth and encourage investment that will facilitate the prosperity of their polity. Two critical preconditions for economic development are the existence of predictable laws governing the marketplace and a legal regime that protects capital formation and ensures property rights. The entrenchment of constitutional rights and the establishment of independent judicial monitoring of the legislative and executive branches are seen as ways of increasing a given regime's credibility and enhancing the ability of its bureaucracy to enforce contracts. This encourages the trust of investors and enhances their incentive to invest, innovate, and develop.

Indeed, as Max Weber noted, the fundamental building block of every successful capitalist market is a secure "predictability interest" based on formal, unambiguous rules and a rational legal system (as opposed to arbitrary, ad-hoc norms), as well as on rational (as opposed to traditional or charismatic) political authority. Without this, potential investors lack the incentive to invest. Scholars have shown how entrenched legal rights that enhance investors' trust, mainly the constitutional protection of property rights, have led to economic growth in various historical contexts. Nobel Prize laureate Douglass North, for example, has illustrated how legal limitations on rulers' arbitrary power in early capitalist Europe increased the legal security and predictability of external lenders who were protected by law from the seizure of their capital.[25] This allowed polities where such limitations existed to borrow capital and to better their position vis-à-vis their rival polities where the arbitrary power of the ruler ("irrational systems," in Weber's terminology) had not been restricted by law. More recent empirical studies have established a positive correlation between the existence of institutional limitations on government action (constitutional provisions and judicial review, for example) and economic growth.[26] And there are other arguments of a similar nature that consider the impact of constitutional structures on the consolidation of democracy: one need only think of prominent scholars of comparative politics, from William Riker to the more recent "transitology" literature as fruitful examples.

## The Missing Link: Courts as Political Institutions

### The Political Construction of Judicial Review

Evolutionists treat law as the indicator or reflection of development. Functionalists treat modern legal institutions as preconditions of development. The third post-Montesquieu branch of comparative legal studies sees law and legal institutions, mainly constitutions and constitutional courts, as derivative of political vectors and interests. Here, law is treated as a dependent variable. Addressing a major lacuna in Montesquieu's work—the political construction of law and the courts, this branch of scholarship explains variance in the scope and nature of judicial power across societies through political variables.

The first step in this direction was made by Robert Dahl's conceptualization of the U.S. Supreme Court as a mainly political, not juridical, institution.[27] Martin Shapiro's classic *Courts: A Comparative and Political Analysis* was the first thorough application of Robert Dahl's theory of courts as political institutions to the study of comparative public law.[28] Shapiro argues that courts worldwide should be thought of as political agencies of government; and moreover, judges should be perceived as political actors functioning largely in support of political regimes. "Most fundamentally," argues Shapiro, "the role of courts and judicial processes is to maintain the legitimacy of the regime, and most elements of the court system serve to advance this function."[29] Common characteristics and images of court systems worldwide (for example, judicial independence, judicial selection processes, perceptions of impartiality, and procedural fairness, appellate processes, etc.) are politically constructed in order to support political hierarchy, stability, and legitimacy.

To illustrate the applicability of his "courts as political institutions" argument in diverse legal contexts, Shapiro analyzes the main institutional, jurisprudential, and sociolegal characteristics of four prototypical cases, each representing a major and distinct legal tradition. He takes the case of the English legal system as the prototype of a common law system, characterized by a political construction of judicial independence and the image of judicial impartiality. France and Italy serve as prototypical illustrations of how judges in civil law systems (who are commonly perceived as bound by preexisting rules) adjust their jurisprudence to accord with regime interests. Imperial China represents a very different kind of regime again: the political construction of Confucian ethics and nonlitigious mediation in Asian law. Finally, the Ottoman Empire is an example of a decentralized political system resulting in a mosaic of secular and religious jurisprudence; in addition, appellate-less "kadi justice" in Islamic jurisprudence reflects the absence of a central political authority. Shapiro's conclusion is blunt: despite the variance in the legal cultures and traditions within which they operate, judicial tribunals in each of these prototypical cases—and by extension in many other cases—reflect and promote broad socio-political interests.

Another illustration of the "courts as political institutions" argument comes out of the more recent strategic approach to judicial empowerment. Tom Ginsburg's *Judicial Review in New Democracies* examines the evolution of independent constitutional courts during early stages of democratic liberalization in postauthoritarian polities.[30] In a nutshell, Ginsburg argues that the establishment of constitutional review in new democracies is largely a function of politics and interests, not a reflection of macrocultural or societal factors. Specifically, judicial review may provide "insurance" for self-interested, risk-averse politicians, who are negotiating the terms of new constitutional arrangements under conditions of political deadlock or systemic uncertainty.

Ginsburg substantiates this argument through an exploration of the rarely discussed establishment of constitutional courts, and the corresponding judicialization of politics, in three new Asian democracies: Taiwan, Mongolia, and Korea. All three countries share a roughly similar cultural context. Each country underwent a transition to democracy in the late 1980s and early 1990s. Newly established constitutional courts in all three countries have struggled to maintain and enhance their stature within political environments that lack an established tradition of judicial independence and constitutional supremacy. Despite these commonalities, there has been a significant variance in judicial independence among the three countries.

In Taiwan, the democratization process was governed by a single dominant party (KMT) with an overwhelmingly powerful leader (Chiang Kai-shek). The result has been a very gradual constitutional reform and the evolution of a relatively weak and politically dependent court (the Council of Grand Justices). In Mongolia, the former Communist Party was in a strong position during the constitutional negotiation stage but was nonetheless unable to dictate outcomes unilaterally because of a newly emergent set of opposition parties. This resulted in the 1992 creation of a "middle of the road," quasi-independent court (the Constitutional Tsets). In Korea, constitutional transformation took place amidst embedded uncertainty stemming from political deadlock among three parties of roughly equal strength. As a result, in 1988, a strong and relatively independent constitutional court emerged as political insurance against electoral uncertainty.

In a recently published book—*Towards Juristocracy: The Origins and Consequences of the New Constitutionalism*—I suggest that judicial empowerment through constitutionalization in many "new constitutionalism" countries resulted from self-interested actions taken by hegemonic, yet threatened, sociopolitical groups fearful of losing their grip on political power.[31] Constitutionalization may provide an effective solution for influential groups who possess better access to, and influence upon, the legal arena, and who—given serious erosion in their popular support—may seek to entrench their policy preferences against the growing influence of "peripheral" groups and interests. Such a strategic, counterintuitive self-limitation may be beneficial to threatened sociopolitical elites and those who hold power when the limits imposed on rival elements within the body politic outweigh the limits imposed on themselves. Strategic, self-interested legal innovators—threatened political elites in association with economic and judicial elites who have compatible interests—determine the timing, extent, and nature of the constitutional reforms. Judicial empowerment through the constitutionalization of rights is often not a reflection of a genuinely progressive revolution in a polity; rather, it is evidence that the rhetoric of rights and judicial review has been appropriated by certain groups to bolster their own position in the polity.

Understanding constitutionalization as a form of political entrenchment by self-interested, risk-averse politicians representing threatened elites may shed light on the political vectors behind the constitutional revolutions in formerly Westminster-style polities such as Canada, South Africa, and Israel. Canada's adoption of the Charter of Rights and Freedoms in 1982, I argue, was part of a broader strategic response by the federalist, anglophone, business-oriented elites to the growing threat of Quebec separatism and the rapidly changing demographics of Canadian society. The near-miraculous conversion to constitutionalism and judicial review among South Africa's white political and business elites during the late 1980s and early 1990s occurred when it became clear that the days of apartheid were numbered and an ANC-controlled government was inevitable. Israel's 1992 adoption of two new basic laws protecting core rights and liberties, the corresponding establishment of constitutional review in 1995, and the Israeli Supreme Court's continuous antireligious jurisprudence over the past fifteen years were all part of a strategic response by Israel's secular bourgeoisie, who had been rapidly losing its historical political dominance in Israel's majoritarian decision-making arenas.

These works, along with other recent publications that examine in a comparative context the political construction of judicial review, suggest that the existence of an active, nondeferential constitutional court is a necessary, but *not a sufficient condition*, for persistent judicial activism and the judicialization of megapolitics. Assertion of judicial supremacy cannot take place, let alone be sustained, without the support (tacit or explicit) of influential political stakeholders. A political sphere that is conducive to constitutionalization and judicial activism is at least as significant to its emergence and sustainability as the contribution of courts and judges, before even considering the contribution of factors identified by Montesquieu.

*Theories of Judicial Behavior*

Akin to studies of the political origins of judicial review, this emerging area of scholarship challenges Montesquieu's view of the judiciary as the least political branch of the trio. It treats the legal doctrine of *stare decisis* and the mainstream view of judges as rule and precedent followers or as framers of legal policies as a benchmark against which to develop its antithesis: judges do not reach decisions in a way that is fundamentally different from any other branch of government. Courts are political institutions not merely because they are politically constructed but also because the determinants of judicial behavior do not vary considerably from the determinants that affect decision making by other public officials. Reflection of national metanarratives[32]; responsiveness to public opinion[33]; personal ideological preferences[34]; path dependence and cost-benefit calculus[35]; intracourt interactions[36]; and strategic considerations vis-à-vis other branches of government are important determinants of judicial behavior.

The strategic approach to the study of judicial behavior, to pick one example, casts doubt on the prevalent apolitical view of the judiciary. It suggests that judges are not only precedent followers, framers of legal policies, or even ideology-driven decision makers but also sophisticated strategic decision makers who realize that their range of decision-making choices is constrained by the preferences and anticipated reaction of the surrounding political sphere.[37] Accordingly, constitutional court rulings may not only be analyzed as mere acts of professional, apolitical jurisprudence (as doctrinal legalistic explanations of court rulings often suggest) or reflections of judicial ideology (as "attitudinal" models of judicial behavior might suggest) but also a reflection of judges' own strategic choices. Because justices do not have the institutional capacities to enforce their rulings, they must take into account the extent to which popular decision makers will support their policy initiatives.[38] Strategic justices must gauge the prevailing winds that drive election-minded politicians and make decisions accordingly. Judges may also vote strategically to minimize the chances that their decisions will be overridden; if the interpretation that the justices favor is likely to elicit a reversal by superior branches, they will compromise by adopting the interpretation closest to their preferences that could be predicted to withstand reversal. As recent studies show, credible threats to the court's autonomy and harsh political responses to unwelcome activism or interventions on the part of the courts have chilling effects on judicial decision-making patterns.[39] Likewise, judges in certain legal systems may vote strategically, especially in politically charged cases, in order not to diminish their chances for promotion.[40] Supreme Court judges may also be viewed as strategic actors to the extent that they seek to maintain or enhance the Court's independence and institutional position vis-à-vis other major national decision-making bodies.[41] Finally, judges seem to care about their reputation within their close social milieu, court colleagues, and the legal profession more generally.[42] In other words, strategic judges may recognize when the changing fates or preferences of influential political actors, or gaps in the institutional context within which they operate, might allow them to strengthen their own position by extending the ambit of their jurisprudence and fortifying their status as crucial national policy makers.

In sum, while many of Montesquieu's insights did not withstand the acid test of time, we can still hear echoes, in some cases more distant than in others, of Montesquieu's seminal work in each of the social science streams of comparative law studies surveyed above. Although post-Montesquieu comparative sociolegal scholarship challenges, if not outright refutes, most of the empirical arguments put forth in *The Spirit of Laws*, and despite the fact that research design and data analysis methods have become far more sophisticated since Montesquieu's time, the epistemological pillars of Montesquieu's work—comparative research, taxonomy, and the interdependence of law and society—continue to serve as the bedrock of contemporary study of law and legal institutions. Typology of legal systems serves as the basis for both the evolutionist and functionalist approaches. The former treats law as an indicator of development. The latter sees law as a determinant of development. More recent comparative studies treat law and legal institutions as a dependent variable and view law as politics by other means. Judges are not only bound by political constraints, but equally are not always free of self-interested strategic considerations. These studies emphasize a critical missing link in Montesquieu's impressive sociolegal work—the role of politics and power struggles in shaping law, courts, and judicial behavior. At any rate, either as the bedrock of comparative sociolegal inquiry or as the benchmark against which we can develop novel theses, Montesquieu's seminal work has had a lasting impact on the field.

## The Selective Adaptation of Montesquieu in Legal Academia

Canonical American constitutional theory, from the founding fathers to Alexander Bickel, Ronald Dworkin, and John Hart Ely, has endorsed Montesquieu's "separation of powers" argument and his view of the judiciary as the "least dangerous" and most enlightened branch of government.[43] However, although there is considerable resonance with his thinking among social scientists studying legal institutions, the impact of Montesquieu's epistemological framework on comparative constitutional law scholarship produced by legal academics has been far less significant.

It is true that last decade has seen the heyday of comparative public law scholarship. After nearly a century of embedded parochialism and intellectual stalemate, the field has recently undergone a certain renaissance. Scholarly interest in comparative constitutional jurisprudence and the international migration of constitutional concepts has been growing steadily over the last decade. From a relatively obscure topic studied by the devoted few, comparative constitutional law has emerged as one of the more fashionable subjects in contemporary public law scholarship. More constitutional lawyers than ever before now pay attention to constitutional law and politics abroad. Top-ranked law schools now regard courses on comparative constitutionalism as essential additions to the curriculum. Even the United States Supreme Court—perhaps the last bastion of parochialism among the world's leading constitutional courts—has recently joined the comparative reference trend. But in spite of the growing interest in comparative constitutional systems, little has changed in the epistemology and methodology of comparative constitutional law. Fundamental questions concerning the very purpose and rationale of comparative inquiry (and how that enterprise is to be undertaken) remain largely outside the purview of mainstream constitutional law scholarship.

First, there is a persisting resistance among the legal academia to accept the notion that law is a species of politics and that courts are a part of the political system, not a thing apart. This doctrinal separation of law and politics has not passed over most scholars of constitutional law—perhaps the most observably political branch of law. Even as we are witnessing an ever-accelerating reliance worldwide on courts and judicial means for articulating and dealing with the most contentious political questions a democratic polity can contemplate, dozens of lengthy articles published in America's leading law reviews every year continue to portray an almost exclusively court-centric picture of constitutional law. Most of these articles focus mainly on the compatibility of past or present American constitutional jurisprudence with grand constitutional theory. Almost none pay any attention to the critical institutional and political conditions within which constitutional courts operate and judicial review is exercised. Fundamental questions are rarely addressed by constitutional theorists. Where, for example, does judicial power originate? What accounts for the significant variance in the timing, scope, and nature of constitutional reform across the world of new constitutionalism? What are the political conditions that support the maintenance and expansion of judicial power? What are the determinants of judicial decision making? Even more concrete questions such as the effect of institutional features of judicial review on judicial engagement with politics are addressed almost exclusively by political scientists or political economists, not by constitutional theorists. None of Ronald Dworkin's six books on constitutionalism, for example, refer to any of these fundamental questions, nor do they even cite any secondary sources dealing with positive questions or empirical findings concerning the origins and consequences of constitutionalization and judicial review.[44] And Dworkin—arguably the most prominent contemporary constitutional theorist—is certainly not alone in this. In fact, power relations or strategic choices have always been at best a peripheral component of constitutional theory. Indeed, the entire enterprise of canonical constitutional theory seems to be caught up with the idealist notion of constitutional law as sovereign virtue or as an enterprise unto itself. At least in that respect, Montesquieu's understanding of constitutionalism was more realistic than that of many contemporary constitutional theorists.

Even those who are skeptical of the belief that constitutionalism is an all-out "good thing" have given little consideration to the actual political origins or consequences of judicial empowerment. Instead, they have been almost exclusively preoccupied with the well-rehearsed normative debate over the "countermajoritarian" nature of judicial review and the "democratic deficit" inherent in transferring important policy-making prerogatives from elected and accountable politicians, parliaments, and other majoritarian decision-making bodies to the judiciary. Indeed, it is possible to count on the fingers of one hand the empirical and inductive inquiries that question the democratic credentials of constitutionalism and judicial review, let alone the concrete political origins of judicial empowerment.

From Robert Bork on the right to Jeremy Waldron on the left, constitutional theorists critical of judicial activism often blame "power hungry" courts and judges for being too assertive and excessively entangled with moral and political decision making. Subsequently, they are charged with disregarding fundamental separation of powers and democratic governance principles.[45] Even more politically astute critics of the U.S. Constitution's expropriation by the United States Supreme Court are more concerned with the Supreme Court's "imperialist" impulse than with the political conditions that promote judicial activism and the ever-accelerating judicialization of politics.[46]

Second, confusion surrounds the very definition of the term *comparative*. Indeed, in the field of comparative constitutional law 'comparative' is often used indiscriminately to describe what are, in fact, four different types of scholarship: (1) freestanding, single-country studies mistakenly characterized as comparative only by virtue of dealing with any country other than the author's own; (2) surveys of foreign law aimed at finding "the best" or most suitable rule across cultures; (3) comparative reference aimed at self-reflection through analogy, distinction, and contrast; and (4) concept formation through multiple descriptions of the same constitutional phenomena across countries. Genuinely comparative, problem-driven, and *inference-oriented* scholarship is still difficult to come by. Most leading works in the field continue to lag behind the social sciences in their ability to trace causal links among pertinent variables, let alone contribute to theory building through substantiation or refutation of testable hypotheses. The aspiration to *explain* (rather than merely label, survey, or describe) constitutional phenomena through the validation or refutation of pertinent propositions has not, by and large, been shared by most legal academics working in the area.[47]

More specifically, comparative constitutional law scholarship produced by legal academics often either neglects, or in fact seems altogether unaware of, basic methodological principles of controlled comparison, research design, and case selection. To the extent that case selection principles receive any attention, the focus is often on cases that involve current policy concerns in the author's own polity. Too many constitutional comparativists still adhere to a convenient "cherry-picking" approach to case selection, failing to follow basic case selection principles commonly adhered to in the social sciences. Continuous reliance on such an asysystematic and methodology-light practice of research design and case selection does not serve the cause of serious theory-building well. Indeed, it is precisely due to its traditional lack of attention to principles of controlled comparison and case selection that comparative constitutional law scholarship produced by legal academics—progress in recent years notwithstanding—often falls short of advancing knowledge in the manner sought by most social scientists.[48]

There is also a problem, admittedly to a lesser extent, with research methods used by legal comparativists. From *The Spirit of Laws* to the still prevalent armchair anthropology approach to comparative constitutional law, too little has changed, so it seems, in the way some comparative constitutional lawyers pursue their research. Studying comparative constitutionalism is a serious undertaking, a labor of love for this and other authors, but still a difficult, labor-intensive, and time-consuming endeavor. Akin to social and cultural anthropology, it requires a tremendous investment of one's material and intellectual resources. The modern comparativist's basic toolkit must include pertinent linguistic and legal skills; detailed knowledge of foreign legal systems, jurisprudence, and legacies (as opposed to a sketchy acquaintance with two dozen foreign cases); familiarity with basic comparative methodologies, quantitative and qualitative (as opposed to an "E-Z Pass" methodology-light approach to comparative constitutional law scholarship); the ability to remain constantly informed about often underreported constitutional developments overseas (as opposed to a Montesquieulike selective reliance on secondary and easily attainable sources that all too often adhere to the author's normative predispositions and support his or her arguments); cultural sensitivity; and the willingness to spend lengthy periods of time doing field work in less than dazzling conditions (as opposed to "armchair" anthropology research with little or no fieldwork). It is no wonder, then, that sophisticated, genuinely comparative, problem-driven, and inference-oriented scholarship (as opposed to primarily descriptive, single-country studies mistakenly characterized as comparative only by the virtue of dealing with any country other than the author's own) is still difficult to come by.

The difference in the resonance of *The Spirit of Laws* for comparative social science studies of legal institutions and studies of comparative constitutional law by legal academics may be explained, in part, by traditional doctrinal boundaries; trajectories of academic training; and the different epistemologies, functions, and goals of social and legal inquiry. Perhaps the 250th anniversary of the death of the founding master of comparative sociolegal inquiry—suggests that the time is ripe for a sea change in current approaches to comparative study of constitutional law. Legal academics studying comparative constitutional law should release themselves further from traditional doctrinal constraints and contribute more significantly to theory building through the deployment of genuinely comparative, and more methodologically rigorous, principles of research design and case selection. Not only would such a convergence help bridge the gap between constitutional theory and constitutional politics, but it would also create a unified enterprise of comparative constitutional law, with an epistemological framework closer to the one envisioned and practiced by its first master.

## Notes

I thank Simone Chambers, Rebecca Kingston, Steve Newman, and especially Ayelet Shachar for their thoughtful comments, as well Joanna Langille and Tom Rowe for their useful research assistance.

1. Montesquieu, *The Spirit of the Laws*, trans. Anne Cohler (Cambridge: University of Cambridge Press, 1989), 3.
2. Ibid., 9.
3. Ibid., 157.
4. Ibid., 8.
5. Ibid., 659.
6. Robert Launay, "Montesquieu: The Specter of Despotism and the Origins of Comparative Law," in *Rethinking the Masters of Comparative Law*, ed. Annelise Riles (Oxford: Hart, 2001), 28–29
7. *The Spirit of the Laws*, 20.
8. Judith Shklar, *Montesquieu* (Oxford: Oxford University Press, 1987), 85.
9. In the *Persian Letters* Montesquieu engages in another purpose of comparative inquiry: self-reflection through analogy and contrast, in this case, reflection on Louis XVI France through the "outsider" observations of Persian merchants, Usbek and Rica.
10. Launay, "Montesquieu," 30.
11. Ibid., 31; cf. Catherine Volpilhac-Auger's chapter in this volume.
12. See Peter Stein, *Legal Evolution: The Story of an Idea* (Cambridge: Cambridge University Press, 1980) for a general survey of this approach.
13. Sir Henry Maine, *Ancient Law* (Washington, DC: Beard Books, 2000), 1861.
14. Joan Vincent, "Lewis Henry Morgan," *Encyclopedia of Social and Cultural Anthropology*, ed. Alan Bernard and Jonathan Spencer (London: Routledge, 2004), 381.
15. Emile Durkheim, *Montesquieu and Rousseau: Forerunners of Sociology* (Ann Arbor: University of Michigan Press, 1960, 1892), 1.
16. Emile Durkheim, *The Division of Labor in Society* (New York: Free Press, 1964, 1893).
17. Thomas Pangle, *Montesquieu's Philosophy of Liberalism* (Chicago: University of Chicago Press, 1973).
18. For similar arguments in the broader context of economic and political development, see Samuel Eisenstadt, *Modernization: Protest and Change* (Englewood Cliffs, NJ: Prentice-Hall, 1966), Samuel Eisenstadt, ed., *Readings in Social Evolution and Development* (Oxford: Pergamon Press, 1970); Talcott Parsons, *The Evolution of Societies* (Englewood Cliffs, NJ: Prentice-Hall, 1977). Maine's evolutionary thesis of the development of law is echoed by structural functionalist legal sociologists such as

Niklas Luhmann and his theory of the evolution of law as a function of the increasing complexity and contingency in modern societies. See Niklas Luhmann, *A Sociological Theory of Law* (London: Routledge, 1985).

19. For a general survey of this approach see Michele Graziadei, "The Functionalist Heritage," in *Comparative Legal Studies: Traditions and Transitions*, ed. Pierre Legrand and Roderick Munday (Cambridge: Cambridge University Press, 2003).

20. Alan Watson, *Legal Tansplants*, 2nd ed. (Athens: University of Georgia Press, 1993).

21. Paul Rubin, *Business Firms and the Common Law: The Evolution of Efficient Rules* (New York: Praeger Press, 1983).

22. Douglass North and Robert Thomas, *The Rise of the Western World* (Cambridge: Cambridge University Press, 1973).

23. Max Weber, *Economy and Society: An outline of interpretive sociology* (Berkeley: University of California Press, 1978, 1914).

24. North and Thomas, *The Rise of the Western World*; Oliver Williamson, "Credible Commitments: Using Hostages to Support Exchange," *American Economic Review* 73 (1983): 519–40; Barry Weingast, "Constitutions as Governance Structures: The Political Foundations of Secure Markets," *Journal of Institutional and Theoretical Economics* 149 (1993): 286–311; Barry Weingast, "The Political Foundations of Democracy and the Rule of Law," *American Political Science Review* 91 (1997): 245–63.

25. Douglass North and Barry Weingast, "Constitutions and Commitment: The Evolution of Institutions Governing Public Choice in Seventeenth Century England," *Journal of Economic History* 49 (1989): 803–33.

26. Rafael La Porta, Florencio Lopez de Silanes, Andrei Shleifer, and Robert Vishy, "Law and Finance," *Journal of Political Economy* 106 (1998): 1113–55; Rafael La Porta, Florencio Lopez de Silanes, Andrei Shleifer, and Robert Vishy, "The Quality of Government," *Journal of Law, Economics and Organization* 15 (1999): 222–79; Paul Mahoney, "The Common Law and Economic Growth: Hayek Might Be Right," *Journal of Legal Studies* 30 (2001): 503–25; Andrei Shleifer, Rafael La Porta, Florencio Lopez de Silanes, and Cristian Pop-Eleches, "Judicial Checks and Balances," *Journal of Political Economy* 112 (2004): 445–70.

27. Robert Dahl, "Decision-Making in a Democracy: The Supreme Court as a National Policy-Maker," *Journal of Public Law* 6 (1957): 279–95.

28. Martin Shapiro, *Courts: A Comparative and Political Analysis* (Chicago: University of Chicago Press, 1981).

29. Hebert Kritzer, "Martin Shapiro: Anticipating the New Institutionalism," in *The Pioneers of Judicial Behavior*, ed. Nancy Maveety (Ann Arbor: University of Michigan Press, 2003), 397.

30. Tom Ginsburg, *Judicial Review in New Democracies: Constitutional Courts in Asian Cases* (Cambridge: Cambridge University Press, 2003).

31. Ran Hirschl, *Towards Juristocracy: The Origins and Consequences of the New Constitutionalism* (Cambridge: Harvard University Press, 2004).

32. Gary Jacobsohn, *The Wheel of Law* (Princeton: Princeton University Press, 2003); Mitchel Lasser, *Judicial Deliberations: A Comparative Analysis of Judicial Transparency and Legitimacy* (Oxford: Oxford University Press, 2004).

33. William Mishler and Reginald Sheehan, "The Supreme Court as Countermajoritarian Institution? The Impact of Public Opinion on Supreme Court Decisions," *American Political Science Review* 88 (1993): 87–101.

34. Jeffrey Segal and Harold Spaeth, *The Supreme Court and the Attitudinal Model Revisited* (Cambridge: Cambridge University Press, 2002).

35. Cass Sunstein and Edna Ullmann-Margalit, "Second-Order Decisions," in *Behavioral Law and Economics*, ed. Cass Sustein (Cambridge: Cambridge University Press, 2000); Oona Hathaway, "Path Dependence in the Law: The Course and Pattern of Change in a Common Law Legal System," *Iowa Law Review* 86 (2001), 601.

36. Forest Maltzman, James Spriggs, and Paul Wahlbeck, *Crafting Law on the Supreme Court: The Collegial Game* (Cambridge: Cambridge University Press, 2000).

37. William N. Eskridge, "Reneging on History? Playing the Court/Congress/President Civil Rights Game," *California Law Review* 79 (1991): 613–84; Lee Epstein and Jack Knight, *The Choices Justices Make* (Washington, DC: CQ Press, 1998); Cornel Clayton and Howard Gillman, eds. *Supreme Court Decision-Making: New Institutionalist Approaches* (Chicago: University of Chicago Press,1999); Lee Epstein and Jack Knight, "Towards a Strategic Revolution in Judicial Politics: A Look Back, a Look Ahead," *Political Research Quarterly* 53 (2000): 625–61.

38. Kevin McGuire and James Stimson, "The Least Dangerous Branch Revisited: New Evidence on Supreme Court Responsiveness to Public Preferences," *Journal of Politics* 66 (2004): 1018–35.

39. Lee Epstein, Jack Knight, and Olga Shvetsova, "The Role of Constitutional Courts in the Establishment and Maintenance of Democratic Systems of Government," *Law and Society Review* 35 (2001): 117–63; Gretchen Helmke, "The Logic of Strategic Defection: Court-Executive Relations in Argentina under Dictatorship and Democracy," *American Political Science Review* 96 (2002): 291–303; Georg Vanberg, *The Politics of Constitutional Review in Germany* (Cambridge: Cambridge University Press, 2005).

40. Mark Ramseyer and Eric Rasmusen, "Why Are Japanese Judges so Conservative in Politically Charged Cases?" *American Political Science Review* 95 (2001): 331–44.

41. The establishment of an international rule of law in the EU, for example, was driven in no small part by national judges' attempts to enhance their independence, influence, and authority vis-à-vis other courts and political actors. For an elaboration of this point see Karen Alter, *Establishing the Supremacy of European Law: The Making of an International Rule of Law in Europe* (Oxford: Oxford University Press, 2001).

42. Laurence Baum, *Judges and Their Audiences: A Perspective on Judicial Behavior* (Princeton, NJ: Princeton University Press, 2006).

43. The works that adopt one version or other of this approach are too numerous to cite. See. e.g., Alexander Bickel, *The Least Dangerous Branch: The Supreme Court at the Bar of Politics* (Indianapolis: Bobbs-Merrill Bickel, 1962); Ronald Dworkin, *Freedom's Law* (Cambridge: Harvard University 1996); John Hart Ely, *On Constitutional Ground* (Princeton, NJ: Princeton University Press Ely, 1996); and Andras Sajó, *Limiting Government: An Introduction to Constitutionalism* (Budapest-New York: CEU Press, 1999). For a discussion of the impact of Montesquieu's "least dangerous branch" idea on the founding fathers of the American Constitution, see Paul Carrese, *The Cloaking of Power: Montesquieu, Blackstone, and the Rise of Judicial Activism* (Chicago: University of Chicago Press, 2003).

44. Mark Graber, "Constitutional Politics and Constitutional Theory: A Misunderstood and Neglected Relationship," *Law and Social Inquiry* 27 (2002): 315

45. See, e.g., Jeremy Waldron, "Judicial Review and the Conditions for Democracy," *Journal of Political Philosophy* 6 (1998): 335–55; Jeremy Waldron, "Judicial Power and Popular Sovereignty," in *Marbury v. Madison: Documents and Commentary*, ed. Mark Graber (Washington, DC: CQ Press, 2002); Robert H. Bork, *The Tempting of American: The Political Seduction of the Law* (New York: Free Press, 1990); Robert H. Bork, *Coercing Virtue: The Worldwide Rule of Judges* (Toronto: Vintage Canada, 2002).

46. See, e.g., Larry Kramer, *The People Themselves: Popular Constitutionalism and Judicial Review* (Oxford: Oxford University Press, 2004); Mark Tushnet, *Taking the Constitution Away from the Courts* (Princeton, NJ: Princeton University Press, 1999).

47. Ran Hirschl, "The Question of Case Selection in Comparative Constitutional Law," *American Journal of Comparative Law* 53 (2005): 125–55; Ran Hirschl, "On the Blurred Methodological Matrix of Comparative Constitutional Law," in *The Migration of Constitutional Ideas*, ed. Sujit Choudhry (Cambridge: Cambridge University Press, 2006).

48. Two notable exceptions to this observation are the genuinely theory-oriented, economic analyses of constitutionalism, e.g., Robert Cooter, *The Strategic Constitution* (Princeton, NJ: Princeton University Press, 2000) and studies of law and development, e.g., Torsen Persson and Guido Tabellini, *The Economic Effects of Constitutions* (Cambridge: MIT Press, 2003).

# 11

# Free Speech and *The Spirit of Laws* in Canada and the United States

## A Test of Montesquieu's Approach to Comparative Law

*Stephen L. Newman*

Montesquieu was unique among the great legal theorists of his age in viewing the laws of particular nations in terms of the political requirements of local institutions and the always distinctive force exerted on law and politics by local culture. In this respect, as Ran Hirschl's contribution to the present volume illustrates, *The Spirit of Laws* made a seminal contribution to the sociology of law. But how well has Montesquieu's theory stood the test of time? How useful might it be to the modern student of comparative law?

I attempt an answer to this question by examining two landmark cases, one American, the other Canadian, each bearing on the constitutionality of laws criminalizing hate speech. The comparison is apt because Canada and the United States have remarkably similar "natures," to use Montesquieu's term for regime type. Both are descended from the English system of divided powers, both entrench the right to freedom of expression in their constitutions,[1] and both create the judiciary as a de jure coequal third branch of government armed with the power of judicial review.[2] What makes these particular cases of interest for my purposes is that the Canadian high court upheld the criminal ban on hate speech, while its American counterpart found a similar law to be unconstitutional. If Montesquieu's theory of law continues to have relevance it should be able to help explain this seemingly contradictory result.

The Canadian case, *R. v. Keegstra* (1990)[3] concerned the actions of one James Keegstra, a high school social studies teacher in Ecksville, Alberta, who over a period of ten years routinely taught his students that Jews were out to destroy Christianity by war, depression, and other nefarious means. He also taught that the Holocaust was a fabrication invented to garner sympathy for the Jewish people. Students who failed to parrot his views received lower grades. At length his unorthodox lessons became a public issue, and he was dismissed from his post. Subsequently, he was charged under sec. 319(2) of the federal *Criminal Code*, which penalizes the willful promotion of hatred against "an identifiable group," a category defined by the statute as "any section of the public distinguished by colour, race, religion, or ethnic origin." Keegstra challenged the constitutionality of the law claiming that it violated sec. 2(b)—the free speech provision—of the *Canadian Charter of Rights and Freedoms*. In upholding the impugned statute the Canadian Supreme Court acknowledged its adverse impact on sec. 2(b) but nonetheless found it allowable under sec. 1 of the charter, known as the reasonable limits clause, which provides that government may impose restrictions on protected freedoms so long as these can be "demonstrably justified in a free and democratic society."[4]

In the parallel American case, *R.A.V. v. St. Paul* (1992),[5] the juvenile petitioner, Robert Viktora, was charged under a municipal Bias Motivated Crime Ordinance proscribing the display of symbols, including but not limited to a burning cross or Nazi swastika, that are known or reasonably ought be known to arouse "anger, alarm or resentment" on the basis of race, color, creed, religion, or gender. Viktora had participated with other youths in burning a cross, crudely fashioned from pieces of broken furniture, on the lawn of a black family in his neighborhood. He subsequently explained their actions as a prank committed under the influence of alcohol and drugs. The trial judge dismissed the charges on First Amendment grounds, finding there is no power under the Constitution to suppress speech or expressive conduct, like the act of burning a cross, solely on account of the state's disapproval of the message; however, on appeal by the city the Minnesota State Supreme Court reinstated the charges, arguing that the impugned ordinance could be made to fit within a narrowly tailored exception to the First Amendment known as the "fighting words" doctrine. The question before the United States Supreme Court was whether in fact St. Paul's ordinance could be saved by reading it as pertaining only to fighting words.

Montesquieu's theory, as laid out in *The Spirit of Laws*, alerts us to the importance of what he calls the "nature" and "principle" of government as well as the influence on the laws of a host of environmental factors.[6] Regime type would not seem to be a factor in distinguishing the American and Canadian cases. Differing principles, by which Montesquieu means the passions that motivate participants in the political system, together with environmental factors, among which he includes the manners and mores of the people, may hold greater explanatory power.[7] Indeed, Chief Justice Dickson of the Canadian

Supreme Court appears to follow Montesquieu's theory in his majority opinion. Acknowledging his disagreement with First Amendment jurisprudence, Dickson speaks of differing "constitutional visions" rooted in the two nations' different historical experiences and political traditions. In the story he tells, Canada is unlike the United States in at least two important respects. First, in contrast with the American melting pot, Canada's experience of racial, ethnic, religious, and linguistic pluralism makes the Canadian polity significantly more fragile. Because various subnational group identities are stronger and the national civic identity weaker in Canada than in the United States, the Canadian government has good reason to suppress speech that by its nature would threaten the comity among groups. Second, Canada's normative commitments to multiculturalism and equality, which find expression in sections 27 and 15 of the *Charter* respectively, mandate a heightened judicial sensitivity to the affronts suffered by historically oppressed or otherwise vulnerable minorities.[8] For a people who value diversity and equality as highly as, to Dickson's way of thinking, Canadians do (or ought to do), preserving the self-esteem of those targeted by hate speech is more important than protecting the free speech of hate mongers.

Montesquieu may be understood to refer to principles in two senses, ideal and empirical. In the former sense, principles are passions dictated by the logic of the regime type.[9] Thus, for example, the success of a republic requires that citizens have a passion for equality.[10] If this passion is lacking, republican virtue succumbs to corruption, and the regime is endangered. Empirically speaking, principle refers to people's actual motives, which frequently deviate from what they ought to be. Dickson's majority opinion, through the stress it lays on the normative importance of egalitarianism and multiculturalism, implicitly theorizes the principles that provide, in Montesquieu's terms, the springs of government. Dickson's primary focus, however, is on the danger posed by antagonistic passions.

Hate speech, or hate "propaganda," as Dickson refers to it, is said to harm the Canadian polity in two ways. First, it does "emotional damage" to those persons targeted by hate mongers, having "a severely negative impact on the individual's sense of self-worth and acceptance." Second, the injury done by this assault on the "self-dignity of the target group" is exacerbated "by the possibility that prejudiced messages will gain some credence [within the general public], with the attendant result of discrimination, and perhaps even violence, against minority groups in Canadian society." The latter is taken to have broad implications for the stability of the nation: "[I]t is not inconceivable," Dickson writes, "that the active dissemination of hate propaganda can attract individuals to its cause, and in the process create serious discord between various cultural groups in society."[11]

Given the severity of the threat he claimed to discern, the tentative nature of Dickson's language here is striking. We are not told that hate propaganda has led to a contagion of hatred, resulted in acts of discrimination, or provoked violence against vulnerable minority groups, only that it might *possibly* do so. The rift between cultural groups that would result in "serious discord" is not presented as imminent, but rather as something that is *not inconceivable*. Even where Dickson's language is more assured there is a curious lack of substance. We are told that hate propaganda is emotionally damaging to its victims, that it lowers their self-esteem and engenders a sense of alienation from the broader society, but no evidence is presented in support of these assertions. The one empirical study on which the Court relied, the report of the Cohen Committee (Special Committee on Hate Propaganda in Canada, 1966), spoke in the same dire tones as Dickson's majority opinion, but its two-year survey uncovered relatively few pieces of hate literature to complain of and counted an insignificant number of dedicated hate mongers and their hangers-on.[12]

Anxiety over the power of modern propaganda to sway public opinion colors the Cohen Commission's report. The spectres hovering in the background would appear to be Nazi Germany and Soviet Russia, and for his part Dickson seems all too ready to assimilate Keegstra's pathetic classroom diatribes to the totalitarian Big Lie. Quoting the Cohen Commission, he tells us that "individuals can be persuaded to believe 'almost anything' if information or ideas are communicated using the right technique and in the proper circumstances." For the authors of the commission's report the horrors of the twentieth century have falsified the comfortable Enlightenment belief that man is a rational creature, whose mind, if "trained and liberated from superstition by education . . . would always distinguish truth from falsehood, good from evil." Although Dickson sides with the report in affirming humanity's tendency to reject falsehood and evil "in the long run," he accepts its glum admonition that in the short run it is too often true "that emotion displaces reason and individuals reject the demonstrations of truth put before them and forsake the good they know." "We act irresponsibly," he writes, "if we ignore the way in which emotion can drive reason from the field."[13] Dickson's lack of faith in the power of human reason to resist malevolent ideas retailed as slick propaganda may be a reaction to political events of the late twentieth century, but in tone as well as substance his complaint is reminiscent of Edmund Burke, the great eighteenth-century critic of the "empire of light and reason."[14] Political scientist Peter Russell has described the Canadian constitutional tradition as Burkean in spirit if not by design, and it may be that Dickson echoed Burke's complaint against the meager strength of human reason unaware that he was drawing on a theme deeply woven in the fabric of Canadian constitutionalism.[15]

There is still something more to be said about the way the majority opinion in *Keegstra* glosses the concept of 'liberty.' Following Isaiah Berlin, it is useful to think about liberty in two senses, one positive, the other negative.[16] Negative liberty is experienced by the individual as freedom from coercive laws or the forcible interference of private persons. Liberty understood in this sense means that we are free to act (or refrain from acting) as we will, subject only to the caveat that our actions do not limit the like freedom of others. Positive liberty is experienced as the freedom of individuals to act in ways that realize something essential about their nature or well-being. Understood in this sense liberty pertains to a goal that transcends the arbitrary will of the individual. Thus, while negative liberty may enable positive liberty (by giving individuals scope to realize their highest good), conflict between the two concepts of liberty is also possible insofar as the negative liberty of individuals to do as they will can result in behaviors that are self-defeating from the standpoint of positive liberty.

There are elements of Dickson's opinion that appear to make freedom of expression subordinate to an overriding civic purpose. Two related assertions are of particular importance. First, he claims that because exposure to hate propaganda lowers the self-esteem of minority group members, it lessens the likelihood that they will participate in civic affairs. Second, he links the propaganda effects of hate speech on the general public to the creation of a chilly climate for minority group members, who correctly infer that their speech will not be welcomed by the majority. Thus, Dickson concludes, hate speech adversely affects the quality of civic membership for persons belonging to minority groups in Canadian society. The crucial assumption in this chain of reasoning is that the individual's sense of dignity and self-worth are tied to "the ability to articulate and nurture an identity derived from [group] membership."[17] It becomes important, therefore, to protect the status of vulnerable groups so that their members have an opportunity to develop the personal resources needed to flourish as human beings. Only by securing their group identity can they be assured entrance into the political life of the nation on an equal basis with the majority. On this logic the state is justified in limiting the expressive freedom of those who engage in hate speech in order protect the equality rights of targeted minorities, thus serving "the legitimate Parliamentary objective of protecting target group members and fostering harmonious social relations in a community dedicated to equality and multiculturalism."[18] In effect, Dickson's opinion justifies contracting the sphere of negative liberty protecting Keegstra's speech in order to secure positive liberty for politically marginal groups.

Contemporary First Amendment jurisprudence is far less open to making such trade-offs. Its core doctrines were fashioned by the United States Supreme Court in the first half of the twentieth century in response to government efforts to suppress overtly political, albeit allegedly subversive, speech. Faced with claims that the national security was at stake, the Court eventually came around to adopting the formula proposed by Justice Holmes in *Schenck v. United States* (1919). According to Holmes, the question "is whether the words are used in such circumstances and are of such a nature as to create a clear and present danger that they will bring about the substantive evils that Congress has a right to prevent."[19] Subsequent decisions applied Holmes's clear and present danger rule more broadly, reaching actions taken by the state governments as well as Congress, and established that the evils to be prevented must be tangible, usually in the form of violence against persons or property, and also that the danger apprehended must be grave and imminent. There was a time at midcentury when the court substituted a less restrictive test of "grave and probable" harm; however, that deviation from the trajectory established by the clear and present danger rule was soon abandoned.[20] Today, in marked contrast with Dickson's reasoning in *Keegstra*, the U.S. Court no longer treats fear of some merely *conceivable* harm associated with speech as sufficient to override the First Amendment guarantee.

The libertarian philosophy underlying the Supreme Court's approach to the First Amendment is perhaps best illustrated by Holmes's colleague on the Court and frequent collaborator, Justice Brandeis. It is not the evil inherent in certain ideas that poses a danger, Brandeis insisted in *Whitney v. California* (1927),[21] but rather the lack of time and opportunity to subject those ideas to full public examination. Brandeis attributed to the framers of the Constitution the belief that "discussion affords ordinarily adequate protection against the dissemination of noxious doctrine."[22] Building on this depiction of the framers' constitutional faith, he insisted that "no danger flowing from speech can be deemed clear and present, unless the incidence of the evil apprehended is so imminent that it may befall before there is opportunity for full discussion. If there be time to expose through discussion the falsehood and fallacies, to avert the evil by the process of education, the remedy to be applied is more speech, not enforced silence. Such must be the rule if authority is to be reconciled with freedom."[23] More speech seemed an adequate defence against the spread of noxious doctrine to Brandeis because he had confidence in the capacity of ordinary citizens to engage in rational deliberation. His trust in deliberative rationality and commitment to the efficacy of public discussion remain fundamental precepts of First Amendment law.[24]

Fighting words—words that "by their very utterance inflict injury or tend to incite an immediate breach of the peace"—play no part in rational deliberation and consequently have been determined by the Court to fall outside the protection of the First Amendment.[25] In R.A.V., the nine Justices of the Supreme Court had no difficulty agreeing that symbolic value of the burning cross Viktora erected on his neighbour's property fell within the category of fighting words and could lawfully be proscribed by the city of St. Paul. To this extent, at least, the American Court agreed with its Canadian counterpart that racist hate speech may be outlawed without running afoul of the constitutional right to freedom of expression. Nonetheless, the *R.A.V.* Court was unanimous in striking down St. Paul's Bias Motivated Crime Ordinance. Four members of the Court, led by Justice White, argued that the ordinance was void for being overbroad because it expressly proscribed the display of racist symbols that elicit "resentment" along with those causing "anger and alarm." While the latter struck White and his colleagues as suggestive of fighting words, the former seemed to them to put at risk protected speech that merely gave offence or engendered hurt feelings.[26]

Justice Scalia's majority opinion took a different tack, choosing this opportunity to rethink the scope and application of the Court's fighting words doctrine. It is not true, he argues, that fighting words are "entirely invisible to the Constitution," nor is it the case that they have "at most a 'de minimus' expressive content, or that their content is in all respects 'worthless and undeserving of constitutional protection.'" Rather, fighting words are categorically excluded from the protection of the First Amendment, because "their content embodies a particularly intolerable (and socially unnecessary) mode of expressing whatever idea the speaker wishes to convey."[27] In other words, it is not the message, however noxious, that distinguishes fighting words from protected speech, but rather the speaker's unduly provocative presentation of her ideas. Scalia, then, is willing to extend the protection of the First Amendment to the expression of racist ideas; however, at the same time he sees no constitutional objection to having the city of St. Paul proscribe cross burnings and the public display of other symbols of hate insofar as these constitute a particularly intolerable mode of communicating the speaker's message. What he finds unacceptable about the ordinance in question is that, in his judgment, the city had applied its ban selectively, singling out disfavored speech on the basis of its content and point of view. In essence, it appeared to Scalia that the city had taken sides in a partisan dispute over racial, religious, and gender equality by penalizing one side for the use of fighting words while leaving the other side free to indulge in abusive personal invective. The city, he complains, had no authority "to license one side of a debate to fight freestyle, while requiring the other to follow Marquis of Queensberry rules."[28] The logic of Scalia's argument would in effect require St. Paul to ban *all* fighting words in order to reach the injuries specifically associated with hate speech.[29]

Whether or not Scalia's revision of the Court's fighting words doctrine will stand the test of time is open to question. His attempt to distinguish the ideational content of the message from its mode of expression appears on its face to be difficult to sustain. How does one separate a racial slur from the racist idea it communicates? Moreover, his analysis of the St. Paul ordinance would appear on its face to be seriously flawed. As Justice Stevens argues in his concurring opinion, the city would not be guilty of impermissible content or viewpoint discrimination if it had legitimately determined that "fighting-word injuries 'based on race, colour, creed, religion or gender' are qualitatively different and more severe than fighting-word injuries based on other characteristics."[30]

Scalia himself is compelled to admit under pressure from Stevens's argument that content-based regulation of a subclass of fighting words "poses no significant danger of idea or viewpoint discrimination"—and is thus allowable—when "the basis for the content discrimination consists entirely of the very reason the entire class of speech at issue is proscribable."[31] Surely, this condition is met in regard to the suppression of hate speech as a subclass of fighting words. If so, then Scalia was wrong to accuse St. Paul of viewpoint discrimination. The ordinance was even-handed in as much as it forbade *both* sides in the debate over equality to employ provocative symbols of hate. As Stevens explains, extending Scalia's pugilistic metaphor, the ordinance simply banned "punches 'below the belt'—by either party."[32]

An analysis rooted in Montesquieu's theory of comparative law resists attributing the divergent trajectories of the Canadian and American Courts to rival political philosophies or the weight of precedent. Rather, an explanation must be sought first and foremost in the social facts and cultural norms that distinguish Canada from the United States. Montesquieu's theory would appear to have its charms for Samuel LaSelva of the University of British Columbia, who argues that the Canadian and American Courts perceived the problem posed by hate speech differently because the self-understandings and lived political experiences of the two nations are fundamentally unalike. LaSelva insists that while Canada and the United States are pluralistic societies, "Canada is a different kind of society, and its pluralism is unlike the American variety."[33] To use now familiar tropes, America is a melting pot, and Canada, a mosaic.[34] As Seymour Martin Lipset argues in his comparative sociological study of the two nations, the United States is disinclined to perpetuate parochial group identities, and Canada refuses to assimilate groups into a monolithic national identity.[35] For LaSelva, and those Canadian scholars who think as he does, the distinctiveness of Canadian pluralism dictates an equally distinctive approach to regulating the freedom of expression.[36]

This explanation would perhaps be more persuasive if the *Keegstra* Court had been unanimous in its decision. In fact, the Court split four to three with the dissenters voting to disallow the impugned statute. Moreover, Justice Beverley McLaughlin, speaking for the minority, drew on the logic of First Amendment jurisprudence, and in particular the clear and present danger test, to argue that the criminal suppression of hate speech "may well have a chilling effect on defensible expression by law-abiding citizens."[37] Her analysis found the provisions of the *Criminal Code* penalizing hate speech void for vagueness and overbreadth, concluding that this attempt to stifle the wilful promotion of hatred resulted in an assault on all the basic values underlying free speech.[38] McLaughlin's dissent, and especially its reliance on the example set by First Amendment law, points to the contestable and inherently political nature of the Supreme Court's decision in *Keegstra*.

As Montesquieu knew full well, laws do not merely reflect a society's character; they also help to shape its character by virtue of the fact that the laws educate. While Montesquieu's remarks on this subject were intended for legislators, they would seem to apply equally well to judges who "make" constitutional law by interpreting the constitutional text. Because the act of judicial interpretation almost invariably relies on a political philosophy that both grounds and illuminates the text, we need to look yet again at Dickson's majority opinion for some sign of its (implicit) theoretical leanings. Here I take my bearings from the normative weight Dickson assigns to the group rights that he reads into the *Charter*'s equality and multiculturalism clauses and the priority he gives to protecting the civic capacities of Canada's cultural minorities. As against the liberal understanding of rights associated with First Amendment law, it seems to me that the *Keegstra* decision takes a republican approach to rights.[39] The republican and liberal traditions share many of the same features, including a historical commitment to constitutionally entrenched rights and liberties. In republican thought, however, liberty is believed to be realized through citizens' participation in the public life of the nation and not through the individual's unfettered pursuit of his or her private interests, as in the liberal conception of freedom. In republicanism, rights serve to empower a politically active citizenry; in liberalism, rights operate as a check on political power, limiting the reach of the state and protecting the individual from a tyranny of the majority.[40] Viewed through the lens of republicanism, Dickson's concern with the effects of hate speech on the self-perceptions of minority groups makes perfect sense. To the extent hate propaganda lowers the self-esteem of members of minority groups and thereby deters them from participating in public life, it does them (and the state) a grievous civic injury; should the contagion of hate infect the majority, it would weaken the bonds of civic friendship and expose the republic to the danger of factional conflict.

In contrast, McLaughlin's dissent adopts a decidedly liberal outlook. Her dissent is largely dismissive of Dickson's concerns. If groups targeted by hate mongers were to find their credibility undermined with the majority, as the chief justice feared would be the case, that would be unfortunate but hardly a reason to engage in censorship, she argues, for no individual, whatever his or her status, has a right "to be listened to or to be believed." If there are persons "gullible enough" to believe hate propaganda, censorship will be of little use as a prophylactic, for these same persons "might be just as likely to believe that there must be some truth in the racist expression because government is trying to suppress it."[41] Unlike Dickson, McLaughlin sees no conflict between the free speech and equality clauses of the *Charter*. The latter, she insists, guarantees the right to be free from state-sponsored discrimination; it does not, as the majority opinion suggests, offer a basis for denying protection to the expression of disfavored ideas. On the contrary, as she reads the Court's previous free speech decisions, the Canadian state, like its American counterpart, is required to observe strict content and viewpoint neutrality in regulating expression. Reflecting on the implications for the right to free expression of the *Charter*'s multicultural clause, McLaughlin offers a decidedly different take on the social and political ramifications of Canadian pluralism. In her view, diversity implies disagreement and an unavoidable degree of hostility among groups. The "expression of derogatory opinion about other groups," she writes, is "a necessary correlative of a multicultural society" and tolerance of these mutual antagonisms, far from indulging a threat to the survival of Canada's multicultural heritage, constitutes the very "essence of multiculturalism."[42]

Apparently, the differing "constitutional visions" Dickson invoked to distinguish the Canadian and American approaches to free speech vie for supremacy on the Canadian Court itself! Indeed, it bears remarking that the distinctive "Canadian" vision articulated by Dickson owes a rather large intellectual debt to American critical race theorists, whose defence of campus speech codes and municipal ordinances such as the one that figures in *R.A.V.* inform Dickson's rationale for suppressing racist hate speech.[43] The choice between the rival constitutional visions at stake in these cases is real and important, for it has the power to shape the political environment in which future choices will be made. Partisans of the approach favored by the Canadian Court believe it will empower socially disadvantaged groups at the expense of their oppressors;[44] critics of this approach believe it will only encourage the intergroup hostility it is intended to prevent by fanning the flames of a combative "identity politics."[45]

As boundary-setting exercises, neither the Canadian nor the American hate speech cases yields an entirely satisfactory result. The majority in *R.A.V.* refused even to consider that the historical oppression of racial minorities in the United States and their continuing experience of discrimination might justify affording them special protection from the harms of hate speech, at least in the narrow sense provided for by the Court's traditional fighting words doctrine, much as Justices White and Stevens argued in their concurring opinions.[46] Meanwhile, the *Keegstra* majority can be faulted for accepting a purely conjectural harm in place of a proven or even probable injury.[47] Is it any less reasonable to suppose that the solidarity of the targeted group will insulate its members from the sting of hurtful words or that the nation's democratic traditions will inoculate the majority against the contagion of hate? To paraphrase Brandeis, surely it requires something more substantial than a speculative threat for the courts to recommend an enforced silence as the appropriate reply to noxious doctrine.[48]

If I have understood Montesquieu's theory of comparative law correctly, it remains useful insofar as it directs our attention to politically relevant facts and norms that powerfully influence (even if they do not determine) constitutional lawmaking. The sociocultural differences between the Canadian mosaic and the American melting pot at least partially explain why hate speech is more readily tolerated in the United States than in Canada. The disparate outcomes in *R. v. Keegstra* and *R.A.V. v. St. Paul* have far-reaching implications for the nature and limits of freedom of expression as it is practiced in Canada and the United States, and this, in turn, will contribute over time to each nation's political self-understanding, perhaps further distancing the two societies. There is, then, a genuine clash of constitutional visions at the heart of the cases discussed in this chapter. I have argued, however, that these competing visions are rooted in rival philosophic traditions that have deep roots in *both* countries. Moreover, the impetus to penalize hate speech is the same in both as politically mobilized minority groups and the political Left put pressure on government to rein in offensive speech.[49] Montesquieu's theory, for all of its impressive sociological insight, tends to obscure the pure politics of law. Cultural norms and social characteristics may indeed influence the spirit of the laws, but it is politics that sets limits to the judicial imagination and constrains constitutional choice.

## Notes

This chapter draws on my "American and Canadian Perspectives on Hate Speech and the Limits of Free Expression," in *Constitutional Politics in Canada and the United States*, ed. Stephen L. Newman (Albany: State University of New York Press, 2004), 153–74.

1. The First Amendment to the *United States Constitution* states that "Congress shall make no law . . . abridging the freedom of expression." Section 2(b) of the *Canadian Charter of Rights and Freedoms* guarantees "freedom of thought, belief, opinion and expression."

2. It is only since the patriation of the *Canadian Constitution* in 1992 that the Canadian Supreme Court gained the power of judicial review. On the changed role of the Canadian Court and its larger political significance, see Peter McCormick, *Supreme at Last: The Evolution of the Supreme Court of Canada* (Toronto: James Lorimer, 2000).

3. 3 S.R.C. 697. Cf. *R. v. Zundel*, [1992] 2 S.C.R. 731, in the Court struck down a related provision of the *Criminal Code* barring the spread of false news.

4. The test for whether a limit on a right or freedom guaranteed by the *Charter* can be "demonstrably justified" derives from *R. v. Oakes*, 1 S.C.R. 103 (1986). Under the *Oakes* test government must show (1) that it has undertaken to limit the right or freedom in question in order to achieve "an objective of pressing and substantial concern"; (2) that there is "proportionality" between this legitimate objective and the impugned measure. The balancing of individual and group interests that is the hallmark of sec. 1 analysis occurs in assessing proportionality, which proceeds in three stages. First, it must be demonstrated that the means chosen is rationally related to the end. Second, the impairment of the right or freedom must be shown to be the least

possible consistent with the objective. Third, there must be a proportionality between the effects of the impugned measure and the compelling objective that justifies infringing the right or freedom in question. See Ian Greene, *The Charter of Rights* (Toronto: Lorimer, 1989), 55.

5. 505 U.S. 377 (1992).

6. All references are to the Cambridge edition of *The Spirit of the Laws*, ed. A. Cohler, B. Miller, and H. Stone (Cambridge: Cambridge University Press, 1989). The environmental factors Montesquieu considered were both physical (e.g., climate and terrain, which are addressed in Books XIV and XVIII respectively) and moral (e.g., the effects of popular mores and manners, which are addressed in Book XIX, and the influence of religion, which is addressed in Books XXIV and XXV). Melvin Richter suggests that of the two, Montesquieu placed the greater emphasis on moral factors. See his "An Introduction to Montesquieu's 'An Essay on the Causes That May Affect Men's Minds and Characters,'" *Political Theory* 4.2 (1976): 132–33. Following Richter, I have chosen to emphasize their influence here.

7. On Montesquieu's view of the influence of mores and manners, see especially Book XIX. There Montesquieu explains, "Many things govern men: climate, religion, laws, the maxims of government, examples of past things, mores, and manners; a general spirit is formed as a result," adding a bit later on that the legislator (and dare I say, the judge) "is to follow the spirit of the nation when doing so is not contrary to the principles of government, for we do nothing better than what we do freely and by following our natural genius" (310).

8. Section 15 of the Charter, which is similar to the Equal Protection Clause of the U.S. Fourteenth Amendment, guarantees equality "before and under the law." Section 27 states that the Charter is to be interpreted "in a manner consistent with the preservation and enhancement of the multicultural heritage of Canadians." Unlike the provisions of the Fourteenth Amendment, section 15 expressly permits affirmative action; however, neither section 15 nor section 27 mandates differential treatment of minority groups. Cf. Justice McLaughlin's dissenting opinion in *Keegstra* at sections II B(1) and (2).

9. "There is this difference between the nature of the government and its principle: its nature is that which makes it what it is, and its principle, that which makes it act. The one is its particular structure, and the other is the human passions that set it in motion" (*The Spirit of the Laws*, III, 1, 21).

10. In chapter 3 of Book V Montesquieu writes, "Love of the republic in a democracy is love of democracy; love of democracy is love of equality" (*The Spirit of the Laws*, 43).

11. *R. v. Keegstra*, 748.

12. Terry Heinrichs discusses the paucity of the empirical evidence adduced by the commission in support of its position in "*Gitlow* Redux: 'Bad Tendencies' in the Great White North," *The Wayne Law Review* 48.3 (2002): 1146–53.

13. *R. v. Keegstra*, 747.

14. Edmund Burke, *Reflections on the Revolution in France*, ed. John G. A. Pocock (Indianapolis and Cambridge: Hackett Publishing, 1987), 67.

15. See Peter H. Russell, "Can the Canadians Be a Sovereign People? The Question Revisited," in Stephen L. Newman, *Constitutional Politics in Canada and the United States*, 9–34.

16. Isaiah Berlin, "Two Concepts of Liberty," in *Four Essays on Liberty* (Oxford: Oxford University Press, 1969): 118–72.

17. *R. v. Keegstra*, 763.

18. Ibid., 763. In essence, Dickson argues that hateful utterances silence the targeted individuals and groups. The silencing argument has been most powerfully developed by a group of legal scholars in the United States known as critical race theorists, several of whom are cited favorably in Dickson's footnotes. For a statement of their position, see Mari J. Matsuda, Charles R. Lawrence III, Richard Delgado, and Kimberle Williams Crenshaw, *Words That Wound: Critical Race Theory, Assaultive Speech, and the First Amendment* (Boulder: Westview Press, 1993). But see also the critical reply to their position by Henry Louis Gates Jr., "War of Words: Critical Race Theory and the First Amendment," in H. L. Gates Jr., A. Griffin, D. E. Lively, R. C. Post, W. B. Rubenstein, and N. Strossen, *Speaking of Race, Speaking of Sex: Hate Speech, Civil Rights, and Civil Liberties* (New York: New York University Press, 1994), 17–58. For a critique of Dickson's appropriation of critical race theory, see Terry Heinrichs, "Censorship as Free Speech! Free Expression Values and the Logic of Silencing in *R. v. Keegstra*," *Albany Law Review* 36.4 (1988): 337–70.

19. 249 U.S. 47, 52 (1919).

20. The relaxed standard was articulated in *Gitlow v. New York*, 268 U.S. 652 (1925). On the decisive shift away from the "grave and probable" danger test, see Terry Heinrichs, "*Gitlow* Redux: 'Bad Tendencies' in the Great White North."

21. 274 U.S. 357 (1927).

22. *Whitney*, 274 U.S., 375.

23. Ibid., 377.

24. The importance of public debate and the capacity of ordinary citizens to sort through even highly emotional claims and counterclaims was affirmed in the infamous Skokie case from the late 1970s, which dealt with the controverted right of a group of neo-Nazis to hold a public demonstration in a heavily Jewish Chicago suburb. Federal District Court Judge Bernard Decker, in ruling against the municipality's attempt to bar the demonstration, acknowledged that "the incitement of hatred is often a byproduct of vigorous debate on highly emotional subjects"; nonetheless, he insisted that in keeping with First Amendment jurisprudence "a great deal of useless, offensive *and even potentially harmful* language must be tolerated as part of the 'verbal cacophony' that accompanies uninhibited debate, not for its own sake, but because any attempt to excise it from public discourse with the blunt instrument of criminal sanctions must inevitably have a dampening effect on the vigor of that discourse" (Quoted in Philippa Strum, *When the Nazis Came to Skokie: Freedom for the Speech We Hate* [Lawrence: University Press of Kansas, 1999], 104 [emphasis added]).

25. The Court's fighting words doctrine was articulated in *Chaplinsky v. New Hampshire*, 315 U.S. 568, 572 (1942). In *Gooding v. Wilson* 405 U.S. 518, 524 (1972), the Court further narrowed the doctrine's application to utterances that "have a direct tendency to cause acts of violence by the person to whom, individually, the remark is addressed."

26. Separate concurrences were filed by Justices White, Blackmun, and Stevens. White stayed closest to the traditional fighting words doctrine with an emphasis on a narrow, categorical exception to the First Amendment guarantee; however, all three

justices, together with Justice O'Connor, agreed that the St. Paul ordinance was overbroad and thus facially invalid. See *R.A.V. v. St. Paul*, 411–14.

27. Ibid., 383, 385, 393.

28. Ibid., 393.

29. The breathtaking scope of the ban on fighting words necessary to reach the injuries inflicted by racist speech under Scalia's revised doctrine was pointed out by Justice White in his concurring opinion (ibid., 404–05).

30. Ibid., 425.

31. Ibid., 388.

32. Ibid., 435.

33. Samuel V. LaSelva, "Pluralism and Hate: Freedom, Censorship, and the Canadian Identity," in *Interpreting Censorship in Canada*, ed. K. Peterson and A. Hutchinson (Toronto: University of Toronto Press, 1999), 48.

34. On the melting pot versus the mosaic, see Seymour Martin Lipset, *Continental Divide: The Values and Institutions of the United States and Canada* (New York: Routledge, 1991), 172–92. Intriguingly, Lipset argues that in the past few decades insurgent minority groups have challenged the melting pot ideal in the United States, while at the same time Canada has experienced a political backlash against the mosaic concept under the pressure of recent immigration.

35. See Lipset, *Continental Divide*, 173, on the Canadian preference for a group-centered approach to rights in contrast with the American emphasis on individual liberties.

36. Cf. Alan C. Cairns, *Disruptions: Constitutional Struggles from the Charter to Meech Lake*, ed. Douglas E. Williams (Toronto: McClelland & Stewart, 1991); Irwin Cotler, "Hate Speech, Equality, and Harm under the Charter: Towards a Jurisprudence of Human Dignity for a 'Free and Democratic Society,' " in *The Canadian Charter of Rights and Freedoms*, Student Edition, ed. G. A. Beaudoin and E. Mendes (Toronto: Carswell, 1996), ch. 20; Peter H. Russell, "Can the Canadians Be a Sovereign People? The Question Revisited"; and Lorraine Eisenstat Weinreb, "Hate Promotion in a Free Society: *R. v. Keegstra*," *McGill Law Journal* 36 (1991): 1416–49.

37. *R. v. Keegstra*, 852.

38. Ibid., 862. Dickson attempts to minimize the implications of the majority's decision by reading the statute as placing a ban on only the most extreme forms of hate speech, noxious utterances "clearly associated with vilification and detestation" that tend toward the "destruction of both the target group and the values of [Canadian] society" (ibid., 777). McLaughlin appears troubled by the inherent difficulty of distinguishing permissible expressions of dislike and disapproval from impermissible "vilification and detestation."

39. Consider Dickson's assessment of the stakes in *Keegstra* in light of what Maurizio Viroli has to say about republicanism: "Those who hark back to the republican tradition must choose policies that attenuate domination rather than those that try to attenuate civic obligation in the guise of being free from impediments... if liberty as the absence of domination for some conflicts with liberty as the absence of restraint or interference for others, then we must place the former above the latter, since that is more in keeping with the ideal of the *res publica*, a community of individuals in which no one is forced to serve and no one is allowed to dominate, an ideal that has been

and remains the core of the republican utopia" (Maurizio Viroli, *Republicanism* [New York: Hill & Wang, 1999], 53–54).

40. On the opposition between liberal rights and the republican tradition in the Canadian context, see Charles Taylor, "Alternative Futures: Legitimacy, Identity, and Alienation in Late Twentieth-Century Canada," in *Constitutionalism, Citizenship, and Society in Canada*, ed. A. Cairns and C. Williams (Toronto: University of Toronto Press, 1985), 183–229.

41. *R. v. Keegstra*, 853.

42. Ibid., 110, 111.

43. See note 19.

44. In addition to the critical race theorists cited previously, see American legal theorist Catharine MacKinnon, *Only Words* (Cambridge, MA: Harvard University Press, 1993), which contains praise for the Canadian Court's decision in *Keegstra*.

45. See Stefan Braun, "Freedom of Expression and Hate Propaganda Laws: Striking a Balance in Canadian Democracy" (PhD diss., York University, 2000), chs. 4 and 5; also Reg Whitaker, "Chameleon on a Changing Background: The Politics of Censorship in Canada," in *Interpreting Censorship in Canada*, 19.

46. Justice Stevens cast this argument somewhat more broadly in his Ralph Elliot First Amendment Lecture at Yale Law School: "We should at least consider the possibility that racial, religious, and gender-based invectives can cause distinct and especially grievous injury, particularly when used by members of a powerful group against an individual already disadvantaged by a hostile environment. Most obviously, it is in that posture that an epithet comes closest to a threat, by evoking the ever-present spectre of bias-motivated violence, and, with it, real fear in the recipient" ("*The* Freedom of Speech," *Yale Law Journal* 102 [1993]: 1311).

47. Cf. *Landmark Communications Inc. v. Virginia*, 435 U.S. 829 (1978). Clarifying what it called the "proper" application of the clear and present danger test the Supreme Court said that "the test requires a court to make its own inquiry into the imminence and magnitude of the danger said to flow from the particular utterance and then to balance the character of the evil as well as its likelihood against the need for free and unfettered expression" (Quoted by Floyd Abrams in *Speaking Freely, Trials of the First Amendment* [New York: Viking Penguin, 2005], 79).

48. Montesquieu did not have much to say about freedom of expression in *The Spirit of Laws*; however, in chapter 12 of Book XII he addresses the just treatment of "indiscreet speech." In context, it is apparent that he has in mind a distinction between speech critical of the ruler and insurrectionary speech, or incitement to high treason. He is at pains to insist that mere speech by itself can be no crime, for words carry multiple meanings, and what may give offense to the ruler might in fact carry no intent to disturb the government. However, "a man who goes into the public square to exhort the subjects to revolt becomes guilty of high treason, because the speech is joined to the act and participates in it. It is not speech that is punished but an act committed in which speech is used. Speech becomes criminal only when it prepares, when it accompanies, or when it follows a criminal act" (198–99). If words directed by citizens toward one another are treated in the same manner, then hate speech intended to incite violence against members of the targeted group may legitimately be proscribed. Nonetheless, it is far from clear that speech expressing and promoting hatred would by

itself constitute a crime in Montesquieu's terms. The key question would seem to be an empirical one: under the circumstances, do the speaker's utterances tend to incite to violence, or do they (merely) express a disfavored opinion?

49. On the politics of hate speech in the United States, see Samuel Walker, *Hate Speech: The History of an American Controversy* (Lincoln: University of Nebraska Press, 1994). On the politics of hate speech in Canada, see Stefan Braun, "Freedom of Expression and Hate Propaganda Law."

Part IV

# Montesquieu and Modern Liberalisms

# 12

# Montesquieu's *Persian Letters*
## A Timely Classic

### Fred Dallmayr

> If I knew something useful to my nation but ruinous to another nation, I would not propose it to my ruler because I am a human being before I am a Frenchman.
>
> —Montesquieu, *Mes Pensées*, ed. Roger Caillois
> (Paris: Gallimard 1949), n.10, 980

The age of Enlightenment is often portrayed as the upsurge of an abstractly rational universalism completely oblivious of, and even hostile to, historical tradition and especially to the rich welter of regional and local ways of life. In its home country, the age of *lumières* led eventually to a complete break with, and attempted eradication of, the past—a rupture that stood in sharp contrast to developments in the English-speaking world. Latter-day devotees of Enlightenment often propagate a bland universalism on the Jacobin model—an outlook that ignores the circumstance that the rays of *lumières* are always necessarily refracted in the diversity of concrete practices and experiences on the ground. Quite apart from its general disdain for history, the Jacobin model also shortchanges the refracted character of enlightened thought in eighteenth-century France, the fact that French intellectual life during the period was by no means monopolized by a handful of *philosophes* in Paris. A prominent exemplar of nonconformist thought was the Baron de Montesquieu who, throughout his life, maintained somewhat strained relations both with ruling orthodoxies and with the Parisian salons. Precisely by virtue of his nonconformism, his work reemerges today—in our "postmodern" times—as an important guidepost pointing (however vaguely) in the direction of an "alternative modernity" or "alternative modernities."[1]

Montesquieu's concern with cultural alternatives was particularly demonstrated in his attention to non-Western societies and cultures, especially in his reflections on Persia, assembled in his famous *Persian Letters* (*Lettres Persanes*) first published in 1721. In the following I hope to do three things. First, I want to discuss some of the distinctive features of Montesquieu's general *oeuvre*, limiting myself to a few salient points. Next, I want to pinpoint or lift up some particularly instructive passages of his *Persian Letters* illustrating his talent as a thoughtful and critical comparativist. Finally, I want to highlight aspects that, in my view, demonstrate Montesquieu's continuing *relevance* and especially the importance of his *Letters* as a "timely classic" in the contemporary context.

## Montesquieu as a Practical Philosopher

Montesquieu's work is complex and multifaceted, but it is by no means devoid of an overall philosophical coherence. Although a relatively youthful and experimental text, the *Persian Letters* illustrate and fit into this overall coherence—whose design has been too often either dismissed or badly misconstrued. Born and raised in a country deeply imbued with Cartesian teachings, Montesquieu was sufficiently a Frenchman and a modernist to stand opposed to oppressive prejudices of the past and to political despotism (especially the despotism of Louis XIV's later reign); at the same time, however—partly under the influence of British empiricism—he was sufficiently endowed with common sense to appreciate the role of history and culture, and hence to resist an abstract rationalism operating deductively from first principles. This middle position made Montesquieu an odd figure located outside the usual battle lines of his period and certainly outside the Cartesian bifurcations of mind and matter, reason and sense experience. Several modern philosophers—including Hobbes and Spinoza—had placed history outside the pale of philosophy properly speaking, the latter seen as deductive argumentation; in response or in retaliation, empirical historians sometimes expelled philosophy from real-life history, the latter seen as a jumble of contingent data. Neither the *Persian Letters* nor *The Spirit of Laws* fits into these schemes. If Hannah Arendt was correct in saying that genuine thinking means reflecting on "what we are doing" or what is going on in concrete praxis, then Montesquieu was in Arendt's sense an eminently practical thinker or philosopher.[2]

Montesquieu's unconventional position—unconventional in terms of the paradigm of Western modernity—has given his interpreters endless headaches, leading them to strange conclusions.³ While some of the *philosophes*, such as d'Alembert, attempted to read him in their own light, many nineteenth-century interpreters such as Auguste Comte, construed him as an empirical sociologist and positivist—which was only a short step to his reputation as a radical historicist and perhaps even a relativist and materialist. During the twentieth century, Montesquieu came into a juggernaut of neo-Kantian antinomies, especially the antinomies of universalism and particularism, of moral absolutism and relativism—with the relativist verdict usually prevailing. A case in point is George Healy, the able translator of the *Persian Letters*, whose introduction begins by stressing a judicious balance or tension but ends with a dismissive verdict. Although, like most *philosophes*, Montesquieu was weary of "traditional 'absolutes' "—Healy notes—he could not accept the contrary position "that there are no values in human relationships except those imposed by force or agreed upon in selfish and expedient conventions." Hence, like many of his contemporaries, he upheld the notion of "natural law" or of laws of nature—although he quickly insisted that in human society "natural laws will vary in their explicit content as the material and historical conditions of societies vary." In this manner, his work sought to "unify radically opposed directions" and to balance the notion of natural law with its concrete application. Despite this noted effort, however, Healy in the end allows relativism to triumph. "On careful reading," he observes, many of Montesquieu's arguments "turn out to be full of unresolved problems" and he was often led "toward a position of complete moral relativism." His mature thought, above all, "increasingly turned from 'nature' to 'utility' as the basic test of the worth of an idea or institution."⁴

My point here is not to deny certain "unresolved problems" in Montesquieu's work but to remonstrate against the lop-sided final verdict. What the verdict tacitly assumes is the binding character of the neo-Kantian bifurcation of norms and facts, of universal rules and contingent data—an assumption that is by no means warranted. Clearly, norms, to be binding or even relevant, must relate to the human condition in the world, which is inevitably concrete and varied from time to time and place to place. Even the most lofty maxims lose their traction unless they are practiced by people in their ordinary lives; moreover, unless linked with ordinary lives, maxims easily become punitive or despotic. Recognition of this connection had been the hallmark of the Aristotelian legacy, which had been completely shunted aside at the dawn of Western modernity. As Hans-Georg Gadamer notes, the concept of 'ethos' central to Aristotelian ethics made precisely the following explicit: that " 'virtue' does not consist merely in knowledge [of norms], for the possibility of knowing depends, to the contrary, on what a person is like, and the being of each person is formed beforehand through his or her education and way of life." Hence, the crux of Aristotelian ethics resided in the "mediation between *logos* and *ethos*," between knowing and being.⁵ Seen in this light, Montesquieu may be viewed as a budding Aristotelian "out of season," a fact that is recognized by Kingsley Martin when he presents him as a philosophical Montaigne. Montesquieu, Martin writes, "did indeed share Montaigne's eager interest in the diversity of things; he enjoyed collecting and relating the various customs of people." However, bitten by the rational "virus" of his generation, he could not remain "an essayist or a skeptic: he was forced to attempt for the modern world the task which Aristotle had performed for the ancients."[6]

The Aristotelian legacy is evident in the opening books of *The Spirit of Laws* where Montesquieu discusses the nature of law, the different types of political regimes, and their animating "spirit." The very first sentence of the text establishes the tonality pervading the rest of the work: "Laws in their most general signification are the necessary relations derived from the nature of things." With this sentence a basic insight is affirmed: that laws or norms are not simply commands or arbitrary conventions but rather "relations" or the outgrowth of complex relationships. For Montesquieu, everything is relational and not atomistic or individualistic. Hence, the first sentence is immediately followed by the observation that God has his relational laws (often called "covenants"), the natural universe has its relational laws, and so does the animal kingdom and the human community—the latter aspect testifying to the "sociable" character of human beings (an insight derived from Aristotle).[7] Somewhat later in the text Montesquieu elaborates on the complex character of the relational "nature of things." Human beings, he writes, "are influenced by various causes, by the climate, religion, the laws, the maxims of government; by precedents, morals and customs, from whence is formed a general spirit that takes its rise from these." In this passage, the crucial idea of a "general spirit" underlying laws and political regimes is put forward, an idea that served as a leitmotif throughout the author's entire life. More than a decade earlier, in his essay on the "greatness and decline" of Rome, he had stated the idea in these terms: "There is in each nation a general spirit upon which power itself is founded; when this power shocks this spirit, if suffocates itself, and it necessarily comes to a halt." What is advanced in these passages is a conception which is entirely outside the pale of an arid, analytical rationalism: that, to be workable and beneficial, norms, power, and rationality itself need to be undergirded by a living spirit or *ethos* oriented toward some form of the (Aristotelian) good life.[8]

With some modifications, the Aristotelian legacy persists in the discussion of types of governmental regimes and their animating principles. The text distinguishes among only three types of government (collapsing somewhat the traditional classification of regimes): namely, monarchical, despotic, and republican or democratic governments. Each one of these types is undergirded—for good or ill—by an animating "ethos" or motivating principle. In monarchies, the principle is said to be "honor," predicated on the prevailing hierarchy of ranks and estates. In despotic regimes, people are basically motivated by "fear" (a reference to the later years of Louis XIV and probably to the theories of Thomas Hobbes). It is only in republics or democracies that Montesquieu singles out "virtue" as the well-spring of public life—where virtue means something like equal respect or mutual recognition coupled with affection. As Book V of his text makes clear, "virtue" here is not merely a theory but a practice, not merely a form of knowledge but a mode of feeling and sensation. "Virtue in a republic," he states, in a prominent anti-Cartesian passage, "is a most simple thing: it is a love for the republic; it is a sensation and not merely a consequence of acquired knowledge—a sensation that may be felt by the meanest as well as by the highest person in the state." Needless to say, love is a relational bond, and hence virtue in a republic is a deeply mutual or relational commitment: "Love of the republic in a democracy is love of the democracy, and love of the democracy is that of equality." Montesquieu does not tire to stress the affective and relational character of democratic bonding. "Love of equality in a democracy," he states in another famous passage, "limits individual ambition to the sole desire, the sole happiness of doing greater services to the country than the rest of our fellow citizens. They cannot all render her equal services, but they ought all to serve her with equal alacrity." From this affective bonding a basic pedagogical principle can be derived: "Everything depends on fostering this love in a republic, and to inspire it ought to be the principal business of education; but the surest way of instilling it into children, is for parents to set them an example."[9]

There is no need here to discuss in detail the various constitutional and institutional arrangements examined or recommended in Montesquieu's work. The need is all the less pressing as many of his recommendations have become nearly "common sense" by being adopted by many modern governments in Europe, America, and beyond. Prominent among these recommended arrangements are the separation or at least differentiation of governmental powers, the distinction between religious and political authority, and the stress on the importance of liberty (or liberties) in a well-constituted republic or democracy, with liberty meaning "the power of doing what we ought to will [in accordance with democratic virtue] and not being constrained to do what we ought not to will."[10] Montesquieu's constitutional observations found a particularly receptive audience in America, both during the colonial period and at the time of the founding of the new republic. In the words of Norman Torrey: "The founders of the American commonwealth, especially Franklin, Jefferson, and Madison, were imbued with the principles of *The Spirit of Laws*." Above all, the idea of the balance and separation of powers found "ready soil" in America and became a guiding principle of the constitution of 1789. Even before that, Torrey notes, the Frenchman's influence was felt in colonial charters and state constitutions, such as in Franklin's Pennsylvania and Jefferson's Virginia, especially in the fields of civil liberties and criminal justice—an influence culminating in the later *Bill of Rights*.[11]

Quite apart from his legal and institutional contributions, Montesquieu's work also found genuine resonance among later philosophers both at home and abroad. A prominent case in point is Hegel whose *Philosophy of Right* pays tribute to the French thinker in numerous ways, while bending the latter's views in the direction of his own absolute idealism. Already in his introduction Hegel focuses on the character of "law" and its relation to the "nature of things." "Natural law or law from the philosophical point of view," he writes (honoring but also undercutting Kantian bifurcations), "is distinct from positive law; but to pervert their difference into an opposition and contradiction would be a gross misunderstanding." Turning to the opening pages of *The Spirit of Laws*, he adds that, on this point, "Montesquieu proclaimed the true historical view and the genuinely philosophical position, namely, that legislation [or law] both in general and in its particular provisions is to be treated not as something isolated and abstract but rather as a subordinate moment in a whole, interconnected with all the other features which make up the character of a nation and an epoch." It is only when seen in this connectedness or relationship that laws acquire "their true meaning and hence their justification." At a later point, in the section on "constitutional law," Hegel repeats the tribute by stating that it was "Montesquieu above all" who kept in sight both the "connectedness of laws" and the "philosophical principle of always treating the part in its relation to the whole." With minor reservations, the praise extends also to the notion of a "general spirit" or ethical well-spring animating political regimes. "We must recognize," the section on the "constitution" (*Verfassung*) affirms, "the depth of Montesquieu's insight in his now famous treatment of the animating principles of forms of government." This insight was particularly evident in the discussion of democracy where "virtue" was extolled as the governing principle—"and rightly so because that constitution rests in point of fact on moral sentiment (*Gesinnung*) seen as the purely substantial form in which the rationality of absolute will appears in democracy."[12]

## The Persian Letters

Although presented as a series of written exchanges, the *Persian Letters* are by no means a random assortment of stray observations, but rather reflect the overall coherence of Montesquieu's general position. Perhaps more clearly than *The Spirit of Laws*, the *Letters* reveal Montesquieu's cosmopolitan (or non-Eurocentric) outlook, his taste for cross-cultural comparison, and his keen eye for societal differences and their roots. In this respect, the Baron was definitely ahead of most of his French contemporaries. As George Healy pointedly observes: "The French Enlightenment was densely populated with men who spoke of the world, yet remained, essentially, incorrigible little-Europeans." By contrast, "notwithstanding the Cartesian side of his mind," Montesquieu was "sincerely committed to the empirical and comparative method that most *philosophes* extolled but comparatively few really understood and fewer really practiced." His taste for cross-cultural comparison was nurtured by his own frequent travels abroad—to Austria, Hungary, Italy, Germany, Holland, and England. In addition, he was an avid reader of travelogues which at that time were flooding bookstores in France; with particular regard to Persia, historians of ideas have noted the influence of a number of books popular during the Baron's youth. Needless to say, Montesquieu's acquaintance with Persia was entirely secondhand, which explains many shortcomings of his text. Nevertheless, to quote Healy again, "his failure to depict an authentic Persia was due more to inadequacies in his sources than to his motives or energies."[13]

As indicated before, the *Persian Letters* are a series of exchanges whose topics are varied and do not follow a single story line. Some of the letters deal with provocative or exotic topics that probably titillated eighteenth-century readers but are no longer of great interest today. On this issue I agree with the translator's comment that the burden of the *Letters* is not to be found in "irrerevant observations on popes and kings, or in the tangled story of Usbek's frustrated wives and eunuchs." Leaving these topics aside and proceeding very selectively, I want to lift up instead passages that, in my view, illustrate the broad coherence of Montesquieu's outlook mentioned above. Regarding the relation between law and "ethos" or practical life, no story is more instructive than the story of the ancient Troglodytes, a tribe of people inhabiting the southern edge of Arabia. Usbek, the Persian traveler who tells the story, first notes that, in an early time, the tribe lived in a Hobbesian kind of condition with everybody in fear of others and trying to subdue or kill everybody else. Eventually they succeeded in nearly exterminating the tribe, leaving just two families as survivors. Having barely survived disaster, the two families embarked on a completely new path: they were "humane, just, and lovers of virtue" and "labored together for their mutual benefit." Each family was united by bonds of love, and the attention of parents was solely directed to "educating their children in ways of virtue." Children were taught "that individual interest is always bound to the common interest" and "that justice for others is a blessing for ourselves." Guided by this common ethos, the tribe lived a joyful and happy life, and in this condition, the people "could not fail to gain the gods' favor." Their relation to the gods was likewise free of selfishness, for they "knew only how to request good for their fellows." Greed and cupidity were alien to this happy land, and in giving presents to each other, "he who presented the gift always believed himself the favored one."

So far the story teaches the benefits or blessings accruing from a good ethical life in opposition to a selfish and violent one. Unfortunately, the story does not end there. As the Troglodyte nation grew larger and larger every day, the people at one point thought it appropriate that they should have a king with formal laws and structures of government. They decided to choose as king an old man respected for both his age and his virtue; but he was deeply distressed and did not wish to meet with them. When the people sent deputies to him, he addressed them saying: "You offer me a crown, and if you absolutely insist, I must of course accept it; but rest assured that I will die of grief to see the Troglodytes, free since my birth, submit now to a master." Growing still more distressed and agitated the old man exclaimed: "I see ... your virtue is beginning to burden you. For in your present leaderless state you must be virtuous on your own; for if you were not you could not survive." This condition, however—he continued—now seemed too onerous to the people: "You prefer to submit yourselves to a prince and his laws, which would be less exacting than your own morality. You know that, under such laws, you will be able to indulge your ambition, acquire riches, and languish in mean pleasures; you know that, so long as you avoid actual crime, you will no longer need virtue." At this point the deeper lesson of Usbek's story emerges into plain view: that people should not abandon the practice of ethical life in favor of formal legal structures and procedures behind whose screen they might sink into lethargy or selfish greed. To this extent, the story concurs with the opening of The Spirit of Laws: that law must be seen as embedded in concrete ways of life, a point that does not necessarily militate against laws or law-making as such but certainly against granting them priority status. Laws can be "known" without being followed, but ethics requires self-motivated practice. Usbek's story actually begins with a maxim that anticipates its ending and that ethicists might fruitfully ponder: "There are certain truths which one must not only cognitively accept but must feel; such are the truths of morality."[14]

The benefits of ethically good regimes—or regimes grounded in an ethical way of life—are extolled in several letters. Writing to his Persian friend Rhedi in Venice, Usbek praises the enlightened conditions in some European countries, especially in republican regimes. "Benign government," he observes, "contributes marvelously to the propagation of the species. All the republics are constant proof of this, and especially Switzerland and Holland, which are the two worst countries in Europe with respect to terrain and yet are the most heavily populated." The reason for the latter is the attractiveness of the two countries: their commitment to individual liberty combined with the cultivation of equality or equal respect characteristic of democracies: "The very equality of the citizens, which normally also results in an equality of wealth, brings abundance and life into all parts of the body politics and spreads them everywhere." This stands in stark contrast to countries under arbitrary or despotic rule "where the prince, the courtiers, and a few other individuals possess all the wealth, while all the rest groan under a crushing poverty." This comparison leads Usbek to venture some general reflections on the relation between nature and nurture, innate dispositions and external conditions. In opposition to a kind of "essentialism" assuming a fixed human "nature" persisting under any and all conditions, Usbek admits the role of conditioning factors either fostering or obstructing human dispositions—an admission stopping far short of an external determinism. "Men," he states, "are like plants and never flourish unless well cultivated. Among poverty-stricken people the species falters and sometimes even degenerates." This passage may be compared with a statement in *The Spirit of Laws* that treats human "nature" not as a fixed entity but more like a possibility or potentiality for good or ill—with good or bad outcomes being traceable to the manner of cultivation. "Before there were intelligent beings," we read there, "they were possible; they had therefore possible relations, and consequently possible laws. Before laws were made, there were relations of possible justice."[15]

As a central attribute of good regimes, justice is a topic frequently mentioned in the *Letters*. As Usbek remarks in another message to his friend: "If there is a God, my dear Rhedi, he must necessarily be just" because otherwise he would be "the worst and most imperfect of all beings." Quite in accord with the later *Spirit of Laws*, justice is found to reside not in the command of a superior nor in arbitrary convention but in a relationship: "Justice is the proper relationship actually existing between two things; this relationship is the same whoever contemplates it, whether God, or an angel or, finally, man." Under the impulse of self-interest, greed, or ambition, human beings can lose their way and turn away from justice, whose voice "can hardly make itself heard in the tumult of the passions." This does not mean that human beings are "naturally" wicked or evil but only that their better inclinations can be derailed by adverse influences: "No one is gratuitously wicked; there must be a determining cause, and that cause is always narrow self-interest." In a bold passage, Usbek—or Montesquieu through the mouth of Usbek—places justice on a par with religious faith or even above it. "Even if there were no God," he asserts, "we ought to love justice always—which is to say, to try to resemble that being of whom we have such a beautiful idea and who, if he existed, would necessarily be just." Thus, even though we might exit from "the yoke of religion," we would still be "bound by that of justice." Growing even bolder, Usbek/Montesquieu attacks a certain brand of extreme fideism that, in elevating God beyond all worldly relationships, transforms him into a despotic monster: "All these thoughts lead me to oppose those metaphysicians who represent God as a being who exercises his power tyrannically, who make him act in a way we would not wish to act ourselves for fear of offending him." In opposition to this distant tyrant-God, it is comforting to turn one's glance toward human beings in whom justice is present at least as a possibility: "How satisfying it is when a man examines himself and finds a just heart!"[16]

For Usbek/Montequieu, justice is a quality or virtue applicable not only to domestic society but also to the relations between societies and countries.

In this respect, the *Letters* strongly oppose the Hobbesian conception equating interstate relations with a natural state of war. "Magistrates," Usbek affirms, "ought to administer justice between citizen and citizen; and each nation ought to do the same between itself and other nations. In this second administration of justice, only maxims applicable to the first can be used." This affirmation leads Usbek into the issue of war and peace between nations. Replicating almost verbatim the teachings of Vitoria and Hugo Grotius, he draws very tight limits around the notion of "just" warfare. "There are only two kinds of just war," he states, "those undertaken in self-defense and those which aid an attacked ally." Hence, there is no justice in an offensive or aggressive war nor in making war "for the private quarrels of a prince (or ruler)" because someone has refused an honor due to the ruler or has treated his ambassadors without proper respect or any similar motive. The reason for these restrictions, Usbek adds, is that "a declaration of war ought to be a just act in which the punishment is always in proportion to the crime"; hence, a prior determination has to be made whether the infliction of death is warranted—"for to make war against someone is to will a death penalty." Given its gravity and finality, willing the death penalty must always be a last resort—because both virtue and religion impel us to seek life and its preservation in peace. Seen from this angle, conquest by itself "does not establish any right." As long as the subdued people persist, conquest contains "a pledge of peace and reparation for wrongs committed"; but if the people are destroyed, it is simply "a monument of tyranny." "This, my dear Rhedi"—Usbek concludes—"is what I call international law, the law of nations, or rather, the law of reason."[17]

At the time of the composition of the *Letters*, European nations were involved in frantic efforts to expand colonial or imperial domination in the non-Western world. Usbek/Montesquieu shows as little sympathy for these colonizing ventures as for unjust warfare. The reason for the distaste is both ethical and practical or utilitarian: ethically, the imposition of dominion on foreign populations shows a lack of that equality or equal respect demanded in republics; practically, colonialism usually backfires. In Usbek's words: "The usual effect of colonization is to weaken the home country without populating [or advancing] the colony." His letter on the topic to his friend draws attention particularly to the conquest of the Americas by the Spanish colonizers, an event following on the heels of the discovery of the "New World." The verdict is stern and uncompromising; in fact, it is difficult to find in the literature of the eighteenth century a condemnation of the conquest as forceful as this passage penned by Usbek/Montesquieu:

> The Spanish, despairing of keeping these vanquished nations subservient to themselves, decided to exterminate them and to send out loyal people from Spain to take their place. Never was

a horrible plan more punctually executed. A people, as numerous as the entire population of Europe, was seen to disappear from the earth at the approach of these barbarians who, in discovering the Indies, seemed only to have thought of disclosing to mankind the final degree of cruelty. By such barbarism they retained the land under their dominion.

In the long run, however, the Spanish venture in the Americas was bound to fail, because the homeland was incapable of replenishing the huge gap left by the destruction of indigenous peoples. Even when pursued with less cruelty, as in the case of the Portuguese, far-flung colonizing efforts were liable to run into similar dilemmas. Drawing the lesson from a large number of ancient and modern examples, Usbek reaches the conclusion that rulers should shy away from colonization, especially if the latter requires military subjugation: "What prince would envy the lot of these conquerors?... It is the fate of colonizing heroes to ruin themselves either by conquering lands they soon lose or by subduing nations they are then obliged to destroy."[18]

Apart from their critique of colonialism and unjust wars, the *Letters* are eloquent in their denunciation of religious fanaticism and their defense of religious toleration. Repeatedly, Usbek cites historical examples demonstrating both the inequity and the social costs of religious intolerance. One example is that of Shah Suleiman, in the late seventeenth century, who had contemplated either expelling all Armenians from Persia or else forcing them to become Muslims—in the belief that the country "would remain polluted so long as it kept these infidels in its bosom." If this policy had been carried out (which in this case did not happen)—Usbek comments—"this would have been the end of Persian greatness"; for, by exiling the Armenians nearly "all the merchants and most of the artisans would have been eliminated in a single day." Another example—where policy was actually implemented—was the persecution of the Parsees (the followers of Zoroaster) by Muslim rulers, leading to their exodus in large numbers to India. As a result of this religious zealotry, Persia was deprived of "a hardworking people who, by their labor alone, were close to victory over the sterility of the soil." These and similar examples persuade Usbek of the moral as well as practical superiority of religious toleration and, in fact, of the desirability of having several religions in a country side by side. For, he states, "members of tolerated religions usually render more service to their country than do those of the dominant religion," because, cut off from "customary honors," they can distinguish themselves only by their hard work. Moreover, the coexistence of several religions in a country encourages a healthy competition between religious groups, with each group being eager to prove its worth and the purity of its beliefs. Thus, it has often been noted that the introduction of a new faith or sect in a country is "the surest way to correct abuses in the old." To the argument that the diversity of faiths leads inevitably to conflict and warfare, Usbek has a quick rejoinder: "It is not the multiplicity of religions which has produced wars, but the spirit of intolerance stirring those who believe themselves to be in a dominant position," a spirit that, like "a kind of madness," testifies to a "total eclipse of human reason."[19]

Preference for religious toleration does not exclude criticism of perceived blemishes or possible abuses—especially since such blemishes rarely touch the core of a religious faith. Usbek's letters frequently single out dubious or harmful practices both in the case of Christianity and in that of Islam. Thus, in the example of the Spanish conquest, Catholic faith was involved at least as a pretext for invasion and plunder, a fact that tarnished the faith because of its complicity; a similar stain marking Catholic faith was the expulsion of Muslim and Jews from Spain prior to the conquest. A somewhat less grievous stain on Catholicism is the practice of celibacy among priests and monks, whom Usbek calls Christian "eunuchs." This practice is hard to understand, he writes, "since I do not see how something which produces nothing can be a virtue." Obviously, Catholic theologians are involved in a contradiction when they say "that marriage is sacred and that its opposite, celibacy, is even more so." In the case of Islam, objections to certain policies of Persian rulers have been mentioned above. Some other objections are more light-hearted and perhaps even playful. On a par with the issue of Catholic celibacy is the Muslim practice of polygamy. "I find nothing more contradictory," Usbek confides to his friend, "than the plurality of wives permitted by the holy Koran and the order, given in that book, to satisfy them all." This order, he continues, makes a good Muslim look like "an athlete, destined to compete without letup" but who, overburdened and weakened by his efforts, "languishes even on the field of victory." More seriously damaging is a pervasive religious arrogance that treats Muslims as invariably destined for paradise while consigning Christians to eternal hell fire. "Do you really think," Usbek asks a Muslim dervish in Tauris, "that they will be condemned to eternal punishment because they have been so unfortunate as not to have mosques in their country? Will God punish them for not practicing a religion which he has not made known to them?"[20]

Critique of blemishes and abuses does not interfere with respect for religions in their diversity—especially when a distinction is made between core and periphery, between the basic meaning of faith and its accidental or ephemeral dross. In one of his letters to Rhedi, Usbek seeks precisely to disentangle the basic core of faith as a lived practice from marginal accretions. Commenting on Christian people in Europe, he detects an overabundance of rhetoric and a dearth of practice: "I see here people who dispute endlessly about religion, but at the same time apparently compete to see who can least observe [or practice] it." In all religions, however, irrespective of doctrinal differences, it is practice that ultimately counts: "Whatever religion one professes, its principal parts consist always in obedience to divine ordinance [that is, law as relationship], love of fellow men, and reverence for one's parents." With growing maturity, this insight is slowly spreading among people in Europe and hopefully elsewhere. There is a growing awareness, Usbek states, that it was "a mistake to chase the Jews from Spain" and to persecute the Huguenots in France. More and more people come to realize that "zeal for the expansion of one's religion is different from dutiful devotion to it" and that "love and observance of a religion need not involve hatred and persecution of people who do not so believe." If such awareness were to take hold everywhere, then the day would dawn when the inner bond among religions would become manifest, and people everywhere would worship the divine in truth and spirit. This day was already at hand between Christians and Muslims. For, as Usbek writes to the dervish: "Everywhere [in all religions] I find Islam, although I cannot find Muhammad everywhere." The reason, he adds, is that "truth cannot be contained, and always breaks through the clouds surroundings it. Hence, a day will come when the divine will behold only true believers on earth—for time, which consumes everything, eventually also destroys error."[21]

## A Timely Classic

Read in conjunction with portions of *The Spirit of Laws*, Montesquieu's *Persian Letters* are not merely an entertaining period piece but a storehouse of insights containing important lessons not only for his period but for our time as well. For this reason, the *Letters* can be considered a timely classic today. Foremost among Montesquieu's lessons is the primacy assigned to ethics or ethical conduct over formal laws and procedures, that is, to lived practice over abstract knowledge. In both texts, "law" is treated as a relationship, as an ingredient embedded in a web of related factors that ultimately constitute a way of life. With this accent on practical conduct, Montesquieu's work stands in sharp contrast to recent and contemporary moral theory, which, almost uniformly, tends to privilege formal procedures and maxims over practice. The outcome of this privilege is a hypertrophy (or overabundance) of theoretical formulas coupled with the widespread, and widely noted, atrophy of ethical behavior in most Western societies. The likelihood of this decay—of the replacement of virtue by abstract rules—is bemoaned with dramatic intensity in the final episode of the story of the Troglodytes (a story philosophers would do well to remember in our time). To be sure (and to avoid misunderstanding), emphasizing lived practice does not simply make Montesquieu an anarchist or anti-institutionalist, a reading that would render unintelligible his concern with the separation of public powers and with the role of intermediary bodies on the regional and local levels.

An equally timely and crucial lesson to be derived from Montesquieu's work is the need for cross-cultural understanding and interfaith toleration. Together with Leibniz, Herder, and Goethe, the French Baron ranks (at least incipiently) among the great cosmopolitan and ecumenical thinkers of the modern age. What is particularly noteworthy here is that cosmopolitanism and interfaith tolerance in his case were linked with a deep appreciation of cultural and religious traditions and hence not predicated on an abstract rationalism or universalism aloof from the past and prone to reduce tolerance to mere neutral indifference. Just as in the case of Herder, cosmopolitan and interreligious engagement for Montesquieu was a matter of pedagogy working "from the ground up" and hence could not be imposed "top down" by abstract rules. It was only by taking one's own cultural background seriously that one could come to see why tradition matters to other people; and it was only by probing one's own faith (beyond its ephemeral dross) that one could penetrate to the inner well-spring of all faiths—which, for Usbek/Montesquieu, resides in piety and good conduct rather than theoretical knowledge. In the language of contemporary theologians, one might say that the French thinker preferred *orthopraxis* to *orthodoxy* in interfaith relations. In a similar manner, cosmopolitan or cross-cultural relations involved a balanced progression from local to regional to global attachments, that is, from family and town to country and finally to the world. In no case, however, were primary attachments allowed to veto or thwart broader humanitarian loyalties. As he wrote forcefully at one point: "If I knew something useful to my country but prejudicial to Europe, or useful to Europe but prejudicial to humankind, I would consider it a crime."[22]

Closely connected with his cosmopolitanism is Montesquieu's celebration of international law and his condemnation of unjust warfare—aspects that today have acquired again crucial significance. Following the great founders of the modern law of nations, his letter to Rhedi states unequivocally: "There are only two kinds of just wars: those undertaken in self-defense and those which aid an attacked ally"—a statement that renders unlawful and hence criminal all kinds of offensive wars (and especially preventive or "preemptive" wars). On this issue, too many contemporaries are willing to sacrifice their loyalty to humanity to an ill-conceived patriotism or rather chauvinism—as if licensing offensive warfare could not easily boomerang against one's home country. In this regard, Montesquieu's stress on the relational character of law remains compelling, which, in the case of the law of nations, means that its rules must be binding equally on strong and weaker nations, on hegemonic and nonhegemonic powers in our shared world. A corollary of his championing of international bonds is the warning against foreign adventures and conquests, and especially against policies of colonization, which, in Usbek's view, only tend to "weaken the home country" without benefiting the colony. In our time, colonialism is no longer openly propagated or defended but persists in many covert and subtle forms. A prominent contemporary variant is the quasi-missionary spreading of ideologies or worldviews around the globe, in neoimperialist fashion. In his *Persian Letters* and elsewhere, Montesquieu is no partisan of empires. As Usbek complains to Rhedi: "Empires may be compared to a tree in which the overly extended branches deprive the trunk of all its sap and are useful only to provide shade."[23]

Usbek's comments are not a marginal gloss but reflect one of Montesquieu's life-long preoccupations: his concern about the frequent sliding of democracies or republics into tyranny or despotic imperialism. The classical illustration of this decay was the transformation of the Roman republic into a far-flung empire, a topic to which he devoted one of his longer historical studies (*Considerations on the Causes of the Grandeur of the Romans and of Their Decline*, of 1734). Even prior to the completion of this study, the concern surfaced eloquently in *Persian Letters*. As we read there in one of Rhedi's letters: "The astounding expansion of the Roman republic would have been a great blessing to the world, if it had not involved the unjust distinction between Roman citizens and the conquered peoples," and if the republic thus had been able to preserve its "virtue" (of democratic equality). This preservation, however, was impossible: "Caesar crushed the Roman republic and subjected it to an absolute power. Hence, for a long time Europe groaned under a violent military government, and Roman benevolence was changed into cruel oppression." Rhedi's comments strike a theme which the French thinker subsequently reiterated in many variations. In Kingsley Martin's judicious words:

> From the history of Rome, Montesquieu developed one of his most famous generalizations. Beginning with a small territory, Rome attained strength as a republic founded upon the virtue of its citizens. When its territory had been everywhere extended, the old methods of government were no longer adequate, the spirit of the republic was corrupted, and new vices accompanied the growth of imperialism. Constitutional monarchy soon degenerated into despotism, relying no longer on virtue but on force and fear.[24]

Martin's statement, summarizing Montesquieu's deep apprehensions, should give contemporary readers pause. If it is true—as some observers claim—that the "New World" is tending to replicate the example of ancient Rome, then there is ample reason to share the French thinker's worries. Moreover, the retreat of republicanism is cause for alarm for citizens and noncitizens alike, because the rise of unchecked power threatens the liberties of both. In this respect, recent developments in Western societies are by no means reassuring, that civic equality is increasingly allowed to decay, and the "virtue" of democracy—which, as Montesquieu says, is love of equality—is shunted aside in favor of the unleashing of egotism and individual greed. When under the aegis of so-called privatization, civic republican bonds give way to the upsurge of a renewed Hobbesian state of nature where "the big fish eat the little fish," democracy or republican government is imperiled. Here is a passage from *The Spirit of Laws* that seems to be written for all times and especially for our time: "When virtue is banished, ambition invades the hearts of those who are capable of receiving it, and avarice dominates the whole community. Desires of people then change their objects: what they were fond of before, now becomes indifferent. They were free with laws, now they want to be free without them. Every citizen is like a slave who has escaped from his master's house. What was an accepted maxim now is called harsh rigor. Rules are given the name of constraints, and loyalty the name of fear."[25]

The decay of civic virtue and equality is one of the greatest calamities befalling a democracy, because there is virtually no remedy in sight. With the growing despotism of ruling elites, voices willing and able to remonstrate are increasingly silenced; hence, little or no room is left for citizens to "speak truth to power" and to urge a change of course, particularly a return to democratic virtue. Those daring to speak up increasingly face the risk of harsh persecution—a fact vividly illustrated by experiences recounted in *Persian Letters*. As Usbek confides to a friend in Isfahan: "From my earliest youth I have been a courtier—yet, I can say that I was not in the slightest corrupted by it. Indeed, I formed the great plan of daring to be virtuous even at court." In his effort to implement this plan, Usbek "carried truth even to the foot of the throne and spoke a language previously unknown there," thereby disturbing flatterers and confounding "idolaters and their idol." Eventually, however, the plan could no longer be maintained because of growing intimidation and threats of reprisals. "When I saw that my sincerity made enemies," the letter continues, "that I provoked the jealousy of the ministers but not the favor of the prince, . . . I resolved to withdraw" by going into "self-exile from my country"—an experience paralleling innumerable similar self-exiles and expatriations in our own time. Given its likely severe consequences, truth-telling in front of princes or rulers must not be done lightly or frivolously but out of moral responsibility and following the voice of conscience. "Truth is a heavy burden, my dear Usbek," fellow traveler Rica reminds him, "when it must be carried even to princes! Therefore, it ought to be remembered that those who do so are constrained to it and that they would never have decided to take a step so unfortunate for themselves in its consequences, were they not compelled by their sense of duty, their respect, and even their love."[26]

What Rica beautifully expresses in these lines is that dissidents and truth-tellers do not love their country less than others but more, because they wish their country to return to the path of civic virtue and to abandon its errancy in the wasteland of despotism and imperial power. Moral dissidents are sometimes described as people offering "prophetic witness" and rightly so because they confront rulers on the plane not of power but of justice. *Persian Letters* contains a marvelous phrase testifying to the importance of such witnessing: "I would have men speak to kings as the angels spoke to our holy Prophet." The words are put in the mouth of Rica, Usbek's Persian friend. But the words reflect not only the sentiments of one particular Muslim; they can (and should) reflect also the sentiments of believers of different faiths and of citizens in different countries around the world.

To be sure, prophetic witnessing seems to be a solitary activity, reserved for only a few individuals, but not necessarily so. Particularly among people still remembering the benefits of democracy, witnessing may take the form of a broader social engagement. Everything depends here on proper education or pedagogy, on the ability to arouse among people the recollection of, and renewed desire for, civic virtue and equality. The real difficulty lies in the task of educating rulers and privileged elites—that is, people whose ambition and greed have been magnified beyond all sensible proportions and whose democratic sensibilities have been largely or wholly extinguished. All efforts for improvement must concentrate on curbing the excesses of these powerful elites; for their bad example is prone to corrupt everything. As Usbek writes in his final letter to Rhedi: "What crime can be greater than that committed by a minister [or ruler] when he corrupts the morals of an entire nation, degrades the hearts of the most upright, ... and obliterates virtue itself? What will posterity say when it blushes over this shame of its forbears?"[27]

## Notes

This chapter was presented at a conference on Montesquieu held in Toronto in September 2005 in commemoration of the 250th anniversary of his death.

1. I follow here the writings of Charles Taylor on alternative or multiple modernities. See his *Sources of the Self: The Making of Modern Identity* (Cambridge: Harvard University Press, 1989), 509–13; *A Catholic Modernity?* ed. James L. Heff (New York: Oxford University Press, 1999), 16–19; and "Two Theories of Modernity," *Public Culture* 11 (1999): 153–73. Compare also Scott Lash, *Another Modernity, a Different Rationality* (Oxford: Blackwell, 1999), and Dilip Gaonkar, ed., *Alternative Modernities* (Durham, NC: Duke University Press, 2001). The general theme of the Toronto conference mentioned above was "Modernity in Question: Montesquieu and His Legacy."

2. See Hannah Arendt, *The Human Condition* (Chicago: University of Chicago Press, 1958), 6; also *Between Past and Future: Six Exercises in Political Thought* (Cleveland and New York: Meridian Books, 1963), 14.

3. His contemporary and kingpin *philosophe* Voltaire once remarked that Montesquieu was "Michel Montaigne turned legislator"—a comment meant as a jesting critique of the Baron's oddity (with "Montaigne" standing for skeptical empiricism and

"legislator" for the chief ambition of progressive *philosophes*). See Kingsley Martin, *The Rise of French Liberal Thought*, ed. J. Mayer (New York: New York University Press, 1954), 153. Montesquieu reciprocated by stating (p. 150, note 2): "As for Voltaire, he has too much wit to understand me. He reads no books but those he writes, and he then approves or censures his own progeny as the wind takes him."

4. See Montesquieu, *The Persian Letters*, trans. with introduction by George R. Healy (Indianapolis, IN: Hackett Publishing, 1964), xv–xviii. For a similar verdict see Werner Stark, *Montesquieu: Pioneer of the Sociology of Knowledge* (Toronto: University of Toronto Press, 1960). In his introduction to his translation of *The Spirit of Laws*, David W. Carrithers presents Montesquieu as navigating uneasily between the poles of "rationalism" and "relativism"; see Montesquieu, *The Spirit of Laws*, ed. with introduction by Carrithers (Berkeley: University of California Press, 1977), 34–44.

5. Hans-Georg Gadamer, "On the Possibility of a Philosophical Ethics," in his *Hermeneutics, Religion, and Ethics*, trans. Joel Weinsheimer (New Haven, CT: Yale University Press, 1999), 28–29.

6. Martin, *The Rise of French Liberal Thought*, 153.

7. *The Spirit of Laws*, I, 1. Although accepting the notion that humans are "naturally" sociable, Montesquieu recognizes that in this case nature has to be supplemented or perfected through culture, that is, through government and civil laws (p. 101). The conception of law as relational resonates with Confucian ethics as well as with the classical Indian notion of dharma. Compare, e.g., *The Politics of Affective Relations: East Asia and Beyond*, ed. Chaihark Hahm and Daniel A. Bell (Lanham, MD: Lexington Books, 2004).

8. In our time, this needed underpinning has been clearly recognized by Charles Taylor in his insistence that rules and principles only make sense in a broader "horizon of significance." See Taylor, *The Ethics of Authenticity* (Cambridge, MA: Harvard University Press, 1992), 35–37, 66. See also *The Spirit of Laws*, 289 (Book XIX, 4). The passage from *Considerations on the Causes of the Greatness of the Romans and Their Decline* (1734) is taken from the introduction of Carrithers, 25.

9. See *The Spirit of Laws*, 107 (II, 1), 117–24 (III, 3–9), 130, 132–33 (IV, 5, V, 2, 3).

10. *The Spirit of Laws*, 200 (XI, 3).

11. For the above points see *Les Philosophes: The Philosophers of the Enlightenment and Modern Democracy*, ed. Norman L. Torrey (New York: Capricorn Books, 1960), 90–91.

12. See *Hegel's Philosophy of Right*, trans. T. M. Knox (Oxford and New York: Oxford University Press, 1967), 16 (introduction, paragraph 3), 161 (paragraph 261), 177–78 (paragraph 273). Hegel's appreciation of Montesquieu's work was not complete, however. A main point of disagreement concerned the "separation of powers" and "checks and balances." As Hegel states sharply (p. 282, paragraph 300, addition 178): "The idea of the so-called 'independence of powers' contains a fundamental error of supposing that the powers, though independent, are to check one another. This independence, however, destroys the unity of the state." On the other hand, Hegel fully shared Montesquieu's concern about the proper functioning of "intermediary bodies," especially on the local and regional levels—a concern traceable to the Baron's early service as counselor of the Parlement of Bordeaux and later as "*président*" of the Parlement of Guyenne. On this

point see Carl J. Friedrich, *The Philosophy of Hegel* (New York: Random House/Modern Library, 1954), xxiii.

13. Montesquieu, *The Persian Letters*, xi–xii. Among books that may have influenced the Baron, Healy mentions Antoine Galland's translation of *The Thousand and One Nights* (Paris: Barbin, 1704) and Jean Chardin's *Voyages en Perse et autre lieux de l'Orient* (Rouen: Ferrand, 1723).

14. *The Persian Letters*, 22–30 (letters 11–14). In a cross-cultural perspective, Montesquieu's preference for ethical practice over formal laws resonates to some extent with Confucian teachings and definitely with the words of Lao tzu: "When people lost sight of the way to live (*tao*), came codes of love and honesty; learning came, charity came, hypocrisy took charge." See *The Way of Life according to Lao tzu*, trans. Witter Bynner (New York: Periger Books, 1972), 46.

15. See *The Spirit of Laws*, 99 (I, 1); *The Persian Letters*, 205–06 (letter 122).

16. *The Persian Letters*, 139–41 (letter 83). Although the reference is elusive, one can probably link the fideist target with certain extreme forms of Augustinianism and Jansenism prevalent during the Reformation period.

17. *The Persian Letters*, 156–58. Compare also my "Law of Peoples: Civilizing Humanity," in *Peace Talks: Who Will Listen?* (Notre Dame: University of Notre Dame Press, 2004), 42–63.

18. *The Persian Letters*, 202–05 (letter 121). For similar sentiments expressed half a century later by Johann Gottfried Herder see my "Truth and Difference: Some Lessons from Herder," in *Alternative Visions: Paths in the Global Village* (Lanham, MD: Rowman & Littlefield, 1998), 36–38. Compare also Sankar Muthu, *Enlightenment against Empire* (Princeton: Princeton University Press, 2003).

19. *The Persian Letters*, 142–44 (letter 85). Quite plausibly, Healy perceives in the example of Shah Suleiman a veiled reference to the revocation of the Edict of Nantes in 1685 by Louis XIV, a revocation that ended the toleration of Protestants in France (p. 142, note 2).

20. *The Persian Letters*, 60 (letter 35), 191 (letter 114), 196 (letter 117). Another letter to the Persian friend in Venice criticizes among Muslims a certain other-worldly orientation, an eagerness to reach paradise which shortchanges this-worldly tasks and obligations: "Hard and useful work, concern about an assured fortune for our children, all projects which carry beyond a short and fleeting life, seem somehow absurd to us. Tranquil in the present, free from worry about the future, we cannot be bothered to repair the public buildings, to reclaim wasteland, or cultivate land which is ready for our care. We live in a kind of general insensitivity, and leave everything to providence" (letter 119, 200).

21. *The Persian Letters*, 61 (letter 35), 75 (letter 46), 101–02 (letter 60). The comments on the future of faith are not wistful ruminations but backed up by scripture—especially by the words of Jesus to the woman at Jacob's well: "The hour is coming, and now is, when the true worshippers will worship [God] in spirit and truth" (John 4:23). At one point (letter 60, 102), Usbek expresses the hope that the divisions within Islam may also be healed and that "peace were established once and for all between Ali and Abu Bakr," that is, between Shiites and Sunni Muslims. I am aware that *The Spirit of Laws* often reveals a less ecumenical outlook and even an occasional prejudice against Islam; see, e.g., *The Spirit of Laws*, 122–23 (XXIV, 3).

22. See Montesquieu, *Pensées* (Paris: Belles Lettres, 1925); cited from *Les Philosophes*, 84.

23. *The Persian Letters*, 204 (letter 121). Regarding the recent reemergence of empire compare Michael Hardt and Antonio Negri, *Empire* (Cambridge: Harvard University Press, 2000); also Benjamin R. Barber, *Fear's Empire: War, Terrorism and Democracy* (New York: Norton, 2003).

24. See Martin, *The Rise of French Liberal Thought*, 156; *The Persian Letters*, 223 (letter 131).

25. *The Spirit of Laws*, 118–19 (III, 3).

26. *The Persian Letters*, 17 (letter 8), 237 (letter 140).

27. Ibid., 261 (letter 146).

# 13

# Montesquieu and Us

## Jean Ehrard

These days Montesquieu is certainly not the most ubiquitous or publicized among the great writers of the French Enlightenment, much less so than Voltaire, Rousseau, or even Diderot. Nevertheless we read and reedit his works. It seems that this author who died two hundred and fifty years ago, having lived in a social and intellectual context so different from our own, not only remains a source of literary pleasure or an object of erudite curiosity for the happy few,[1] but also has a lot to teach us. The first publication of a truly comprehensive and critical edition of his *Complete Works*, a project being carried out by the Société Montesquieu for the Voltaire Foundation,[2] is a rather sure sign that he continues to belong, or has resumed belonging, in the present. A panoramic glance at comparable initiatives taken since 1758 will reveal that they were never without a link to the present, whether there were many such initiatives, such as after Thermidor, during the Restoration, or at the end of the nineteenth century, with the renaissance of political liberalism and the Republic, or few, such as under the authoritarian regimes of the First and Second Empires or the Vichy government.[3] Consequently, it appears necessary to make as precise an inquiry as possible into, on one hand, the effective presence of Montesquieu among us, and on the other, the reasons for that presence, or the meaning of our *need for Montesquieu* that such presence reveals to us now, at the dawn of the twenty-first century.

Of course the "us" just used does not refer only to the French but to many different nationalities, including but not limited to Europeans. Montesquieu and *The Spirit of Laws* are very present in Germany, for example, at least among politicians. In 1949 Montesquieu was praised as being one of the "Founding Fathers" of the Basic Law for the Federal Republic of Germany.[4] More recently, the February 5, 2005, edition of *Der Spiegel*, quoting French president Jacques Chirac in reference to the then Minister of the Interior, Nicolas Sarkozy—"I decide, he executes"—invoked the authority of *The Spirit of Laws* against the current French constitutional practice, asking if in 2005 we are really in Paris or still at the court of Louis XIV in Versailles. Is it really up to the president of a republic to make all the decisions?[5] On another subject, President Horst Köhler made reference to the wisdom of Montesquieu, who warned against the excesses of bureaucracy; two days later, on March 17, 2005, Chancellor Gerhard Schröder echoed the same warning: "Useless laws weaken necessary laws."[6]

What is true of France's close neighbors is true also of distant countries around the world. In 2001, Uruguayan researcher Héctor Gros Espiell, studying the role of the doctrine of the separation of powers in the constitutional tradition of his country for the *Revue Montesquieu*, concluded: "Thus, for us, the republican and democratic State governed by the rule of law was, is and will remain inseparable from the thought of Montesquieu in political theory and history."[7] It is unnecessary to comment on the numerous works, some of which have become classics, that address the question of the relationship between Montesquieu and the American Federal Constitution; the presence of *The Spirit of Laws* in the Canadian history of political ideas is attested to by Thomas Pangle's book on Montesquieu and the origins of liberal democracy.[8] More unexpectedly, Montesquieu has made an appearance in what was the country of the Taliban: in 1995 an Afghan film maker, Akram Barmak, directed a nineteen-minute film entitled *Persian Letters*, which allows the spectator to witness a group of Afghan musicians, who have been invited to perform at the Théâtre de la Ville, discover Paris, its streets, its crowds, its trains—"the fastest in the world." We see them walking in Paris dressed in traditional costumes, receiving only slightly surprised glances from Parisian passers-by, in contrast to their own amazement to see their portraits on the walls and in the press; they are amused by the display windows and the advertisements and worried about the rain damaging their string and percussion instruments. A subtle sense of humor accompanies the tragic, as images of Kabul crushed by war intermingle with the Parisian scenes.[9]

In France Montesquieu remains in numerous cases a useful if not necessary reference. The Société Montesquieu, created by a member of the family and the namesake of the director of the publication of the *Complete Works*, coordinates the sale of wine. In Paris the Cercle Montesquieu organizes gatherings of corporate attorneys from major French firms. Also in the corporate domain, the 2001 law governing economic regulations (known as the NRE law for "Nouvelles Régulations Economiques") is sometimes hailed as the Montesquieu Law, insofar as it moves in the direction of the separation of economic power by dissociating the functions of chairman and chief executive officer of a corporation.[10] But, not surprisingly, it is in the political sphere that Montesquieu's presence is the most pronounced. In the fall of 2005 the brilliant *Dialogue in Hell between Machiavelli and Montesquieu*, which landed the pamphleteer Maurice Joly in prison in 1865, was played in Paris.[11] We might also note that starting in 1997, one year before the 250th anniversary of the publication of *The Sprit of Laws*, the present author employed a convenient instrument of analysis to sound Montesquieu's continuing influence: the annual number of references to Montesquieu, to his life and works, in *Le Monde*.[12] The choice of this daily is easily explained by its intellectual level and by the place it leaves, aside from current events and on-the-spot commentary, for more reflective analyses and the debate of ideas. The numbers yielded by this study are modest: from 1997 to 2003, they range from 17 to 45 references annually. Voltaire performed at least twice as well during the same time period. Nevertheless, the results for Montesquieu are not without interest. First, because they are due to two sorts of texts in *Le Monde*: the "Debates/Analysis" section and "Reader's Mail." Second, because of the nature of the questions in which his name is implicated: the political-financial "affairs" that all too often disquiet or scandalize public opinion, while reminding, *a contrario*, of the Republic's need for virtue; the tax system in relation to freedom; the construction of the European Union and federalism; globalization and the World Trade Organization (WTO); French political institutions, be it a question of the legitimacy of the Senate and bicameralism, the rejection of direct democracy by fear of populism, or the preeminence of the Constitutional Council, whose mission is to safeguard the "spirit of the law"; and especially the balance of powers—often mistakenly referred to as the "separation of powers"—including the consideration of three other powers, in addition to the three analyzed by Montesquieu, which he could not have known: the power of science, the power of technology, and the power of the media; and finally, the functioning of the judicial system and the relations between the Office of the Public Prosecutor and the Ministry of Justice. We will return to this last point below. Let us also mention two major issues that go far beyond the borders of the Hexagon: the relationship between political liberalism and economic liberalism and the place that the population of foreign origin occupies in a nation, on which subject Montesquieu's universalism is set against Le Pen.

So it seems that Montesquieu is solidly ensconced in French political culture, and it is hardly surprising that in addition to the articles mentioned, there are books that ask questions of Montesquieu regarding the present. Catherine Larrère demonstrates how he helps us think about the universal and the particular at the same time: diversity comes first and must be respected, and the universal cannot be its negation; the universal manifests itself through diversity in two ways, in the reciprocity of rights, on one hand, and in the rejection of certain practices, on the other. According to Montesquieu, there is no universalism through uniformity, but there exists a negative universal.[13]

Another book published in 1999, doubtlessly inspired by the anniversary the preceding year as well, is that of Alain Juppé.[14] One might be surprised that a former prime minister, not yet retired from public life, found the time and freedom of mind necessary for the writing of his book; one could ask mean-spiritedly if he was hoping thereby to forget the electoral disappointments of his party or his own legal troubles. But one has to acknowledge that for an *agrégé* of letters and former mayor of Bordeaux, the project was practically self-evident. Nevertheless, even if the specialists are still hungry after having read the book, in the absence of teaching us a lot about Montesquieu, it renders Juppé more familiar, more sympathetic. One will remember in particular the appendix, *Some of My Favorite Citations*, and notably the following aphorism: "When a man has nothing new to say, why doesn't he keep quiet?"

What is most interesting about Juppé's book is that it was written—that a prominent politician felt the need for this intimate confrontation, this encounter. Such an encounter with Montesquieu is possible for every citizen today who inquires into the realities and problems of his time. Montesquieu can play an active role in our civic reflection, on the condition that we make correct use of his *œuvre*. This requirement evidently means excluding all anachronisms, all temptations to expect ready-made solutions to problems that were not his. But if he cannot resolve our problems for us, two and a half centuries after his death, he can at least help us to reflect upon them, and in the first place, to formulate them correctly. I will give two examples of this, relating to two burning questions that have cropped up in France in recent years: the initiation of legal proceedings and religious symbols in public schools.

The old question of the relation between executive power and the judicial system is resolved in France, as in all states governed by the rule of law, according to the principle of the separation of powers. It imports little that the *Constitution of 1958* reserves the word *power* for the executive and the legislative, while referring to simple judicial *authority*. The *judicial system that judges* is independent of the government; the judges are irremovable; and the High Council of the Magistracy is there to safeguard that independence. Montesquieu would be satisfied by this arrangement, being someone who so rarely used the word *separated* in a positive sense but nonetheless wrote: "There is no liberty if the power of judging is not separate from legislative power and from executive power."[15] But what about the *judicial system that prosecutes*? The public prosecutor, the "standing judge," is much more dependent on the Ministry of Justice which, in the management of the judges' careers, must consult the High Council of the Magistracy but is not required to follow its recommendations. This gives rise to a recurring suspicion that the general prosecutors, and substitutes would be able to act—or not act—on ministerial instructions. This old suspicion was revived in the 1990s and early 2000s by the political-financial "affairs" of Paris and the region of Ile-de-France. In general, people agree that the Ministry of Justice has the right and the duty to give general instructions to the public prosecutors of France; these instructions define a penal code for the entire national territory without which there would no longer be, in practice, equality of citizens before the law. It is a different thing to expedite a helicopter to the Himalayas to try to bring back a prosecutor who was on vacation, presumed to be more indulgent with the powerful than his assistant and replacement! This fantastic—some would say "abracadabrantesque"[16]—incident resulted in the creation of a commission charged with reviewing the rules, presided over by a judge with a reputation for his competence and integrity, Pierre Truche.

Now this is where Montesquieu comes in. I myself was only a former local elected official, a modest university professor in the province, already retired. Great was my surprise when one day, I was approached by the general prosecutor of the Court of Appeals of Riom (my town) who essentially said to me: "I am a member of the Truche Commission. I intend to mention Montesquieu, in one sense or another. In my opinion he would not have defended the independence of the public prosecutor, since he considers "admirable" the institution of a "public avenger" who prosecutes in the name of the French monarch. But what do you think Montesquieu would say, you who are, so I am told, a Montesquieu specialist?" I requested time to reflect, and the next day (we saw each other at Clermont at the same history colloquium), I responded that in effect, *The Spirit of Laws* marked a clear preference for the public accusations of the French monarchy rather than the system of individual denunciation in practice in ancient cities (VI, 8, XII, 20). However, I objected that under a moderate government, prosecuting *in the name of the prince* is not to prosecute according to the arbitrary will of an individual but *in the name of the law*. Moreover, the "public avenger" is designated as an "officer," that is to say, as someone who is owner of his office and who, as such, is independent of the reigning power. We know how Montesquieu defends the venality of offices, a factor of social mobility (V, 19). One takes less notice of his condemnation of recourse to "commissioners" transformed into judges (XII, 22). The distinction is nevertheless enlightening: a *commissioner* is entirely dependent on the power that nominated him and can dismiss him at any moment; his only defense is an excess of zeal! An *officer* is irremovable, a characteristic that contributes to the stability of the orders of the state, a stability that distinguishes, fortunately, monarchy from despotism (II, 4). One of the laws of despotism is that "the prince must place or displace subjects in an instant" (V, 19). Thus, having assigned the initiation of legal proceedings to an officer rather than a commissioner, Montesquieu, it seemed to me, would have supported the independence of the office of the public prosecutor.

A more emotionally charged and complex question, that of the Islamic headscarf in public schools and in other public workplaces, poses the general problem of the place that it is legitimate to reserve for or refuse to community-specific practices in a modern republic. This same problem arose in the state of Florida, in relation to the identity photo of a young woman wearing a headscarf, and also in the Canadian province of Ontario, where a recently proposed law, which was withdrawn in the end, would have authorized the application of Sharia law to marriage and family law for Muslims.[17] And of course in France, the issue has arisen since the influx of Muslims from the Maghreb, Africa, and Asia Minor made Islam the second French religion. Now the presence of veiled students in middle schools and high schools has troubled many teachers, because it is contrary to *laïcité*[18]—that is to say, the ideological and religious neutrality of the republican school—and also because it is seen as a sexist symbol affirmative of the inferiority of women. After several years of attempts to resolve the problem, starting from ministerial memoranda and dialogues within educational institutions, the government had recourse, in this case as well, to a commission of experts, the Stasi Commission, named after its president, Bernard Stasi, charged with writing a report. The commission's report, the conclusions of which were not followed in their entirety, invited the National Assembly to vote on the matter: thus a law prohibiting "conspicuous" religious symbols in public educational institutions was enacted. Perhaps the imprecision of the word *conspicuous* encouraged a flexible implementation of the law; nonetheless, some girls who insisted on wearing their headscarves to school were expelled, and it is not at all certain that the problem has been definitively resolved.

What would Montesquieu say about this issue? Even accustomed as I am to going back and forth from his past and our present, I have not concealed from myself the absurd character of the question. For it is difficult to interpret *The Spirit of Laws* as a feminist work. And while it is true that the work tends toward the secularization (*laïcisation*) of public life, denouncing any amalgamation of the temporal and spiritual, and in this way contributes to the secularization (*laïcisation*) of minds, despite the author's desire to appear Christian, it would perhaps be to overinterpret the texts and history to consider Montesquieu as being at the origin, even remotely, of the 1905 law instituting the separation of churches and state.[19] At the same time, it is not forbidden to look for the starting points of reflection in Montesquieu's work. Going in the direction of the rejection of the headscarf, one should remember his profound wariness with respect to religious proselytism, which he suspects of intolerance. Intolerance is a double attack on civic concord and the liberty of others: "A citizen does not satisfy the laws by contenting himself with not agitating the body of the State; he must also not disturb any citizen whatsoever" (XXV, 9). According to our legislators and to our principle of secularism, any propaganda at school, be it by virtue of a simple piece of clothing, constitutes an attack against the liberty of the students, whose school's mission is precisely to form critical minds.

In addition, "there are scarcely but intolerant religions that are greatly zealous to establish themselves elsewhere" (XXV, 10).

However, *The Spirit of Laws* gives us a whole set of suggestions going in the other direction as well. Montesquieu warns us against legislative inflation, as was noted earlier. He also tells us that if the law crosses over the boundary of its domain of legitimacy—the public interest—it becomes oppressive: "The law is not a pure act of power; things indifferent by their nature are not within its scope" (XIX, 14). To be sure, the question of whether the wearing of the Islamic headscarf is *indifferent* or not with respect to the common good warrants discussion: Montesquieu invites us to go deeper into the matter. All the more since, being an exponent of diversity, he warns against any artificial attempt at standardization, what he considers to be an indication of a despotic deviation of the use of power (XXIX, 18). We know to what degree this chapter, whose author goes so far as to impugn the standardization of weights and measures, would have run up against Condorcet. In the dialogue, or rather the posthumous controversy, between the historian-philosopher and the philosopher-geometer, two practices of reason oppose each other, the rational and the reasonable.[20] Adhering to the second one, Montesquieu does not hesitate to make statements that clash with our contemporary principles of equality before the law, as in the past he clashed with Condorcet: "When the citizens observe the laws, what does it matter if they observe the same ones?" (XXIX, 18).

Montesquieu does not see any difficulty in principle with different rules of behavior coexisting in the same country: "In China, the Chinese are governed by Chinese ceremonies, and the Tartars by Tartar ceremonies; they are, however, the people in the world which most have tranquility as their purpose" (XXIX, 18). The same holds for Roman Gaul, after the arrival of the Barbarians: "[T]he Salic law had been established for the Franks, and the Theodosian code for the Romans" (XXVIII, 4). Moreover, the wearing of the headscarf depends first and foremost on mores, before depending on the law as enacted through the will of the legislator. Now we are told that "when one wants to change mores and manners, one must not change them by the laws, as this would appear to be too tyrannical; it would be better to change them by other mores and other manners" (XIX, 14). Peter the Great's law obliging the Muscovites to cut their beards was therefore tyrannical. Today, Montesquieu would perhaps ask himself whether the chador is not the equivalent for Muslims. And he would add that in France every attack on the liberty to wear it would be a useless tyranny. Would not the process of cultural assimilation have gone at more or less the same speed in France as in the Russia of the eighteenth century?

> The ease and promptness with which this nation has become orderly has shown that this prince [Peter I] had too low an opinion of it and that these peoples were not beasts as he said. The violent

means he employed were useless; he would have accomplished his purpose as well by gentleness.

He himself saw how easy it was to make changes. The women had been enclosed and in a way enslaved; he called them to court, he had them dress in the German way, and he sent them fabrics. They immediately appreciated a way of life that so flattered their taste, their vanity, and their passions, and they made the men appreciate it.

What made the change easier was that the mores of that time were foreign to the climate and had been carried there by the mixture of nations and by conquests. (XIX, 14)

Let us leave aside the sequel, the explanation related to the climate, already old fashioned in 1748. What remains is the essential point, seen correctly by Montesquieu: the capacity of a dominant sociocultural system to assimilate, little by little, and without coercion, mores imported by the population. Will someone reply that all that belongs to the past, that in a modern republic there is no longer room for fashion or for feminine coquetry? Yet there remains a grave, and unsettling, question that Montesquieu obliges us to ask: by enacting a law on the Islamic headscarf, have not our legislators, like our teachers, demonstrated a lack of confidence in the cultural vitality of our country and its schools?

However, this question, along with the points that led us to it, is not the only concluding inquiry. It is necessary to return to liberty, "this good which allows the enjoyment of the other goods."[21] Montesquieu is aware of the attachment of peoples to their customs; he also knows that true liberty cannot be reduced, like in old Russia, to "the usage of wearing a long beard" (XI, 2). There are, in his judgment, universal values that transcend the diversity of customs, and by this measure, all usages are not equal. There are multiple false conceptions of liberty, but only one true liberty: "the right to do everything the laws permit" (XI, 3), which "consists in security or, at least, in the opinion one has of one's security" (XII, 2). Now from this perspective alone all customs are not equivalent. Everything depends on the political context: "The customs of a slave people are a part of their servitude; those of a free people are a part of their liberty" (XIX, 27). It belongs to each individual to judge whether the Muslims of France come from free countries. This is in any case a supplementary aspect of the headscarf issue that must be examined. We have just seen the complexity of this issue, and it is not easy, through an analysis of opposing considerations, to put oneself in Montesquieu's place and draw conclusions in his stead. The same doubt would probably subsist if we were to inquire into other customs that have been brought to France in recent date, which French law prohibits. For example, what would Montesquieu say of the ban on polygamy, a practice used more or less secretively by certain Africans of France? He would undoubtedly repeat that the climate and the demography of Europe promote monogamy (XVI, 2, 4). Is it then necessary to enact laws to this end? As to forced marriages, in certain cases imposed on young French women whose families come from Morocco or Africa, it is uncertain whether they would have posed a problem for either a subject of Louis XV, for whom such practices were part of the habitual order of things, or a philosopher particularly attached to the authority of the father and the preservation of patrimonies (XXIII, 7, 8). In contrast, one can have no doubt as to the horror with which Montesquieu would have looked upon the practice of excision, an intolerable mutilation inflicted upon the woman's body and dignity; here we would find at work the negative universal of which Catherine Larrère speaks.

Thus Montesquieu's thought is constantly defined and redefined by the tension between antithetical pairs, less by the contradiction of the real and the ideal, as was said in the time of Gustave Lanson, than by the marriage of the universal and the particular, the diverse and the singular. His thought is paradoxical. We who sometimes dispute about the state being *too big* or *not big enough* could be reminded of the paradox of the state, as it is articulated by Montesquieu: a state is at once a threat and a protection, a constant potential threat against liberty and at the same time an indispensable guarantor of the liberty and security of all. But to think paradoxically is to deny one's reader—and oneself—the possibility of establishing any certitude whatsoever. A paradoxical manner of thinking always produces thought in movement, in the incessant pursuit of a problematic equilibrium, thought that is not didactic but heuristic, like that of Diderot, and thus still stimulating and living even two and a half centuries later. With Montesquieu the possibility of dialogue is unlimited: he is one of us.

## Notes

1. "Happy few" is in English in the original.
2. Under the direction of Jean Ehrard, then Ehrard and Catherine Volpilhac-Auger, then Volpilhac-Auger and Pierre Rétat. Seven of the twenty-two scheduled volumes have been published from 1998 to 2005.
3. See *Œuvres complètes*, vol. 1. *'Lettres persanes' et introductions générales* (Oxford: Voltaire Foundation, 2004), xv–xxii.
4. Edgar Mass, "Montesquieu et la loi fondamentale de la RFA," *Dix-Huitième Siècle* 21 (1989): 163–77.
5. See Nicolas Weill's brief review of the *Spiegel* article in the March 26, 2005, edition of *Le Monde*. Weill's article deals primarily with the rehabilitation of Cartesianism by the senate of the University of Utrecht three days earlier.

6. *The Spirit of Laws*, XXIX, 16. In German: "Ein Gesetz, das nicht notwendig ist, unterbleibt besser" (G. Schröder, speech to the Bundestag, Berlin, Die Bundesregierung, 16); "Wenn es nicht notwendig ist, ein Gesetz zu erlassen, dann ist es notwendig, kein Gesetz zu erlassen" (H. Köhler, speech to the Forum of Entrepreneurs, edited by the Services of the Presidency, 5). I owe these references to Mr. Berthold Falk of Berlin, someone who knows Montesquieu well.

7. See Espiell's article, "Le principe de la division des pouvoirs, la Révolution d'émancipation latino-américaine et le droit constitutionnel de l'Uruguay," *Revue Montesquieu* 5 (2001), 123.

8. Thomas L. Pangle, *Montesquieu's Philosophy of Liberalism: A Commentary on the Spirit of the Laws* (Chicago: University of Chicago Press, 1973).

9. Film production, 1995. Let us recall the following little-known anecdote: upon arrival, having presented their Afghan passports, they were detained by the authorities. It was something they were not expecting in a "democratic country."

10. Michel Germain, *Bulletin de l'ILEC* (Paris: Institut de Liaison et d'Etudes des Industries de Consommation, 2001). See *Revue Montesquieu*, 6 (2002): 277–78. Michel Germain teaches corporate law at the University of Paris II (Panthéon–Assas).

11. Paris, Théâtre du Lucernaire. Directed by Hervé Dubourjal, with Jean-Paul Bordes in the role of Machiavelli and Jean-Pierre Andréani as Montesquieu. As Michel Cournot notes (*Le Monde*, October 9, 2005), the text had been adapted for stage performance by Pierre Fresnay in 1968, and again by Pierre Tabard in 2001. There was also a dramatic reading of a part of the text performed by the organizers of the theater workshop at the University of Clermont-Ferrand (Service Universités—Culture).

12. Jean Ehrard, "Montesquieu dans les débats politiques français d'aujourd'hui," *Studies on Voltaire and the Eighteenth Century* (Oxford: Voltaire Foundation, 2003), 455–64; "Montesquieu dans *Le Monde* en 1998," *Revue Montesquieu* 3 (1999), 99–108; "Montesquieu dans *Le Monde* en 1999," *Revue Montesquieu* 4 (2000): 115–23; "Montesquieu dans *Le Monde* en 2000," ibid. 5 (2001): 147–53; "Montesquieu dans *Le Monde* en 2001," ibid. 6 (2002): 59–67; "Montesquieu dans *Le Monde* en 2002," Ibid. 7 (2003–2004): 159–67.

13. Catherine Larrère, *Actualité de Montesquieu* (Paris: Presses de Sciences Po, 1999).

14. Alain Juppé, *Montesquieu le moderne* (Paris: Perrin-Grasset, 1999).

15. *The Spirit of Laws*, XI, 6. On the use of the different forms of the verb *to separate* in *The Spirit of Laws*, see Jean Ehrard, *L'esprit des mots. Montesquieu en lui-même et parmi les siens* (Geneva: Droz, 1998), 159–60.

16. A neologism used by Jacques Chirac in response to an accusation related to this affair.

17. On the first point, this information was gleaned from *USA Today* (September 8, 2005). On the second point, which provoked lively debate in Ontario, see the *National Post*, September 9 and 10, 2005. The proposition came from the province's premier, who withdrew it in the end. See *Le Monde* (October 22, 2005).

18. The definition of *laïcité* provided in the Robert dictionary is: "A political concept which implies the separation of civil society from religious society, the State exercising no religious power, and Churches exercising no political power" (*Le Petit*

*Robert* [Paris: Robert, 2003]). The legal basis of French *laïcité* is the 1905 law on the separation of church and state.

19. See *Montesquieu, the State and Religion. Actes du colloque à Sophie* (Paris: Société Montesquieu, 2005).

20. The distinction between the *rational* and the *reasonable*, introduced in the beginning of the twentieth century by the American philosopher John R. Commons and revisited in 2000 in the commentary of Laure Bazzoli (*L'économie politique de John R. Commons. Essai sur l'institutionnalisme en sciences sociales* [Paris: L'Harmattan, 1999]), comes to light as particularly pertinent when we apply it to *The Spirit of Laws*. Unlike Condorcet, Montesquieu esteems that the rational is not always reasonable. This explains why Paul Vernière could have entitled one of his last books *Montesquieu et l'Esprit des lois ou la raison impure* (Paris: Société d'Edition d'Enseignement Supérieur, 1977). On the divergence between Condorcet and Montesquieu, see Robert Niklaus, "Condorcet et Montesquieu: Conflit idéologique entre deux théoriciens rationalistes," *Dix-Huitième Siècle* 25 (1993): 399–409; Catherine Kintzler, "Condorcet, critique de Montesquieu et de Rousseau," *Bulletin de la Société Montesquieu* 6 (1994): 10–31; and Jean Ehrard, "L'aune ou le mètre," *L'Esprit des mots*, 295–306.

21. Montesquieu, *Oeuvres complètes*, 14, 15. *Mes Pensées*, (Oxford: Voltaire Foundation, forthcoming), n. 1874.

# 14

# Montesquieu and the Future of Liberalism

### Ronald F. Thiemann

Montesquieu continues to fascinate interpreters in a broad range of fields and disciplines. Working as we do in this odd modern/postmodern era, Montesquieu intrigues in part because his writings resist easy categorization. While fully at home in eighteenth-century France, Montesquieu's thought comprises classical, medieval, modern, and even postmodern themes. His reflections are unsystematic and remarkably diverse in both content and form. His style is primarily descriptive, though normative implications seem always to lie just beneath the surface of his elegant prose. At times brilliantly perspicacious, at times maddeningly obscure, he is a rhetorical master, rivaling Spinoza and Hume in his employment of ironic tropes. Montesquieu beckons us to understand, then eludes our attempts to do so. No wonder he continues to fascinate.

How might Montesquieu assist us in reconstructing liberal political theory in our times? For centuries liberal theory has been central to the building of democratic and capitalist regimes worldwide, but for the past two decades it has come under severe attack by critics from both the Right and the Left. Communitarian critics bemoan liberalism's excessive individualism and its apparent disregard for virtue and community.[1] Postcolonial critics point to liberalism's deep complicity with imperialism and colonialism and seek means of building democratic societies independent of liberalism's ethnic chauvinism and excessive rationalism.[2]

In this chapter I will examine three basic dilemmas of liberal theory and then ask how Montesquieu might assist us in moving beyond liberalism's aporias. The three dilemmas are the right relation between freedom and equality, the necessity of virtue yet the incapacity to cultivate it, and the challenge of pluralism and the need for social cohesion.

These dilemmas emerge out of the basic tenets of liberal political theory and thus define fundamental tensions within liberal theory classically conceived. The tenets of classical liberal theory[3] are:

- Society is an association of free and equal citizens, and political, economic, and social structures are built to ensure a fair system of cooperation among free and equal persons.

- The fundamental moral norm of liberal societies is social justice: the right of every person to equal concern and respect.

- Because of the "fact of pluralism" no one comprehensive view of the good life should be implemented through the force of law or state power. "The priority of the right to the good" (John Rawls).[4] *Corollary 1*: "Government must be neutral on questions of the good life and political decisions must be independent of any conception of the good life or what gives value to life" (Ronald Dworkin).[5] *Corollary 2*: church and state must be rigorously separated and religion relegated to the realm of the private.

- Disproportionate or unequal outcomes due to circumstance of birth, talent, or economic advantage or disadvantage should be counteracted by appropriate societal intervention. "Difference principle" (Rawls).[6]

Society as conceived by liberal theory is an association of free and equal citizens in which all persons have a right to equal concern and respect, in which no comprehensive view of the good can be enforced by law, and in which state intervention is permitted to overcome significant disparities, especially, economic.

## First Dilemma

Freedom and equality as conceived by liberalism are in fundamental tension with one another. If freedom is given full sway—without the balancing intervention of government action—then equality is virtually impossible to achieve. Those who by virtue of wealth, genetic predisposition, social status, and education begin life with an advantage over those who lack such things will, if given full freedom, simply expand the gap between them and the disadvantaged, thus vitiating the hope of equality. Similarly, if government intervenes with too heavy a hand in order to guarantee equality, then freedom will inevitably suffer, as the unhappy history of Communist regimes clearly indicates.

Political debates in the United States from the New Deal to the present have often been disputes within liberal political theory (libertarian, conservative, progressive) concerning the balance between freedom and equality. The laissez-faire economic policies of the Hoover administration of the 1930s were countered during the Great Depression by the New Deal economic reforms of the Roosevelt administration (social security, graduated income tax, public works administration) and the later Great Society programs of the Johnson administration designed to create greater economic equality. The racial discrimination of the Jim Crow era was modified by the post–civil rights movement political reforms (*Brown v. Board of Education*, the Civil Rights Act, the Voting Rights Act, affirmative action) designed to create greater political equality. The Reagan and Bush eras have seen the progressive dismantling of both forms of equality in the name of liberty. Thus the pendulum swings back and forth between equality and freedom thereby rendering American politics increasingly unstable and lacking in common ground.

## Montesquieu on Freedom and Equality

Here as in most instances Montesquieu refuses to side with any of the positions (libertarian, conservative, progressive) within contemporary liberal political theory. Like the *libertarians* Montesquieu identifies freedom as the highest good of a republic in which freedom is defined as not living under the constraint or rule of another person (Berlin's "negative freedom").[7] Political liberty (in contradistinction to "independence") is "that tranquility of mind which comes from the opinion that each has of his security" (XI, 6). In order to achieve "this liberty it is necessary that the government be such that one citizen be unable to fear another citizen" (XI, 6).

Like the *conservatives*, however, Montesquieu also believes that freedom must be constrained because of the ever-present possibility of corruption, negligence, and a "certain tepidness of love of country" (V, 19). For this reason Montesquieu proposed the need for both a senate of elders and a body of censors who would maintain the austere moral discipline required of democratic republics. In like manner he advocated a form of virtue that subjugates personal self-interest to well-being of the common good. "This virtue can now be defined as love of the laws and of country" (IV, 5). A self-abnegating patriotism is central to Montesquieu's understanding of political virtue.

Despite these similarities to both libertarians and conservatives, Montesquieu also holds principles dear to contemporary *progressives*, most notably economic equality. One of the most striking aspects of his political philosophy is his unabashed commitment to economic equality. The stability of the democratic republic depends fundamentally on a combination of frugality and equality. Montesquieu insisted that inheritances should pass not to one's heirs but to the needy of society. Wealth, Montesquieu argued, undermines the virtues essential to a republic. Everyone must work and toil so that all citizens might eschew luxury and indolence.

For Montesquieu then liberty and equality are kept in precarious balance through the virtues of patriotism (love of laws and country), frugality, and the desire to serve the common good. Genuine liberty can be achieved only in a nation of laws, because only in such a nation can citizens be secure and thus free from the fear of other citizens. True political virtue involves the subjugation of one's own desires to those of the common good, thus yielding a "chastened patriotism." Finally, such virtue encourages the frugality and rejection of luxury that creates the conditions for a secure, stable, and economically egalitarian society.

## Second Dilemma

Liberalism argues for the necessity of civic virtues but has shown a consistent incapacity to cultivate them. The founders of the American republic shared with Montesquieu a conviction that effective government requires civic virtue among the populace. "Is there no virtue among us?" asked James Madison. "If there be not, no form of government can render us secure. To suppose that any form of government will secure liberty or happiness without virtue in the people is a chimerical idea."[8] While American constitutional democracy presupposes a virtuous public life, the founders were at best ambivalent about how such virtue was to be fostered.[9]

Madison drew heavily upon Montesquieu in his description of the human condition and the necessity of governmental safeguards against human passions. Like Montesquieu Madison developed a theological argument to assert his view of human beings as free and equal bearers of natural rights. Rights are inalienable, Madison argued, because they come from the hand of a Creator God; human beings are free because conscience alone should dictate "what homage" each person should return "to the Creator." The violation of freedom of conscience is "an offense against God, not against man."[10]

At the same time Madison, even more than Montesquieu, feared the negative consequences of human passions and self-interest. Madison, too, saw that "the various and unequal distribution of property" would be "the most common and durable source of factions" that would render citizens "more disposed to vex and oppress each other than to co-operate for their common good."[11] Thus he draws directly from Montesquieu the conception of the division and balance of powers in the construction of a constitutional republic. Unlike Montesquieu, however, Madison and the other founders do not return to the question of virtue and its cultivation among the populace. With the exception of Benjamin Franklin, the American founders give little or no attention to virtues such as frugality and moderation and provide no recommendations on how the virtues necessary for self-governance can be nurtured within the fledgling republic. American political theory has thus always been vexed by the question of how to nurture the civic virtues necessary for effective self-governance.

## Montesquieu on Virtue

Montesquieu may be more the source of this dilemma than a resource for its resolution. On the one hand, Montesquieu clearly admires the commercial republic of eighteenth-century England, a form of government that has no apparent reliance upon civic virtue. He develops his theory of the division and balance of powers by construing the English republic as one in which security is maintained by the balance of selfish competitive factions and the creation of nonpopular representative governmental institutions. The American founders clearly lifted their view of separation of powers directly from this portion of Montesquieu's *The Spirit of Laws*, without resolving the obvious tension between Montesquieu's treatment of the commercial republic and his earlier discussion of classical virtuous republics. By failing to address this fundamental tension within their own political theory, the American founders created a dilemma between virtue and power that continues to this very day. The founders rejected two of Montesquieu's basic ideas: the formation of a noble or aristocratic class of governors within whom the appropriate virtues might be cultivated and the creation of a board of censors who would enforce such virtuous behavior in the populace, but they found no ready replacement for these ideas in their own political theory, thus leaving the question "whence virtue?" unanswered.

## Third Dilemma

According to liberal theory, pluralism is a "given" of contemporary democratic life, but such cultural, moral, and religious diversity also undermines the social cohesion needed for a viable government of law and consent. Liberalism as a polity is designed in large part to address the conditions for social cohesion in light of the "fact of pluralism." Because every modern society will have various competing and conflicting understandings of the ultimate ends or goods of human life (what Rawls calls "comprehensive schemes"), a liberal polity requires such goods to be subordinated to those ends upon which all reasonable citizens can agree. All comprehensive schemes must be eliminated from the realm of the political, though they may be allowed to flourish within the personal and associational life of citizens. For some liberal theorists this implies the "priority of the right to the good," the "neutrality" of government toward all comprehensive schemes, and the "privatization" of religion (see the *corollaries* under the "tenets of classical liberalism" listed above).

Liberalism is thus willing to sacrifice public virtue for social cohesion under the conditions of modern pluralism. Some theorists such as John Rawls grant to "background culture"—that is, churches, universities, civic clubs—a role in "endorsing" the fundamental "overlapping consensus" of liberal societies, but they cannot play a constituting role in providing the content of that consensus. (This is what Rawls means when he calls the overlapping consensus "freestanding.")[12] Liberal theorists construe pluralism not only as a *fact* of modern social life but as the essential *problem* facing modern governments. If governments are to provide security for their citizens, they must limit the influence of comprehensive schemes in the realm of the political, even at the expense of emptying public life of the very virtues Madison thought to be fundamental to the health of modern republics.

The vacuum created by the relegation of morality, virtue, and religion to the private realm creates a fundamental instability in liberal societies, especially when citizens remain deeply attached to the primary commitments of their local moral communities. The remarkable rise of the so-called religious Right in the United States over the past twenty-five years illustrates how vulnerable liberal public life is to significant incursions by organized politico-religious forces within civil society. Citizens with strong moral and religious convictions will not long be willing to leave those convictions at the boundary of the public square. Liberalism demands of its citizens a bifurcation of the self that cannot easily be sustained by a populace with deep and widespread moral and religious convictions. Liberalism needs to devise a way in which such convictions can be incorporated into the public sphere without allowing any single religious or moral community to dominate public life. Liberalism needs to "pluralize" its public life by incorporating the manifold moral and religious voices into its polity. Liberalism is self-deluding when it believes that it can maintain social stability by relegating such forces to some imagined "private" realm.

## Montesquieu on Virtue and Social Cohesion

Once again Montesquieu provides mixed resources for addressing this third dilemma. We have already seen how Montesquieu requires the subjugation of personal self-interest to the national common good and insists upon a self-abnegating form of patriotism. Like other "classical liberals," Montesquieu asserts the primacy of social cohesion over any individual need or interest. Montesquieu does not, however, relegate virtue, morality, and religion to the private realm. Indeed, his views on religion set him apart from other advocates of liberal political theory.[13]

As a classical liberal theorist Montesquieu understands that the tenets of religion cannot serve as the primary basis for law in a modern political society. "However respectable may be the ideas that spring directly from religion, they should not always serve as the basis for civil law, because civil laws have another basis which is the general good of society" (XXVI, 9). Demonstrating a subtlety only rarely found in contemporary liberal theorists, Montesquieu refuses simply to *separate* religion and politics, preferring rather to assign independent jurisdictions to religious and political institutions. Moreover, he does not consider religion to exercise its function merely in the private or personal realm. For Montesquieu religious institutions are public, and religious laws can provide support for the general laws of morality even if they do not provide the ultimate warrant or grounding for those laws. In this regard, Montesquieu's position resembles the arguments offered by John Rawls in his final revision of *Political Liberalism*. Wherever religion functions to bolster the laws of civil society, there religious and political ends are complementary. But when religious practice or dogma undermines social or political ties, Montesquieu shows no reluctance to criticize those beliefs and practice. Thus Montesquieu demonstrates a subtle and dialectical understanding of the relation between religion and politics, one from which contemporary liberal theorists could learn.[14]

For Montesquieu it is not religion, diverse moral opinions, or comprehensive views of the good that provide the primary challenge to social cohesion; rather, as we discussed earlier, it is economic inequality or great disparities in wealth that threaten the social ties of modern societies. But Montesquieu may have underestimated the corrosive effect of greed, self-interest, and acquisitiveness in modern commercial republics. Modern capitalist societies have shown little interest during the past century in encouraging the traits of frugality, self-control, and asceticism that both Montesquieu and later Max Weber thought essential to the moral well-being of modern commerce. The recent horror experienced by the victims of hurricane Katrina has brought to the world's attention the problems of poverty, race, and economic inequality that have always plagued the American experiment in democracy. If liberal political theory is to have a viable future, then advocates of liberal republicanism would do well to sit again at the feet of one of the great teachers of the modern era. The passage of centuries has served to show us that Montesquieu has lessons we desperately need to learn and relearn. Perhaps the future of liberalism depends in part in looking again to its past.

## Notes

1. The literature produced by communitarian critics of liberal theory is vast, but some of the most influential works in this genre are Michael Sandel, *Liberalism and the Limits of Justice* (Cambridge: Cambridge University Press, 1998), and *Democracy's Discontent: America in Search of a Public Philosophy* (Cambridge: Harvard University Press, 1996); Alisdair MacIntyre, *After Virtue: A Study in Moral Theory* (Notre Dame: University of Notre Dame, 1997), and *Whose Justice? Which Rationality?* (Notre Dame: University of Notre Dame, 1989). I have commented extensively on this debate in *Religion and American Public Life: A Dilemma for Democracy* (Georgetown: Georgetown University Press/Century Fund, 1996).

2. See especially Uday Singh Mehta, *Liberalism and Empire: A Study in Nineteenth Century British Liberal Thought* (Chicago: University of Chicago Press, 1999).

3. In *Religion and Public Life* I distinguish between "classical" and "revisionist" liberalisms, 72–120. See also Ronald F. Thiemann, "Public Religion: Bane or Blessing for Democracy," *Obligations of Citizenship and Demands of Faith: Religious Accommodation in Pluralist Democracies*, ed. Nancy L. Rosenblum (Princeton: Princeton University Press, 2000), 73–89.

4. "The Priority of the Right and Ideas of the Good," *Philosophy and Public Affairs* 17.3 (1988). Cf. *Political Liberalism* (New York: Columbia University Press, 1996), 173–211.

5. Ronald Dworkin, "Liberalism," *A Matter of Principle* (Cambridge: Harvard University Press, 1983), 191.

6. John Rawls, *A Theory of Justice* (Cambridge: Harvard University Press, 1999).

7. Isaiah Berlin, "Two Concepts of Liberty," *Four Essays on Liberty* (Oxford: Oxford University Press, 1979), 118–72.

8. *The Debates in the Several State Conventions on the Adoption of the Federal Constitution*, ed. Jonathan Elliot (Philadelphia: Lippincott, 1836), III, 536–37.

9. This is the "dilemma" that I discuss in *Religion and Public Life: A Dilemma for Democracy*.

10. "Memorial and Remonstrance against Religious Assessments, 1785," *The Mind of the Founder: Sources of the Political Thought of James Madison*, ed. Marvin Meyers, rev. ed. (Hanover-London: University Press of New England, 1981), 8–9.

11. *The Federalist Papers*, ed. Clinton Rossiter (New York: NAL Penguin, 1961), 79.

12. John Rawls, *Political Liberalism* (New York: Columbia University Press, 1993), 131–72.

13. The best treatment of Montesquieu on religion is Rebecca E. Kingston, "Montesquieu on Religion and on the Question of Toleration," *Montesquieu's Science of Politics: Essays on the Spirit of Laws* (New York: Rowman & Littlefield, 2001), 375–408.

14. There is a deep compatibility between Montesquieu's views on religion and the arguments I have made in *Religion and Public Life: A Dilemma for Democracy*. Cf. also Jeffrey Stout, *Democracy and Tradition* (Princeton: Princeton University Press, 2004).

# 15

# Montesquieu and Liberalism
## The Question of Pluralism

### Catherine Larrère

## Montesquieu and the Liberal Tradition

Concerning the question of Montesquieu's contribution to the liberal tradition, there is general agreement as to three points of emphasis: constitutional law, commercial humanism, and the defense of individual liberties and rights.

Constitutional law: the reference here is the chapter of *The Spirit of Laws* on the "constitution of England" (XI, 6) and the role played by the distribution of powers in the establishment of the rule of law. In addition to this undisputed contribution, one could add the study of the "federal republic" (IX, 1–3), that is, of the role of the federation in the republican constitution, but this would be more controversial, particularly in France.

Commercial humanism, rather than economic liberalism: Montesquieu, in effect, is neither a defender of free trade nor a free market theorist. But he emphasized the civilizing effects of commerce, namely, its capacity to make *moeurs* more mild and to contribute to peace on an international level (by rendering nations dependent on one another) as well as domestically: commercial interests regulate political passions and prevent the violence of states.[1]

Last, the defense of individual liberties and rights: according to Voltaire, "man had lost his rights; Montesquieu gave them back to him." Voltaire's statement sums up what earned Montesquieu the approbation and support of the philosophes of his time (notably when he was attacked by the Church after the publication of *The Spirit of Laws*). While one does not find in Montesquieu a general theory of the rights of man, he showed himself to be extremely sensitive to the defense of liberties, particularly with respect to the issues of slavery, which he was the first to condemn unconditionally, and of penal law ("the citizen's liberty depends principally on the goodness of the criminal laws" [XII, 2]). The accentuated homage that Beccaria pays to him at the beginning of the *Essay on Crimes and Punishments*, like the recurring references to his passage on arbitrariness made by the late eighteenth-century reformers of penal law ("It is the triumph of liberty when criminal laws draw each penalty from the particular nature of the crime. All arbitrariness ceases [...] man does not do violence to man" [XII, 4]), demonstrate Montesquieu's influence on the reform of criminal legislation, even if he himself was not a reformer (in *The Spirit of Laws* he gives a very tempered assessment of Colbert's 1663 Criminal Ordinance, which was a target of the reformers).[2]

All of this is well known. As Isaiah Berlin reminds us, Montesquieu's contribution to the liberal tradition is indisputable, but formulated in this way, it does not have a lot to teach us. It is, according to Berlin, because "the essentials of Montesquieu's teaching formed the heart of the liberal creed everywhere," that the "liberal aspects of his teaching" had "degenerated into commonplaces of liberal eloquence" as early as the middle of the nineteenth century.[3] One must then ask the question, does an original Montesquieuian contribution to liberalism exist, above and beyond these "commonplaces," that is still pertinent today? It is more difficult to answer this question.

This difficulty stems from the term itself. While the use of "liberal" in its current meaning of the defense of liberties (and not only in the older sense of generous, which is preserved in the word liberality) is attested to circa 1750, that is, at the time of the publication of *The Spirit of Laws* (1748), "liberalism" (like many "-isms") is a nineteenth-century invention. Thus the context of this term, that of the aftermath of the revolutions at the end of the eighteenth century (American, French, European) and of the democratic equality they introduced, is completely foreign to Montesquieu. Then the question of the continuation was posed: should we terminate the Revolution—this was the liberal position—by accepting its heritage, that of individual liberties? Or should we continue toward socialism, in search of greater equality? If liberalism, in the nineteenth century, defines itself in opposition to socialism, it does not make much sense to set Montesquieu against socialism. When Tocqueville, in 1848, criticizes the "droit au travail," which, in his view, constitutes a "socialist" measure, he equates the role that the state would have to play in upholding such a right to that played by the monarchy of the Ancien Régime. Montesquieu, in his chapter "On poorhouses" (XXIII, 29), defends the idea of the intervention of the state to prevent the distress of those deprived of work. Are we therefore obliged to consider him as a "socialist" or, more modestly, as the promoter of a "social" policy, which liberals of strict obedience could not support? This would be, in our view, anachronistic.

For the same reasons, it seems to us objectionable to want to situate Montesquieu within a conflict between liberty and equality, which does not appear explicitly in this form until after the French Revolution (and Tocqueville, in this respect as well, played an important role). Doubtless Montesquieu accommodates social inequalities all the more easily given that he was convinced that equality (such as it was sought in the ancient democracies) can only be the fragile result of extremely coercive policies. At the same time, he poses the question of the potential positive effects of these inequalities for the most destitute, which is what leads him to emphasize the function of the redistribution of wealth that luxury can exercise. Should we then understand him to be a precursor of the difference principle, defended by John Rawls in *A Theory of Justice* (inequalities that benefit the least advantaged are acceptable)? This would be to confuse two very different questions: the one that Montesquieu poses (Can the poor derive more advantages from inequality than from strict equality?) and the one that Rawls confronts (What degree of inequality can we tolerate in societies whose principle is equality?).

Rather than confronting Montesquieu with a conception of liberalism that is largely posterior to him (which easily leads to anachronisms and does not allow one to make a comprehensive judgment), it is preferable to place Montesquieu at the very root of the modern adoption of liberal values. This is what Thomas Pangle has done, and his book, *Montesquieu's Philosophy of Liberalism*[4] is the most far-reaching attempt to inscribe Montesquieu in liberalism, understood through its origins.[5] He identified Montesquieu with liberalism so well that, to inquire into the pertinence of liberal values becomes, finally, the same thing as to investigate the limits of the thought of Montesquieu, and this leads us to ask the same question: in expelling religion, have we not forgotten about evil?[6] According to Pangle, Montesquieu rallies behind the values of modernity, those of individual liberty and security, of each person's right to achieve happiness, to satisfy her own aspirations (or selfish desires). It is in the opposition between ancients and moderns that Montesquieu founds his liberalism: renouncing the ancient search for perfection, denouncing the constraints of virtue, Montesquieu defends the modern values of liberty. Hence his political preferences, which England embodied: he praises England's constitution for achieving the rule of law by limiting the various powers; he announces the pacifying and civilizing merits of its commercial values.

The famous speech in which Benjamin Constant presents the opposition between the liberty of the ancients and that of the moderns owes much to Montesquieu, and this is particularly true when it comes to the opposition between war and commerce, which gives the first opposition its social content. However, it is difficult to find in Montesquieu oppositions (between the ancients and the moderns, between liberty as participation in political power and liberty as private enjoyment) as sharply contrasted as those established by Constant.

"The political men of Greece who lived under popular government recognized no other force to sustain it than virtue. Those of today speak to us only of manufacturing, commerce, finance, wealth, and even luxury" (III, 3). Montesquieu put forward the opposition between virtue and commerce in such a striking manner that Rousseau reused the phrase in his *Discourse on the Sciences and the Arts*.[7] We would be mistaken, nonetheless, to think that this is Montesquieu's last word; the highly rhetorical presentation of this opposition leads one rather to suppose the opposite. The opposition between virtue and commerce is surmountable.[8] There exist in antiquity commercial republics that are also virtuous. Montesquieu introduces the expression "spirit of commerce" to explain what could appear to be a paradox: "the spirit of commerce brings with it the spirit of frugality, economy, moderation, work, wisdom, tranquility, order, and rule. Thus, as long as this spirit continues to exist, the wealth it produces has no bad effect" (V, 6). And it is because republics are compatible with commerce that the time of republics is not past, contrary to what Louis Althusser affirms.[9] The Dutch Republic shows that there is a place in modernity for encounters among republican values (virtue, a certain frugality), the development of commerce, and the existence of public and individual liberties (religious liberty in particular). The distinction, in Book XX, between commerce founded on economy (specific to republics) and commerce founded on luxury (suitable to monarchies) indicates that there are several paths commerce can take in modern times and that one of them is more properly republican.

Montesquieu does not present as rigid an opposition between two forms of liberty as Constant does any more than he establishes a strict separation between antiquity and modernity, republics and monarchies. Certainly, the definition given in Books XI and XII of liberty as security points in the direction of a liberty conceived as private enjoyment, sheltered from incursions of power: "[P]olitical liberty is that tranquility of spirit which comes from the opinion each one has of his security" (XI, 6). But such a conception of liberty often leads to presenting it as a natural power, whose existence is independent of the law. This is what Hobbes does, situating liberty in the state of nature and positing that, in the civil state, liberty can only consist in "the silence of the law." Montesquieu rejects this conception of liberty: "One must put oneself in mind of what independence is and what liberty is" (XI, 3); liberty is the "right to do everything the laws permit" (XI, 3). It is not realized outside of the law, but with the law: "therefore, we are free because we live under civil laws" (XXVI, 20).

We will not, then, be surprised to see Montesquieu present another conception, after having given a definition of liberty that seems characteristic of the liberty of the moderns, which turns toward the republican tradition, toward the liberty of the ancients: "As, in a free State, every man, considered to have a free soul, should be governed by himself, the people as a body should have legislative power" (XI, 6). This formulation, in which the metaphor of the free rule of each individual over himself introduces the affirmation of the political power of the people, is characteristic of what Quentin Skinner calls the "Roman model" of republican liberty, defended by the radical English republicans at the end of the seventeenth century.[10]

It is very difficult to inscribe Montesquieu in an opposition between the ancients and the moderns, which has been said to be "the product of the liberal ideology [which] has no meaning outside of it."[11] This does not make Montesquieu an antiliberal, but it shows that he rejects strict oppositions and the simplification of choices that characterize ideological positions. Certainly, Montesquieu makes choices (and it is one of the great merits of Thomas Pangle's book to have called into question the idea of a neutral Montesquieu, purely descriptive and refusing all normative judgments), and he is all the more inclined to make choices given that there is always, in his view, a plurality of solutions. This is, at any rate, the thesis we would like to defend: Montesquieu's contribution to liberalism consists in his pluralist vision of the political good.

Pluralism is the acknowledgment of the plurality of conceptions of the good, an acknowledgment rendered necessary by the collapse of the religious vision of the unity of the good with the crisis of the Reformation, such that pluralism appears to be the political, liberal solution to the religious crisis.[12] If this is the case, we cannot but find it striking that Montesquieu contrasts the plurality of the political good with the unity of the religious good: "Human laws enact about the good; religion, about the best. The good can have another object because there are several goods, but the best is one alone and can, therefore, never change" (XXVI, 2). To this, one can add the political, not metaphysical, conception that Montesquieu has of liberty. The definitions of political liberty that we find in this period are inseparable from fundamental philosophical positions: thus one can contrast the materialist vision of Hobbes, that of liberty as the absence of physical obstacles to movement, with the more spiritual and moral conception of Rousseau, who ties liberty to the capacity for self-determination, for giving oneself one's own law. Montesquieu, for his part, intends to "speak in all systems" (XII, 2) and to give a definition of political liberty that is distinct from the philosophical definition of liberty and is therefore not dependent on a given philosophical system. One can therefore accept the political definition of liberty that Montesquieu gives, without adhering to a particular philosophical system. There is a good example of pluralism in political philosophy.

Of course, pluralism is a very contemporary question, and in directly relating the current debate on pluralism to this or that statement of Montesquieu, we do not intend to expose ourselves to the anachronisms previously denounced. Montesquieu's pluralism can only be established by starting from a comprehensive study of his method, situated in the philosophical and historical context that is his own, putting aside references to contemporary questions for the duration of such a study, which is all the more necessary given that Montesquieu's pluralism is a controversial question among his commentators. Isaiah Berlin is convinced that he "is not a monist but a pluralist."[13] However, Thomas Pangle's interpretation of Montesquieu's liberalism is resolutely monist: he sees in Montesquieu the defender of a unique model (commercial England) and the theoretician of a "unitary principle of political psychology,"[14] that of selfish motivation. In a critical reading of Thomas Pangle's study, Bernard Manin is led to defend the idea that we find in Montesquieu, "a liberalism of plurality."[15]

It is this path of inquiry into the "liberalism of plurality" that we would like to pursue in turn, in attempting to show how the pluralism of Montesquieu is inseparable from the method that he adopts in *The Spirit of Laws*, that of the study of types (or of the search for "principles"). We will thus seek to present the different forms of pluralism that one can find in Montesquieu. This will lead us to examine what is often called his "relativism." If one admits the plurality of the good, can one avoid the conflict of values, what Max Weber called the "war of the gods"? Does Montesquieu have something to teach us concerning this question? Our interest in Montesquieu, in effect, is not purely erudite or "antiquarian." We are studying him from the starting point of our contemporary preoccupations, and this is precisely the reason why we want to avoid a retrospective reading which, projecting onto Montesquieu what we already know, would lead us to turn in circles around our own thoughts, far from giving us the necessary distance to put them to the test. This is why our first part, the inquiry into pluralism, will be followed by a second part, which will examine its contemporary relevance. Adopting the distinction that Bernard Manin establishes between the liberalism of unity and the liberalism of plurality, we would like to suggest that if pluralism and liberalism are not always in agreement today, it is perhaps because contemporary liberalism remains dependent on a unitary rather than a pluralist model.

## From Diversity to Plurality

Montesquieu takes interest in the diversity of human things, so as to find an order in them. This is what he announces in the Preface of *The Spirit of Laws*: "I began by examining men, and I believed that, amidst the infinite diversity of laws and mores, they were not led by their fancies alone." He returns to this idea in the *Défense de L'Esprit des lois*: "[T]his work has as its object the laws, customs, and diverse usages of all the nations on earth."[16] But Montesquieu does not, as a result, seek to reduce this multiplicity to unity; he wishes to put it in order with the help of a small number of forms or principles. As Raymond

Aron explains, "One renders diversity intelligible when one organizes it with the help of a small number of types or concepts" and he specifies that the principles or types, thus drawn out, "constitute an intermediary level between incoherent diversity and a universally valid framework."[17]

One can take "universally valid framework" to mean not only the unique form of the diversity of phenomena that one would draw out but also the elementary component that the analysis would isolate. Montesquieu is often considered close to Bacon in his empiricism, in opposition to Descartes.[18] While this is surely true, it is hardly original. The "Discours préliminaire" of the *L'Encyclopédie* consecrates Bacon's triumph and, after Locke, who would defend the existence of innate ideas? And even before Locke, Hobbes, as much as he was an adept of deduction, placed sensation at the origin of ideas. But all these empiricists do not follow the same method, and there is the important difference. Montesquieu does not adopt Hobbes' resolutive-compositive method, that of decomposing the multiplicity by analysis, isolating the elementary form, and reconstructing, with this building block, forms that are more complex, but in which one can find the same structure and the same components. This is not the way in which Montesquieu proceeds; he does not seek the unique principle, the elementary motivation common to all. Doubtless, as Isaiah Berlin notes, Montesquieu remarks in passing that "men [are] made for self-preservation" (XXIV, 11)[19] or that "happiness and unhappiness consist in a certain disposition, favourable or unfavourable, of the organs" (*Pensées*, 30), or that "interest is the greatest monarch on earth" (*Lettres persanes*, 106). But, comments Berlin, "these are the typical maxims of almost any eighteenth-century moralist."[20] It did not occur to Montesquieu to do as Bentham did, that is, to make of similar remarks the founding principle of an entire edifice.[21] Montesquieu's method is not reductionist.

Of these types, or principles, which Montesquieu uses to order the diverse, Raymond Aron mentions the most significant: the different types of government, the enumeration of which opens Book II ("there are three kinds of government: republican, monarchical, and despotic" [II, 1]). This typology remains in place as a reference until the end of the work. But it is not the only one: each stage of the exposition introduces a new typology and new principles of classification. In going from the first part (Books I–VIII) to the second (Books IX–XIII), one sees a new typology of governments introduced, one that distinguishes between despotic governments and moderate governments (which group republics and monarchies into one). With the third part (Books XIV–XIX), new references are taken into account: climates, as a way of indexing diversity ("As one distinguishes climates by degrees of latitude, one could distinguish them by degrees of sensitivity, so to speak [XIV, 2]); the distinctions, in Book XVIII, among savage, barbarian, and civilized peoples (or hunting, pastoral, and agricultural peoples); the trilogy, in Book XIX, of laws, mores, and manners.

The fourth part (Books XX–XXIII), dedicated to commerce, brings into play the distinction between the commerce of economy and the commerce of luxury, and so on. In truth, only religions (Books XXIV–XXV) are not ordered in this way. For the distinction between true and false religions is imposed upon Montesquieu, a distinction whose heterogeneity contravenes the rules of his classifications, which consider as equal the different types distinguished. Doubtless the distinction between moderate and despotic governments is also a heterogeneous distinction, differentiating between good and bad governments. But this is a secondary distinction, which emerges out of the first one, namely, the original typology that distributes equally, or indifferently, the three "kinds" of government it distinguishes. Montesquieu's attempt to equalize the different religions, by considering them all as "human institutions," is made to fail by the injunction of the Church to treat "true" religion apart (but the books on religion occur sufficiently late in the work so as to enable the reader, informed by the usage of the other typologies, to correct this herself).

These different types are as many explanatory frameworks: each is defined by a certain number of characteristics that we can expect to find in the different phenomena grouped under a given type. The method of stating general characteristics and then confirming them in the phenomena studied appears frequently in Montesquieu (see, for example, the occurrence of a "what I say is confirmed by the entire body of history" [III, 3] after the statement that virtue is the principle of democratic government). The different types furnish comparative frameworks, even more than separate explanatory models; this makes it possible to relate two types to one another in opposition ("That virtue [the principle of democratic government] is not the principle of monarchical government" [III, 5]), or, inversely, in conciliation ("The people, in a democracy, are, in certain respects, the monarch; in other respects, they are the subjects." [II, 2]). The multiplicity of typologies envisaged allows for the multiplication of points of view on the phenomena (or groups of phenomena), thus avoiding subjecting them all to a given type. From the point of view of the typology of governments, there is no comparison possible between Sparta and China: the former is a republic, and the latter is a despotic regime. But both confuse laws, mores, and manners. This does not lead to the conclusion that they are similar but rather to a better comprehension of each of them.

The objective of all of these comparisons is, in effect, to bring out differences; one must be careful "not to consider as similar those cases with real differences or to overlook differences in those that appear similar," as Montesquieu announces in his Preface. The symmetrical construction of this sentence is misleading: it is not a matter of comparing two symmetrical dangers, the one consisting in seeing what is different as similar, the other in seeing what is similar as different; the real danger, repeated twice, consists in overlooking the differences. Illusion lies in resemblance; Montesquieu is not preoccupied with seeking the similar. The typological method, in this respect, is not inductive; it does not aim to draw out, by generalization or the selection of similar characteristics, general types or models that would represent as many results of the process of accumulating knowledge. Being means of comparison, types are only an intermediary step in an approach that aims at the knowledge of particulars. This renders the design of *The Spirit of Laws*, often denounced as incoherent, intelligible. As Bernard Manin reminds us, having begun with the presentation of laws in the universality of their extension, the work concludes, in Books XXX and XXXI, by the study of a singular case ("an event which happened once in the world and which will perhaps never happen again" [XXX, 1]): the ancient laws of the French monarchy.[22]

Hence the importance of the typology of governments for an approach oriented by the observation of particularities: the typology delimits the unit of that which one seeks to know. The climatic determinations serve as bearings in large geographical zones (North/South), and they even serve to divide large regions (Europe/Asia, in Book XVII). The typology of the governments applies to the entities that Montesquieu studies, what Galiani (a good reader of Montesquieu) characterizes by the following expression: "separated countries which govern themselves with their laws and which form a whole."[23] These "peoples" or "nations" (to use Montesquieu's terms) are characterized at once by their unity and by their complexity. The notion of "general spirit" (XIX, 4) accounts for this double aspect. "Many things govern men: climate, religion, laws, the maxims of the government, examples of past things, mores, and manners": that is, complexity. The role of the "general spirit" is to designate, for each "nation," which factor, among the set of these various factors, is dominant, bestowing upon each its particularity: "Nature and climate almost alone dominate savages; manners govern the Chinese; laws tyrannize Japan; in former times mores set the tone in Lacedaemonia; it was set by the maxims of government and the ancient mores in Rome" (XIX, 4). Each unity is characterized and particularized by the mode of connection and the organization of its constituent parts. Hence the rule governing comparison, when it comes to judging the laws of different countries: one must not compare them one by one but "take them all together and compare them all together" (XXIX, 11).

This ambition to identify unities and to grasp their differences, each in relation to one another as well as within each (one must not, in confusing laws and mores, regulate by laws what is in the domain of mores), has indisputable normative implications. It makes it possible to make nuanced evaluations, to determine degrees of evil (from the least bad to the worst) instead of sticking to strict black and white oppositions. "Much of good sense consists in knowing the nuances of things,"[24] Montesquieu soberly remarks, in response to accusations made by the Church, for whom not to condemn is necessarily to approve (Montesquieu objects, "But if I were to say that I prefer a fever to the scurvy, would that mean that I am fond of a fever; or only that the scurvy is more disagreeable to me than a fever?").[25] Faced with these religious criticisms, Montesquieu does not appeal to his neutrality as an observer; he indicates another, more nuanced mode of evaluation. This appears to him to be "more useful."[26]

In effect, to ignore these differences is to expose oneself to great dangers. Not only must one not confuse moderate governments with despotic ones, good with evil, but one must also be attentive to the plurality of goods. All moderate governments are not equivalent. "Mr. Law, equally ignorant of the republican and of the monarchical constitutions, was one of the greatest promoters of despotism that had until then been seen in Europe" (II, 4). The accusation is clarified when, in Book XX, Montesquieu develops the distinction between the commerce of economy and the commerce of luxury, explaining how institutions that are suited to the former (which one tends to encounter in republics) do not have their place in the latter (in which monarchies indulge). Now, among these institutions, one finds those which Law, at the time of the System, had wanted to introduce in France: a central bank, a large company in a monopoly position. One sees to what extent the desire to align France along the English commercial model (and from this point of view, England is closer to republics) could produce negative consequences, far from being favorable to liberty.

Montesquieu does not elaborate models, either in the cognitive sense of the term (models as stable forms that emerge through the process of induction and that one can study in and of themselves) or in the normative sense of a model to imitate. One could object that this is not the case for the English constitution, and it is certainly as a constitutional model that it has very often been interpreted (the English model consisting in the independence of the judiciary, two chambers, an executive that can intervene in the legislative). This is doubtless due to the fact that Montesquieu tends to abstract his analysis of England from this nation's history. While the debate concerning English politics and institutions had been rooted in a historical study of England, be it on the English side (the ancient constitution)[27] or the French side (the historical studies—divergent from one another—of Rapin-Thoyras or Voltaire),[28] Montesquieu reduces to nothing, or almost (the allusion at the end of the chapter to the fact that "this fine system was found in the forests" [XI, 6]), the historical integration of the English constitution (as opposed to his historical analysis of the French laws at the end of *The Spirit of Laws*). Can one then conclude that, thus detached from its historical context, the English constitution presents a pure constitutional model, exportable at leisure? Charles Eisenmann's study showed, on the contrary, that in his chapter on the constitution of England, Montesquieu does not so much present a pure juridical or institutional apparatus as he studies the relations between social forces.[29]

What Montesquieu retains from his analysis of England is not so much a constitutional model as a new indicator of diversity: the plurality of powers and social forces. This framework serves as his point of reference in the remainder of Book XI, in which, having moved from the study of England to that of Rome, he examines the distribution of powers there. And at the end of Book XI, he gives an outline of a research plan (leaving it to his reader to develop it): "I should like to seek out in all the moderate governments we know the distribution of the three powers and calculate thereupon the degrees of liberty each one of them can enjoy" (XI, 20). Thus there is no proposal of a model but rather the exposition of a framework that would permit a systematic study of cases and an indexing of liberty.

The passionate attention Montesquieu pays to the diversity of human things ("everything interests me, everything amazes me")[30] is therefore inseparable from a valorization of plurality. To give an order to diversity using a small number of types, frameworks, or principles, instead of seeking to reduce the multiple to one, leads to the isolation of units ("separated countries which govern themselves with their laws") that are characterized at once by their particularity and by their complexity. Hence the two levels of plurality that Bernard Manin distinguishes: the diversity of particular entities ("external plurality") and the social complexity proper to each ("internal plurality").[31]

## External Plurality

Different countries have different objectives. This is why the political good is plural: there are as many political goods as there are situations in place or time. This leads Montesquieu to reject the idea of a unique good, applicable to all places and times alike. Consequently, he praises Solon: "Solon was asked if the laws he had given to the Athenians were the best; 'I have given them the best laws they could endure,' he replied: this is a fine speech that should be heard by all legislators" (XIX, 21). Montesquieu's implicit criticism is aimed primarily at religious universalism—Catholic in particular—as well as at the religious aims of the colonizers. He thus takes the side of those who wanted to resist conversion: "[W]hen Montezuma persisted in saying that the religion of the Spaniards was good for their country and that of Mexico for his own, he was not saying an absurd thing" (XXIV, 24). But Montesquieu's criticism applies to all universalisms, including the universalist rationalism of the Enlightenment. Condorcet was not mistaken about this. According to him, Montesquieu, in taking interest in the diversity of laws and customs, leaves aside the question of their justice, which can only be universal: "A good law must be good for all men, just as a true proposition is true for all."[32] Montesquieu's pluralism is often interpreted as a form of relativism, which deprives the good of all content, either by reducing it to a matter of mere preference or by rendering it contradictory. This is what leads some to consider Montesquieu to be a sociologist and not a moralist; according to this view, his empirical interest in the diversity of situations overrides his moral preoccupations.

If one can speak of relativism (in the sense of the good being relative to the circumstances of time and place in which it can be judged), it is necessary to note that it is tempered by two sorts of naturalism. All customs can find an explanation, a raison d'être. Notwithstanding, all are not acceptable. There are limits fixed by nature. "I was going to say that it [torture or the question] might be suitable for despotic governments [...] ... But I hear the voice of nature crying out against me" (VI, 17). Therefore, there are universal norms, founded on nature (and grasped by sentiment or reason), but they prohibit or fix limits; they do not prescribe content. As Raymond Aron remarks, "The rational laws of human nature, in Montesquieu, are all conceived in a manner sufficiently abstract so as to exclude the deduction from them of what particular institutions must be, and to authorize the condemnation of certain practices."[33] The condemnation of slavery is a good example of the application of these negative prescriptions. Slavery is against nature (all men are born equal), but it can happen that it exists, and Montesquieu finds "a natural reason" (XV, 7) for it: there are climates that are so hot that men will not work unless forced. As debatable as this reason is (does not Montesquieu add immediately after that in the majority of countries "however arduous the work that the society requires there, everything can be done by freemen"? [XV, 8]), it also provides a limit: this reason only exists in rare climates, excluding any generalization of the measure. Montesquieu is thus able to denounce the projects to extend slavery to Europe that some defended.[34] To explain slavery by the diversity of the climate is thus a way of naturalizing differences, which, having been assigned a specific place, are prevented from being generalized. In the same manner, differences are prevented from hostile encounters. One does not then necessarily find oneself exposed to this "war of the gods," which, for Max Weber, is the necessary consequence of the admission of the plurality of values. This is perhaps also the result of the fact that, for Montesquieu, the different values to which different peoples adhere are not necessarily contradictory. He holds that one of the advantages of development is to put men in contact with one another and to allow them to compare their mores: "great things have resulted from this," remarks Montesquieu (XX, 1). The problem is not so much the encounter of different values, as their authoritarian imposition, as in the case of religious conversions imposed by force.

What allows Montesquieu, finally, to evade relativism (and not only to temper it) is his conception of the political project, proper to each nation. According to him, each state has an object that is particular to it: "Expansion was the object of Rome; war, that of Lacedaemonia; religion, that of the

Jewish laws; commerce, that of Marseilles; public tranquility, that of the laws of China." Montesquieu concludes his enumeration by introducing England (whose constitution he will present): "There is also one nation in the world whose constitution has political liberty for its direct object" (XI, 5). Such a presentation might surprise minds like that of Condorcet. On the one hand, if liberty is to be the object of one single nation, the implication seems to be that liberty cannot be a universal aspiration, which one could qualify as a conservative position. On the other hand, in introducing liberty at the end of an enumeration that includes neutral projects (commerce, public tranquility), as well as dubious projects or even projects fatal to liberty (the expansion at which Rome aimed led to the loss of her political liberty), does not one deprive liberty of all value? It becomes merely a project like any other.

This is certainly the case if one stops at an objective enunciation, made from the exterior. As Montesquieu enumerates them, there is no reason to say that one of these "objects" is worth more than another. But at the same time, these are projects. As such, they are irreducible to one another; the attachment of a nation to them, in and of itself, gives value to them, whatever their objective value. This suffices for Montesquieu to name the tyranny "which is felt when those who govern establish things that run counter to a nation's way of thinking" a "tyranny of opinion" (XIX, 3). A nation's way of thinking is perhaps not good, but one cannot change it in a coercive manner. The good cannot be imposed: this goes to support our contention that Montesquieu does not propose a model to imitate. That there is no uniform situation to which one could apply a uniform model is a further reason. Each state has its proper object, distinct from that of others. It is insufficient, therefore, to suppose that states, or each of their objects, have a univocal intention, such as self-preservation, that it would suffice to render possible. That is Hobbes' solution: the good state is the one capable of guaranteeing the coexistence of liberties; everything that goes beyond security belongs in the private sphere. This is not the case for Montesquieu: the distinction between projects shows, as Bernard Manin writes, that "the idea of happiness or living well that each people forges for itself is an integral part of the political object; it is not confined to the private sphere."[35]

External pluralism is the consequence of the diversity of objects of each state. Out of complexity arises internal pluralism. This is the famous thesis of the distribution of powers, which makes possible the rule of law, the necessary condition of liberty (one is only free with the law). As Eisenmann has demonstrated,[36] this distribution of powers does not effect a rational attribution of competences so much as it aims at a dynamic equilibrium of powers, each counteracting the other: "The form of these three powers should be rest or inaction. But as they are constrained to move by the necessary motion of things, they will be forced to move in concert" (XI, 6). Not only is it a matter of an equilibrium between institutional powers (lower chamber, upper chamber, and the king), but it is also a matter of the social relations among different powers: the people, the nobility, and the king in England, patricians and plebeians in Rome.

## Internal Plurality

Societies are socially differentiated, and this plurality is favorable to liberty. This conception of internal pluralism can be juxtaposed to the thesis that Aristotle defends against Plato: the city does not have as its task to be a unity; it is composed of heterogeneous parts, and each part has different claims to make concerning justice, none of which can be rejected a priori.[37] One finds a similar idea in Machiavelli, who affirms, early in the *Discourses on the First Decade of Titus Livius*, that in Rome the conflict between patricians and plebeians, far from having put liberty in danger, as the historians of Rome claimed, was in fact the surest guarantee ("the guard," says Machiavelli) of liberty.[38] To the merits of plurality, Machiavelli thus adds those of conflict and makes this notion a central part of his republican theory. The thesis of the positive effects of social conflicts in Rome is used again by Montesquieu, against Bossuet this time, in a famous passage of the *Considérations*: "And, as a general rule, every time one sees everyone tranquil in a State which calls itself a republic, one can be assured that liberty does not exist there. What one calls union in a political body is a very equivocal thing. True union is a union of harmony which makes all the parts, as opposed as they appear to us to be, participate in the general good of the society, just as dissonances in music participate in the overall harmony. There can be union in a State in which one thinks one sees only discord, that is to say, a harmony from which results the happiness which alone is true peace."[39] One can thus consider internal pluralism as the heritage that Montesquieu retains from a republican tradition he knows well but in relation to which he shows himself, most often, to be distant or critical.[40]

This conception of the equilibrium of social forces is, for Raymond Aron, what makes it possible to affirm that "the essence of the political philosophy of Montesquieu is liberalism."[41] He emphasizes the "heterogeneous and hierarchical," "aristocratic," that is, strongly inegalitarian dimension of this presentation of the plurality of powers. Indeed, is not this dimension a constant for Montesquieu? "In a State there are always some people who are distinguished by birth, wealth or honors" (XI, 6). Montesquieu's thought is, in this respect, strongly opposed to the values that triumphed after the French Revolution: "He is to no degree a doctrinaire of equality, still less of popular sovereignty. Linking social inequality to the essence of social order, he is very accommodating toward inequality."[42] The fact that Montesquieu finds himself in an ambiguous position with respect to the dominant values of contemporary France could explain certain interpretations. Either one does not mention the social dimension, and one interprets the distribution of powers as a rational attribution of competences. One then attributes to Montesquieu a theory of the "separation of powers." It is this interpretation that is the most widely received, despite the rectifications made to it, starting with that of Eisenmann. Or one pays attention to the social analysis, but one sees in it an indication of Montesquieu's aristocratic or even reactionary positions. This is Althusser's reading of Eisenmann. In both cases, the liberal dimension of Montesquieu's pluralism is misunderstood.

## Plurality of Juridical Regimes

It is perhaps necessary, in order to better apprehend Montesquieu's pluralism, to envisage a third form of it. It is mainly developed in Book XXVI (the book in which Montesquieu affirms the plurality of the political good): Montesquieu distinguishes different domains of law (international, religious, political, civil, domestic) and affirms the necessity, for the legislator, to take into consideration this diversity, not to confuse the different objects. It is another form of internal pluralism, but it does not take into account the diversity of social groups, but rather that of normative domains. To this distinction already established in Book XIX between what depends on the laws and what depends on mores (one must not regulate by laws what belongs in the domain of mores, such as whether or not to have a beard) is added the distinction of the different domains of the law (one must not regulate domestic affairs as if they were political affairs). It is thus a matter of distinguishing normative domains, and the unresolved question is that of the *good* law. Contrary to what Condorcet affirms, Montesquieu is not disinterested when it comes to the question of what is a good law. He envisages it differently from what appears to Condorcet to be the only possible solution.

Whether it is a matter of treating the diversity of facts, or that of norms, the method is the same. The point of departure is the often conflictual diversity of laws and the multiplicity of possible choices for the lawmaker. The objective is to render this diversity intelligible, that is to say, to be able to differentiate between a good and a bad law (or between a good law and one that is less good). The way to achieve this objective is not to reduce diversity to unity (adopting a universal criterion, as does Condorcet, for whom there is only one good law) but to bring order to the diversity by utilizing a plurality of frameworks, what Montesquieu, in this case, calls "principles." Each domain of the law has its principle. That of the law of peoples (what we call "international law") is thus, for example, that "the various nations should do to one another in times of peace the most good possible, and in times of war the least harm possible, without harming their true interests" (I, 3). To make a good law is to understand to which juridical domain it belongs, to consider the principle that governs it, and to conform the formulation of the law to it.

Hence the necessity to not confuse the laws and their different domains of application. The most striking case (Montesquieu begins with this one) is that of the distinction between religious law and political law. If the political law has jurisdiction over the good and acknowledges its plurality and the possibility of its changing, while the religious law presides over the best and desires invariable laws, then to regulate by religious laws what belongs to the domain of political laws can only be harmful (XXVI, 2). But the distinction must be made between different human laws as well. The relations between states are not regulated by any civil law; they are, says Montesquieu, in a "forced state," and thus the law of peoples cannot regulate their relations in the manner that relations between individuals subject to the civil law are regulated within states (XXVI, 20). Thus the principle of the law of peoples has a purely prudential character (to do to one another the least harm in times of war and the most good in times of peace), while the civil laws can command unconditionally. Neither is there any reason to treat the relations between heads of state in the same manner as the relations between individuals: the succession of kings is not determined (when that succession could include an entire country) in the same way as that of individuals (XXVI, 16, 23).

Things would be rather simple if it were enough to distinguish among the different domains and to apply to each the corresponding law. But there are numerous acts to which several laws lay claim. Such is the case with marriage, which is, "of all human acts, the one that is of the most interest to society"; it is thus under the jurisdiction of civil laws,[43] but since it is also considered to be "the object of a particular benediction," it is also under the jurisdiction of religion (XXVI, 13). It is therefore necessary to establish a hierarchy in order to avoid conflicts. Civil law must have priority over religious law. It is a matter of principles: the principle of civil laws is "the general good of society" (XXVI, 9), while religious law is concerned rather with individual cases and is regulated by "purely spiritual ideas" (XXVI, 8). It belongs to human, civil laws (be it political, civil, or domestic law) to regulate what is concerned with earthly life. Another rule subjects civil law to natural law: civil law must not be contrary to natural law (XXVI, 3, 4).

Nevertheless, Montesquieu does not establish a rigid hierarchy that would lead to a fixed order, in which one law is completely subordinated, or even reduced, to the other. Even the religious law preserves a certain independence: Montesquieu acknowledges that it belongs to the "law of religion" to make decisions concerning the indissolubility of marriage[44] (XXVI, 13). But it is especially concerning the relation between natural law and civil law (in the broad sense) that Montesquieu demonstrates his choice in favor of plurality and his rejection of reductionism. For the natural law theorists (like Pufendorf), natural law fixes a framework of obligations, of which political and civil laws are merely particular applications. This is not what Montesquieu thinks: for him, natural law leaves large areas of indetermination, which rely entirely on the competence of political and civil law. This is also the case with respect to the relation between parents and children: "Natural law orders fathers to feed their children, but it does not oblige them to make them their heirs" (XXVI, 6). All inheritance laws are thus under the jurisdiction of the civil law: one cannot judge civil law from the standpoint of the principles of the natural law, which has nothing to say about the matters under the jurisdiction of the civil law. This amounts to leaving a great deal of latitude to political inventiveness, but it also means that the harmony among the principles of different laws is very fragile.

This is certainly true in the case of the Voconian law, a Roman law that "did not permit one to appoint a woman heir, not even one's only daughter" (XXVI, 6). After having alluded to this law in Book XXVI, Montesquieu dedicates nearly the totality of Book XXVII to it (which treats "the origin and revolutions of the Roman laws on inheritance"). As early as Book VI, Montesquieu shows that the civil laws (regulating the relations between individuals) depend on the political laws: the same civil laws do not exist in a monarchy, in a republic, and in a despotic government. There is therefore nothing surprising in the fact that, in Rome, the manner of making wills and their importance depended on the constitution and that wills were a political act, intended to maintain the division of property in a republic, the principle of which was equality. The Voconian law, "made to prevent women from having excessively great wealth" (Book XXVII) by preventing them from becoming heirs, is, from this point of view, a good law, in conformity with the spirit of the Roman laws. Nevertheless, it was continually eluded. Roman fathers spent their time finding ways to get around it and to make their daughters their heirs. Montesquieu explains that this law combatted "natural feelings" (those of fathers for their daughters): "[T]he law sacrificed both the citizen and the man and thought only of the republic" (Book XXVII). We have here the very example of a defective resolution of the conflicts between different normative domains. And one lesson: finally, it is the liberty of individuals that decides. Whatever the validity of a principle (such as that of the Voconian law, the aim of which was the salvation of the republic), it cannot be imposed if it enters into a contradiction with other principles (like those that are at the origin of the moral sentiments of the fathers).

What Montesquieu means by "principles" in Book XXVI are not universal rules (like those that Condorcet had in mind), but finalities (like the good of the society in general for civil law, or the least harm—or the most good according to the situation—for the law of peoples). A good law is a law that satisfies its end. Moral rationality, for Montesquieu, could be considered consequentialist (it aims at maximizing the good); one could thus compare it to utilitarian moral rationality, especially given that the political end is not limited to security for Montesquieu but includes happiness. But while utilitarianism, in assigning itself the rule of achieving the greatest happiness for the greatest number, seeks to maximize an aggregate of individual ends perceived as homogenous,[45] and thus places itself in a unifying reductionist perspective, Montesquieu's consequentialism aims at a qualitative result that does not consist in maximizing one sole end but in harmonizing divergent ends (the Voconian law is not a good law). This is why it does not seem to us that Montesquieu's moral rationality, as consequentialist as it is, can be called "instrumental." It is a matter not only of maximizing effects but also of attaining something that has meaning. Relating laws to their finality is not to grasp a relation of cause and effect but a relation of suitability, which makes it possible to situate an element in a meaningful whole. "Everything is closely linked together" (XIX, 15): one can never isolate a law from its context; one can only compare meaningful wholes among them.

## The War of the Gods Will Not Occur

To acknowledge the plurality of the good exposes one to two types of consequences, which one can consider regrettable: a form of relativism that leads to moral skepticism, on one hand; a confrontational clash of conflicting and competing values—what Max Weber called the "war of the gods," on the other hand. Montesquieu avoids these two consequences. His relativism does not consist in juxtaposing contradictory moral judgments, in the manner in which the skeptical argumentation proceeds (Pascal's "truth on this side of the Pyrenees, error on the other side"), but rather in showing that the good only defines itself *in situ*, in a situation that is characterized by objective circumstances as well as by the project of those who desire to achieve their good. Montesquieu's examination of the plurality of the domains of law, and the principles that govern them, shows that one can assign diverse and even opposite values without subordinating them or reducing them to only one of them. Just as Montesquieu affirms in the *Persian Letters* that "it is not the multiplicity of religions that has produced wars, it is the spirit of intolerance animating the one which believed itself to be dominant" (*Lettres persanes*, LXXXV), one could say that it is not the multiplicity of ends that runs the risk of causing a difficulty but the fact that certain ones are violently imposed as the only true ones.

## Contemporary Pluralism

What can we learn from the liberalism defended by Montesquieu, this liberalism of plurality? It is perhaps not the most widespread form of liberalism. "Liberalism is not necessarily pluralist," concludes Bernard Manin, at the end of his study in which he sets in opposition the political thought of plurality and that of unity.[46] This duality traverses the opposition between the ancients and the moderns (on the side of the monists, one finds Plato as well as Rousseau, and on the side of the pluralists, Aristotle as well as Montesquieu). In modern times, this opposition not only separates theorists of absolute, monarchical, or popular sovereignty, like Hobbes or Rousseau, from a partisan of the limitation of power, like Montesquieu; it also divides liberalism. All liberal thinkers do not share Montesquieu's idea that there are several manners of achieving the political good. For many of them, there exists a unique form, a "constitutional model" apt to achieve liberty.[47] Ironically, it is often thought that Montesquieu made an important contribution to the elaboration of such a model with the English constitution. This shows well to what extent the monist vision has gained ascendance over the pluralist vision.

That political liberty is today recognized as a universal aspiration and that everyone agrees that all the peoples of the world should have access to democracy in no way implies that these goals are to be achieved by the adoption of a unique democratic institutional model. It is against this unitary vision that Amartya Sen raises his voice in an article questioning the way in which many (especially in the United States) conceive of the extension of the democratic model to the entire world: the exportation of an institutional model (electoral procedures and constitutional mechanisms) the origin of which is thought of as European or Western.[48]

In response to this view, Amartya Sen objects that one cannot reduce democracy to mere electoral practices, that the conception of democracy must be widened to include public debate or what John Rawls calls the exercise of "public reason."[49] It is only on this level that one can take into account the participation of citizens in public discussions and the possibility of their influencing political decisions, both necessary conditions to safeguard the diversity of doctrines and their expression in the political domain. Without the dimension of public debate, of its pluralist interactions, we cannot speak of democracy. Now, as soon as we situate ourselves on this level, the idea of a unique model or a purely Western origin can no longer hold up: it is incumbent upon us to take into account the richness and the diversity of the traditions of public debate in different parts of the world (Africa, India, Japan): fifth-century Athens is not the only place where ways of exposing arguments in common and seeking consensus were invented.

Amartya Sen does not cite Montesquieu, and nothing in what he says refers directly to Montesquieu. This is of little importance. His criticism of the imposition of a formal universal, which reveals itself finally to be but a particular view of things (the Western view); this notion that one can only arrive at the universal (democratic liberty) by way of particular situations and traditions; this conviction that to be able to enjoy the political good, a people must make it their own, in accordance with their vision of things; all of these ideas appear to us to be faithful to the spirit of Montesquieu, to the spirit of the liberalism of plurality. External pluralism remains pertinent today.

The contemporary pertinence of internal pluralism is perhaps more difficult to apprehend. What we mean by internal pluralism today, in political terms, is a multiplicity of doctrines, rather than a social diversity; it means relations between individuals rather than between social groups. Now, social groups are what retain Montesquieu's attention: his analysis is not situated on the level of the individual, and he is not particularly interested in the diversity of conceptions of the good within a given country. His conception of internal plurality is social and objective rather than individual and subjective. For this reason, one can call it "sociological." In particular, Montesquieu's presentation of internal pluralism is sociological (from our contemporary point of view) because his analysis does not integrate a normative dimension: Montesquieu's language is that of interest and not rights; he does not in any way moralize his presentation. This allows him to say, for example, that the prerogatives of the nobility in a "free State" are "odious" (XI, 6). What characterizes the current conception of democracy, however, is its inclusion of a normative dimension, in the form of a theory of individual rights.[50] As attuned as he was to the problem of individual liberties, Montesquieu never puts in place a formal structure built around individual rights, in the manner of contemporary political theory.

It is in Rousseau's *Social Contract* that we find such a structure: the political question of this work is that of the equal distribution of rights among free subjects. The individual is at once a methodological and an axiological reference; political reflection includes the normative dimension. From this point of view, contemporary theorists of political liberalism and democracy are much more the heirs of Rousseau than of Montesquieu. However, one can raise a question as to whether such a normative structure does not lead quite easily to a unitary rather than a pluralist vision. This is undoubtedly the case in Rousseau: all intermediary associations (the "cabals," the "partial associations")[51] between individuals and their common or general will are banished; only interindividual differences are taken into account. These, in turn, are neutralized: the general will is formed when each finds in himself what renders him similar to all the others. Doubtless there are other ways besides Rousseau's to conceive of the formation of a common will, starting from this normative structure. It remains true, however, that its individualistic dimension makes it difficult to take differences into account. Understood on an individual level, these differences can only be perceived as preferences, as data that can be observed. Ends cannot be discussed at this level. The reductionist, unitary vision thus prevails: differences become nothing more than particular variations of one sole purpose (interest, self-preservation).

What this study reveals about Montesquieu's normative internal pluralism is that ends can be discussed, and ends can be known. This surely derives from the fact that Montesquieu does not apprehend ends on an individual level but grasps them on a collective level (that of a country or social group) or on an objectifiable level (that of a juridical domain suited to regulate a set of activities). Does not the orientation of the examination of liberty in a pluralist direction lead to the taking into account of a collective or objective dimension in a normative individualistic approach? This could be one of the teachings of Montesquieu's pluralism.

## Notes

1. Albert O. Hirschman, *The Passions and the Interests: Political Arguments for Capitalism before Its Triumph* (Princeton: Princeton University Press, 1977).

2. David Carrithers, "La philosophie pénale de Montesquieu," *Revue Montesquieu* 1 (1997): 39–64.

3. Isaiah Berlin, "Montesquieu" (1955), in *Against the Current: Essays in the History of Ideas* (Oxford: Clarendon Press, 1991), 131.

4. Thomas L. Pangle, *Montesquieu's Philosophy of Liberalism: A Commentary on the Spirit of the Laws* (Chicago: Chicago University Press, 1973).

5. For a critical presentation of the liberal interpretation of Montesquieu, see Céline Spector, *Montesquieu, Pouvoirs, richesses et sociétés* (Paris: PUF, 2004), 19–24.

6. See Thomas Pangle, talk delivered on September 10, 2005 at the Munk Centre, University of Toronto, as part of the conference entitled "Modernity in Question: Montesquieu and His Legacy."

7. Jean-Jacques Rousseau, *Discours sur les sciences et les arts*, part 2: "The ancient political men spoke incessantly of morals and virtue; ours speak only of commerce and money," in *Œuvres complètes* (Paris: Gallimard, Bibliothèque de la Pléiade, 1969), III, 19.

8. Bernard Manin, "Montesquieu, la République et le commerce," *Archives européennes de sociologie* XLII.3 (2001): 573–602.

9. Louis Althusser, *Montesquieu, la politique et l'histoire* (Paris: PUF, 1964), 59.

10. Quentin Skinner, *Liberty before Liberalism* (Cambridge: Cambridge University Press, 1998).

11. Yan Thomas, "Le sujet de droit, la personne et la nature," *Le Débat* 10 (1998): 105.

12. See Charles Larmore, *Modernité et morale* (Paris: PUF, 1993).

13. Berlin, "Montesquieu," *Against the Current*, 157.

14. One finds the same affirmation in Paul Rahe, who speaks of "a unitary principle of political psychology." See his chapter "Forms of Government," in *Montesquieu's*

*Human Science: Essays on the Spirit of the Laws (1748)*, ed. David W. Carrithers, Michael A. Mosher, and Paul A. Rahe (Boston: Rowman & Littlefield, 2001), 100.

15. Bernard Manin, "Montesquieu et la politique moderne," in *Cahiers de philosophie politique de l'Université de Reims* (Bruxelles: Ousia, 1985), 213.

16. Montesquieu, *Défense de L'Esprit des lois*, in *Œuvres complètes II* (Paris: Gallimard, 2000), part II.

17. Raymond Aron, *Les étapes de la pensée sociologique* (Paris: Gallimard, 1967), part I, Les Fondateurs, Charles Louis de Secondat, baron de Montesquieu, 29.

18. Bertrand Binoche, *Introduction à De l'esprit des lois de Montesquieu* (Paris: PUF, 1998).

19. See also *Lettres persanes*, 143.

20. Berlin, "Montesquieu," *Against the Current*, 142.

21. See, for example, the following formulations in Jeremy Bentham: "*Pleasures and Pains the Basis of all the other Entities*" (*A Table of the Springs of Action*, 1815), or, "Nature has placed mankind under the governance of two sovereign masters, *pain* and *pleasure*. It is for them alone to point out what we ought to do, as well as to determine what we shall do" (*An Introduction to the Principles of Morals and Legislation*, 1789, ch. 1).

22. Manin, "Montesquieu et la politique moderne," 166.

23. Ferdinand Galiani, *Dialogues sur le commerce des bleds* (1770), 3rd Dialogue (Paris, ed. Fayard, 1984), 50.

24. Montesquieu, *Défense*, Part II.

25. Ibid.

26. Ibid.

27. J. G. A. Pocock, *The Ancient Constitution and the Feudal Law* (Cambridge: Cambridge University Press, 2nd edition, 1987).

28. Edouard Tillet, *La constitution anglaise, Un modèle politique et institutionnel dans la France des Lumières* (Aix-en-Provence: Presses Universitaires d'Aix-Marseille, 2001).

29. Charles Eisenmann, "L'*Esprit des lois* et la séparation des pouvoirs," *Mélanges Carré de Malberg* (Paris: Sirey, 1933); "La pensée constitutionnelle de Montesquieu," *Bicentenaire de l'Esprit des lois: La pensée politique et constitutionnelle de Montesquieu* (Paris: Sirey, 1952).

30. *Lettres persanes*, 48.

31. Manin, "Montesquieu et la politique moderne," 206–29.

32. Condorcet, *Observations sur le vingt-neuvième livre de L'Esprit des lois* (1780), in Condorcet, *Œuvres Complètes*, (Paris: Firmin-Didot, 1847–1849), I, 378.

33. Aron, *Les étapes de la pensée sociologique*, 65.

34. *The Spirit of Laws*, XV, 9: "Every day one hears it said that it would be good if there were slaves among us." Montesquieu could have had in mind J. F. Melon (*Essai sur le commerce en général*, 1734) and Mably (*Le Droit public en Europe*, 1748; ch. 9 is added in the edition of 1757).

35. Manin, "Montesquieu et la politique moderne," 214.

36. Eisenmann, "L'*Esprit des lois* et la séparation des pouvoirs," and "La pensée constitutionnelle de Montesquieu."

37. Aristotle, *Politics*, book III. See on this subject Bernard Manin, "Montesquieu et la politique moderne," 202–06; Pierre Manent, "La démocratie comme régime et comme religion," in *La pensée politique* no. 1, *Situations de la démocratie* (Paris: Hautes Etudes, Gallimard-Le Seuil, 1996), 62–75.

38. Machiavelli, *Discourses on the First Decade of Titus Livius*, book I, ch. 4, "That the disputes between the people and the Roman Senate made this republic free and powerful."

39. Montesquieu, *Considérations sur les causes de la grandeur et de la décadence des Romains*, ch. 9.

40. Catherine Larrère, "République et démocratie," Acts of the Colloquium "République et démocratie aujourd'hui," organized by the Cercle Clermontois de Philosophie Politique, Clermont-Ferrand, May 21–22, 1993, in *Les Annales de Clermont*-Ferrand, 32 (Clermont-Ferrand: Les Presses Universitaires de la Faculté de droit de Clermont-Ferrand, 1996), 13–31.

41. Raymond Aron, *Les étapes de la pensée sociologique*, 63.

42. Ibid., 62.

43. Throughout Book XXVI, Montesquieu speaks of civil laws in two different senses. On one hand, civil laws designate laws instituted by human beings in opposition to natural law and religious law. On the other hand, civil law is distinct from political law and domestic law: political law deals with the attribution of political power and the way in which subjects are subject to it; civil law deals with the relations between individuals who are subject to the law, while "domestic law" deals with relations among family members.

44. The interpretation of this passage is, however, controversial. How could Montesquieu, a partisan of divorce, leave it to the Church to decide? Two editors of *The Spirit of Laws* disagree on this point: Brèthe de la Gressaye thinks that Montesquieu is hostile to the secularization of marriage, while Robert Derathé considers him to be favorable to the institution of civil marriage, distinct from religious marriage (see Robert Derathé's edition of *De l'esprit des lois* [Paris: Garnier, 1973], vol. II, 537).

45. This is the notion put forward by Bentham according to which all pleasures have the same value, a notion summarized in the formulation, "Prejudice apart, the game of push-pin is of equal value with the arts and sciences of music and poetry. If the game of push-pin furnish more pleasure, it is more valuable than either" (*The Rationale of Reward* [London, 1825], book III, ch. 1). In his essay, "Bentham," John Stuart Mill paraphrases this formulation: "quantity of pleasure being equal, push-pin is as good as poetry."

46. Manin, "Montesquieu et la politique moderne," 214, 224.

47. Manin cites Hayek on this subject, "Montesquieu et la politique moderne," 213.

48. Amartya Sen, "Democracy and Its Global Roots: Why Democratization Is Not the Same as Westernization," *New Republic* 6 (2003): 28–35.

49. John Rawls, lecture 6, "The Idea of Public Reason," in *Political Liberalism* (New York: Columbia University Press, 1993), 212–54.

50. Hence Jürgen Habermas's criticism that sociological analyses of contemporary democracies ignore their normative dimension. See Jürgen Habermas, *Between Facts and Norms: Contributions to a Discourse Theory of Law and Democracy* (1992) (Cambridge: MIT Press, 1998), particularly chs. 7 and 8.

51. Rousseau, *Du Contrat social*, Book II, ch. 2.

# Bibliography

Abrams, Floyd. *Speaking Freely, Trials of the First Amendment*. New York: Viking Penguin, 2005.
Adams, John. "Novanglus; or a History of Dispute with America." In *The Revolutionary Writings of John Adams*, ed. Bradley Thompson. Indianapolis: Liberty Fund, 2000.
Alter, Karen. *Establishing the Supremacy of European Law: The Making of an International Rule of Law in Europe*. Oxford: Oxford University Press, 2001.
Althusser, L. *Montesquieu, la politique et l'histoire*. Paris: PUF, 1964.
Arendt, Hannah. *Between Past and Future: Six Exercises in Political Thought*. Cleveland and New York: Meridian Books, 1963.
———. *The Human Condition*. Chicago: University of Chicago Press, 1958.
———. *Origins of Totalitarianism*. New York: Harcourt, Brace, 1951.
Aristotle. *Nicomachean Ethics*. Trans. J. Tricot. Paris: Vrin, 1987.
———. *The Politics*. Trans. and ed. Ernest Barker. Oxford: Oxford University Press, 1958.
Aron, Raymond. *Les étapes de la pensée sociologique*. Paris: Gallimard, 1967.
Ashworth, John. "The Relation between Capitalism and Humanitarianism." *American Historical Review* 92 (1987): 813–28.
Baker, Keith Michael. *Inventing the French Revolution*. Cambridge: Cambridge University Press, 1990.
Baranger, Denis. *Parlementarisme des origines*. Paris: PUF, 1999.
Barber, Benjamin R. *Fear's Empire: War, Terrorism and Democracy*. New York: Norton, 2003.
Barker, Ernest "A Huguenot Theory of Politics." *Church, State, and Study*. London: Methuen, 1930.
Baron d'Holbach. *Système social*. Paris: Fayard, 1994.
Bartlett, Robert C. *The Idea of Enlightenment: A Post-mortem*. Toronto: University of Toronto Press, 2001.
Bayle, Pierre. *Pensées diverses sur la comète*, ed. P. Rétat. Paris: Nizet, 1984.
Bazzoli, Laure. *L'économie politique de John R. Commons. Essai sur l'institutionnalisme en sciences sociales*. Paris: L'Harmattan, 1999.

Benítez, M. "Montesquieu, Fréret et les remarques tirées des entretiens avec Hoangh." *Actes du colloque de Bordeaux (1998)*. Bordeaux: Académie nationale des sciences, belles-lettres et arts de Bordeaux, 1999.

Benrekassa, G. "De Montesquieu à Benjamin Constant: La fin des Lumières?" *Dix-Huitième Siècle* 21 (1989): 117–33.

Bentham, Jeremy. *Introduction to the Principles of Morals and Legislation (1789)*. London: W. Pickering, 1823.

———. "Pleasures and Pains the Basis of All the Other Entities." *A Table of the Springs of Action*. London: R. and A. Taylor, 1817.

———. *The Rationale of Reward*. London: Robert Heward, 1830.

Berger, Peter. "On the Obsolescence of the Concept of Honor." In *Revisions: Changing Perspectives on Moral Philosophy*, eds. S. Hauerwas and A. MacIntyre. Notre Dame: University of Notre Dame Press, 1983.

Berlet, Charles. *Les Provinces au XVIIIe siècle et leur division en departments*. Paris: Bloud, 1913.

Berlin, Isaiah. "Deux conceptions de la liberté." *Eloge de la liberté*. Trans. J. Carnaud and J. Lahana. Paris: Calmann-Lévy, 1988.

———. "Montesquieu." *A contre-courant*. Trans. A. Berelowitch. Paris: Albin Michel, 1988.

———. "Montesquieu." *Against the Current: Essays in the History of Ideas*. Oxford: Clarendon Press, 1991 (1955).

———. "Two Concepts of Liberty." *Four Essays on Liberty*. Oxford: Oxford University Press, 1969.

Bernard, Jean Frédéric. *Recueil des Voyages au Nord contenant divers mémoires très utiles au commerce et à la navigation*. Paris: J. F. Bernard, 1725–38.

Bernier, François. *Voyages*. Amsterdam: Paul Marret, 1710.

Beyer, C.-J. "Montesquieu et la censure religieuse de *L'Esprit des lois*." *Revue des Sciences Humaines* (1953): 105–31.

Bickel, Alexander. *The Least Dangerous Branch: The Supreme Court at the Bar of Politics*. Indianapolis, IN: Bobbs-Merrill, 1962.

Binoche, Bertrand. *Introduction à De l'esprit des lois de Montesquieu*. Paris: PUF, 1998.

Birnbaum, Pierre. *The Idea of France*. Trans. M. B. DeBevoise. New York: Hill & Wang, 2001, original French pub. 1998.

Blackell, Mark. "Symptoms of Democracy: Ambivalence and Its Limits in Modern Liberal Conceptions of the Liberal Democratic Bond." Ph.D. diss., York University, 2004.

Blackstone, William. *Commentaries on the Laws of England (1765–1769)*. Chicago: University of Chicago Press, 1979.

Bloom, Allan. *Love and Friendship*. New York: Simon & Schuster, 1993.

Boesche, Roger. "Why Did Tocqueville Think a Successful Revolution was Impossible?" In *Liberty, Equality, Democracy*, ed. Eduardo Nolla. New York: New York University Press, 1992.

Boltanski, Luc, and Laurent Thévenot. *De la justification. Les économies de la grandeur*. Paris: Gallimard, 1991.

Bonno, Gabriel. *La Constitution britannique devant l'opinion française de Montesquieu à Bonaparte*. Paris: Champion, 1932.

Bork, Robert H. *Coercing Virtue: The Worldwide Rule of Judges*. Toronto: Vintage Canada, 2002.
———. *The Tempting of America: The Political Seduction of the Law*. New York: Free Press, 1990.
Braun, Stefan. "Freedom of Expression and Hate Propaganda Laws: Striking a Balance in Canadian Democracy." Ph.D. diss., York University, 2000.
Burke, Edmund. *Reflections on the Revolution in France*. Ed. J. G. A. Pocock. Indianapolis and Cambridge: Hackett Publishing, 1987.
Burton, John Hill. *The Life and Correspondence of David Hume*. Edinburgh: W. Tait, 1846.
Cairns, Alan C. *Disruptions: Constitutional Struggles from the Charter to Meech Lake*. Ed. Douglas E. Williams. Toronto: McClelland & Stewart, 1991.
Cambiano, G. *Polis. Histoire d'un modèle politique*. Trans. S. Fermigier. Paris: Aubier, 2003.
Carcassonne, E. "La Chine dans *L'Esprit des lois*." *Revue d'histoire littéraire de la France* (1924): 193–205.
Carrese, Paul. *The Cloaking of Power: Montesquieu, Blackstone, and the Rise of Judicial Activism*. Chicago: University of Chicago Press, 2003.
Carrithers, David, Michael Mosher, and Paul Rahe, eds. "Introduction." *The Spirit of Laws by Montesquieu*. Berkeley: University of California Press, 1977.
———. "Montesquieu's Philosophy of History." *Journal of the History of Ideas* 47.1 (1986): 61–80.
———. *Montesquieu's Science of Politics*. Lanham, MD: Rowman & Littlefield, 2001.
———. "Not So Virtuous Republics: Montesquieu, Venice, and the Theory of Aristocratic Republicanism." *Journal of the History of Ideas* 52 (1991): 245–68.
———. "La philosophie pénale de Montesquieu." *Revue Montesquieu* 1 (1997), 39–64.
Carrithers, David, and Patrick Coleman, eds. *Montesquieu's Spirit of Modernity*. Oxford: Voltaire Foundation, 2002.
Cassirer, Ernst. *The Philosophy of the Enlightenment*. Boston: Beacon Press, 1960.
Chardin, Jean. *Voyages de Mr. le Chevalier Chardin, en Perse, et autres lieux de l'Orient*. Amsterdam: Delorme, 1711.
Chinard, Gilbert. *Jefferson et les Ideologues*. Paris: Les Presses Universitaires de France, 1925.
———. "Montesquieu's Historical Pessimism." In *Studies in the History of Culture*. Menasha, WI: American Council of Learned Societies, 1942.
Clayton, Cornel, and Howard Gillman, eds. *Supreme Court Decision-Making: New Institutionalist Approaches*. Chicago: University of Chicago Press, 1999.
Coleman, Patrick, and David Carrithers, eds. *Montesquieu and the Spirit of Modernity*. Oxford: Voltaire Foundation, 2002.
Condorcet, Jean-Antoine-Nicolas de Caritat. *Observations sur le vingt-neuvième livre de L'Esprit des lois* (1780). *Œuvres Complètes*, Vol. I. Paris: Firmin-Didot, 1847–1849.
Constant, Benjamin. *De l'Esprit de conquête et de l'usurpation dans leurs rapports avec la civilisation européene*. Paris: GF-Flammanon, 1986.
Constant, Benjamin. *Oeuvres*. Ed. Alfred Roulin. Paris: Gallimard, 1957.
Cooter, Robert. *The Strategic Constitution*. Princeton: Princeton University Press, 2000.

Corwin, Edward. "The 'Higher Law' Background of American Constitutional Law." *Harvard Law Review* 42 (1928–29): 149–85, 365–409.
Cotler, Irwin. "Hate Speech, Equality, and Harm under the Charter: Towards a Jurisprudence of Human Dignity for a 'Free and Democratic Society.' " In *The Canadian Charter of Rights and Freedoms*, eds. G. A. Beaudoin and E. Mendes. Toronto: Carswell, 1996.
Cotta, Sergio. "L'Idée de parti dans la philosophie politiquue de Montesquieu." *Actes du Congrès Montesquieu réuni à Bordeaux du 23 au 26 mai 1955*. Bordeaux: Delmas, 1956.
Courtney, C. "L'Image de l'Angleterre dans *L'Esprit des lois*." *Actes du Colloque international tenu à Bordeaux, du 3 au 6 décembre 1998 pour commémorer le 250ème anniversaire de la parution de L'Esprit des lois*. Bordeaux: Académie des Sciences, Belles-Lettres et Arts, 1999.
———. "Montesquieu and the Problem of *la diversité*." In *Enlightenment Essays in Memory of Robert Shackleton*, eds. Giles Barber and C. Courtney. Oxford: Voltaire Foundation, 1988.
Courtois, J.-P. *Inflexions de la rationalité dans "L'Esprit des lois."* Paris: PUF, 1999.
Craiutu, Aurelian. *Liberalism under Siege: The Political Thought of the French Doctrinaires*. Lanham, MD: Lexington Books, 2003.
d'Iribane, Phillipe. *La Logique de l'honneur: Gestion des entreprises et traditions nationales*. Paris: Seuil, 1989.
Dahl, Robert. "Decision-Making in a Democracy: The Supreme Court as a National Policy-Maker." *Journal of Public Law* 6 (1957): 279–95.
Dallmayr, Fred. "The Law of Peoples: Civilizing Humanity." *Peace Talks: Who Will Listen?* Notre Dame, IN: University of Notre Dame Press, 2004.
———. "Truth and Difference: Some Lessons from Herder." In *Alternative Visions: Paths in the Global Village*. Lanham, MD: Rowman & Littlefield, 1998.
Dalrymple, John. *An Essay towards a General History of Feudal Property in Great Britain*. Littleton CO: Fred Rothman, 1979, 1758.
Dampier, William. *New Voyage around the World*. London: J. Knapton, 1699.
de Casabianca, Denis. *Le sens de l'esprit. Les sciences et les arts: formation du regard dans "L'Esprit des lois."* Ph.D. diss., Université d'Aix-Marseille I, 2002.
de la Porte, Fr. Joseph. *Observations sur la littérature moderne*. Amsterdam: Pierre Mortier, 1750, III, art. V, 73–96. Published also as *Observations sur "L'Esprit des lois."* Amsterdam: Pierre Mortier, 1751.
de Montluc, Blaise. *Commentaires*. Paris: A. Picard, 1911.
de Tracy, Destutt. *Commentaire de L'Esprit des lois (1819)*. Caen: Centre de philosophie politique et juridique de l'Université de Caen, 1992.
———. *A Commentary and Review of Montesquieu's* The Spirit of the Laws. Trans. Thomas Jefferson. New York: Burt Franklin 1969, 1811.
Descartes, Rene. *The Philosophical Works of Descartes*. Trans. Elizabeth S. Haldane and G.R.T. Ross. Cambridge: Cambridge University Press, 1972, 1911.
Desgraves, Louis. *Inventaire des documents manuscrits des fonds Montesquieu de la bibliothèque municipale de Bordeaux*. Geneva: Droz, 1998.
Dodds, Muriel. *Les Récits de voyages, sources de* L'Esprit des lois *de Montesquieu*. Paris: Honoré Champion, 1929.

Dresher, Seymour. "Foreward." In *Tocqueville and the French*, ed. Françoise Mélonio. Trans. Beth G. Raps. Charlottesville: University Press of Virginia, 1998.
Du Halde, Jean-Baptiste, ed. *Description de la Chine*. Paris: G. Lemercier, 1735.
———. *Lettres édifiantes et curieuses écrites des missions étrangères par quelques missionnaires de la Compagnie de Jesus*. Paris: s.n., 1703.
Du Cerceau, Jean Antoine, *Histoire de la revolution de Perse*. Paris: Briasson, 1728.
Durkheim, Emile. *The Division of Labor in Society*. New York: Free Press, 1964, 1893.
———. *Montesquieu and Rousseau: Forerunners of Sociology*. Ann Arbor, MI: University of Michigan Press, 1960, 1892.
Dworkin, Ronald. *Freedom's Law*. Cambridge, MA: Harvard University Press. 1996.
———. "Liberalism." *A Matter of Principle*. Cambridge, MA: Harvard University Press, 1983.
Echeverria, Durand. *The Maupeou Revolution. A Study in the History of Libertarianism France, 1770–1774*. Baton Rouge: Louisiana State University Press, 1985.
Ehrard, Jean. *L'esprit des mots. Montesquieu en lui-même et parmi les siens*. Geneva: Droz, 1998.
———. "Montesquieu dans *Le Monde* en 1998." *Revue Montesquieu* 3 (1999): 99–108.
———. "Montesquieu dans *Le Monde* en 1999." *Revue Montesquieu* 4 (2000): 115–23.
———. "Montesquieu dans *Le Monde* en 2000." *Revue Montesquieu* 5 (2001): 147–53.
———. "Montesquieu dans *Le Monde* en 2001." *Revue Montesquieu* 6 (2002): 59–67.
———. "Montesquieu dans *Le Monde* en 2002." *Revue Montesquieu* 7 (2003–2004): 159–67.
———. "Montesquieu dans les débats politiques français d'aujourd'hui." *Studies on Voltaire and the Eighteenth Century*. Oxford: Voltaire Foundation, 2003.
———, ed. *Montesquieu, l'Etat et la religion. Actes du colloque à Sophie*. Paris: Société Montesquieu, 2005.
Ehrenberg, Alain. *La Fatigue d'être soi*. Paris: Odile Jacob, 1998.
Eisenmann, Charles. "*L'Esprit des lois* et la séparation des pouvoirs." In *Mélanges Carré de Malberg*. Paris: Sirey, 1933.
———. "La pensée constitutionnelle de Montesquieu." In *La Pensée politique et constitutionnelle de Montesquieu*. Paris: Sirey, 1952.
Eisenstadt, S. N. *Modernization: Protest and Change*. Englewood Cliffs, NJ: Prentice-Hall, 1966.
———, ed. *Readings in Social Evolution and Development*. Oxford: Pergamon Press, 1970.
Ely, John Hart. *On Constitutional Ground*. Princeton: Princeton University Press, 1996.
Epstein, Lee, and Jack Knight. *The Choices Justices Make*. Washington, DC: CQ Press, 1998.
———. "Towards a Strategic Revolution in Judicial Politics: A Look Back, a Look Ahead." *Political Research Quarterly* 53 (2000): 625–61.
Epstein, Lee, et al. "The Role of Constitutional Courts in the Establishment and Maintenance of Democratic Systems of Government." *Law & Society Review* 35 (2001): 117–63.
Eskridge, William N. "Reneging on History? Playing the Court/Congress/President Civil Rights Game." *California Law Review* 79 (1991): 613–84.

Espiell, M. Gros. "Le principe de la division des pouvoirs, la Révolution d'émancipation latino-américaine et le droit constitutionnel de l'Uruguay." *Revue Montesquieu* 5 (2001): 93–124.

Etiemble, René. *Les Jésuites en Chine. La querelle des rites (1552–1772)*. Paris: R. Julliard, 1966.

Fatica, Michele. "Le fonti orali della sinofobia di Ch.-L. Secondat de Montesquieu." In *L'Europe de Montesquieu, Cahiers Montesquieu*, 4, eds. M. G. Bottaro Palumbo and A. Postigliola. Napoli-Oxford: Liguori-Voltaire Foundation, 1995.

Felice, D. "Voltaire lettore e critico dell'*Esprit des lois*." *Oppressione e libertà*. Pisa: ETS, 2000.

Ferguson, Adam. *An Essay on the History of Civil Society* (1767). Ed. Duncan Forbes. Edinburgh: Edinburgh University Press, 1966.

———. *Principles of Moral and Political Science*. Edinburgh: W. Creech, 1792.

Fletcher, F. T. H. *Montesquieu and English Politics (1750–1800)*. London: Arnold, 1939.

Fontaine de la Roche, Jacques. "Examen critique de *L'Esprit des lois*." in *Nouvelles ecclésiastiques* 9 and 16 (1749).

Fontenelle. "Dialogue entre Charles Quint et Erasme." *Dialogues des morts anciens et modernes (1683)*. Paris: Fayard, 1990.

Franklin, Julian H. "Sovereignty and the Mixed Constitution: Bodin and His Critics." In *The Cambridge History of Political Thought 1450–1700*, ed. J. H. Burns. Cambridge: Cambridge University Press, 1991.

Friedrich, Carl J. *The Philosophy of Hegel*. New York: Random House/Modern Library, 1954.

Furet, François. "The Intellectual Origins of Tocqueville's Thought." *The Tocqueville Review/La Revue Tocqueville* 26.1 (2005): 122.

———. *Interpreting the French Revolution*. Trans. Elborg Forster. Cambridge: Cambridge University Press, 1981.

Gadamer, Hans-Georg. "On the Possibility of a Philosophical Ethics." In *Hermeneutics, Religion, and Ethics*. Trans. Joel Weinsheimer. New Haven, CT: Yale University Press, 1999.

Galiani, Ferdinand. *Dialogues sur le commerce des bleds* (1770), 3rd Dialogue. Paris: Fayard, 1984.

Gannett Jr., Robert T. *Tocqueville Unveiled: The Historian and His Sources for the Old Regime and the Revolution*. Chicago: University of Chicago Press, 2003.

Gaonkar, Dilip, ed. *Alternative Modernities*. Durham, NC: Duke University Press, 2001.

Gargan, Edward. *De Tocqueville*. New York: Hillary House, 1965.

Gates, Henry Louis, Jr. "War of Words: Critical Race Theory and the First Amendment." In *Speaking of Race, Speaking of Sex: Hate Speech, Civil Rights, and Civil Liberties*, eds. H. L. Gates, Jr., A. Griffin, D.E. Lively, R. C. Post, W. B. Rubenstein, and N. Strossen. New York: New York University Press, 1994.

Gatrell, V. A. C. *The Hanging Tree: Execution and the English People, 1770–1868*. Oxford: Oxford University Press, 1994.

Gautier, Claude. *L'Invention de la société civile*. Paris: PUF, 1993.

Ghazi, Abu'l. *Histoire généalogique des Tatars traduite du Manuscript Tartare d'Abulgasi Bayadur Chan*, par D*** [i.e., Bentinck]. Leyde: Abraham Kallewier, 1726.

Gibbon, Edward. *An Essay on the Study of Literature*. London: T. Beckett and P.A. De Hondt, 1764.

Ginsburg, Tom. *Judicial Review in New Democracies: Constitutional Courts in Asian Cases*. Cambridge: Cambridge University Press, 2003.

Girard d'Albissin, Nelly. *Un précurseur de Montesquieu: Rapin Thoyras, premier historien français des institutions anglaises*. Paris: Klincksieck, 1969.

Graber. Mark A. "Constitutional Politics and Constitutional Theory: A Misunderstood and Neglected Relationship." *Law & Social Inquiry* 27 (2002): 309–38.

Graziadei, Michele. "The Functionalist Heritage." In *Comparative Legal Studies: Traditions and Transitions*, eds. Pierre Legrand and Roderick Munday. Cambridge: Cambridge University Press, 2003.

Greene, Ian. *The Charter of Rights*. Toronto: Lorimer, 1989.

Grosrichard, Alain. *Structure du sérail. La fiction du despotisme asiatique dans l'Occident classique*. Paris: Seuil, 1979.

Gunn, J. A. W. *Queen of the World: Opinion in the Public Life of France from the Renaissance to the Revolution*. Oxford: Voltaire Foundation, 1995.

Gwyn, William B. *The Meaning of the Separation of Powers*. New Orleans: Tulane University; The Hague: Nijhoff, 1965.

Haakonssen, Knud. "Dugald Stewart and the Science of a Legislator." In *Natural Law and Moral Philosophy: From Grotius to the Scottish Enlightenment*. Cambridge: Cambridge University Press, 1996.

Habermas, Jürgen. *Between Facts and Norms: Contributions to a Discourse Theory of Law and Democracy* (1992). Cambridge, MA: MIT Press, 1998.

Hahm, Chaihark, and Daniel A. Bell, eds. *The Politics of Affective Relations: East Asia and Beyond*. Lanham, MD: Lexington Books, 2004.

Hardt, Michael, and Antonio Negri. *Empire*. Cambridge, MA: Harvard University Press, 2000.

Haskell, Thomas. "Capitalism and the Origins of the Humanitarian Sensibility." *American Historical Review* 90 (1985): 339–61, 547–66.

Hathaway. Oona. "Path Dependence in the Law: The Course and Pattern of Change in a Common Law Legal System." *Iowa Law Review* 86 (2001): 601ff.

Hegel. *Hegel's Philosophy of Right*. Trans. T. M. Knox. Oxford and New York: Oxford University Press, 1967.

Heinrichs, Terry. "Censorship as Free Speech! Free Expression Values and the Logic of Silencing in R. v. Keegstra." *Albany Law Review* 36.4 (1988): 337–70.

———. "'Gitlow Redux: 'Bad Tendencies' in the Great White North." *The Wayne Law Review* 48.3 (2002): 1146–53.

Helmke, Gretchen. "The Logic of Strategic Defection: Court-Executive Relations in Argentina under Dictatorship and Democracy." *American Political Science Review* 96 (2002): 291–303.

Hirschl, Ran. "On the Blurred Methodological Matrix of Comparative Constitutional Law." In *The Migration of Constitutional Ideas*, ed. Sujit Choudhry. Cambridge: Cambridge University Press, 2006.

———. "The Question of Case Selection in Comparative Constitutional Law." *American Journal of Comparative Law* 53 (2005), 125–55.

———. *Towards Juristocracy: The Origins and Consequences of the New Constitutionalism*. Cambridge: Harvard University Press, 2004.

Hirschman, Albert O. *The Passions and the Interests: Political Arguments for Capitalism before Its Triumph*. Princeton: Princeton University Press, 1977. [Translated as *Les Passions et les Intérêts*. Trans. Andler (Paris: PUF, 1997)].

Hochard, Claudine. "La compassion comme amour social et politique de l'autre au XVIIIème siècle." In *La Solidarité: Un Sentiment Républicain?* ed. Jacques Chevallier. Paris: PUF, 1992.

Hofstadter, Richard. *The Idea of a Party System: The Rise of Legitimate Opposition in the United States, 1780–1840*. Berkeley: University of California Press, 1969.

Howard, Charles. "Letter of 3 February 1730 to the earl of Carlisle." *The Manuscripts of the Earl of Carlisle*. London: Historical Manuscripts Commission, 1897, Fifteenth Report, Appendix, part VI.

Hulliung, Mark. *Montesquieu and the Old Regime*. Berkeley: University of California Press, 1976.

———. *The Social Contract in America*. Lawrence: University Press of Kansas, 2007.

Hume, David. *The Letters of David Hume*. Ed. J. Y. T. Greig. Oxford: Clarendon Press, 1932.

———. "Of the Populousness of Ancient Nations." In *Political Discourses*. Edinburgh: A. Kincaid and A. Donaldson, 1752.

———. *Political Essays*. Ed. Knud Haakonssen. Cambridge: Cambridge University Press, 1994.

Hume, David, Thomas Hill Green, and Thomas Hodge Grose. *An Enquiry concerning the Principles of Morals*. London: Scientia Verlag, 1964.

Jacobsohn, Gary. *The Wheel of Law*. Princeton: Princeton University Press, 2003.

Jardin, André. *Tocqueville: A Biography*. Trans. Lydia Davis. Baltimore, MD: Johns Hopkins University Press, 1998.

Jones, Peter. *Hume's Sentiments: Their Ciceronian and French Context*. Edinburgh: Edinburgh University Press, 1982.

Jouanna, A. *Le Devoir de révolte*. Paris: Fayard, 1989.

Juppé, A. *Montesquieu le moderne*. Paris: Perrin-Grasset, 1999.

Kaempfer, Engelbert. *Historia imperii japonici*. La Haye: P. Gosse and J. Neaulme, 1729.

Kames, Lord Henry Homes. *Essays on the Principles of Morality and Natural Religion*. Edinburgh: G. Hamilton and J. Balfour, 1751.

———. *Essays upon Several Subjects concerning British Antiquities*. Edinburgh: A. Kincaid, 1747.

———. *Historical Law Tracts*. Edinburgh: A. Kincaid, 1758.

———. *Sketches of the History of Man*. Edinburgh: Creech, 1774.

Katz, Stanley. "Constitutionalism, Contestation and Civil Society." *Common Knowledge* 8.2 (2002): 287–303.

Kelly, Christopher. *Rousseau as Author: Consecrating One's Life to the Truth*. Chicago: University of Chicago Press, 2003.

Kemp, Betty. *King and Commons, 1660–1832*. London: Macmillan, 1957.

Keohane, N. O. "Virtuous Republics and Glorious Monarchies: Two Models in Montesquieu's Political Thought." *Political Studies* 20 (1972): 383–96.

———. "The President's English: Montesquieu in America." *Political Science Reviewer* 6 (1976): 355–87.

Kingdon, Robert. "Calvinism and Resistance Theory, 1550–1580." In *The Cambridge History of Political Thought 1450–1700*, ed. J. H. Burns. Cambridge: Cambridge University Press, 1991.

Kingston, Rebecca E. "L'Intérêt et le bien public dans le discours du Parlement de Bordeaux." In *Le Temps de Montesquieu*, eds. C. Volpilhac-Auger and M. Porret. Geneva: Droz, 2002.

———. *Montesquieu and the Parlement of Bordeaux*. Geneva: Librairie Droz, 1996.

Kintzler, Catherine. "Condorcet, critique de Montesquieu et de Rousseau." *Bulletin de la Société Montesquieu* 6 (1994): 10–31.

Kramer, Larry. *The People Themselves: Popular Constitutionalism and Judicial Review*. Oxford: Oxford University Press, 2004.

Krause, Sharon. *Liberalism with Honor*. Cambridge, MA: Harvard University Press, 2002.

———. "The Politics of Distinction and Disobedience: Honor and the Defense of Liberty in Montesquieu." *Polity* 31.3 (1999): 469–99.

———. "The Spirit of Separate Powers in Montesquieu." *The Review of Politics* 62 (2002): 231–65.

Kritzer, Herbert. "Martin Shapiro: Anticipating the New Institutionalism." In *The Pioneers of Judicial Behavior*, ed. Nancy Maveety. Ann Arbor: University of Michigan Press, 2003.

La Loubère. *Du royaume de Siam*. Paris: Coignard, 1691.

La Mothe le Vayer. "Dialogue traitant de la politique sceptiquement." *Dialogues faits à l'imitation des anciens, 1630–1631*. Paris: Fayard, 1988.

La Porta, Rafael, et al. "Law and Finance." *Journal of Political Economy* 106 (1998): 1113–55.

———. "The Quality of Government." *Journal of Law, Economics and Organization* 15 (1999): 222–79.

Labrousse, Elisabeth. *Pierre Bayle: Heterodoxie et Rigorisme*. The Hague: Martinus Nijhoff, 1964.

Lambert, Jean-Claude. *Tocqueville and the Two Democracies*. Trans. A. Goldhammer. Cambridge, MA: Harvard University Press, 1989.

Landi, Lando. *L'Inghilterra e il pensiero politico di Montesquieu*. Padova: Cedam, 1981.

Landry-Deron, Isabelle. *La Preuve par la Chine. La Description de J.-B. Du Halde, Jésuite, 1735*. Paris: Éditions de l'EHESS, 2002.

Lao tzu. *The Way of Life according to Lao tzu*. Trans. Witter Bynner. New York: Periger Books, 1972.

Larmore, Charles. *Modernité et morale*. Paris: PUF, 1993.

Larrère, Catherine. *Actualité de Montesquieu*. Paris: Presses de Sciences Po, 1999.

———. "Introduction to the *Réflexions sur la monarchie universelle* (1734)." In *Œuvres completes*, vol. II. Oxford: Voltaire Foundation, 2000.

———. "Montesquieu: L'éclipse de la souveraineté." In *Penser la Souveraineté*, eds. Gian-Mario M. Cazzaniga and Yves-Charles Zarka. Paris: Vrin, 2002.

———. "République et démocratie." Actes du colloque République et démocratie aujourd'hui." Clermont-Ferrand, 21–22 May 1993. *Les Annales de Clermont-Ferrand*, vol. 32. Clermont-Ferrand: Les Presses Universitaires de la Faculté de droit de Clermont-Ferrand, 1996.

———. "Les Typologies des gouvernements chez Montesquieu." *Textes et documents*. Clermont-Ferrand: Faculté des lettres et sciences humaines de Clermont-Ferrand, 1979; reprinted in the *Revue Montesquieu* 5 (2001): 157–72.

LaSelva, Samuel V. "Pluralism and Hate: Freedom, Censorship, and the Canadian Identity." In *Interpreting Censorship in Canada*, eds. K. Peterson and A. Hutchinson. Toronto: University of Toronto Press, 1999.

Lash, Scott. *Another Modernity, a Different Rationality*. Oxford: Blackwell, 1999.

Lasser, Mitchel. *Judicial Deliberations: A Comparative Analysis of Judicial Transparency and Legitimacy*. Oxford: Oxford University Press, 2004.

Launay, Robert. "Montesquieu: The Specter of Despotism and the Origins of Comparative Law." In *Rethinking the Masters of Comparative Law*, ed. Annelise Riles. Oxford: Hart Publishing, 2001.

Lehmann, William. *John Millar of Glasgow*. Cambridge: Cambridge University Press: 1960.

Leibniz. *Discours de métaphysique*. Trans. G. Le Roy. Paris: Vrin, 1988.

———. *Nouveaux Essais sur l'entendement humain*. Paris: Flammarion, 1990.

Lipset, Seymour Martin. *Continental Divide: The Values and Institutions of the United States and Canada*. New York: Routledge, 1991.

Lloyd, Howell A. "Constitutionalism." In *The Cambridge History of Political Thought 1450–1700*, ed. J. H. Burns. Cambridge: Cambridge University Press, 1991.

Lowenthal, D. "Montesquieu." In *Histoire de la philosophie politique*. Trans. O. Sedeyn. Paris: PUF, 1994.

Luhmann, Niklas. *A Sociological Theory of Law*. London: Routledge, 1985.

Lynch, A. J. "Montesquieu's Ecclesiastical Critics." *Journal of the History of Ideas* 38 (1977): 487–500.

Mably, abbé de. *Le Droit public en Europe*. Amsterdam: Meynard Uytwerf, 1748.

MacIntyre, Alisdair. *After Virtue: A Study in Moral Theory*. Notre Dame, IN: University of Notre Dame, 1997.

———. *Whose Justice? Which Rationality?* Notre Dame, IN: University of Notre Dame, 1989.

MacKinnon, Catharine. *Only Words*. Cambridge, MA: Harvard University Press, 1993.

Madison, James. *The Debates in the Several State Conventions on the Adoption of the Federal Constitution*. Ed. Jonathan Elliot, vol. 3. Philadelphia: Lippincott, 1836.

———. *The Federalist Papers*. Ed. Clinton Rossiter. New York: Penguin, 1961.

———. "Memorial and Remonstrance against Religious Assessments, 1785." In *The Mind of the Founder: Sources of the Political Thought of James Madison*, ed. Marvin Meyers. Hanover-London: University Press of New England, 1981.

Mahoney, Paul. "The Common Law and Economic Growth: Hayek Might Be Right." *Journal of Legal Studies* 30 (2001): 503–25.

Maine, Sir Henry. *Ancient Law*. Washington, DC: Beard Books, 2000, 1861.

Malebranche, Nicolas. "Traité de la nature et de la grace." In *Oeuvres complètes II*. Paris: Gallimard, 1992.
Maltzman, Forest, et al. *Crafting Law on the Supreme Court: The Collegial Game*. Cambridge: Cambridge University Press, 2000.
Mandeville, Bernard. *Recherche sur l'origine de la vertu morale*. In *La Fable des abeilles*. Trans. L. Carrive. Paris: Vrin, 1990.
Manent, Pierre. *La Cité de l'homme*. Paris: Fayard, 1995. (Translated as *City of Man*. Trans. Marc LePain. Princeton: Princeton University Press, 1998).
———. "La démocratie comme régime et comme religion." In *La pensée politique No. 1, Situations de la démocratie*. Paris: Hautes Etudes, Gallimard-Le Seuil, 1996.
Manin, Bernard. "Montesquieu, la république et le commerce." *Archives européennes de sociologie* 42.3 (2001): 573–602.
Marin, Louis. *Le Portrait du roi*. Paris: Editions de Minuit, 1981.
Markovits, Francine. "Montesquieu: L'esprit d'un peuple, Une histoire expérimentale." In *Former un nouveau peuple?* ed. Josiane Boulad Ayoub. Sainte-Foy: Presses Universitaires de Laval, 1996.
Martin, Kingsley. *The Rise of French Liberal Thought*. Ed. J. P. Mayer. New York: New York University Press, 1954.
Mason, S. M. *Montesquieu's Idea of Justice*. La Haye: Martinus Nijhoff, 1975.
Mass, Edgar. "Montesquieu et la loi fondamentale de la RFA." *Dix-Huitième Siècle* 21 (1989): 163–77.
Matsuda, Mari J., Charles R. Lawrence III, Richard Delgado, and Kimberle Williams Crenshaw. *Words That Wound: Critical Race Theory, Assaultive Speech, and the First Amendment*. Boulder, CO: Westview Press, 1993.
McCormick, Peter. *Supreme at Last: The Evolution of the Supreme Court of Canada*. Toronto: James Lorimer, 2000.
McDougall, Warren. "Gavin Hamilton, Bookseller in Edinburgh." *The British Journal for Eighteenth-century Studies* 1 (1978): 1–19.
McGuire, Kevin, and James Stimson. "The Least Dangerous Branch Revisited: New Evidence on Supreme Court Responsiveness to Public Preferences." *Journal of Politics* 66 (2004): 1018–35.
McIlwain, Charles Howard. *The American Revolution: A Constitutional Interpretation*. New York: Macmillan, 1923.
———. *Constitutionalism Ancient and Modern*. Ithaca: Cornell University Press, 1947.
Meek, Ronald. *Social Science and the Ignoble Savage*. Cambridge: Cambridge University Press, 1976.
Mehta, Uday Singh. *Liberalism and Empire: A Study in Nineteenth Century British Liberal Thought*. Chicago: University of Chicago Press, 1999.
Melon, J. F. *Essai politique sur le commerce*. Amsterdam: F. Changuion, 1735.
Melzer, Arthur. "The Origin of the Counter-Enlightenment: Rousseau and the New Religion of Sincerity." *American Political Science Review* 90 (1996): 344–60.
Millar, John. *Historical View of the English Government*. London: A. Millar, 1749.
Mishler, William, and Reginald Sheehan. "The Supreme Court as Countermajoritarian Institution? The Impact of Public Opinion on Supreme Court Decisions." *American Political Science Review* 88 (1993), 87–101.

Molesworth, Robert. *An Account of Denmark, as it was in the Year 1692.* London: Timothy Goodwin, 1694.

———. *The Principles of a Real Whig.* London: J. Williams, 1775.

———. "Translator's Preface." In *Franco-Gallia, or, an account of the ancient free state of France, and most other parts of Europe, before the loss of their liberties.* London: Edward Valentine, 1721 (1574).

Montaigne. *Essais.* Ed. Pierre Villey. Paris: PUF, 1992.

Montesquieu, Charles Louis Secondat, Baron de. *Considerations on the Causes of the Greatness of the Romans and Their Decline.* Trans. and ed. David Lowenthal. Ithaca: Cornell University Press, 1965.

———. *De l'Esprit des lois.* Ed. Jean Brethe de La Gressaye. Paris: Les Belles Lettres, 1950–1961, 4 vols.

———. *De l'Esprit des lois.* Ed. Robert Derathé. Paris: Garnier, 1973.

———. *Mes Pensées et le Spicilège.* Ed. Louis Desgraves. Paris: Robert Laffont, 1991.

———. *Oeuvres complètes.* Ed. André Masson. 3 vols. Paris: Nagel, 1950–1955.

———. *Oeuvres complètes.* Ed. Jean Ehrard and Catherine Volpilhac-Auger. Oxford: Voltaire Foundation, Naples: Istituto per gli studi filosofici, 1998–.

———. *Œuvres complètes.* Ed. Roger Caillois. 2 vols. Paris: Bibliothèque de la Pléiade, 1949–1951.

———. *Pensées.* Paris: Belles Lettres, 1925.

———. *The Persian Letters.* Trans. George R. Healy. Indianapolis, IN: Hackett Publishing, 1964.

———. *The Spirit of the Laws.* Trans. and ed. Anne M. Cohler, Basia Carolyn Miller and Harold Samuel Stone. Cambridge: Cambridge University Press, 1989.

———. *The Spirit of the Laws.* Trans. Thomas Nugent. New York: Hafner, 1949.

———. *A View of the English Constitution. By the late Baron De Montesquieu. Being A Translation of the Sixth Chapter of the Eleventh Book of his celebrated Treatise, intitled L'Esprit des Loix.* London: Sold by B. White, Horace's Head, Fleet-Street; and H. Payne, in Pall-Mall, 1781.

Moore, James. "Hume's Political Science and the Classical Republican Tradition." *Canadian Journal of Political Science* 10 (1977): 809–39.

Mosher, Michael. "The Judgmental Gaze of European Women: Gender, Sexuality, and the Critique of Republican Rule." *Political Theory* 22.1 (1994): 25–44.

———. "The Skeptic's Burke: Reflections on the Revolution in France, 1790–1990." *Political Theory* 9.3 (1991): 391–418.

Mosner, Ernest Campbell. *The Life of David Hume,* 2nd ed. Oxford: Clarendon Press, 1980.

Murphy, Walter. "Civil Law, Common Law, and Constitutional Democracy." *Louisiana Law Review* 91 (1991).

———. "Constitutions, Constitutionalism, and Democracy." In *Constitutionalism and Democracy. Transitions in the Contemporary World,* ed. Douglas Greenburg et al. New York: Oxford University Press, 1993.

Muthu, Sankar. *Enlightenment against Empire.* Princeton: Princeton University Press, 2003.

Neely, Sylvia. *Lafayette and the Liberal Ideal, 1814–1824.* Carbondale: Southern Illinois University Press, 1991.

Nenner, Howard. "The Later Stuart Age." In *The Varieties of British Political Thought, 1500–1800*, ed. J. G. A. Pocock. Cambridge: Cambridge University Press, 1993.
Newman, Stephen L. "American and Canadian Perspectives on Hate Speech and the Limits of Free Expression." In *Constitutional Politics in Canada and the United States*, ed. Stephen L. Newman. Albany: State University of New York Press, 2004.
Niklaus, Robert. "Condorcet et Montesquieu: Conflit idéologique entre deux théoriciens rationalistes." *Dix-Huitième Siècle* 25 (1993): 399–409.
Norman L. Torrey, ed. *Les Philosophes: The Philosophers of the Enlightenment and Modern Democracy*. New York: Capricorn Books, 1960.
North, Douglass, and Barry Weingast. "Constitutions and Commitment: The Evolution of Institutions Governing Public Choice in Seventeenth Century England." *Journal of Economic History* 49 (1989): 803–33.
North, Douglass, and Robert Thomas. *The Rise of the Western World*. Cambridge: Cambridge University Press, 1973.
Oakeshott, Michael. *De la conduite humaine*. Trans. O. Seyden. Paris: PUF, 1995.
Orwin, C. "Compassion and the Softening of Mores." *Journal of Democracy*, Tenth Anniversary Issue (*Democracy in the World: Tocqueville Reconsidered*), 11.1 (2000): 142–48.
———. "Rousseau and the Discovery of Political Compassion." In *The Legacy of Rousseau*, eds. Clifford Orwin and Nathan Tarcov. Chicago: University of Chicago Press, 1997.
Pangle, Thomas L. *Montesquieu's Philosophy of Liberalism: A Commentary on the Spirit of the Laws*. Chicago: Chicago University Press, 1973.
Pappas, John. "La campagne des philosophes contre l'honneur." *Voltaire Studies* 205 (1982): 40–43.
Parsons, Talcott. *The Evolution of Societies*. Englewood Cliffs, NJ: Prentice-Hall, 1977.
Pascal, Blaise. *Pensées*. Ed. Leon Brunschvig. Paris: Hachette, 1968.
Percival, John. *Diary of Viscount Percival, afterwards first Earl of Egmont*, vol. I, 1730–1733. London: Historical Manuscripts Commission, 1920.
Pernot, Camille. *La Politesse et sa philosophie*. Paris: PUF, 1996.
Persson, Torsen, and Guido Tabellini. *The Economic Effects of Constitutions*. Cambridge, MA: MIT Press, 2003.
Plumb, J. H. *The Growth of Political Stability in England, 1675–1725*. London: Macmillan 1767.
———. *Sir Robert Walpole, the King's Minister*. London: Cresset Press, 1960.
Pocock, John G. A. *The Ancient Constitution and the Feudal Law*. Cambridge: Cambridge University Press, 1957.
———. *Barbarism and Religion*. Cambridge: Cambridge University Press, 1999–.
———. *The Machiavellian Moment*. Princeton: Princeton University Press, 1975. (Translated as *Le Moment Machiavélian*. Trans. L. Borott. Paris: PUF, 1997).
———. *Virtue, Commerce and History*. Cambridge: Cambridge University Press: 1988. (Translated as *Vertu, Commerce et Histoire*. Trans. H. Aji. Paris: PUF, 1998).
Radner, John. "The Art of Sympathy in Eighteenth-Century British Moral Thought." *Studies in Eighteenth-Century Culture* 9 (1979): 189–210.

Rahe, Paul A. "The Book That Never Was: Montesquieu's *Considerations on the Romans* in Historical Context." *History of Political Thought* 26.1 (2005): 43–89.

Ramseyer, Mark, and Eric Rasmusen. "Why Are Japanese Judges so Conservative in Politically Charged Cases?" *American Political Science Review* 95 (2001): 331–44.

Rawls, John. *The Law of Peoples*. Cambridge: Harvard University Press, 1999.

———. *Political Liberalism*. New York: Columbia University Press, 1993.

———. "The Priority of the Right and Ideas of the Good." *Philosophy and Public Affairs* 17.3 (1988). *Political Liberalism*. New York: Columbia University Press, 1996.

———. *A Theory of Justice*. Cambridge: Belknap Press of Harvard University Press, 1971, 2nd edition, 1999.

Raynal. *Histoire philosophique et politique des [. . .] deux Indes*. La Haye: Gosse Fils, 1774.

Reid, John Philip. *The Ancient Constitution and the Origins of Anglo-American Liberty*. DeKalb: Northern Illinois University Press, 2005.

Renaudot, Eusèbe. *Anciennes relations des Indes et de la Chine de deux voyageurs mahométans, qui y allèrent dans le neuvième siècle*. Paris: Coignard, 1718.

Ricault, Paul. *État présent de l'Empire ottoman*. Paris: S. Mabre-Crmoisy, 1670.

Richter, Melvin. "Comparative Political Analysis in Montesquieu and Tocqueville." *Comparative Politics* 1 (January 1969): 129–60.

———. "An Introduction to Montesquieu's 'An Essay on the Causes That May Affect Men's Minds and Characters.'" *Political Theory* 4.2 (1976): 132–33.

———. "Montesquieu, the Politics of Language, and the Language of Politics." *History of Political Thought* 10 (1989): 71–88.

———. "The Uses of Theory: Tocqueville's Adaptation of Montesquieu." In *Essays in Theory and History*, ed. Melvin Richter. Cambridge: Harvard University Press, 1970.

Riley, Patrick *The General Will before Rousseau*. Princeton: Princeton University Press, 1986.

Roche, Daniel. *France in the Enlightenment*. Trans. Arthur Goldhammer. Cambridge: Harvard University Press, 1998.

Ross, Ian. *Lord Kames and the Scotland of His Day*. Oxford: Clarendon Press, 1972.

Rousseau, Jean-Jacques. *Œuvres completes*. Paris: Gallimard, Bibliothèque de la Pléïade, 1969.

Rubin, Paul. *Business Firms and the Common Law: The Evolution of Efficient Rules*. New York: Praeger Press, 1983.

Russell, Peter H. "Can the Canadians Be a Sovereign People? The Question Revisited." In *Constitutional Politics in Canada and the United States*, ed. Stephen L. Newman. Albany: State University of New York Press, 2004.

Sajó, Andras. *Limiting Government: An Introduction to Constitutionalism*. Budapest-New York: CEU Press, 1999.

Salmon, J. H. M. "Catholic Resistance Theory, Ultramontanism, and the Royalist Response, 1580–1620." In *The Cambridge History of Political Thought 1450–1700*, ed. J. H. Burns. Cambridge: Cambridge University Press, 1991.

Sandel, Michael. *Democracy's Discontent: America in Search of a Public Philosophy*. Cambridge: Harvard University Press, 1996.

———. *Liberalism and the Limits of Justice*. Cambridge: Cambridge University Press, 1998.

Schaub, Diana J. *Erotic Liberalism. Women and Revolution in Montesquieu's Persian Letters*. Lanham, MD: Rowman & Littlefield, 1995.

Schleifer, James T. *The Making of Tocqueville's Democracy in America*. Chapel Hill: University of North Carolina Press, 1980.

Scott, James. *Seeing Like a State*. New Haven: Yale University Press, 1997.

Segal, Jeffrey, and Harold Spaeth. *The Supreme Court and the Attitudinal Model Revisited*. Cambridge: Cambridge University Press, 2002.

Sen, Amartya. "Democracy and Its Global Roots: Why Democratization Is Not the Same as Westernization." *New Republic* 6 (2003): 28–35.

Shackleton, Robert. "Allies and Enemies: Voltaire and Montesquieu." In *Essays on Montesquieu and the Enlightenment*, eds. David Gilson and Martin Smith. Oxford: Voltaire Foundation, 1988.

———. *Montesquieu: A Critical Biography*. Oxford: Oxford University Press, 1961. (Translated as *Montesquieu, Biographie critique*. Trans. J. Loiseau. Grenoble: PUG, 1977).

———. "Montesquieu, Bolingbroke and the Separation of Powers." *French Studies* (1948).

Shapiro, Martin. *Courts: A Comparative and Political Analysis*. Chicago: University of Chicago Press, 1981.

Shennan, James H. *The Parlement of Paris*. Ithaca: Cornell University Press, 1968.

Sher, Richard B. "From Troglodytes to Americans: Montesquieu and the Scottish Enlightenment on Liberty, Virtue and Commerce." In *Republicanism, Liberty and Commercial Society, 1694–1776*, ed. David Wootton. Stanford: Stanford University Press, 1994.

Shklar, Judith N. *Montesquieu*. Oxford: Oxford University Press, 1987.

———. "Montesquieu and the New Republicanism." In *Machiavelli and Republicanism*, eds. Gisela Bock et al. Cambridge: Cambridge University Press, 1990.

Silver, Allan. "Friendship in Commercial Society: Eighteenth Century Social Theory and Modern Society." *American Journal of Sociology* 95.6 (1990): 1474–1504.

Singer, Brian. "Montesquieu, Adam Smith and the Discovery of the Social." *Journal of Classical Sociology* 4.1 (2004): 31–57.

Skinner, Quentin. *The Foundations of Modern Political Thought: Volume 2: The Age of Reformation*. Cambridge: Cambridge University Press, 1978.

———. *Liberty before Liberalism*. Cambridge: Cambridge University Press, 1998.

———. "The Republican Ideal of Political Liberty." In *Machiavelli and Republicanism*, eds. Gisela Bock et al. Cambridge: Cambridge University Press, 1990.

Smith, Adam. *An Inquiry into the Nature and Causes of the Wealth of Nations* (1776). Indianapolis: Liberty Classics, 1979.

———. *Lectures on Jurisprudence*. Ed. R. L. Meek, D. D. Raphael, and P. G. Stein. Oxford: Clarendon Press, 1978.

———. *The Theory of Moral Sentiments*. Ed. D. D. Raphael and A. L. Macfie. Indianapolis: Liberty Classics, 1982.

Somerville, J. P. "Absolutism and Royalism." In *The Cambridge History of Political Thought 1450–1700*, ed. J. H. Burns. Cambridge: Cambridge University Press, 1991.

Speck, W. A. *Stability and Strife, England 1714–1760*. London: Arnold, 1977.

Spector, Céline. "Cupidité ou charité? L'ordre sans vertu, des moralistes du grand siècle à *L'Esprit des lois* de Montesquieu." *Corpus* 43 (2003): 23–69.
———. *Montesquieu et l'émergence de l'économie politique*. Paris: Champion, 2006.
———. *Montesquieu, les "Lettres persanes."* Paris: PUF, 1997.
———. *Montesquieu, Pouvoirs, richesses et sociétés*. Paris: PUF, 2004.
———. "Quelle justice? Quelle rationalité? La mesure du droit dans *L'Esprit des lois*." *Montesquieu en 2005*, ed. C. Volpilhac-Auger. Oxford: Voltaire Foundation, 2005.
———. *Le Vocabulaire de Montesquieu*. Paris: Ellipses, 2001.
Spector, Céline and Thierry Hoquet, eds. *Lectures de L'Esprit des Lois*. Bordeaux: Presses Universitaires de Bordeau, 2004.
Spitz, Jean-Fabien. *La Liberté politique*. Paris: PUF, 1995.
Stark, Werner. *Montesquieu: Pioneer of the Sociology of Knowledge*. Toronto: University of Toronto Press, 1960.
Stein, Peter. *Legal Evolution: The Story of an Idea*. Cambridge: Cambridge University Press, 1980.
Stevens, John Paul. "The Freedom of Speech." *Yale Law Journal* 102 (1993): 1311.
Stewart, Dugald. *The Collected Works of Dugald Stewart*. Farnborough, UK: Gregg International, 1971.
Stewart, M. A. "The Dating of Hume's Manuscripts." In *The Scottish Enlightenment*, ed. Paul Wood. Rochester, NY: University of Rochester Press, 2000.
Stoner, James. *Common Law and Liberal Theory: Coke, Hobbes, and The Origins of American Constitutionalism*. Lawrence: University Press of Kansas, 1992.
Stout, Jeffrey. *Democracy and Tradition*. Princeton: Princeton University Press, 2004.
Strum, Philippa. *When the Nazis Came to Skokie: Freedom for the Speech We Hate*. Lawrence: University Press of Kansas, 1999.
Sunstein, Cass, and Edna Ullmann-Margalit. "Second-Order Decisions." In *Behavioral Law and Economics*, ed. Cass Sunstein. Cambridge: Cambridge University Press, 2000.
Sznaider, Natan. *The Compassionate Temperament: Care and Cruelty in Modern Society*. Lanham, MD: Rowman & Littlefield, 1994.
Taylor, Charles. "Alternative Futures: Legitimacy, Identity, and Alienation in Late Twentieth-Century Canada." In *Constitutionalism, Citizenship, and Society in Canada*, eds. A. Cairns and C. Williams. Toronto: University of Toronto Press, 1985.
———. *A Catholic Modernity?* Ed. James L. Heff, S. M. New York: Oxford University Press, 1999.
———. *The Ethics of Authenticity*. Cambridge, MA: Harvard University Press, 1992.
———. *Multiculturalisme. Différence et démocratie*. Trans. D.-A. Canal. Paris: Champs Flammarion, 1994.
———. *Sources of the Self: The Making of Modern Identity*. Cambridge: Harvard University Press, 1989.
———. "Two Theories of Modernity." *Public Culture* 11 (1999): 153–73.
Thiemann, Ronald F. "Public Religion: Bane or Blessing for Democracy." In *Obligations of Citizenship and Demands of Faith: Religious Accommodation in Pluralist Democracies*, ed. Nancy L. Rosenblum. Princeton: Princeton University Press, 2000.

———. *Religion and American Public Life: A Dilemma for Democracy*. Georgetown: Georgetown University Press/Century Fund, 1996.

Thomas, Yan. "Le sujet de droit, la personne et la nature." *Le Débat* 10 (1998), 105.

Tillet, Edouard. *La constitution anglaise, Un modèle politique et institutionnel dans la France des Lumières*. Aix-en-Provence: Presses Universitaires d'Aix-Marseille, 2001.

Tocqueville Alexis de. *Democracy in America*. The Henry Reeve Text as Revised by Francis Bowen. Further Corrected and edited by Phillips Bradley. New York: Vintage Books, 1945.

———. *Democracy in America*. Trans. George Lawrence, ed. J. P. Mayer. New York: HarperCollins, 1988.

———. *Democracy in America*. Ed. and trans. Harvey C. Mansfield and Delba Winthrop. Chicago: University of Chicago Press, 2000.

———. "The European Revolution" & "Correspondence with Gobineau." Ed. and trans. John Lukacs. Glouster, MA: Peter Smith, 1968.

———. *Journey to America*. Trans. George Lawrence. Ed. J. P. Mayer. New Haven: Yale University Press, 1960.

———. *Journeys to England and Ireland*. Ed. Jacob-Peter Mayer. Garden City, NY: Doubleday, 1968.

———. *Œuvres complètes*. Ed. J. P. Mayer. Paris: Gallimard, 1951–.

———. *The Old Regime and Revolution*. Ed. François Furet and Françoise Mélonio. Trans. Alan S. Kahan. Chicago: University of Chicago Press, 1998–2001.

———. *The Old Regime and the French Revolution*. Trans. Stuart Gilbert. Garden City, NY: Doubleday, 1955.

———. *Recollections*. Trans. George Lawrence. Ed. J. Mayer and A. Kerr. Garden City: Doubleday, 1970.

———. *Selected Letters on Politics and Society*. Trans. James Toupin and Roger Boesche. Ed. Roger Boesche. Berkeley: University of California Press, 1985.

———. *The Two Tocquevilles. Father and Son. Hervé and Alexis de Tocqueville on the Coming of the French Revolution*. Ed. and trans. R. R. Palmer. Princeton: Princeton University Press, 1987.

———. *Writings on Empire and Slavery*. Ed. and trans. Jennifer Pitts. Baltimore: Johns Hopkins University Press, 2001.

Tully, James. *Strange Multiplicity: Constitutionalism in an Age of Diversity*. Cambridge: Cambridge University Press, 1995.

Tushnet, Mark. *Taking the Constitution Away from the Courts*. Princeton: Princeton University Press, 1999.

Vanberg, Georg. *The Politics of Constitutional Review in Germany*. Cambridge: Cambridge University Press, 2005.

Vernière, Paul. *Montesquieu et L'Esprit des lois ou la raison impure*. Paris: Société d'Edition d'Enseignement Supérieur, 1977.

Vile, M. J. C. *Constitutionalism and the Separation of Powers*. Oxford: Clarendon Press, 1967.

Vincent, Joan. "Lewis Henry Morgan." In *Encyclopedia of Social and Cultural Anthropology*, eds. Alan Bernard and Jonathan Spencer. London: Routledge, 2004.

Viroli, Maurizio. *Republicanism*. New York: Hill & Wang, 1999.

Volpilhac-Auger, Catherine. "Du bon usage des *Geographica*." *Revue Montesquieu* 3 (1999): 169–78.

———. "Une nouvelle 'chaîne secrète' de *L'Esprit des lois*: L'histoire du texte." In *Montesquieu en 2005*, ed. C. Volpilhac-Auger. Oxford: Voltaire Foundation, 2005.

———. "L'ombre d'une bibliothèque. La bibliothèque manuscrite de Montesquieu." In *Lire, copier, écrire. Les bibliothèques manuscrites et leurs usages au XVIII$^e$ siècle*, ed. É. Décultot. Paris: CNRS Editions, 2003.

Volpilhac-Auger, Catherine, with Hélène de Bellaigue. *Les plus belles pages des manuscrits de Montesquieu confiés à la bibliothèque municipale de Bordeaux par Jacqueline de Chabannes*. Bordeaux: William Blake, 2005.

Voltaire. "Honneur." In *Questions sur l'Encyclopédie*, eds. Nicholas Cronk and Christiane Mervaud. Oxford: Voltaire Foundation, 2007.

———. *Supplément au Siècle de Louis XIV* (1753), III, in *Œuvres historiques*. Paris: Gallimard, 1957.

Waddicor, M. H. *Montesquieu and the Philosophy of Natural Law*. La Haye: Martinus Nijhoff, 1970.

Waldron, Jeremy. *The Dignity of Legislation*. Oxford: Oxford University Press, 1999.

———. "Judicial Power and Popular Sovereignty." In *Marbury v. Madison: Documents and Commentary*, ed. Mark Graber. Washington, DC: CQ Press, 2002.

———. "Judicial Review and the Conditions for Democracy." *Journal of Political Philosophy* 6 (1998): 335–55.

Walker, Samuel. *Hate Speech: The History of an American Controversy*. Lincoln, NE: University of Nebraska Press, 1994.

Wallace, Robert. *A Dissertation on the Numbers of Mankind in Ancient and Modern Times*. Edinburgh: G. Hamilton and J. Balfour, 1753.

Waluchow, Wil. "Constitutionalism." *Stanford Encyclopedia of Philosophy*. Internet: http://plato.stanford.edu/entries/constitutionalism/.

Wansleben, Johann Michael. *Nouvelle relation de l'Égypte*. Paris: Compagnie des libraries associés, 1698.

Ward, Lee. "Montesquieu on Federalism and Ango-Gothic Constitutionalism." *Publius* 37 (2007): 551–77.

Watson, Alan. *Legal Transplants*. 2nd ed. Athens: University of Georgia Press, 1993.

Weber, Max. *Economy and Society: An Outline of Interpretive Sociology*. Berkeley: University of California Press, 1978, 1914.

Weingast, Barry. "Constitutions as Governance Structures: The Political Foundations of Secure Markets." *Journal of Institutional and Theoretical Economics* 149 (1993): 286–311.

———. "The Political Foundations of Democracy and the Rule of Law." *American Political Science Review* 91 (1997): 245–63.

Weinreb, Lorraine. "Hate Promotion in a Free Society: R. v. Keegstra." *McGill Law Journal* 36 (1991): 1416–49.

Welch, Cheryl B. *Liberty and Utility: The French Ideologues and the Transformation of Liberalism*. New York: Columbia University Press, 1984.

Weston, Corinne. "England: Ancient Constitution and Common Law." In *The Cambridge History of Political Thought 1450–1700*, ed. J. H. Burns. Cambridge: Cambridge University Press, 1991.

Whitaker, Reg. "Chameleon on a Changing Background: The Politics of Censorship in Canada." In *Interpreting Censorship in Canada*, ed. K. Peterson and A. C. Hutchinson. Toronto: University of Toronto Press, 1999.

Williamson, Oliver. "Credible Commitments: Using Hostages to Support Exchange." *American Economic Review* 73 (1983): 519–40.

Winch, Donald. "The System of the North: Dugald Stewart and His Pupils." In *That Noble Science of Politics: A Study in Nineteenth-Century Intellectual History*, eds. Stefan Collini, Donald Winch and John Burrow. Cambridge: Cambridge University Press, 1983.

Wokler, Robert. "Apes and Races in the Scottish Enlightenment: Monboddo and Kames on the Nature of Man." In *Philosophy and Science in the Scottish Enlightenment*, ed. Peter Jones. Edinburgh: John Donald, 1988.

Wolin, Sheldon. *Tocqueville between Two Worlds: The Making of a Political and Theoretical Life*. Princeton: Princeton University Pres, 2001.

Wootton, David. "Leveller Democracy and the Puritan Revolution." In *The Cambridge History of Political Thought 1450–1700*, ed. J. H. Burns. Cambridge: Cambridge University Press, 1991.

Youngson, A. J. *After the Forty-Five*. Edinburgh: Edinburgh University Press, 1973.

Zuckert, Michael. "Natural Rights and Modern Constitutionalism." *Northwestern Journal of International Human Rights* 8 (2004).

# About the Contributors

**David W. Carrithers** is Adolph Ochs Professor of Government at the University of Tennessee at Chattanooga. He is the editor (Berkeley: University of California Press, 1977) of an abridged, critical edition of Montesquieu's *The Spirit of Laws* that includes an English translation of Montesquieu's *Essay on Causes Affecting Minds and Characters (1736–1743)*. He is also the coeditor of two recent publications on Montesquieu: *Montesquieu's Science of Politics: Essays on* The Spirit of Laws, eds. David W. Carrithers, Michael A. Mosher, and Paul A. Rahe (Lanham, MD: Rowman & Littlefield, 2001) and *Montesquieu and the Spirit of Modernity*, eds. David W. Carrithers and Patrick Coleman (Oxford: Voltaire Foundation, 2002). His essays on Montesquieu as a philosopher of history, on Montesquieu's influence on the American founding, on Montesquieu as a theorist of punishment, on Montesquieu's solution to the problem of the French national debt, and on Montesquieu's account of aristocratic republicanism have been published in the *Journal of the History of Ideas*, the *History of Political Thought*, and the *French-American Review*.

**Crystal Cordell** (the translator for various chapters) is a PhD candidate in Political Science at the University of Toronto and at the Ecole des Hautes Etudes en Sciences Sociales, Paris. She has received the Diploma of Advanced Studies (Diplôme d'Etudes Approfondies) with the distinction "Très bien" from the Ecole des Hautes Etudes en Sciences Sociales (thesis title: "Rousseau et Tocqueville. *L'Emile* et l'homme démocratique"). She received her bachelor's from Boston College (*summa cum laude*) in Political Science and French. She has published articles in *Commentaire*.

**Rebecca E. Kingston** is Associate Professor of Political Science at the University of Toronto. She is author of *Montesquieu and the "Parlement" of Bordeaux* (Geneva: Droz, 1996), which was awarded the Prix Montesquieu and of various articles on French criminal justice history and modern political thought. She is editor of a collection of articles (with Leonard Ferry) entitled *Bringing the Passions Back In: The Emotions in Political Philosophy* (Vancouver: UBC Press, 2008) and is currently completing a book on the theme of politics and the emotions in the history of political thought with a focus on Montesquieu, entitled "The Idea of a Public Passion."

**Cecil Patrick Courtney** is Emeritus Reader in French Intellectual History and Bibliography in the University of Cambridge and a Fellow of Christ's College. His publications include *Montesquieu and Burke* (Oxford, 1963), *Isabelle de Charrière (Belle de Zuylen): A Biography* (Oxford, 1993), and numerous articles on eighteenth-century topics, particularly on Montesquieu and Raynal. He is a member of two editorial boards preparing major critical editions: Montesquieu's *Oeuvres complètes* and Raynal's *Histoire philosophique des deux Indes* and is general editor of Benjamin Constant's *Correspondance générale*. He is a corresponding member of the Académie de Bordeaux, has been distinguished visiting professor at the University of Utrecht, and has held visiting fellowships at Harvard and Yale.

**Fred Dallmayr** is Packey J. Dee Professor of Political Science at the University of Notre Dame. He specializes in modern and contemporary European thought but also has a growing interest in comparative philosophy, particularly non-Western political thought (focusing on Islam, Hinduism, Buddhism, and Confucianism), cross-cultural dialogue, and global human rights. In addition to his many articles, he has authored fourteen books, including, most recently, *Achieving Our World: Toward a Global and Plural Democracy* (2001); *Dialogue among Civilizations: Some Exemplary Voices* (2002); *Beyond Orientalism: Essays on Cross-Cultural Encounter* (Lanham, MD: Rowman & Littlefield, 1996); and *Alternative Visions: Paths in the Global Village* (Lanham, MD: Rowman & Littlefield, 1998). He has been the recipient of NEH and Fulbright fellowships and has been a visiting professor at the New School and the University of Hamburg. He has been a fellow of the Kroc Institute since 1994.

**Jean Ehrard** is a graduate of the Ecole Normale Supérieur and former Dean of the Faculty of Arts and Social Sciences of the University of Clermont Ferrand. He is also a former President of the French Society for Eighteenth Century Studies and the honorary President and founding member of the Société Montesquieu. He initiated the publication (still ongoing), through the Voltaire Foundation of Oxford University, of the first critical and complete edition of the works of Montesquieu in twenty-two volumes. His 1964 book, *L'Idée de la nature en France dans la première moitié du XVIIIe siècle* has been reissued twice (Dans: Slatkine, 1981; Albin Michel, 1994) and once in condensed form (1970). In addition, he is author of *Montesquieu critique d'art* (Paris: Presses universitaires de France, 1965); *Le XVIIIe siècle I, 1720-1750* (Paris: Arthaud,

1974); *L'Invention littéraire au XVIIIe siècle: fictions, idées, société* (Paris: Presses universitaires de France, 1997); and *L'Esprit des mots. Montesquieu en lui-même et parmi les siens* (Genève: Droz, 1998).

**Ran Hirschl** is Professor of Political Science and Law at the University of Toronto and holds a senior Canada Research Chair in Constitutionalism, Democracy and Development. He has published extensively on comparative constitutional law and politics in social science journals, law reviews, and edited collections. He is the editor (with Christopher L. Eisgruber) of a special symposium issue of *I-CON International Journal of Constitutional Law* entitled "North American Constitutionalism" and the author of *Towards Juristocracy: The Origins and Consequences of the New Constitutionalism* (Cambridge, MA: Harvard University Press, 2004). He is currently completing two new books (both of which will also be published by Harvard University Press) titled *Sacred Judgments: The Dilemma of Constitutional Theocracy*, and *Lex Comparativus Novo: Comparative Legal Studies for the Twenty-first Century*.

**Catherine Larrère** is professor of philosophy at l'Université de Paris I-Panthéon-Sorbonne. Her notable publications include *L'Invention de l'économie. Du droit naturel à la physiocratie* (Paris: PUF-collection Léviathan-1992); *Actualité de Montesquieu* (Paris: Presses de Sciences PO, 1999); and many articles on Montesquieu. She is a member of the Montesquieu Society and of the editorial board for the *Revue Montesquieu*. She also is participating in the editing of Montesquieu's *Œuvres complètes* with the Voltaire Foundation.

**Jacob T. Levy** is Tomlinson Professor of Political Theory at McGill University, and secretary-treasurer of the American Society for Political and Legal Philosophy. He is the author of *The Multiculturalism of Fear* (New York: Oxford University Press, 2000) and articles including "Beyond Publius: Montesquieu, Liberal Republicanism, and the Small-Republic Thesis" (*History of Political Thought*, 2006) and "Federalism, Liberalism, and the Separation of Loyalties," (*American Political Science Review*, August 2007). He holds a PhD in politics from Princeton University and an LL.M. from the University of Chicago Law School.

**James Moore** is Emeritus Professor of Political Science at Concordia University. He has written extensively on the Enlightenment in Scotland and reformed Europe. His most recent publications include *Natural Rights on the Threshold of the Scottish Enlightenment: The Writings of Gershom Carmichael* (2002), *Francis Hutcheson on Logic, Metaphysics and the Natural Sociability of Mankind* (2006) (both with Michael Silverthorne), and entries in *The Oxford Dictionary of National Biography* (2004) and *The Cambridge History of Eighteenth-Century Political Thought* (2006).

**Michael Mosher** teaches political thought and comparative government at the University of Tulsa where he is department chair. He is coeditor of *Montesquieu's Science of Politics* (Lanham, MD: Rowman & Littlefield, 2001) and has recently contributed "Montesquieu and the Global Reach of Enlightenment: The Anti-Colonialist as Imperial Liberal" to *Empire and Modern Political Thought*, ed. Sankar Muthu (New York: Cambridge University Press, forthcoming); "Montesquieu on Conquest: Three Cartesian Heroes and Five Good Enough Empires," to *Revue Montesquieu*, 8 (2005–2006); and "Free Trade, Free Speech, and Free Love: Monarchy from the Liberal Prospect in Mid Eighteenth Century France," to *Monarchisms in the Age of Enlightenment: Liberty, Patriotism, and the Common Good*, eds. Hans Blom, John Christian Laursen, and Luisa Simonutti (Toronto: University of Toronto Press, 2007).

**Stephen L. Newman** is Associate Professor of Political Science at York University in Toronto where he teaches courses on the history of Western political thought and liberal theory. He is the author of *Liberalism at Wits' End: The Libertarian Revolt against the Modern State* (Ithaca, NY: Cornell University Press, 1984) and editor of *Constitutional Politics in Canada and the United States* (Albany: State University of New York Press, 2004).

**Clifford Orwin** is Professor of Political Science, Fellow of St. Michael's College and Director of the Program in Political Science and International Affairs at the Munk Centre for International Studies at the University of Toronto. He is the author of *The Humanity of Thucydides* (Princeton University Press, 2nd. ed. 1997) and of numerous articles on ancient, modern, and contemporary thought. He is completing a book on the role of compassion in modern politics and political thought.

**Brian C. J. Singer** teaches at Glendon College and is associated with the graduate programs in Sociology and Social and Political Thought at York University, Toronto. He is the author of *Society, Theory and the French Revolution: Studies in the Revolutionary Imaginary* (New York: St. Martin's Press, 1986), and some twenty book chapters or journal articles on diverse topics. He has also translated a number of works from French, including books by Jean Baudrillard and Claude Lévi-Strauss.

**Céline Spector**, a graduate of the Ecole Normale Superieure, is a lecturer in philosophy at l'Université Bordeaux 3. Her work has focused on political philosophy of the eighteenth century and on Montesquieu and Rousseau in particular. Her most recent publications include *Montesquieu. Pouvoirs, richesses et societes* (Paris: Presses Universitaires de France, 2004) and *Montesquieu et l'emergence de l'Economie politique* (Paris: Champion, 2006).

## About the Contributors

**Ronald F. Thiemann**, Professor of Theology and Professor of Religion and Society, has been at Harvard University since 1986, first as Dean of the Divinity School (1986–1998) and then in his current professorial position. He also is a Faculty Fellow at the John F. Kennedy School's Hauser Center for Nonprofit Organizations and serves on the steering committee of the center's Joint Program in Religion and Public Life. He is a faculty affiliate at the Kennedy School's Harvard Center for Public Leadership and has received a fellowship from the center in support of his current research project. An ordained Lutheran and a specialist on the role of religion in public life, he is the author of *Revelation and Theology: The Gospel as Narrated Promise*, *Constructing a Public Theology: The Church in a Pluralistic Culture*; and *Religion in Public Life: A Dilemma for Democracy*. He is also an editor of *Who Will Provide? The Changing Role of Religion in American Social Welfare*. He is currently working on a book-length project entitled *Prisoners of Conscience: Public Intellectuals in a Time of Crisis*, which examines the courageous stance of four public figures—Anna Akhmatova, Albert Camus, Langston Hughes, and George Orwell—during the tumultuous period of 1914–45. Before coming to Harvard, Thiemann taught for ten years at Haverford College, where he also served as acting provost and acting president.

**Catherine Volpilhac-Auger** is Professor of French Literature at the Ecole Normale Supérieur, Lyon, and President of the Société Montesquieu (http://montesquieu.ens-lsh.fr). She is codirector of the publication of the complete works of Montesquieu (now almost half complete through the Voltaire Foundation of Oxford University), and she has published various editions of his manuscripts as well as a number of works on the literature of the seventeenth and eighteenth centuries. Her most recent publications include *L'Atelier de Montesquieu. Manuscrits inédits de La Brède* (Napoli and Oxford: Voltaire Foundation and Liguori Editore, 2001), *Montesquieu. Mémoire de la critique* (Paris: Presses de Paris-Sorbonne, 2003), *Montesquieu en 2005* (Oxford: Voltaire Foundation, 2005), and *Les Plus Belles Pages des manuscrits de Montesquieu confiés à la bibliothèque de Bordeaux par Jacqueline de Chabannes* (Bordeaux: William Blake, 2005).

# Index

absolutism, 43, 99–100, 169; and corruption, 61; of the Stuarts, 42. *See also* Bourbons; monarchy.
Acton, Lord John, 99
Adams, John, 132
Adolfus, Gustavus, 157
affects, 49; and political motivation, 51. *See also* passions; principles; sentiments.
Africa, 202, 297
Alembert, Jean d', 241
Althusser, Louis, 282, 293
ambition, 49–50, 53, 58, 69, 247. *See also* honour.
America, United States of, 152, 153, 160; Bill of Rights, 243; Constitution, 118, 131, 214, 222; First Amendment, 222, 223, 225, 226, 227, 229, 243; founders of, 122, 274, 275; U.S. Supreme Court, 212, 214, 222, 225, 226. *See under* constitutionalism; democracy; liberalism; pluralism; republicanism.
*Ancien Régime*, 53, 68, 107, 141, 167, 280
ancient world, 33, 67, 98, 99, 107, 183; tradition of political philosophy in, 50. *See also* antiquity; republic; Greece; Rome; virtue.
Anson, Admiral George, 82
anthropology, 81; political 69
anti-Jacobinism. *See* Jacobins.

antiquity, classical, 144
appetites, 188. *See also* passions.
Arendt, Hannah, 8, 240
aristocracy, 53, 130, 151, 162. *See also* honour; nobility; republicanism.
Aristotle, 4, 9, 50, 54, 64, 150, 200, 241, 242, 243, 292, 297
Aron, Raymond, 200, 284, 285, 290, 292
Augustine, 64
authority, 3, 61; in Hobbes; political, 206, 207, 208; reconciled with freedom, 226; distinction between religious and political, 243; spiritual, 141; state, 10
autonomy: local, 129; political 66, 67

Bacon, Francis, 285
Barker, Ernest, 121
Bayle, Pierre, 181
Beccaria, Cesare, 280
Beiner, Ronald, 144–45
Benítez, Miguel, 84
Bentham, Jeremy, 133, 285
Berlin, Isaiah, 18, 123, 224–25, 273, 280, 284–85
Blackstone, William, 34, 120, 133
Bodin, Jean, 16, 119, 133
Bolingbroke, Henry Saint John, 37, 40, 182
Bonaparte, Napoleon, 128–30, 152
Bossuet, Jacques-Bénigne, 16, 292
Bourbons, 8, 16, 125, 129

Brandeis, Justice Louis (U.S.), 226, 230
Britain. See England.
Buffon, Comte de (Georges-Louis Leclerc), 149
Burke, Edmund, 10, 12, 120, 128, 129, 224; *Reflections of the Revolution in France*, 12

Canada: Charter of Rights and Freedoms, 210, 222, 223, 229–30; Cohen Commission, 224; Constitutionalism in, 224; history of political ideas in 260; Supreme Court, 222–24, 228–30. See *under* constitutionalism; liberalism; pluralism.
capitalism, 206
caprice, 62, 101; See also passions.
Cartesianism. See Descartes, René.
Catholicism, 54, 250; See also Christianity.
Cerceau, Jean Antoine du, 82
Chardin, Jean, 82
Charles I, 123, 157, 158
checks and balances, 34, 43, 100, 105, 107, 110n12. See also powers.
China, 5, 82–90, 105, 202, 264, 286–87; and empire, 8, 9, 18, 19, 86, 87, 208; enlightened despotism of, 82; customs and mores in, 84–86, 94n36, 94n39, 265; political and judicial institutions of, 88; rites, 86–88 passim. See also despotism.
Christianity, 21, 23–24, 54, 141–45 passim, 250. See also Protestantism; religion.
civil society, 7–12, 15, 22, 49, 55–56, 62, 74n36, 105; equilibrium within, 64–65
civility, 9–10, 86
citizenship, 38–39, 57, 66; republican, 9
climate, 35, 99, 107, 151, 183, 202, 285–87 passim, 290.
Coke, Sir Edward, 117
colonialism. See empire.
commerce, 121–22, 141, 143–44, 151, 183, 190–91, 202, 279, 282, 286; and communication, 13–19 passim; and its impact on citizens, 141, 280. See also communication.
common good, 16, 50–63 passim
communication, 19; culture of; and the "talking cure", 14
communitarianism, 23, 26, 271; spirit of, 19
compassion, 139–45 passim. See also love; virtue.
Comte, Auguste, 200, 241
Condorcet, Marquis de, 3, 127–28, 265, 289, 291, 293
conservatism, 10
Constant, Benjamin, 7, 66–67, 117–18, 128–29, 133, 280
constitutionalism, 1, 118–19; ancient, 115, 117–20, 123, 132; modern, 115, 124–25; contractarian and covenantal, 116–17, 132; British, 116, 120; positivist; French, 117, 133; whiggish, 120; liberal, 128. See also America, United States of; Canada; England; law.
contractarianism. See *under* constitutionalism.
corruption, 43, 45 n.18, 63, 66, 140, 182, 185; in education; in England, 43; in monarchies, 52, 61, 98; in republics, 122
cosmopolitanism, 9, 141, 244, 252
courts: independence of judges, 3, 12, 123, 182, 211, 262; judging as interpretation and education, 229; judicial review, 133, 209, 210, 221; political construction of, 207, 208, 211, 213; public prosecutor, 262, 263; *stare decisis*, 210. See also national courts (e.g. *under* England).
culture, 13. See also customs; manners; mores.
customs, 21, 22, 266. See also manners; mores.

deliberation, 61
democracy, 11, 53, 70, 103, 132, 150, 151, 192, 243, 244; ancient, 41; constitutions and, 214; contemporary, 6,

297–98; establishment of, 46, 47n34; representative, 127. *See also* equality; liberalism; regime typology; republic.
Derathé, Robert, 84
Descartes, René, 23, 24, 26, 70n1, 285; Cartesianism 240, 245; *Discourse on Method*, 23; *Meditations*, 23
despotism, 3, 59, 90, 98, 100–103 passim, 151, 168, 240; citizen as slave under, 41; contradictions in Montesquieu's consideration of, 89–90; as the corruption of monarchy, 52; idea of, 82; "oriental", 11, 15; reason and, 46n25; and revolution, 59; weakness of, 101. *See also* fear; regime typology; tyranny.
determinism, 160, 161, 167
Dicey, Albert Venn, 133
dignity, 68, 223, 225. *See also* rights.
disobedience. *See* obedience.
distribution of powers. *See* checks and balances; powers.
diversity, 3, 4, 127, 129, 130, 133, 223, 239, 242, 250, 261, 265, 284, 289, 293. *See also* pluralism.
division of powers. *See* powers.
Dodds, Muriel, 82–83, 88–89
Durkheim, Émile, 3, 199, 204–205

education, 55, 62, 139, 140, 229, 241, 255; and liberty 8; in monarchies, 62–65; in republics, 243
Eisenmann, Charles, 288, 291, 293
emotion, 224. *See also* passions; sentiments.
empire, imperialism and 26, 248, 252–53, 271. *See also* Rome, China, Ottomans.
empiricism, 240, 285
England, 2, 53, 105, 149, 288; Act of Settlement (1701), 33–34; Act of Union (1707), 119; Bill of Rights (1689), 33; character, 25, 38; Civil War, 123, 157; Commonwealth, 46, 47n34; Constitution of, 3, 33–34, 39, 43, 120, 182; Glorious Revolution, 44, 47n37, 120; Parliament of, 38–39, 119; political system in, 32–40; Reformation in, 157; relation between Crown and Parliament, 35–37, 40, 43, 182; as a republic that hides under the form of a monarchy, 122; Restoration, 34, 42; spirit or principle of regime, 43–44, 106; Tories, 37, 40; Whigs, 37. *See also* Charles I; climate; commerce; suicide.
Enlightenment, 1, 18, 24, 107, 116, 133, 224, 239, 289; Cartesian, 26; French, 244, 259; Scottish, 179–80, 186; tragedy of, 27
equality, 20, 68, 140, 150, 159, 162–63, 225, 243, 246, 253–55, 272–74, 280, 292. *See also* democracy; liberty; republic; virtue.
*esprit*. *See* spirit.
*esprit général*. *See* general spirit.
Estates General. *See* France.
ethos, 241, 245
Etiemble, René, 86
expression, freedom of. *See* speech.

family, 17
fear, 41, 52, 58–59, 72n15, 102–103, 242. *See also* despotism.
federalism 133, 261
*Federalist*, 47n43
Fénelon, Françoise de Salignac de La Mothe, 86
Ferguson, Adam, 179, 181, 184–86
feudalism, 69, 186–91, 206
fighting words, 226–27
France, 18, 26, 87; Bibliothèque nationale, 82; Estates General, 119, 124–25, 162, 165, 168; monarchy in, 54; Parlements, 61–62, 117, 119, 124–27, 150, 168; Revolution, 118–19, 124, 125, 150–52, 161–62, 164–65, 259, 280, 292; secularization, 22–23; Terror, the, 66. *See also* commerce; Enlightenment; Louis XIV; Louis XV; republicanism; sociability.
Franklin, Benjamin, 243, 275

freedom. *See* liberty.
Freemasons, 117
French Revolution. *See* France.
Fréret, Nicholas, 84, 87

Gadamer, Hans-Georg, 241
general spirit, 35, 42, 242, 244, 287
Germany, 43, 259
globalization, 14–15
Glorious Revolution. *See* England.
glory, 52, 56–57, 74n37. *See also* honour; ambition.
Goethe, Johann Wolfgang von, 252
government: mixed, 33, 99; moderate, 16, 43, 51, 65, 288–89; typology, 51. *See also* law; power; powers; regime typology.
Greece, ancient, 12. *See also* republic.
Grotius, Hugo, 50, 248

Habermas, Jürgen, 105
Halde, Jean Baptiste du, 82–90 passim
Hamilton, Alexander, 7, 47n43
Harrington, James, 9, 191
Healy, George, 241, 244–45
Hegel, Georg Wilhelm Friedrich, 3, 13, 38, 66–67, 161, 243–44
Herder, Johann Gottfried von, 252
Hirschman, Albert, 50, 106
historicism, 13
history, 144, 240; philosophical, 151
Hoang, Arcadio, 84–88 passim
Hobbes, Thomas, 50, 119, 133, 143–44, 240, 243, 248, 282, 283, 285, 291, 297
*honnête homme*, 62–64
honor, 17, 19, 41, 49–56 passim, 60, 64, 70, 72n16, 103, 242; as an art of simulacra, 64; as distinct from virtue, 52–56; "false", 56–58; and resistance, 16, 17, 58–60, 76n59, 103. *See also* monarchy; principles of government.
Huguenots, 120–21, 157, 251
human nature. *See* nature.
human rights. *See* rights.
*humanité* (humanism), 139–45 passim

Hume, David, 31, 34, 38–39, 42, 43, 179, 181–84, 188, 191, 271
Hutcheson, Francis, 179

identity politics, 230
imperialism. *See* empire.
inclination, 58. *See also* passions, sentiment.
individual: the monarchic contrasted with the despotic, 58
individualism, 106
inequality, 6, 20, 140–41, 280
interest: public, 38–39, 66, 70; relation between public and private, 49–50, 67; self-, 37–40, 42, 47, 48n44, 49, 55, 247
invisible hand, 50, 66, 70
Islam, 24, 250, 264. *See also* religion.

Jacobins, 3, 4, 22, 129, 239
Jansenists, 17; perspective of the, 54, 64
Japan, 103
Jefferson, Thomas, 127, 131–32, 243
Jesuits, 81–89 passim
Joly, Maurice, 261
Judaism, 250–51
judgment; normative, 63; free, 22
judicial review. *See* courts.
just war. *See* war.
justice, 247–48

Kant, Immanuel, 26; Kantian perspective, 241, 244
Katz, Stanley, 116

Laboulaye, Edouard-René Lefebvre de, 83–84
*laïcité*, 22, 264. *See also* France, secularization in.
Lange, Lorenz, 82, 89
law, 52, 53, 265, 293, 294; comparative, 2, 199, 203–204, 207–208, 212, 214–16, 221, 228, 230–31; constitutional (or fundamental), 5, 123, 207, 244, 279; and despotism, 98–101; feudal, 104; Islamic, 208; of nations,

248, 252; natural, 202, 205, 241, 244, 294–95; nature of, 242, 251; and passion, 74n39; penal, 58, 203, 280; politics of, 231; power of the, 67; rationality of, 50; religious, 10, 294; rule of, 9, 123, 125, 133, 262, 279; separation of power from, 3, 98.
Law, John, 183, 288
legislator, 9, 229; prejudices of the, 10; republican, 58
Leibniz, Gottfried Wilhelm, 56, 252
liberalism, 280; basic dilemmas of, 271, 276; complicity with imperialism, 271; contemporary, 1–3 passim, 69, 141, 271; political, 10.
liberty, 38–41, 60–63 passim, 69–70, 125, 150, 152, 168, 243, 290; and commerce, 14; ancient and modern, 78n80, 108; aristocratic, 104; civil, 66–67; distinguished in liberal and republican traditions, 229, 283; English, 33, 40; political 2, 7, 20, 33, 56, 58, 66–67, 273, 282–83; positive and negative, 65–66, 123, 224–25; Spartan, 15; spirit of, 44, 68; as supreme value, 42, 150. See also liberalism; republic; speech, freedom of.
Locke, John, 22, 24–25, 34, 116, 121, 192, 285
Louis XIV, 11, 18, 86, 158, 240, 243, 260
Louis XV, 17, 158, 166
love, 101–102, 104, 232n10, 243. See also virtue.
Luther, Martin, 24, 26

Mably, Gabriel Bonnet, 67
Machiavelli, Niccolò, 4, 9, 60, 292
Madison, James, 7, 47 n. 43, 117–18, 131–33, 243, 274, 276
Malebranche, Henri Gouhier, 56, 70n1, 86
Mandeville, Bernard, 38
Manin, Bernard, 284, 287, 291, 297
manners, 1, 14–15, 18, 63; and civility, 85; English, 35; and morals of citizens, 2, 32. See also civility; mores.

Marx, Karl, 13, 141; Marxism, 140–41
Maseres, Francis, 34
Masson, André, 84–88 passim
McIlwain, Charles, 115–16
moderation, 53. See under government.
modernity, 1, 3, 145, 240, 280
moeurs, 1, 140–41, 143. See also customs; mores.
Mohammed, the Prophet, 157
Molesworth, Robert, 120–21
monarchy, 16–17, 52, 56, 103–104, 201, 280; commercial, 122; constitutional; and "excellence", 61; privileging prejudice, 21; and public life, 19. See also despotism; education; England; France; regime typology.
monism, 69
Montaigne, Michel de, 242
Montesquieu, Charles-Louis de Secondat: as anti-imperialist, 26; anti-Jacobinism of, 2–4
Montesquieu (works of): Considerations on the causes of the greatness of the Romans and their decline, 142, 149, 151, 153–55 passim, 292; Geographica I, 85; Geographica II, 81–91 passim; Notes sur l'Angleterre, 39–40, 42; Pensées, 42, 49, 58, 87, 91, 168–69, 285; Persian Letters, 18, 22–26, 54–55, 59, 82, 169, 239–55, 285, 296; De la Politique, 157–58 ; Spicilège, 86, 91; Spirit of Laws 1, 3, 8–27 passim, 31–32, 35, 39, 41, 49–70 passim, 81–91 passim, 121, 143, 150, 168–69, 179, 182, 186, 192, 199–201, 211, 215, 221–22, 240, 242–44, 246, 264–65, 279, 284, 288; Voyages, 82
morality, 50, 58, 246. See under law; virtue.
mores, 18, 21, 50, 62–63, 69–70, 86, 100, 140, 151. See also manners.
More, Thomas, 9
Murphy, Walter, 116
Muscovites, 89

Napoleon. See Bonaparte, Napoleon.

natural law. *See under* law.
natural right, 51. *See also* rights.
nature, 51–52, 140, 143, 181–82, 290; human, 89, 246–47, 290; as inseparable from principle, 61; state of, 205; of things, 242
Newton, Isaac, 16, 26, 70n1-2
Nietzsche, Friedrich, 3, 145
nobility, 189; in England, 182; of the sword and the robe, 60; of virtue, 53. *See also* aristocracy.
Nugent, Thomas, 31

Oakeshott, Michael, 65
obedience, 17, 61, 155; affective motivations of, 51–52; religious, 57; and resistance, 58–62. *See also* monarchy; honour.
Old Regime. *See under* France; *Ancien Régime*.
Ottomans, 208
Ouange, M. *See* Hoang, Arcadio.

Paine, Thomas, 132
Pangle, Thomas, 260, 280, 283, 284
parlements. *See under* France.
Parliament, British. *See under* England.
Parrenin, Père Dominique, 90
Pascal, Blaise, 57, 75n41, 296
passions, 3, 9–10, 32, 36, 38, 49, 51–53, 57, 74n39, 97, 101, 106–107, 139, 163, 166, 223, 247, 274. *See also* specific passions (e.g. fear); regime types.
patriotism, 101, 103, 106, 252, 273–74. *See also* virtue.
perfectionism. *See under* politics.
*philosophes*, 8, 26, 128, 163, 239, 241, 245
philosophy: Montesquieu's ambivalence toward, 8
physiocrats, 163–64
Plato, 9, 292, 297; *Republic* 13
pluralism, 4, 6, 20, 68–70, 133, 150, 223, 228, 275, 283, 289; moral, 4–5
Pocock, John G. A., 119–20
politeness, 9, 63, 69, 86
political parties, 36–37, 39

politics, 6; and custom, 22; perfectionist, 7–13 passim, 20; science of. *See also* regime typology; citizenship; liberty; liberalism.
population, 183–84
power: abuses of, 67, 69, 76n59; as a check to power, 33; concentration of, 130; and the courts, 209, 262; despotic, 59, 98–99; limitation of, 40, 99–100; and the passions, 102; as separate from law, 3; symbolic dimension of, 100, 102; will and, 99. *See also* corruption.
powers, 261; distribution of, 36, 62, 291; intermediate or intermediary, 32, 41, 47n5, 61, 123, 127, 150; separation, balance and division of, 7, 11–12, 15, 31, 33–36, 43, 47, 99–100, 106, 110n2, 118, 123, 201, 212, 243, 261–62, 279. *See also* checks and balances.
principles of government, 32–33, 35, 51, 55, 101–102, 182, 185, 201, 223, 296; of English system, 38, 43–44. *See also* fear; honor; moderation; nature; virtue.
privacy. *See* interest.
property, 207, 274
Protestantism, 20, 106, 206
public opinion, 39, 64, 77n62, 223; tyranny of
Pufendorf, Samuel von, 50, 295
punishment, 248. *See under* law.
Puritanism, 8

*R. v. Keegstra* (1990, Canada), 221, 226, 228–31
rationalism: abstract, 50, 242. *See also* Enlightenment; reason.
*R.A.V. v. St. Paul* (1992, U.S.), 222, 226, 230–31
Rawls, John, 10–11, 20, 23, 272, 275, 297; *Political Liberalism*, 23, 277; *Theory of Justice*, 23, 281
reason, 26, 42, 46n25, 57, 144; the cunning of, 56
recognition, politics of, 68

regime typology, 51, 97–98, 201–202, 212, 222, 242, 285; and corresponding principles, 32, 43, 222, 242. See also government; principle.
relativism, 241, 284, 289–90, 296
religion, 4, 10, 151, 202, 247–51, 277, 289; Muslim, 24; and politics, 22, 272, 294–95. See also authority; Christianity; Islam; law.
republic, 58, 98, 149, 223, 234n39, 243, 275; aristocratic and democratic, 185; classical (ancient Greece and Rome), 8–9, 17–18, 66, 154, 156, 183, 282; federation, 122, 168, 279; Dutch, 122, 246, 282; the English Commonwealth, 42, 46, 47n34, 122; French 264; modern, 229, 252–53 260, 277; and over-commitment to public life, 19; Rousseau's version of, 15; Swiss, 246; Venetian, 122. See also virtue.
revolution, 16, 59
Ricault, Paul, 82
Richter, Melvin, xi, 110n18
rights, 99, 116, 121, 192, 210, 279; civic, 68; equality of, 69; in liberal and republican traditions, 229
Rome, ancient, 142, 151–52, 166, 202, 252; Empire of, 11, 153–56, 188. See also republic, virtue.
Rousseau, Jean-Jacques, 15, 22, 55, 67, 139–45, 150, 164–65, 259, 280, 283, 297–98
rule of law. See under law.
Russell, Peter, 224

satire, of aristocratic ethic, 53
Sarkozy, Nicolas, 260
*Schenck v. United States* (1919), 225
Scottish Enlightenment. See under Enlightenment.
security, 67. See also liberty, political.
self: -love, 64, 101–103, 106; -interest (see under interest). See also honor.
Sen, Amartya, 297
sentiments, 1, 131, 244. See also emotion; passions; principles.

separation of powers. See under powers.
Sieyès, Emmanuel-Joseph, 133
skepticism, 8, 23, 25, 51, 242
Skinner, Quentin, 283
slavery, 4, 35, 59, 129, 290
Smith, Adam, 3, 38, 129, 179, 190, 203
sociability, 18, 242; French, 17, 107
society: commercial, 69; monarchic, 56, 62; perfect, 51; republican, 68; stages of, 185–86. See also civil society; power.
Solon, 289
sovereignty, 292; by representation 67
Sparta, 8–9, 15, 122. See also republics; virtue.
speech, freedom of, 221, 228, 231, 235n48
Spinoza, Baruch, 145, 240, 271
spirit, 242. See also general spirit.
*stare decisis*. See under courts.
Strauss, Leo; Straussian tradition, 53
suicide, 25, 35, 107.
sympathy. See compassion.

Tacitus, 47 n. 42, 87
Tartars, 90, 103
Taylor, Charles, 68–69, 255n1
Terror. See France.
Thoyras, Rapin de, 36
Tocqueville, Alexis de, 3, 11, 129, 131, 140, 145, 149, 280
toleration, 4, 121, 230, 249–52, 264
Tracy, Destutt de, 127–28, 132–33
tradition, 164; ancient 50; liberal democratic, 1; Western, 2
Treaty of Utrecht, 40
Troglodytes, 245–46, 251
Tully, James, 116, 132
tyranny, 35, 98, 253. See also despotism.

uniformity, 3, 116, 128–29, 151, 261
United States. See America, United States of.
universalism, 69, 239, 261, 289, 298; negative universal, 267. See also Jacobin; uniformity.

*universitas*: contrasted with *societas*, 65–68
utilitarianism, 296

virtue, 9–10, 20–21, 43, 52–53, 55, 58, 68–69, 101, 243–46; Christian, 54–55; civic, 66, 154, 254–55, 275; commerce and, 67; moral, 21. *See also* regime typology, education.
Voconian law, 295
Voltaire, Jean-François-Marie Arouet, 55, 83, 86, 183, 259, 261, 279, 288

Walpole, Robert 37, 40
war, 248, 252. *See also* law.
Weber, Max, 21, 109n7, 199, 205–207, 277, 284, 290, 296
Weil, Françoise, 84
Whiggism, 120–21. *See also* England.
women, 12, 18, 266; rights of, 11; society of, 18; subordination of, 19, 63

Yorke, Charles, 187

www.ingramcontent.com/pod-product-compliance
Lightning Source LLC
Chambersburg PA
CBHW030127240426

43672CB00005B/55